GREAT GARDEN FORMULAS

GREAT GARDEN FORMULAS

The ULTIMATE BOOK of MIX-IT-YOURSELF CONCOCTIONS for YOUR GARDEN

Joan Benjamin and Deborah L. Martin, Editors

Contributing Writers: Erin Hynes, Tina James, Cheryl Long,
Barbara Pleasant, Trisha Shirey, Debra Warner

Rodale Press
Emmaus, Pennsylvania

©1998 by Rodale Press, Inc.
Interior illustrations ©1998 by Julia Child

Library of Congress Cataloging-in-Publication Data

Great garden formulas / Joan Benjamin and
    Deborah L. Martin, editors.
        p.   cm.
    Includes bibliographical references and index.
    ISBN 0–87596–798–1   (hardcover)
    1. Organic gardening—Formulae.   I.
Benjamin, Joan.
SB453.5.G74   1998
635'.0484—ddc21   98–8915
                                                        CIP

Distributed in the book trade by St. Martin's Press

2   4   6   8   10   9   7   5   3   1   hardcover

Editors: Joan Benjamin, Deborah L. Martin
Contributing Editors: Fern Marshall Bradley,
    Warren Schultz
Senior Research Associate: Heidi A. Stonehill
Cover and Interior Book Designer:
    Randall Sauchuck
Interior Illustrator: Julia Child
Cover Illustrator: Randall Sauchuck
Layout Designer: Susan P. Eugster
Copy Editor: Sara Cox
Manufacturing Coordinator: Patrick T. Smith
Indexer: Lina Burton
Editorial Assistance: Jodi Guiducci, Sarah Heffner

Rodale Home and Garden Books
Vice President and Editorial Director:
    Margaret J. Lydic
Managing Editor, Garden Books: Ellen Phillips
Director of Design and Production: Michael Ward
Associate Art Director: Patricia Field
Production Manager: Robert V. Anderson, Jr.
Studio Manager: Leslie M. Keefe
Copy Director: Dolores Plikaitis
Book Manufacturing Director: Helen Clogston
Office Manager: Karen Earl-Braymer

Rodale Press
Organic Gardening Starts Here!

Here at Rodale Press, we've been gardening organically for over 50 years—ever since my grandfather J. I. Rodale learned about composting and decided that healthy living starts with healthy soil. In 1940, J. I. started the Rodale Organic Farm to test his theories, and today, the nonprofit Rodale Institute Experimental Farm is still at the forefront of organic gardening and farming research. In 1942, J. I. founded *Organic Gardening* magazine to share his discoveries with gardeners everywhere. His son, my father, Robert Rodale, headed *Organic Gardening* until 1990, and today, the fourth generation of Rodales is growing up with the magazine. Over the years, we've shown millions of readers how to grow bountiful crops and beautiful flowers using nature's own techniques.

In this book, you'll find the latest organic methods and the best gardening advice. We know—because our authors and editors are all passionate about gardening! We feel strongly that our gardens should be safe for our children, pets, and the birds and butterflies that add beauty and delight to our lives and landscapes. Our gardens should provide us with fresh, flavorful vegetables, delightful herbs, and gorgeous flowers. And they should be a pleasure to work in as well as to view.

Sharing the secrets of safe, successful gardening is why we publish books. So come visit us at the Rodale Institute Experimental Farm, where you can tour the gardens every day—we're open year-round. And use this book to create your best garden ever.

Happy gardening!

Maria Rodale

Maria Rodale
For Rodale Garden Books

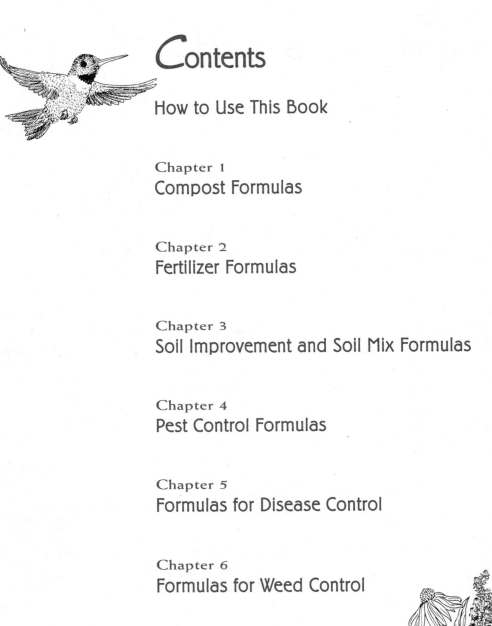

Contents

How to Use This Book

What's your formula for garden success? Perhaps it's a special fertilizer, a homemade pest spray, or a technique for starting seeds that you've developed yourself. Don't you wish you knew more great home-made recipes and techniques? Perhaps you'd like to try "Halloween Leaf Compost," "Fabulous Fertilizer Fix for Bulbs," or a "Weed-Free Lawn Formula." You'll find these and hundreds more secrets to success in this book.

These special "secret formulas" that gardeners concoct are among the things that make gardening so much fun. As you know, gardeners love to experiment and to find new uses for things they have on hand. They also like to share their unique ideas for terrific organic recipes and surefire techniques—and that's what *Great Garden Formulas* is all about.

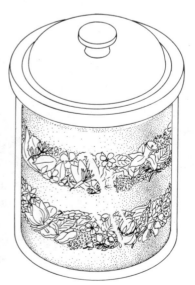

When you read *Great Garden Formulas*, you'll feel as if you've joined a recipe swap with gardeners across the country. You'll find over 350 wonderful garden formulas for everything from compost and soil mixes to pest and disease controls to wildflower meadow mixes and butterfly gardens. As a bonus, we've also collected terrific formulas for things you can make out of the bounty of your garden, from a fertilizer made from Swiss chard leaves to a wealth of herbal seasonings, crafts, and even beauty products.

Finding Formulas Fast

Great Garden Formulas is designed to make it easy to find the formulas you need to garden better, to help solve your garden problems, and simply to let you enjoy your favorite kind of gardening even more. To start, just turn back to the table of contents, where you'll find a list of the chapters. Turn to the opening page of any chapter that interests you, and you'll find a complete listing of the formulas it contains. For instance, if you turn to Chapter 4, "Pest Control Formulas"— you'll see that it includes formulas like "Hot Spray for Flea Beetles" and "Slug-Dissolving Spray." (Ugh!) Or turn to the index to find the formulas you need by looking up keywords such as "slugs" or "compost."

Finding the Right Ingredients

Most of the ingredients listed in these formulas are available at your local garden center or grocery store. But if you're having trouble finding ingredients, check our Sources section beginning on page 308. You'll find an extensive listing of mail-order suppliers of ingredients from soil amendments and seeds to herbal oils.

Finding the Right Technique

Although all the formulas in this book are organic, that doesn't mean they're harmless. For example, while colloidal phosphate and granite dust are part of a great fertilizer mix for tomatoes, they're not a great mixture for you to breathe, and certainly not to eat! And while an herb like Solomon's seal is beneficial in a hand cream or massage oil, it could be toxic if ingested. Check formulas for any special cautions, and be sure to use protective equipment, like rubber gloves or dust masks, when recommended. Follow all instructions carefully and don't assume that ingredients, especially herbs, are interchangeable.

A Word of Thanks

We're thankful to the generous gardeners and garden experts we interviewed for *Great Garden Formulas*. We hope you'll enjoy testing their magic methods and recipes. Keep in mind that no two gardens are ever exactly alike (and who would want them to be?), so you may not get exactly the same results from these formulas as the gardeners who created them. But that's okay. Perhaps one of their ideas will be a springboard to your own brand new formula! Have fun, experiment, and remember: The real formula for garden success is to take plenty of time out from chores to taste your freshly picked vegetables and to smell the flowers.

COMPOST FORMULAS

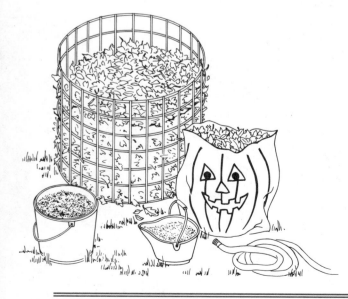

The Joy of Composting

Recycling your food and plant "wastes" by making compost for your garden is the single most important thing you can do to grow bountiful yields of great-tasting food and beautiful flowers. And it's easy, fun, and free! Compost provides a perfectly balanced fertilizer to feed your crops, improve the soil's structure, *and* protect your plants against drought, diseases, and insect pests.

This chapter gives you recipes for the full range of composting techniques. You can use fancy equipment or just pile ingredients directly on the ground. You can use an ultra-easy technique like sheet composting—spreading layers of grass clippings or leaves over the soil where microorganisms and earthworms will break it down. Or you can let a few bags of fall leaves decay behind the garage until they turn into dark, crumbly compost.

Since compost ingredients decompose, or "cook down," fastest when they're combined in just the right proportions, many of these recipes are formulated to help you produce rich, sweet-smelling, finished compost in as little as two weeks! Others take a more relaxed, "let-it-happen" approach that emphasizes ease over speed.

Whether your compost is made quickly or slowly, with carefully measured ingredients or whatever you have on hand, remember that turning organic matter into compost requires water and air. When you're building and tending a compost pile, it's helpful to keep this simple equation in mind:

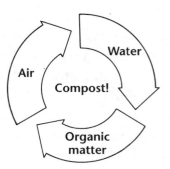

The amount of moisture in your compost pile is almost as important as the ingredients you use. The microorganisms that do all the work in your pile need moisture to survive. But too much water can cause the compost ingredients to mat together, preventing air—another essential ingredient—from circulating. (See "Dry-Weather Compost" on page 2 and "Wet-Weather Compost" on page 3 for the methods that work best in your region's climate.)

Air is necessary because the desirable microorganisms in compost need oxygen in order to do their thing. Without air, other microorganisms will prevail (these will do the decomposition work, too, but with a lot more smell and slime). Use coarse ingredients like straw or cornstalks to keep air flowing all the time, and turn or stir things occasionally to give all the ingredients a breath of fresh air. (See "Just Add Air" on page 13 and "Breathe New Life into Your Compost Pile" on page 7 for ways to aerate your compost.)

Combine these basic composting techniques with any of the following recipes and you'll be spreading nature's best all-natural fertilizer on your crops in no time!

Dry-Weather Compost

Your compost pile can't cook when it's dry and dusty. And it can't become the rich, crumbly soil food you seek when it's wet and waterlogged. The methods you use to keep the moisture in your pile at just the right level—it should be as damp as a wrung-out sponge—will depend on where you live. In a dry climate or during a long period of dry weather, composting in a pit in the ground or in a solid-sided bin will help keep the pile moist. Even frequent turning—with all its benefits—can cause your compost pile to dry out too quickly. Choose from among these moisture-managing methods to keep your microorganisms happy and your compost cooking.

Set your hose attachment on the finest spray, and water your compost pile until it's as wet as a wrung-out sponge. Repeat each time you add new ingredients.

Ingredients and Supplies

Pit or solid-sided bin
Compost ingredients
Pole or stake, approximately 5 feet long

Directions

1. Place ingredients in the pit or bin. Making your compost in a bin with solid sides or in a pit in the ground reduces the amount of moisture that will be lost to evaporation.

2. Spray the pile lightly with water after each addition. It's easier to start your pile with moist ingredients than to get the whole thing wet enough after it's built.

Note: Try one—or both—of these techniques to make the most of rainfall to keep your heap moist:

- Drive the pole or stake into the center of your compost heap to help direct rainfall into the pile.
- Dig a shallow "well" in the top of your compost pile to catch any rain that does fall.

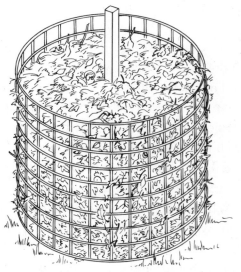

Put raindrops to work by placing an old stake or pole in the center of a compost pile. The rain will travel down along the stake, soaking into the center of the pile.

Wet-Weather Compost

If your weather is wet, cover your compost pile to prevent it from becoming too soggy. A soggy heap will still turn to compost, but the process is a lot smellier and messier. When steady rain threatens to make your compost pile sodden and yucky, top your heap with water-shedding ingredients or a protective tarp.

Ingredients and Supplies

Compost ingredients
Straw, hay, or plastic or canvas tarp

Directions

1. Place ingredients in a pile.

2. Cover the compost pile with a layer of rain-shedding straw or hay (later, it becomes an ingredient in your compost!) or throw a tarp over the pile.

3. Check your heap for moisture periodically. If your pile becomes too wet in spite of your efforts, turn your compost frequently to let in more air and to help return moisture to an appropriate level.

If the forecast calls for steady rain, place a thick layer of straw or hay on top of your compost pile. This rain-shedding layer will help prevent the pile from becoming soaked.

Tarps also protect your compost pile from soggy downpours. Place a tarp over the top of the pile and secure with rocks. Remove the tarp when the weather clears.

The World's EASIEST Compost

"The magical thing about composting is that it happens no matter how much attention you give or don't give to your pile," explains Maria Rodale, author of *Maria Rodale's Organic Garden* and daughter of the late Robert Rodale, long-time editor of *Organic Gardening* magazine. Maria, who gardens at her home in Emmaus, Pennsylvania, just a block away from *Organic Gardening's* editorial offices, says she thinks of her compost pile as her "home waste disposal system."

For no-fuss compost, add materials to the pile without bothering to measure or shred them. Let the pile sit, and in a month or so the bottom will form rich, crumbly compost.

Ingredients and Supplies

All yard wastes, including weeds, spent garden plants, leaves, and grass clippings

Kitchen scraps, including peelings, seeds, rinds, cores, and cobs, but excluding fats, meats, and dairy products

Any corner in the yard, with or without a bin

A little patience

Directions

1. "Just throw everything on the pile," Maria advises. She does recommend keeping meat and dairy products and greasy or fatty foods out of the compost pile, since these break down very slowly and tend to attract pests and pets (like Maria's dog) to the pile.

2. Sit back and wait. Don't bother with measuring, chopping, shredding, turning, or other kinds of compost fussing! In time (within a month or two), dark, rich, crumbly compost will begin to form at the bottom of the pile as the ingredients decompose.

CONTAINING COMPOST-BOUND KITCHEN WASTES

Unless walking to your compost pile is your daily exercise program, you'll want a way to store up a few days' worth of kitchen scraps for less-frequent trips to the heap. In her kitchen, Maria Rodale uses a 5-gallon, lidded bucket to hold scraps for trips to the compost pile every other day or so. "A tight-fitting lid is crucial for controlling odors and fruit flies," she points out. She adds a second container when cold weather arrives: "In the winter, we also keep a medium-size garbage can with a lid outside our back door for kitchen scraps. We take this down to the pile every few weeks or so—if it's cold, there's no smell. That way, we have to take it to the main pile only when we're feeling like a walk and when the weather is cooperating!"

Simple Shovel Compost

You need nothing more than a shovel and a spot to sink it in to put this quick and easy composting technique to work in your garden, says garden writer and photographer Deb Meager of Nevada City, California. Deb's method works well when you have only small amounts of kitchen and garden waste to compost.

Ingredients and Supplies

    1 bucket kitchen scraps and lawn
        and garden wastes
    Shovel

Directions

1. Choose a spot in your garden where you want to improve the soil.
2. Dig a small hole, removing 2 to 5 shovelfuls of soil. The deeper you bury kitchen scraps for composting, the less likely it is that they'll be unearthed by foraging wild animals or pets.
3. Dump the kitchen scraps and yard wastes into the hole and chop them up a bit with the shovel.
4. Return the soil to the hole, covering the scraps and chopping a bit more with the shovel to mix some soil down into the buried scraps. The organic wastes you've put into the hole will gradually become soil-enriching compost—with no pile, no watering, and no turning!
5. Repeat this process as often as possible.

Note: In your garden, it's easy to dig a row of these holes, or a shallow trench, in the path space next to a crop row. Next year, plant your flowers or vegetables in the

Bury chopped kitchen scraps under a layer of sod. The scraps will turn to compost, and your turfgrass will rejoice.

"compost row," and "plant" compostables where your crops once grew.

Variation: Try "Simple Shovel Compost" on your lawn, too. Use your shovel to cut loose a flap of sod, then fold it back and dig a hole. Pour in the kitchen scraps, chop them a little with the shovel, and replace the soil. Then firmly press the sod back into place. Water the spot well. Don't worry if there's a lump left behind when you're through—it will quickly disappear because the scraps shrink as they compost.

Super-Simple Straw Bale Composting

In this method, the straw bales you use to make your compost bin will become ingredients in your next batch of compost. It's recommended by Maine's master organic grower Eliot Coleman in his highly-acclaimed book, *The New Organic Grower*. Eliot says he gets consistently high-quality compost from his straw-bale bins. "I began using this straw bale method after reading about it in a book called *Intensive Gardening*, by Rachel Dalziel O'Brien," he says. "I consider it to be one of the best books ever written on market gardening."

Ingredients and Supplies

8 (or more) straw bales
Loose straw
Assorted green plant wastes
Soil

Directions

1. Stack straw bales like bricks, 2 or 3 bales high, to build a 3-sided enclosure of whatever size you want. You'll need about 8 bales to make a bin that's 2 bales high. The bales make a perfect bin because they keep all the ingredients moist and warm while still letting in plenty of air.

2. Fill the bale enclosure by alternating 2- to 3-inch layers of loose straw with 1- to 6-inch layers of green plant wastes. Make thinner layers of moist materials like grass clippings that might mat together, and thicker layers of loose, open ingredients such as tomato plants or pea vines. Sprinkle a layer of soil over each green layer.

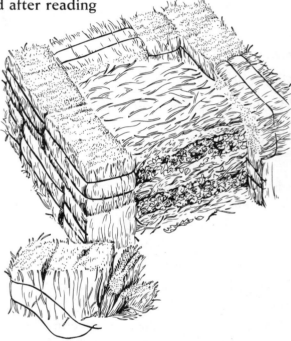

Create a compostable compost bin by using straw bales. Stack them 2 or 3 layers high on 3 sides. After 2 years, use new bales to build another bin, and mix the old straw into your compost pile, or use it for mulch.

3. Let compost happen. Eliot says he prefers to let his compost sit for about 1½ years before he uses it. The straw bales will hold together for at least 2 years. Then you can use them as ingredients in your next heap, with fresh, new bales for the enclosure.

Breathe New Life into Your Compost Pile

You can get compost more quickly if you give your pile some gas—specifically that clear, breathable gas called oxygen. Air in your compost pile makes the ingredients break down faster, so you have finished compost for your garden sooner.

Adding air, by turning or using other ventilation techniques, helps when too many wet ingredients mat down and keep air from circulating through the pile. Too much air, however, can dry out a pile, so you need to be sure to add moisture even when you're turning a pile that's properly moist.

If turning your compost by moving the entire pile to a new spot seems like too much work, don't despair. See "Just Add Air" on page 13 to learn some passive aeration techniques—ways to add air to compost without turning it—that can save your back and your compost pile.

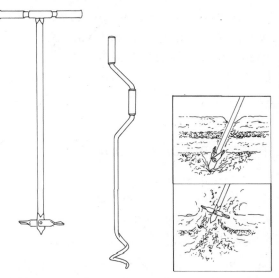

Most compost-aerating tools nave an arrow-shaped tip that's easy to push into the pile and harder to pull out because of the larger hole it makes as it's removed. Look for one with a sturdy handle that lets you get a firm grip on it for pulling.

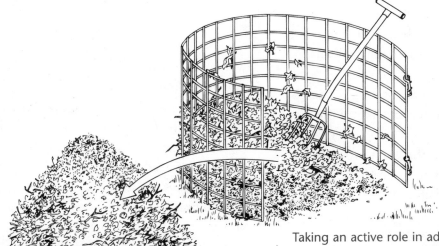

Taking an active role in adding air to your compost can give you a real workout, too: One of the best ways to aerate a compost heap is by turning it—moving the entire pile to a new location.

Basic Backyard Compost

Making your own compost is as easy as pie with this proven recipe from Cyane Gresham, compost specialist at the Rodale Institute Experimental Farm in Berks County, Pennsylvania. Cyane's recipe is based on her 10 years of research to identify the very best composting methods for home gardeners.

Ingredients and Supplies

1 part fresh green materials
1 part dried brown materials
1 part black materials

(See "Compost Choices" on the facing page for examples of green, brown, and black materials)

Directions

1. Build your pile at least 4 feet square and 4 feet high, if possible. When you make your pile this large, temperatures can quickly build up in the center to over 100°F. This rapid warm-up allows heat-loving microorganisms to rapidly turn the ingredients into finished compost.

2. Mix together the ingredients as you go and add enough water to make all the ingredients thoroughly moistened but not soggy. "Don't worry about the exact proportions," Cyane explains. "The composting process is *very* forgiving, and all organic matter will eventually decompose." The closer you can get to equal proportions of greens, browns, and blacks, the faster you'll get finished compost. But even if you made a pile entirely of greens, or entirely of browns, it would eventually turn into good compost. It

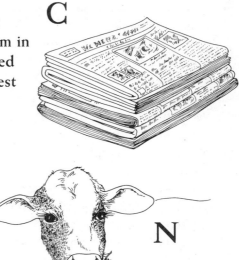

The proper mixture of carbon-rich materials (C), like newspapers, and nitrogen-rich materials (N), like cow manure, encourages compost-forming microorganisms.

will just probably take longer than when you mix the 3 kinds of materials together.

3. You can turn or stir the pile with a garden fork every few weeks if you want to really speed up the process, Cyane says, or you can just let it sit. Either way, make sure that the pile stays moist. If you just let it sit, "it should break down very nicely in a couple of months as long as the weather is warm." (Turning a compost pile "fluffs it up" and introduces more oxygen so that the microorganisms can multiply faster.)

Yield: 2 cubic feet of finished compost

Compost Choices

The "greens" you choose for your compost pile can include any fresh moist organic matter, like grass clippings, weeds, and kitchen scraps. Greens provide necessary nitrogen and moisture to the pile. The "browns" are older, drier, tougher materials like straw, cornstalks, sawdust, fall leaves, and dead plants. You need the browns to keep the pile loose so that air can circulate. The "blacks" can be either garden soil, manure, or chunky incompletely decomposed material from a previous compost pile. "The blacks are the great equalizer in the pile," Cyane Gresham explains. "They absorb and hold moisture, and they also introduce the microorganisms that break down the browns and greens."

Fresh greens

Soil or compost

Dried browns

A key to fast, easy composting is using the right mix. For great results, combine ⅓ fresh green materials, like grass clippings, ⅓ dried brown materials, like straw, and ⅓ black materials, like garden soil.

Things to Keep Out of Your Heap

One of the most satisfying things about making compost is being able to recycle kitchen scraps and garden wastes—stuff you'd probably *throw away* otherwise—into something that's great for your garden. But that doesn't mean that every bit of household waste belongs in your compost pile. Balance the ingredients you add to your heap—you can have too much of a good thing, like grass clippings. And avoid materials that might carry diseases, materials that attract pests, and materials that slow the composting process or make it more difficult.

What to Avoid	Why
Cat droppings	May carry diseases and parasitic organisms; especially dangerous for pregnant women and young children
Coal or charcoal ashes	Contain amounts of sulfur and iron that are toxic to plants
Diseased plants	Require high-temperature (hot) composting to ensure that disease organisms are killed; otherwise may reinfect your garden when compost is spread
Dog droppings	May carry parasitic organisms; unpleasant to handle
Fish, meat, or cheese scraps	Break down slowly; attractive to foraging animals
Grease or oil	Break down slowly; inhibit composting of other materials
Weed seeds/rhizomes	Require hot composting to ensure that seeds are killed; otherwise may sprout wherever compost is applied; weeds like Canada thistle and quackgrass grow back from very small pieces of rhizome and are very hard to control

Loose-Leaf Compost

If rich, soil-building compost fell from the sky every fall, there's no question that you'd gather up some for your garden, right? So why would you even think of disposing of the wealth of free, nutrient-rich leaves that fall from your trees each year?

"Homeowners should *never* throw away their fall leaves," says *Organic Gardening* magazine's research editor Cheryl Long. "Tree roots draw minerals from deep in the soil in order to grow leaves and branches. If you throw away leaves instead of recycling them, you are literally making your soil poorer and poorer every year." Fortunately leaves are *very* easy to compost, very good for your gardens, and often available in large quantities.

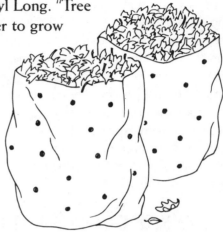

Ingredients and Supplies

Fall leaves
Lawn mower, string trimmer, or
    chipper/shredder

Directions

1. Shred your leaves. The benefits of shredding the leaves are threefold, Cheryl explains: "Shredding makes the volume of leaves much smaller and easier to handle. The shredded leaves are less prone to blowing away. And they decompose faster." Don't despair if you don't have a shredder—you can chop up leaves with your lawn mower. Or put the leaves in a trash can and then use a string trimmer to chop them up. Wear goggles and a dust mask with any of these methods to protect yourself from flying dust and debris.
2. Add the shredded leaves to your compost pile and mix with your other ingredients.

Variation: If you don't have time to shred your leaves, you can still compost them over the winter and add them to your gardens next spring. "All you have to do is pile 'em up, wet 'em down, and let 'em sit," Cheryl says. "If I don't have time to shred my leaves, I just rake them into a pile and put a ring of welded wire fencing around it to keep the leaves from blowing around. Putting them in big plastic trash bags works fine, too."

You can even rescue bags of leaves destined for curbside collection and turn them into compost, Cheryl says. Just poke some holes in the bags to let air and water in and out, then wet the leaves thoroughly. Open the tops of the bags so rain can get in, and let the leaves sit for a few months or more.

Like turning a compost pile, occasionally shaking the bags will help add some air to the mix.

"If I have time, I also mix a few shovelfuls of good garden soil into each pile or bag," Cheryl says. "The soil inoculates the leaves with plenty of the microorganisms and earthworms that help turn them into compost."

When your leaves reach that dark, crumbly state that's called leaf mold, you can use it as a weed-blocking, moisture-conserving mulch. Or mix the leaf mold into your garden beds to improve the soil. Either way, you'll be feeding the soil, the earthworms, and your crops with those treasures from the trees. Leaf mold also makes the perfect ingredient to add to grass clippings over the summer months. "Large amounts of fresh grass clippings alone tend to mat together and don't compost well," Cheryl explains. "If you mix in some leaf mold with the clippings, the pile will cook much better."

MAKE YOUR BEDS WITH SHEET COMPOSTING

Build up your garden beds and send the nutrients in your shredded leaves straight back to the soil with sheet composting. This method of spreading leaves—or other compost materials—directly on top of the soil lets them break down gradually, pretty much the way Mother Nature intended. But shredding gives the process a boost that Mother Nature leaves out.

Rake your leaves into a pile on the lawn or driveway, then run your lawn mower over them in a circle, always blowing them toward the center or against a wall to keep them from spreading out too much.

Halloween Leaf Compost

Transform all those brilliant red and yellow fall leaves into black gold for your garden with this recipe from veteran gardener George Weigel, garden columnist for the *Patriot-News* in Harrisburg, Pennsylvania. George's recipe includes grass clippings, which are high in nitrogen, an ingredient that speeds up the composting of the leaves.

Ingredients and Supplies

> Compost bin
> 4 buckets fall leaves
>   (preferably shredded)
> 2 buckets grass clippings, spent
>   garden plants,
>   or kitchen scraps
> 1 bucket garden soil
> Sprinkling of lime or wood
>   ashes (if available)

When Halloween's over, shred the leaves from your decorative leaf bags and add them to the compost pile.

Directions

1. Dump the ingredients together and mix.
2. Moisten everything well as you mix.
3. Repeat with more layers until you run out of materials, bin space, or energy.

Yield: 3 buckets of finished compost

Note: Mix the finished compost into your beds. George recommends mixing in the compost about 2 weeks before planting.

IN THE BIN

If you don't already have a compost bin, you can just make a pile on the ground, or bend a length of 4-foot-tall welded wire fencing into a circle. Fasten the ends of the fencing together with plastic-coated wire ties or metal clips, and put your compost ingredients inside. To turn or stir your pile, simply unfasten the fencing and move the bin out of the way until you're through.

Just Add Air

The tiny critters that turn your kitchen scraps and yard wastes into compost do their best work when they get plenty of oxygen. Thus, a well-aerated compost pile breaks down much more quickly than one in which the microorganisms are practically gasping for breath. The good news is, you don't have to turn your compost to keep its population of busy microorganisms breathing freely. Instead, do a little advance planning and build in a ventilation system when you build your pile.

Ingredients and Supplies

Several cornstalks, saplings, or sunflower
    stalks, each 4–5 feet long
String or twine

Directions

1. Use string or twine to tie the stalks or saplings into a bundle that is 5 to 6 inches in diameter.

2. Build your compost pile around the bundled stalks, so that the bundle becomes a "chimney" sticking up from the middle of the pile. Air will travel through the hollow stalks and in the spaces between them into the center of your pile.

Variation: Lay 4- to 5-foot-long perforated plastic pipes horizontally at different layers as you build your compost pile. These will also let air into the middle of the pile. As lower layers decompose, pull out the pipes at the bottom of the pile and lay them across the top before adding more ingredients.

Old cornstalks tied together make an economical compost aerator. Simply place them in the center of your compost pile as you build it.

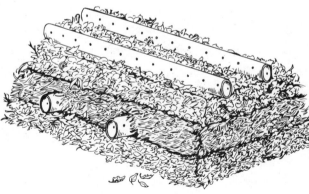

Crisscross horizontal layers of perforated plastic pipes throughout your compost pile to provide excellent aeration.

Chicken and Chips Compost

It's a perfect compost combo—rich chicken manure mixed with wood chips or sawdust. Noted garden experts and authors Doc and Katy Abraham of Naples, New York, explain that both chicken manure and wood chips can burn plants when used alone, but when you mix the two and compost them together, you can produce a safe and effective soil amendment.

Ingredients and Supplies

- 1 part chicken manure
- 1 part wood chips or sawdust

Directions

1. Mix the 2 ingredients together thoroughly and water well.

2. Add them to your existing compost pile, or build a separate pile with them, if you prefer.

3. Let them compost for 6 months or even a year to give the wood wastes plenty of time to break down.

4. Turn the pile occasionally with a garden fork, and add water as needed to keep the material moist. (Or, if the weather is very wet, cover the pile with plastic to keep it from getting too soggy.)

Yield: 1 part of finished compost

Note: It's easy for gardeners to get wood chips or sawdust from tree-trimming companies or local sawmills, say Doc and Katy. "But when wood chips are stored in big piles, they can develop what's called sour mulch syndrome, which produces acetic acid, alcohols, and foul-smelling hydrogen sulfide," Doc explains. These compounds in sour wood mulch can damage plants. But you can

Use a chipper/shredder to turn fallen twigs and branches into compostable wood chips and sawdust.

prevent or cure sour mulch by combining the chips with chicken manure, which is extremely rich in nitrogen and other nutrients (so rich, in fact, that when used full strength it can damage tender seedlings). That chicken manure's nitrogen is exactly what's needed to balance the low nitrogen content of the wood chips. When the manure is mixed together with chips or sawdust and composted, the wood decomposes without producing any sour by-products, and the result is an excellent compost.

Rabbit-Powered Compost Pile

They're cute, they're cuddly, they're composting machines! More than just adorable pals, rabbits are the perfect backyard livestock, says organic gardener K. B. Laugheed of Fortville, Indiana. K. B.'s recipe for top-quality compost starts with high-nitrogen, nonsmelly rabbit manure— it keeps her compost heap hopping! K. B. says her bunnies are every bit as easy-care as the compost pile beneath their cage, and they help her process some compost ingredients, too: "The rabbits never need to be bathed, groomed, or taken for a walk," she says. "And they happily munch on your old lettuce, bruised apples, celery tips, and carrot scrapings."

Ingredients and Supplies

> 1 or 2 rabbits
> Raised hutch with wire bottom
> Kitchen scraps and yard wastes

Directions

1. Lay 8 to 10 inches of kitchen scraps and yard wastes under the rabbits' hutch.

2. Let the rabbits do their thing. As more kitchen scraps and yard wastes become available, add them to the pile.

3. Add water, as needed, to keep the pile moist. In dry climates, dig a hole under the hutch to hold the pile so that it doesn't dry out quickly.

4. About once a year, rake out the finished compost and start again with a fresh base of yard wastes.

For rich compost, build a pile under an outdoor rabbit hutch. Keep adding kitchen scraps and yard wastes to the pile while the rabbits add their contribution.

Always Compost Fresh Manures

Manure from cows, horses, sheep, chickens, and rabbits is an excellent ingredient for your compost pile. The manure from these animals is generally rich in nitrogen and other nutrients, and it will help the other ingredients in your compost pile break down more quickly. In fact, fresh manure *belongs* in your compost pile. Never apply it directly in your garden beds—it can injure your plants and it may carry weed seeds. 🐾

Composting by the Numbers

Knowing that the ideal ratio of carbon to nitrogen in your compost pile is about 30:1 isn't too helpful, unless you also know how to reach that ratio. But if you really want to crank up your compost pile and get it rotting hot and fast, that 30:1 ratio is a good goal to aim for. It provides a balanced "diet" that lets the microorganisms in your pile thrive.

Eric Evans, director of the Woods End Research Laboratory in Mt. Vernon, Maine, offers a few tips to help homeowners make the most of the carbon-to-nitrogen ratio. "The biggest factor in the carbon-to-nitrogen ratio is how much water is present," Eric says. "Dry materials are generally in the range of 40 to 50 percent carbon, and sloppy, wet materials are generally 10 to 20 percent carbon." So the more dry ingredients you have, the quicker you'll reach the 30:1 ratio.

Ingredients and Supplies

Pencil and paper or a calculator

Directions

1. Calculate your pile's total carbon value by multiplying the percentage of carbon of each ingredient by the number of parts (by weight) of that ingredient and then adding up the carbon totals for all the ingredients. (See "Math for Composters" at the right to see how to do the calculations.)
2. Do the same for the nitrogen.
3. Divide the carbon value by the nitrogen value to get the carbon-to-nitrogen ratio. If it's between 25:1 and 35:1, your pile should compost beautifully. If the ratio is higher or lower than that, adjust the proportions of ingredients to bring it into the range of 25 to 35 parts carbon for each 1 part nitrogen.

Math for Composters

Here's an example of how the carbon-to-nitrogen (C:N) ratio works when you apply the formula to real-life amounts of real-life compost ingredients:

Starting with 50 pounds of nonlegume hay (about 1 bale), 10 pounds of kitchen scraps, and 2 pounds of coffee grounds:

50 lbs. hay × 40% C = 20 lbs. C
10 lbs. kitchen scraps × 10% C = 1 lb. C
2 lbs. coffee grounds × 25% C = 0.5 lb. C
20 + 1 + 0.5 = 21.5 total carbon value

50 lbs. hay × 1% N = 0.5 lb. N
10 lbs. kitchen scraps × 1% N = 0.1 lb. N
2 lbs. coffee grounds × 1% N = 0.02 lb. N
0.5 + 0.1 + 0.02 = 0.62 total nitrogen value

21.5 ÷ 0.62 = 34.7 parts carbon to 1 part nitrogen 🐾

Note: "The more dissimilar the materials are in terms of moisture, the bigger the error if you measure by volume and not weight," Eric adds. Even if you're unlikely to weigh every ingredient you add to your heap, this formula will give you an idea how to adjust the proportions of materials in your pile to get finished compost more quickly.

CARBON AND NITROGEN IN COMMON COMPOST INGREDIENTS

This table shows the average percentage of carbon and nitrogen of some common compost ingredients, based on fresh weight. To calculate the carbon-to-nitrogen ratio of your mix, find the approximate percentage of carbon and nitrogen in your ingredients, then follow the steps on the facing page.

MATERIAL	CARBON (%)	NITROGEN (%)
Alfalfa pellets	40.5	2.7
Blood meal	43	13
Coffee grounds	25	1
Cottonseed meal	42	6
Fruit wastes	8	0.5
Fresh grass clippings	10–15	1–2
Dry hay		
Legume	40	2–2.5
Nonlegume	40	1–1.5
Kitchen scraps	10–20	1–2
Fallen leaves	20–35	0.4–1
Fresh manure		
Broiler chicken	20–32.5	1.3–2
Laying chicken	10.5–20	1.5–3
Cow	12–20	0.6–1
Horse	20–35	0.5–1
Dry newspaper or cardboard	40	0.1
Soybean meal	42	6
Vegetable wastes		
Fresh, leafy	10	1
Starchy	15	1
Fresh seaweed	10	1
Fresh weeds	10–20	1–4
Dry wheat or oat straw	48	0.5
Wood chips or sawdust	25–50	0.1

"Roll Out the Redworms" Recycled Barrel Compost

Perfect for small suburban yards, this easy technique from Pennsylvania gardener Jay Jones uses a recycled barrel and redworms to turn kitchen scraps and grass clippings into compost. It works so well for Jay and his wife that they produce *all* their vegetables and fruit year-round (fresh in the summer and canned for the winter) from their small suburban plot.

Ingredients and Supplies

> 55-gallon barrel, without top or bottom
> Kitchen scraps
> Grass clippings and garden waste
> Redworms

Directions

1. Dig a hole about 2 feet deep and set the open-ended barrel over it.

2. Add a couple of inches of grass clippings to the bottom of the hole, then add kitchen scraps and garden waste daily, covering each layer with an inch or so of grass clippings.

3. Once the layers are about a foot deep, add the redworms (the kind usually sold for fish bait). These worms thrive in the warm conditions that will develop in a compost pile, and they speed up the decomposition of the food scraps and grass. (Adding other kinds of earthworms may not work as well as the barrel fills up. Most worm species prefer the cooler temperatures in or near the soil.)

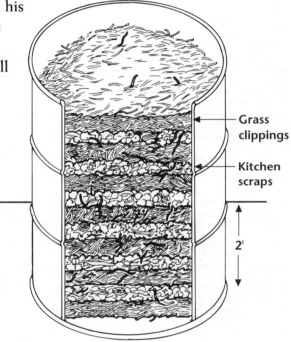

Grass clippings

Kitchen scraps

2'

Plunk an open-ended barrel over a deep hole, add a few kitchen and yard wastes, throw in some redworms, top it off with more scraps, and what do you get? Compost!

4. When the barrel gets full, dig a new 2-foot-deep hole. Lift the barrel off the now-finished compost and set it over the new hole.

5. Add some of the finished compost from the first worm barrel to the new hole to introduce the redworms to their new food supply.

6. Then spread the rich, crumbly compost and worm castings in your garden, where it will provide nutrients, improve soil texture, *and* help prevent disease and insect problems. (And don't be surprised if you soon start finding other kinds of earthworms frolicking in the enriched soil around the barrel.)

THE WORD ON WORMS

When you want to add a little wriggle to your compost, think redworms—also called red wigglers, Georgia reds, or hybrid reds—instead of other kinds of earthworms. The two best kinds for composting are redworms (*Lumbricus rubellus*) and brandling worms (*Eisenia foetida*). Dark red in color and 2 to 3 inches long, these worms are surface dwellers that you can find in fallen leaves in the woods or in manure piles where there is a lot of organic matter. You can also purchase them from garden supply catalogs or bait stores. For a 4 × 6-foot compost pile, you'll need about 1,000 worms. Start with about 500 worms in a compost barrel like the one described on the facing page.

Nightcrawlers (*Lumbricus terrestris*), the worms you see after a rain, tunnel several feet below the ground. They prefer to live where there are large amounts of soil and cool temperatures (not higher than 50°F), so they're not suited for life in a compost bin or wormbox. Use mulch to keep night-crawlers active in your garden during the summer months when warm, dry soil tends to drive them deep under the ground. By keeping the soil cool and moist, a layer of organic mulch makes your garden an inviting place for earthworms to perform their soil-improving magic. Earthworms are especially fond of a newspaper mulch and will flock to spots in your garden where you recycle your daily news as mulch.

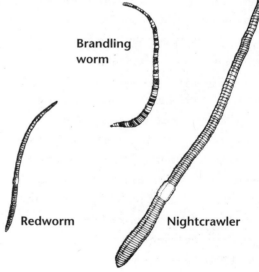

Brandling worm

Redworm

Nightcrawler

Indoor Wormbox Compost

When it comes to composting kitchen scraps, you can always turn to worms. And an indoor wormbox system lets you make compost year-round without even going outdoors. Kitchen scraps are the perfect food for redworms, which will convert the scraps into odorless, nutrient-rich "castings." *Organic Gardening* magazine researcher Diana Erney uses a wormbox composter for wintertime composting right in her basement.

Ingredients and Supplies

Wormbox with drain hole, cover, and
    screened ventilation holes
Redworms

Bedding (shredded leaves or newspapers,
    sawdust, or peat moss)
Kitchen scraps

Directions

1. You can buy a wormbox composter, or make your own from a wooden box or plastic garbage can. "Just be sure it has a drain at the bottom," Diana advises, "because as the worms feed on the food scraps, a lot of moisture is produced." Put something under the drain to catch this moisture—actually "worm tea" (like compost tea)—which makes a great liquid fertilizer for houseplants or transplants!

2. Cover the drainage hole with some small stones or gravel or it just clogs up, Diana says. "I add about 1 inch of gravel to the bottom of the wormbox." She recommends covering this layer of gravel with a screen to avoid getting stones in the castings when you dig them out to use them.

3. Moisten the bedding material and fill the box about ⅔ full. "I also add a bit of finished compost to give the decomposition process a microbial boost," Diana says.

4. Add the worms (you can order them through a mail-order supplier or buy them at a bait shop), and you're ready to begin composting. "My worms absolutely love cukes and melon rinds—they disappear totally in less than a week," Diana reports. Lettuce and coffee grounds also are worm favorites. Always bury the scraps in the bedding to avoid attracting fruit flies to your wormbox.

5. As the worms multiply, the bedding gradually will disappear and the box will become full of worm castings. To harvest the castings, place fresh bedding and scraps in just one spot. As the worms are attracted to the new food, remove some of the castings from the box. Add more bedding to keep the box about ⅔ full, and use the castings to nourish your potted plants, or apply them directly to your garden.

Open This "Can of Worms!"

For ease of harvesting, Diana Erney recommends the unique "Can of Worms" system designed in Australia. "It has three stackable plastic bins with screened bottoms. When the first bin fills up with worm castings, you add the second bin with fresh bedding and food, and the worms will move up into it so you can easily harvest castings from the first bin." (The Can of Worms is available from the Natural Gardening Company, 217 San Anselmo Avenue, San Anselmo, CA 94960.)

The Can of Worms vermicomposter is perfect for small spaces. Worms work their way up through stacked trays of kitchen scraps, leaving rich castings behind.

Foods Worms Love

Don't worry about what to feed your hungry herd of worms. Compost worms love any vegetable or fruit scraps, along with breads, pasta, tea bags, coffee grounds and filters, and any nongreasy leftovers. Eggshells are a particular favorite. Chopping up large scraps like bread slices or melon rinds makes it easier for the worms to turn them into nutrient-rich castings. The worms will also gradually feed on their bedding materials.

Don't ask your worms to compost meat, dairy products, or fatty foods such as peanut butter or mayonnaise. It's not that they don't like them—these foods take a longer time to break down, and they may develop odors or attract insects and rodents to the wormbox. Don't put anything in your wormbox that you wouldn't put into any other compost pile. (See "Things to Keep Out of Your Heap" on page 9.)

Fast, Easy, Pest-Proof Compost in a Drum

Tumbler or drum composters make composting a breeze. They provide easy turning, super-fast compost, and *no* pest problems. Instead of a bin that sits on the ground, drum composters feature a large, barrel-shaped container mounted in a frame that lets you easily aerate the compost by spinning the drum. Since the tumbler is completely enclosed to keep the compost in when it spins, it's perfect for keeping foraging animals out. Drum composting works best when you shred bulky materials before you put them in the tumbler. Mike Peck, president of the PBM Group, Inc., marketers of the ComposTumbler, one of the original drum composters, offers six different recipes that work well in a drum composter.

Ingredients and Supplies

Recipe #1
12 parts fresh grass clippings and/or
   kitchen scraps
3 parts sawdust

Recipe #2
9 parts fresh grass clippings
3 parts kitchen scraps
3 parts straw

Recipe #3
9 parts fall leaves, shredded
3 parts dehydrated cow manure
3 parts fresh weeds

Recipe #4
9 parts fresh grass clippings
3 parts kitchen scraps
3 parts newspaper, wet and shredded

Recipe #5
7 parts fresh or dehydrated horse
   manure
3 parts fall leaves, shredded
3 parts sawdust

Recipe #6
10 bushels fall leaves, shredded
2½ pounds blood meal or alfalfa meal

Directions

1. Choose your recipe and assemble your ingredients. Mike says it's best to moisten dry materials *before* you load them into the drum.
2. As you're loading, close the door and turn the drum several times to mix the materials.
3. Once the composter is loaded, turn it slowly once a day, and it will soon heat up to over 120°F.
4. Check the moisture level every few days and add water if needed. "The material should always be damp, like a wrung-out sponge, but not soggy," Mike says. Tumbled compost will be ready to use in as little as 2 weeks, as soon as the core temperature is no higher than the outdoor temperature during a cool part of the day. (Garden centers and garden supply catalogs sell special thermometers for measuring compost temperature, or you can just stick your hand in and make an educated guess.)

Note: Compared to other composting techniques, drum composting offers the big advantage of producing a batch of finished compost very quickly. That's because it provides the ideal conditions for fast decomposition—even moisture levels, plenty of air, and finely shredded materials. But you can use these recipes to make quick compost in a regular bin, too, because they've been calculated to have the perfect ratio of carbon to nitrogen for rapid microbial growth and decomposition. Just be sure to keep things moist and turn the pile often.

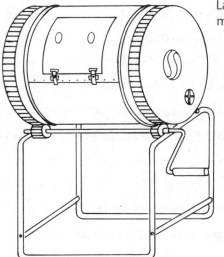

Large, barrel-shaped drum composters, mounted in frames, let you simply spin the drum to aerate the compost.

Chapter 2

FERTILIZER FORMULAS

Fast, Fun, and Fabulous Fertilizer Quick-Fixes

Feed the soil, and the soil will feed your plants. That's one of the basic tenets of organic gardening. In most cases, an annual application of rich compost or well-aged manure will provide enough nutrients and organic matter to sustain your plants all through the growing season. Even so, your garden will probably need a quick pick-me-up from time to time. That doesn't mean that you have to run out to the garden center and drop some cash on an expensive fertilizer. Chances are you have the ingredients for making your own inexpensive, earth-friendly plant food right at hand.

We've polled garden experts from around the country for their favorite fertilizer formulas. Many of these fertilizer mixes, blends, and solutions provide more than the big three nutrients of nitrogen, phosphorus, and potassium. They also include vital micronutrients, plant growth hormones, soil conditioners, and even disease and insect fighters. Some of these time-tested fertilizer formulas include traditional, easy-to-find materials, like fish emulsion and manure. Others make use of more unusual ingredients, like Epsom salts and vinegar. Still others make the most of kitchen and garden wastes, including coffee grounds and weeds.

We hope these gardener-to-gardener formulas will inspire you to cook up some of your own creative mixes by making use of locally available materials for fertilizer. Collect wastes from local breweries, manure from zoos or local farms, leaves from curbsides, and kitchen scraps from restaurants or grocery stores. Many establishments will be glad to have your haul away their wastes for free.

Know Your Ingredients

Some of the recipes in this chapter include fertilizer products that you'll need to buy at a garden center or through a mail-order supply company. If you're new to using organic fertilizers, you may not know the names of some of these products. Here's a rundown of some products you'll use:

Blood meal: dried blood produced as a by-product of the meat industry; contains about 13 percent nitrogen

Colloidal phosphate: clay washed from rock phosphate when the rock phosphate is mined; good source of phosphorus

Cottonseed meal: a waste product left after cottonseed oil is pressed out of cottonseed; may contain chemical residues

Fish emulsion: a liquid by-product of the animal feed industry, made from fish; good source of nitrogen

Greensand: mined mineral deposits; good source of potassium and other minerals

Guano: aged, dried bird or bat droppings; high in nitrogen and phosphate

SOLVING NUTRIENT DEFICIENCY PROBLEMS

When your plants start to look sickly, it could mean that they need a boost of particular nutrients like nitrogen or iron. Observe where the symptoms first appear— whether they're affecting older, lower leaves or younger, upper growth. Then use this table to diagnose your plants' problems and to find a formula for a quick fix.

	Nutrient	Symptoms of Deficiency	Sources of Nutrient	Quick-Fix Formulas (page)
ON OLDER OR LOWER LEAVES	Nitrogen	Leaves yellow; plants light green overall; growth stunted	Alfalfa meal, Blood meal, Fish emulsion, Fish meal, Guano, Soybean meal	Mix and Match Organic Fertilizer (29); Spring-Planting Special Organic Fertilizer (30); Fantastic Foliar Feeding Formula (31); Let Those Grass Clippings Lie! (37); Hay Gives Plants Horsepower (40), Fabulous Fertilizer Fix for Bulbs (43); A Quick Pick-Me-Up for Plants (49); Fruitful Fruit Tree Fertilizer (51)
	Phosphorus	Foliage red, purple, or very dark green; growth stunted	Bonemeal, Colloidal phosphate, Rock phosphate	Mix and Match Organic Fertilizer (29); Spring-Planting Special Organic Fertilizer (30); Swiss Chard Cocktail (36); Hay Gives Plants Horsepower (40); Fabulous Fertilizer Fix for Bulbs (43); Flowering Houseplant Fertilizer (54)
	Potassium	Tips and edges of leaves yellow, then brown; stems weak	Granite meal, Greensand, Sul-Po-Mag, Wood Ashes	Mix and Match Organic Fertilizer (29); Spring-Planting Special Organic Fertilizer (30); Swiss Chard Cocktail (36); Hay Gives Plants Horsepower (40); Fabulous Fertilizer Fix for Bulbs (43); Flowering Houseplant Fertilizer (54)
	Magnesium	Leaves yellow, but veins still green; growth stunted	Dolomitic lime, Epsom salts	The Worms' Turn (42); Medicine Cabinet Micronutrients (50)
	Zinc	Leaves yellow, but veins still green; leaves thickened; growth stunted	Chelated zinc spray, Kelp extract, Kelp meal	Seedling Starter Solution (32); Plant Help from Kelp (33)
ON YOUNGER OR UPPER LEAVES	Calcium	Buds and young leaves die back at tips	Gypsum lime, Oyster shells	Swiss Chard Cocktail (36); Hay Gives Plants Horsepower (40); Fabulous Fertilizer Fix for Bulbs (43)
	Iron	Leaves yellow, but veins still green; growth stunted	Chelated iron spray, Kelp extract, Kelp meal	Fantastic Foliar Feeding Formula (31); Plant Help from Kelp (33)
	Sulfur	Young leaves light green overall; growth stunted	Flowers of sulfur, Gypsum	Fantastic Foliar Feeding Formula (31)
	Copper	Young leaves pale and wilted with brown tips	Kelp extract, Kelp meal	Seedling Starter Solution (32); Plant Help from Kelp (33)
	Manganese	Young leaves yellow, but still green; brown spots scattered through leaves	Kelp extract, Kelp meal	Seedling Starter Solution (32); Plant Help from Kelp (33)
	Molybdenum	Leaves yellow, but veins still green; growth stunted	Kelp extract, Kelp meal	Seedling Starter Solution (32); Plant Help from Kelp (33)

Fine-Tune Your Fertilizing

Our fertilizer formulas include precise measurements, mixing directions, and application rates for many different plants. You'll find all you need to know to make and use your own fertilizers. But don't think of these fertilizers as magic cures. If your plants aren't doing well, fertilizer alone may not solve the problem. It's a good idea to test the soil fertility and pH, too.

To test your soil, contact your local Cooperative Extension office. Most extension offices offer soil tests for a small fee. Soil pH is a measure of the acidity or alkalinity of your soil. You can test soil pH yourself using an inexpensive pH test kit available at most garden centers.

The results from your soil test may include specific recommendations of substances to add to your soil to fix deficiencies, like adding greensand or ground kelp to supply potassium. It's also important to continue building the soil by adding compost or other organic matter every year.

Whenever possible, grow plants that are well adapted to your area and your garden soil. And don't overdo it with fertilizers. Too much of one nutrient may make others unavailable to your plants. For instance, too much potassium may make magnesium unavailable.

When action is necessary, fine-tune your fertilizing to match your plants. Plants grown for lush displays of flowers and bountiful

THE FINE ART OF FOLIAR (LEAF) FEEDING

Plants absorb nutrients very efficiently through their leaves, especially during the first third of the growing cycle. When plants are growing rapidly, are about to bloom, or have just set fruit, they will quickly respond to a technique called foliar feeding, in which you feed your plants by applying fertilizer to the leaves. Spray a fine mist of liquid seaweed, compost tea, or other foliar feed mixture, carefully covering all surfaces of the leaves for best absorption. Early morning and late evening are the best times to foliar feed because that's when the leaf pores open to regulate the passage of water, oxygen, and carbon dioxide through the leaves. So at these times, plants will absorb more of the fertilizer. Don't spray during the heat of the day, when foliar feeding mixtures may burn plants. 🌿

To quickly feed growing plants, spray a fine mist of foliar feed mixture, like liquid seaweed, on all leaf surfaces in early morning or late evening.

harvests of vegetables and fruit will require more frequent fertilizer applications, particularly before and immediately after flowering.

Pick Your Mix

You'll find both dry and liquid fertilizer formulas in this chapter. Dry fertilizers, such as long-lasting granular or powdered mixes, are great for sidedressing actively growing plants. These power-packed organic fertilizers not only supply nutrients, but also improve the texture and moisture retention of the soil by feeding a vast army of beneficial microbes (as many as 900 billion in 1 pound of soil). And these fertilizers will keep on working for weeks, even months.

In most cases, you can just spread dry fertilizer on the soil around individual plants and lightly scratch them into the soil. If your soil is low on any of the major nutrients (nitrogen is especially soluble, so it leaches out quickly from the soil), these dry fertilizers may be the best way to provide them.

The liquid fertilizer formulas we've collected take the form of fast-acting teas and mixtures for foliar feeding (spraying the leaves of a plant) and soil drenches. While it's no substitute for a balanced soil, foliar feeding can be the best way to supplement your plants' diets. Like the vitamin and mineral supplements we humans take to combat high stress levels or to make up for poor eating habits, foliar feedings don't replace good soil fertilizers, they merely supplement them. If major nutrients or trace minerals are missing from the soil, these liquid fertilizers, sprayed directly on the leaves, will provide them fast! Plants will immediately absorb the micronutrients from liquid fertilizers like manure tea, compost tea, and seaweed solutions. Since plants can't store excess nutrients in their leaves and draw on them later, you'll have to repeat foliar feedings at regular intervals.

BUCKETS BEAT BAGS

It's cheaper to buy fertilizer ingredients in bulk and split the costs and the resulting mix with a gardening friend or neighbor. But splitting a batch isn't always possible, and it's a good idea to be prepared in case there are leftovers.

You'll need containers, of course, but labels are just as important. Always label fertilizer containers before you fill them so there's no chance of forgetting a label or confusing the contents with another garden product.

Store homemade fertilizer in 5-gallon plastic buckets with lids. That way, moisture (and pests) can't get into the mix and spoil it. You can get buckets for free—or for a small fee—from grocery stores and restaurants. Attach your labels, or use a permanent marking pen to write the date and ingredients on each bucket. 🌿

Mix and Match Organic Fertilizer

"Make your own custom organic fertilizer for almost any plant," says Bill Wolf, co-author of *Rodale's Chemical-Free Yard and Garden*. In general terms, there are three basic nutrients that a good general organic fertilizer should supply: nitrogen, phosphorus, and potassium. You can save money by buying organic amendments that supply these nutrients and mixing them yourself in the proportions Bill recommends. The specific quantities of each nutrient will vary according to the materials you use, but all will give a balanced supply of nutrients.

Ingredients and Supplies

- 2 parts blood meal or 3 parts fish meal (nitrogen source)
- 3 parts bonemeal, 6 parts rock phosphate, or 6 parts colloidal phosphate (phosphorus source)
- 1 part kelp meal or 6 parts greensand (potassium source)
- Dust mask
- Gloves
- Safety goggles

Directions

1. Choose 1 nitrogen source, 1 phosphorus source, and 1 potassium source from the materials listed above. For example, you could select blood meal for nitrogen, rock phosphate for phosphorus, and greensand for potassium.

2. Mix the 3 materials you've chosen in the proper proportions. Be sure to wear a dust mask, gloves, and safety goggles while mixing the ingredients.

3. Apply the custom fertilizer around the base of established perennials, fruit trees, or roses. You can also mix some of the fertilizer into the soil of a bed before planting vegetable or flower transplants.

KELP HELPS YOUR PLANTS

Kelp meal is the single product that Bill Wolf uses most to fertilize plants because it is such a complete source of the minerals that plants need. He advises applying 10 pounds of kelp per 1,000 square feet for fruit crops, vegetables, lawns, or ornamentals. Adding 1 teaspoon of kelp meal to the potting soil in a 6-inch pot will keep container plants looking their best.

Bill also says that if you can get fresh kelp or seaweed, by all means use it! He recommends rinsing the seaweed to remove salt, then applying it as a mulch or adding it to your compost pile. It decays quickly and is weed and seed free! 🌿

Spring-Planting Special Organic Fertilizer

If you really want to know what kind of organic fertilizer you're putting on your flower and vegetable gardens, quit buying prebagged mixes. Make your own homemade fertilizer and you won't have to wonder about those "extra" ingredients that tend to show up in commercial fertilizers. This mix will give you the "grow power" of a 25-pound bag of 5–10–10 fertilizer—that's 5 percent nitrogen, 10 percent phosphorus, and 10 percent potassium—with no unnecessary additives.

Ingredients and Supplies

17 pounds cottonseed meal
8 pounds colloidal phosphate
45 pounds granite dust
Respirator
Gloves
Safety goggles
Large wheelbarrow or plastic drop cloth
Shovel

Directions

1. Find out what your garden needs before you apply fertilizer. Send a soil sample to a testing lab and ask them for organic recommendations. (See "Organic Soil Testing" on page 57 for labs that offer this service.)
2. Put on the respirator (a more effective form of dust mask), gloves, and goggles, then place all the ingredients in the wheelbarrow or on the drop cloth and mix with the shovel.
3. Before planting in spring, spread the fertilizer over the garden area—the amount

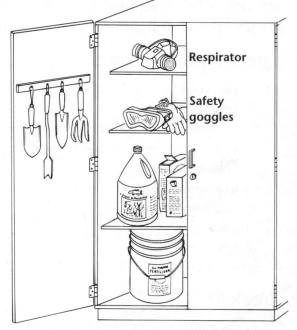

Respirator

Safety goggles

Store fertilizer in a dry place that's out of the sun, like a storage shed or garage. Keep it in a locked cabinet or other secure place so that it's out of reach of children and pets.

you'll need to use depends on your soil test. (Wear gloves, goggles, and a respirator when you work.) Hoe or rake the fertilizer into the top 4 to 6 inches of soil.

Yield: The equivalent of 25 pounds of 5–10–10 commercial organic fertilizer

Fantastic Foliar Feeding Formula

"Foliar (or leaf) feeding is the most efficient way to fertilize," says John Dromgoole, owner of Garden-Ville nursery in Austin, Texas, and host of the "Gardening Naturally" radio program. "When you apply fertilizer to the soil, the roots may take up as little as 10 percent of the nutrients," he explains, "but when fertilizer is applied to the leaves, 90 percent of the material is absorbed." John regularly foliar-feeds all of the nursery stock at Garden-Ville, as well as the plants in his home landscape. His formula includes fish emulsion for nitrogen and seaweed for trace minerals, growth stimulants, and plant hormones. One of John's secret ingredients is blackstrap molasses, which contains iron and sulfur as well as simple sugars that nourish the plants.

Ingredients and Supplies

- 2 tablespoons fish emulsion
- 1 tablespoon liquid seaweed
- 1 teaspoon blackstrap or horticultural-grade molasses
- 1 tablespoon Medina or other biostimulant (if available)
- 1 gallon water (rainwater, if possible)
- Pump spray bottle

Directions

1. Mix all ingredients well.

2. Pour the mixture into a pump sprayer and spray on plants, especially the undersides of the leaves, until the liquid drips off.

Yield: About 1 gallon of liquid fertilizer

Note: You can use this solution on annuals, perennials, roses, vegetables, and fruit trees. Start weekly applications as seedlings develop their first set of true leaves and continue until blooming begins. For vegetables, make one final application when your plants set fruit. Apply to fruit trees as blossoms drop and leaves begin developing. To use as a transplant starter, mix the solution at half strength and apply as a soil drench.

Money-Saving Tip

Instead of using liquid seaweed, buy seaweed powder and mix it with water at home to make your own concentrate. Not only can you mix small amounts as needed, you'll also save up to 30 percent of the cost.

Seedling Starter Solution

It's tough being a transplant. If you've ever moved to a new house or a new town, you know how stressful relocation can be. Moving is just as tough for your plants as it is for you. So give your transplants a break on moving day by serving them a sip of weak "starter solution." Your young plants will recover quickly from the shock of transplanting with this nutrient boost.

Ingredients and Supplies

½ cup fish emulsion
½ cup seaweed extract
Small disposable container,
    like a coffee can
8-ounce jar or bottle with lid

Keep seedlings growing strong by misting them with starter solution every 2 weeks. The light mist from the spray bottle won't disturb roots or leaves like the heavy stream from a watering can would.

Directions

1. Mix the fish emulsion and seaweed extract together in the container.
2. Pour the mix into a jar or bottle. Seal it tightly, label it, and store it in a cool, dark place, like a basement storage cabinet.
3. To use, add 3 tablespoons of starter solution to 1 gallon of water. Use as a soil drench at transplanting time or as a spray for foliar (leaf) feeding.

Yield: 1 cup of fertilizer concentrate

MORE STARTER SOLUTIONS

If you don't have the ingredients to make a fish emulsion–seaweed extract starter solution, you can substitute compost or manure. Don't use manure tea or manure-based compost tea to provide a nutrient boost for your fruit or vegetable crops, since there's a chance manure can carry E. coli bacteria.

To make compost or manure tea, fill a large trash can or other waterproof container one-eighth full of compost or manure. Then fill the container to the top with water. Allow the mixture to steep for a day or two, stirring several times during this period. Dip off the liquid and dilute it with water to a light amber color.

Water each transplant with clear water, then pour about a cup of this solution around the base of each plant. Repeat at 10- to 14-day intervals.

Plant Help from Kelp

Looking for the perfect all-purpose food for your perennials, herbs, shrubs, roses, and fruit trees? Phil Boise of Goleta, California, has concocted an organic mix that keeps his plants healthy and productive all year. Phil and his wife, Ellen McLaughlin, sell organically grown plants, organic pest controls, fertilizers, and seeds at Island Seed and Feed in Goleta.

"Don't skimp on the kelp," Phil says. He uses only cold-water-harvested kelp. "It has a lower salt content and a better nutrient, hormone, and mineral percentage." He's found that kelp also helps to improve the pest and disease resistance of his plants.

Ingredients and Supplies

1 part kelp meal
2 parts alfalfa meal
4 parts any combination cottonseed
    meal, fish meal, and/or soybean meal
1 part rock phosphate
Dust mask
Gloves
Safety goggles

Directions

1. Mix all ingredients thoroughly while wearing a dust mask, gloves, and safety goggles.
2. Use up to 3 cups for each mature rose-bush, perennial, or shrub. For annuals and herbs, use only up to 1½ cups. For midsize fruit trees, you can apply up to 6 cups.
3. Apply 2 or 3 times a year.

Recycled plastic containers like yogurt cups make perfect scoops for measuring fertilizer ingredients in "parts." When mixing fertilizers, wear gloves and a dust mask to protect your skin and to avoid inhaling fine dust particles.

Give Your Plants a Weed Feed

If you can't beat 'em, feed with 'em. That could be the motto of Neil Strickland of Raymond, Mississippi. Neil fertilizes his entire vegetable garden and 3-acre orchard exclusively with a homemade weed tea. Just like cover crops, weeds contain traces of the "big three" nutrients: nitrogen, phosphorus, and potassium. "And fast-growing weeds have many growth hormones and trace minerals," Neil says. He uses whatever is on hand for his brew, including horsetail (*Equisetum arvense*), chickweed, comfrey, nettles, and even willow branches and grass clippings. "If you can use only one plant, make it willow branches," he says, "because they contain many growth hormones that are especially beneficial for transplants."

Ingredients and Supplies

55-gallon drum or several 5-gallon buckets

Silica-rich plants, like stinging or false nettles, or horsetail

Any type of willow branch (watersprouts are especially good)

Green matter, such as fresh lawn clippings, chickweed, and comfrey

Rainwater or chlorine-free water

Stinging nettle

Field horsetail

Directions

1. Coarsely chop some silica-rich plants, willow, and green matter, and fill the drum or buckets ⅓ to ½ full of plant material.

2. Fill the drum or buckets with rainwater or chlorine-free water. It's important to use water that hasn't been chlorinated, because chlorine may kill the microbes that break down the plant matter.

3. Let the mixture stand in the sun for several days (preferably not too close to the house—this is a pretty fragrant fertilizer!).

4. Pour or drain the liquid off the top into a separate container.

5. To use, mix 1 quart of the fertilizer liquid in 5 gallons of water. Spray on plant leaves as a foliar fertilizer, or use as a soil drench for vegetables, fruit trees, and ornamentals. (Neil often uses the liquid full strength on established plants and has not experienced any burning.)

Yield: About 30 gallons of nutrient tea

Note: Add more water and new weed material to the drum or buckets as you use the fertilizer and you'll have a continuous source of plant food. "It's like sourdough starter," explains Neil's friend, Kathleen Chapman, also of Raymond, Mississippi. "You have to keep it going by continuing to add fresh plants and more water. The sludge that remains in the bottom of the container contains microbes that keep the fertilizer cooking." Kathleen says that this weed tea keeps her flower and herb gardens lush and green all season long.

Skeeter Beater

As the weed fibers begin to break down, and the water becomes brown and thickens, algae may grow on the top of your weed-tea container. That's fine. "But mosquitoes can be a problem in the barrels," warns Neil Strickland. He adds minnows to his barrels to feed on mosquito larvae, but suggests that if you don't want to fool with fish, you can cover the containers with screens or lightweight row cover fabric to prevent mosquitoes from laying eggs in the water. Use a transparent or translucent cover and don't seal the top, because the process that breaks down the plant matter requires oxygen and sunlight. Don't use both a cover over your weed barrel and minnows inside it—the poor minnows won't have anything to eat!

   If cold weather forces you to shut down your weed tea preparations for the winter, make good use of the rich sludge at the bottom of the barrel. Add the sludge to your compost pile to get even more benefit from the microbes and nutrients in it. Start a new barrel with fresh weeds when spring arrives.

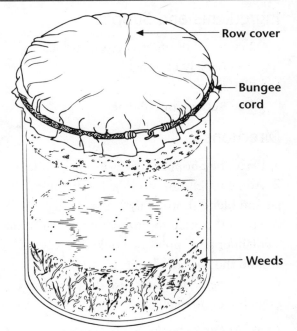

Soak weeds like chopped willow suckers, stinging nettles, and chickweed in water for a few days to make a nourishing tea for plants. A covering of window screen or row cover helps to keep mosquitoes from making a home in your weed-tea barrel.

Swiss Chard Cocktail

Did you go overboard on sowing Swiss chard? Or maybe you're looking for a fast-growing fertilizer source to fill in some empty garden space? You can solve your problems and satisfy your plants' hunger by serving them Swiss chard tea for a quick pick-me-up. Fantastic in salads, stir-fries or just steamed, Swiss chard is great for plants, too. "A happy hour for sad-looking plants" is how Dominique Inge, a self-described "passionate gardener," characterizes her recipe. She uses it regularly on the plants in her organic gardens in Granbury, Texas.

Ingredients and Supplies

2 cups red or green Swiss chard leaves, coarsely chopped
Blender
Cheesecloth or colander

Directions

1. Place the chopped leaves in the blender.
2. Add enough hot water to fill the blender jar and blend thoroughly.
3. Strain the mixture through cheesecloth or a colander and apply the cooked leaves around the base of plants.
4. After the liquid cools, use it as a soil drench around plants.

Yield: About 8 cups of Swiss chard tea

Note: Swiss chard leaves that are longer than 10 inches are best added to the compost pile or used in this tonic tea. You can also use the liquid that's left after cooking Swiss chard in the same way.

Chop your overgrown Swiss chard leaves and process them with hot water in a blender. The cooled cocktail is a great pick-me-up for woebegone plants.

Variation: If all of your chard winds up on the dinner table, you can substitute comfrey in this recipe. Its leaves are high in calcium, phosphorus, potassium, trace minerals, and vitamins A, B-12, and C.

Let Those Grass Clippings Lie!

Grass clippings make great fertilizer, according to Cyane Gresham, compost specialist at the Rodale Institute Experimental Farm in Kutztown, Pennsylvania. Cyane says that it's a crime to waste grass clippings by bagging them up for disposal with household trash because they're such a terrific organic source of nitrogen and other nutrients. "Grass clippings should never leave your property. They are too valuable as a mulch and fertilizer for the lawn, gardens, and landscape," Cyane explains.

Ingredients and Supplies

Lawn mower
Rake
Wheelbarrow or 5-gallon bucket

Directions

1. Mow your lawn.

2. To fertilize the lawn, leave the grass clippings in place. They will break down and add organic matter and nutrients to the soil. To fertilize other areas, rake up some of the clippings (especially in areas where the clippings are dense and might choke out the grass growing underneath them).

3. Put the clippings in a wheelbarrow or bucket and transport them to your garden.

4. Apply the clippings lightly around garden plants. Avoid dense mats of clippings—these can keep water from penetrating the soil. If necessary, mix some fallen leaves into the clippings to create a looser mulch.

MOW IT RIGHT

Some gardeners like to give the lawn a buzz cut when they mow so they won't have to mow as often. But cutting your lawn short is tough on the grass, and it also makes it easier for weeds to grow in your lawn. Ideally, you should remove only one-third of the height of your grass when you mow. For example, if your lawn is 3 inches long at mowing time, you should cut off 1 inch of grass, at most. Mowing high means you can leave your grass clippings in place, which is good for your lawn and less work for you.

If you've missed a mowing or two and have to remove more than one-third of the grass, don't panic. Just rake up the clippings and use them as mulch around your perennials, herbs, or roses. 🌿

Feed Your Garden with Cover Crops

Fifth generation farmer Dean Berden of Snover, Michigan, uses cover crops for fertilizer in his farm fields and his family vegetable garden. Dean produces dry beans, soybeans, wheat, oats, and organically certified cover crop seeds on his 500-acre Thistle Down Farms without using any commercial fertilizer supplements.

In his home garden, Dean also depends on cover crops to build soil fertility. He uses a three-year rotation program, planting a cover crop the first year to build fertility, followed by a "light-feeding" vegetable crop, like peas or beans, in the second year and a "heavy-feeding" crop, like corn or tomatoes, in the third year.

"The microbes in the soil thrive on the habitat created by cover crops," Dean explains. "When the cover crops are cut and tilled under, the microbes greatly increase in numbers and feed themselves on the plant residues." In turn, the microbes generate nutrients in forms that plant roots can absorb.

Ingredients and Supplies

2 pounds per 100 square feet cover crop seed (soybean, oat, and medium red clover seed)

Rotary tiller or digging fork

Directions

1. In the spring, sow ⅓ of your vegetable garden with cover crop seed, spreading the seed lightly by hand and raking it in after planting. Dean recommends combining 2 or even all 3 kinds of cover crops in the same planting.

2. Water the seeded plot well.

3. When the seed has germinated and the cover crop plants are 10 to 12 inches tall, till the plants into the soil. You can also cut the plants to the ground and dig them in by hand, but be forewarned—digging in a

How's That Veggie's Appetite?

To use Dean Berden's soil-building rotation program, you need to know which vegetable crops are heavy feeders and which are light feeders. Here's a rundown of the most common crops by their feeding habits:

Heavy Feeders	Light Feeders
Broccoli	Beans
Cabbage	Beets
Cauliflower	Carrots
Cucumbers	Garlic
Eggplant	Onions
Lettuce	Peas
Melons	Potatoes
Peppers	Radishes
Pumpkins	Turnips
Spinach	
Squash	
Tomatoes	

cover crop by hand can be a tough job! You may want to rent or borrow a tiller instead.

4. At the end of August or in September, re-seed the plot with more cover crops as before. Dean says that, for the second seeding, a combination of oats and red clover is best.

5. Allow this crop to remain in place through the fall and winter. The crop will be killed by frost, but leave the dead plants in place to protect the soil from erosion during the winter.

6. The following spring, till the cover crop under. Allow 2 or 3 weeks for the crop residues to break down, and the plot will be ready to plant. You may want to work the soil lightly again just before planting.

7. Sow seeds or plant transplants of light-feeding vegetable crops (see "How's That Veggie's Appetite?" on the facing page for a list of light-feeding and heavy-feeding crops).

8. Tend and harvest the crops.

9. The following spring, sow seeds or plant transplants of heavy-feeding vegetable crops.

10. Tend and harvest the crops. The following spring, it's time to start again with a year of soil-building cover crops.

Year 1	Cover crops	Heavy feeders	Light feeders
Year 2	Light feeders	Cover crops	Heavy feeders
Year 3	Heavy feeders	Light feeders	Cover crops

A 3-year crop rotation that alternates heavy feeding garden crops like tomatoes with cover crops and then lighter feeders like beans builds and maintains healthy soil, which means more homegrown food for dinner!

Hay Gives Plants Horsepower

Want great performance from your perennials? "Fuel them with high-octane alfalfa hay tea," says John Dromgoole, owner of Garden-Ville nursery in Austin, Texas, and host of the "Gardening Naturally" radio program. Alfalfa has been used for centuries as livestock feed. But John says that everything that makes it a valuable feed— high nitrogen, vitamin A, folic acid, potassium, calcium, and trace minerals—also makes it a great foliar plant food. John says alfalfa tea is especially good for roses and long-blooming ornamentals. You can also substitute bagged alfalfa meal for the hay.

← Panty hose

Strain fertilizer mixes like alfalfa tea through cheesecloth or a piece of panty hose to catch plant debris so that it won't clog your sprayer.

Ingredients and Supplies

5-gallon bucket
1 bale organically grown alfalfa hay,
    coarsely chopped, or 1 bag alfalfa meal
Panty hose or cheesecloth

Directions

1. Fill the bucket ¼ full with alfalfa hay or alfalfa meal.
2. Add water (preferably rainwater) to fill the bucket.
3. Allow the tea to brew for 1 week to 10 days. (This tea smells pretty strong, so don't mix it too near the house!)
4. To make a foliar (leaf) spray or a soil drench, strain the mixture through cheesecloth or a piece of old panty hose. Dilute with water at a ratio of 1 cup of mixture per gallon of water. The final result should look like light transparent tea.

Yield: About 4 gallons of concentrated nutrient tea

BALE BARN

One bale of hay should feed your garden for an entire gardening year. (Or you may be able to collect loose hay from the floor of a local feed store—for free!) Chop and mix the alfalfa as needed. Store the remaining hay under cover to prevent leaching and loss of nutrients. You can keep the hay in a garage or garden shed, or cover it with a tarp in a shady spot.

Note: To replenish the mix, just add more hay and more water to the bucket as needed. When the bucket is full of "used" alfalfa, you can use the dregs to sidedress established plants in the garden.

Compost Is His Plants' Cup of Tea

Malcolm Beck of San Antonio, Texas, knows compost. He is the author of *The Secret Life of Compost,* and he manufactures and sells up to 100,000 cubic yards of it every year. Malcolm believes that compost solubles (the materials that are released when you make the compost tea) are the best part of the pile. He says that these dissolved minerals, microbes, hormones, and other ingredients in compost tea feed the plants, act as a general tonic, and also discourage some pests and diseases. So he makes a simple but effective tea from compost and uses it to feed his plants regularly.

Ingredients and Supplies

5-gallon (or larger) bucket
Compost
1 tablespoon molasses
Biostimulant (optional)

Directions

1. Fill the bucket ¼ full with compost.
2. Fill the bucket to the top with water.
3. Add molasses and biostimulant (optional).
4. Allow the mixture to stand for 2 to 4 days.
5. Strain the mixture through a piece of old panty hose and dilute until the color of iced tea.

Yield: About 4 gallons (or more, depending on the size of the bucket) of compost tea

FUNGUS-FIGHTING TEA

Malcolm Beck says that there are many active ingredients in compost that can help control diseases and deter insect infestations, including many kinds of soil microbes. You can put his basic compost tea to work as a pest fighter, but for fungicidal use, allow the tea to sit for two weeks before using. Malcolm is even using compost tea as an ingredient in a new remedy for repelling imported fire ants.

Note: Apply as a soil drench or foliar (leaf) spray to seedlings, vegetables, and fast-growing plants once a week. Use once a month for slow-growing houseplants.

The Worms' Turn

Jay Mertz always makes room for earthworms at Rabbit Hill Farm in Corsicana, Texas, where he and his wife, Joanne, raise earthworms and sell castings, potting soil, and organically grown plants. He knows that earthworms not only aerate the soil to a depth of 6 feet and make minerals more available in the process, but each earthworm also produces rich fertile castings, or manure, and lots of it—up to its body weight each day! The castings contain several vital nutrients as well as an enzyme that increases the moisture holding capacity of the soil.

"Earthworm castings are the world's best fertilizer," Jay claims. Castings contain all the nutrients plants need for a terrific start, and the additional Epsom salts in his formula provide magnesium for sweet, juicy tomatoes and melons.

A cup of earthworm castings and a teaspoon of Epsom salts sprinkled in the planting hole are all you need to give your tomatoes and melons a great start.

Ingredients and Supplies

    12 cups earthworm castings
    ¼ cup Epsom salts
    Plastic measuring cup or empty 8-ounce
        yogurt container

Directions

1. Put earthworm castings in a bucket or other container and add the Epsom salts. Mix well.

2. Put 1 cup of the mixture in the bottom of each transplant hole as you plant tomatoes and melons.

Yield: 12¼ cups of organic fertilizer mix

YOUR OWN EARTHWORM FARM

You can buy earthworm castings from a garden supply catalog. But it's more fun to build a worm composter to produce a free supply of castings. Earthworms make composting easy—even indoors! Just use a small box to hold earthworms, soil, and kitchen waste. These polite houseguests will consume your kitchen food wastes and shredded newspapers and give you earthworm castings, the world's greatest fertilizer. All they ask for is a nice warm, dark bed and steady meals. To learn more about earthworms and worm bins, see pages 20–21.

Fabulous Fertilizer Fix for Bulbs

Bulbs need more than bonemeal to do their best. Bonemeal does supply daffodils, tulips, and other bulbs with the phosphorus and calcium they crave, but this fertilizer mix offers more. To give your bulbs a more complete diet this fall, add nitrogen (from blood meal) and potash (from greensand or ashes) to your bulbs' bonemeal meal.

Ingredients and Supplies

2–3 pounds blood meal
2–3 pounds bonemeal
2–3 pounds greensand or wood ashes
(use greensand if your soil's pH is near neutral; use wood ashes to raise the pH if your soil is acidic)
Dust mask or respirator
Gloves
Safety goggles
Bucket, washtub, or plastic drop cloth
Shovel

Directions

1. Put on a dust mask or respirator, gloves, and safety goggles (fertilizer materials are dusty), then mix all the ingredients in the bucket or washtub or on the drop cloth, stirring them together with a shovel.
2. Topdress established bulb beds with the mixture in early spring when the foliage starts to emerge from the ground. Broadcast the fertilizer over the soil surface without working it into the soil. Wear your dust mask or respirator, goggles, and gloves for this step, too.

Free Fertilizer Mix

If you have horses or cows—or access to a stable or farm—you can substitute dry manure for the Fabulous Fertilizer mix. (Store-bought manure will work as well.) Use 16 gallons of dry manure, or a ¼-inch layer per 100 square feet of bed. Reapply each spring.

Compost is another great free fertilizer option. Rather than making the Fabulous Fertilizer mix, you can apply 16 gallons (or a ¼-inch layer) of compost per 100 square feet of bulb bed in fall and 2 pounds of blood meal in spring each year. 🐾

Digging around the emerging bulbs can damage roots, so let spring rains wash the fertilizer into the ground.

Yield: Enough fertilizer for 100 square feet

Variation: Substitute 2 pounds colloidal phosphate for the bonemeal. Colloidal phosphate breaks down gradually over about 5 years, so test your soil to see what it needs before fertilizing again.

Roses Respond to Rabbit Manure Tea

"Rocket fuel for roses," is one description for gardener Dominique Inge's favorite compost tea. She and her husband, Charles, use a rabbit manure brew on their antique roses at the Brazos House in Granbury, Texas. Dominique says that the manure tea has never burned any of her plants' roots, but cautions that the tea should be allowed to brew for a few days before application.

Ingredients and Supplies

17-gallon (No. 3) washtub
Composted rabbit manure

Directions

1. Fill the washtub ⅓ full of partially-to-fully composted rabbit manure.

2. Add water to fill the tub the rest of the way.

3. Allow the manure and water mixture to steep in the sun for 2 to 3 days, stirring occasionally.

4. Strain and apply ½ to 1 gallon of the undiluted tea solution around the base of each rose plant.

5. Work the dregs from the container into the soil around the plants.

Yield: About 12 gallons of rabbit manure tea

EASY RABBIT MANURE FERTILIZER

Rabbit manure is just about as close to the ideal organic fertilizer as anything gets—it's high in nitrogen and fairly high in phosphorus (2.4–1.4–.6), nutrients that guarantee healthy foliage, strong roots, and plentiful flowers.

You can make a setup to automatically compost rabbit manure about as fast as your bunnies can make it. All you have to do is keep your bunnies in hutches with hardware-cloth floors like the one shown in "Rabbit-Powered Compost Pile" on page 15. You can start a traditional compost pile below the cages, or even set up a worm composting area below the hutches. As soon as the fresh manure hits the pit, the earthworms will start turning it into nutrient-rich, fully composted castings ready to use in your garden!

Super Food for Roses

"Roses really respond to organic fertilizers," says Judy McKeon, chief horticulturist and rosarian for the Morris Arboretum of the University of Pennsylvania in Philadelphia. "We fertilize all of our roses with this organic blend in early spring and give repeat-bloomers a second application in early summer," she says. "They respond with fantastic foliage and flowers."

Ingredients and Supplies

2-gallon bucket
1 cup alfalfa meal
1 cup fish meal
1 cup greensand
½ cup bonemeal
1 cup gypsum
Dust mask

Directions

1. Mix all ingredients together in the bucket. Wear a dust mask while you work.
2. Pull back mulch and work the mix gently into the soil.
3. Reapply mulch and water well.

Yield: 4½ cups of natural rose food

Note: This formula makes enough fertilizer to feed 1 large rose bush or several small ones. If you prefer, you can triple or quadruple the recipe and store the extra rose food in a sealed, labeled container in a dry, cool place.

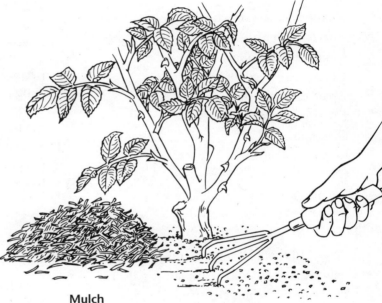

Mulch

Fertilizer

In early spring, push back the mulch around your rose bushes and work organic fertilizer into the top inch of soil. Then remulch the soil and water well. Results—robust roses!

A Bloomin' Wonderful Fertilizer for Roses

Roses have healthy appetites and will put out more blooms if you fertilize them regularly throughout the growing season. Use this formula to keep your roses bursting with blooms.

Ingredients and Supplies

5-gallon bucket or wheelbarrow
2 parts fish meal
2 parts dried blood
1 part cottonseed meal
1 part rock phosphate
1 part greensand
Dust mask
Garden spade
Clean plastic trash bag, plastic trash can, or plastic 5-gallon buckets

FOR HEALTHY ROSES, WATER IN THE MORNING

To avoid disease problems and foil insect pests, water your roses early in the day. Fungal diseases do their worst on cool, damp leaves, but when you water early, the leaves dry quickly in the sun's heat. Spraying your plants with a strong stream of water can knock harmful insects like mites and thrips off the leaves too.

Directions

1. Thoroughly mix all ingredients together in the bucket or wheelbarrow. Wear a dust mask to avoid inhaling dust from the powdered ingredients as you stir.

2. Place the fertilizer in a sealed plastic trash bag, a plastic trash can, or plastic 5-gallon buckets, and label it immediately. Store the fertilizer in a cool, dark place.

3. Every month during the growing season, water your roses, then apply 1 to 3 cups of the fertilizer to each plant. Spread the fertilizer in a circle around each plant, but keep the material off the rose stem. Work the fertilizer into the top inch of soil with a trowel. Then water your roses again.

Note: If your roses are flourishing, 1 cup of fertilizer is enough. But if your plants are extra large or look like they're struggling, give them 2 or 3 cups.

Time your last fertilizer application so that new growth stops several weeks before the first frost hits. In northern garden zones, that means you shouldn't apply fertilizer after August 1; in the middle garden zones, fertilize for the last time around September 1; and in the warmest zones, make the last application by October 1.

Variation: If your soil is very acid, add 1 part wood ashes to the mix.

Mighty Oak Leaf Tea

If highly alkaline water has your plants looking yellow and feeling blue, oak leaf tea can provide an acidic punch. Just keep a few bags of oak leaves handy for making this earthy smelling tea anytime. Acid-loving ferns, azaleas, gardenias, and camellias will really appreciate this one.

Ingredients and Supplies

5-gallon bucket
Dried, brown oak leaves

Directions

1. Fill ⅓ of the bucket with leaves. Add enough water to fill the bucket nearly to the top.

2. Allow to stand in the sun for up to a week until the color of the liquid resembles iced tea. For instant oak leaf tea, pour boiling water over the leaves and allow to cool.

3. Strain the mixture and use it each time your plants need watering.

Yield: About 4 gallons of oak leaf tea

Note: After using all the tea, you can add the leaves to the compost pile or work them into the soil around the base of plants.

To quickly acidify alkaline water for your acid-loving plants, pour boiling water over oak leaves stuffed in a bucket. Allow the liquid to cool, and voilà!

Oak Leaves Make Acid Mulch

Watering with oak leaf tea is good for acid-loving plants, and so is mulching around the plants with dried, shredded oak leaves. The dried leaves have the added benefit of being a high-potassium fertilizer (0.8–9.4–0.1), which promotes strong root growth, disease resistance, and abundant flowering. As shredded oak leaves decompose, they'll lose their acidifying effect, but they'll add valuable organic matter to the soil. Plus, an oak leaf mulch will help keep weeds under control. 🍂

The Vinegar Cure
for Acid-Loving Plants

It sometimes seems impossible to grow azaleas and other acid-loving plants in the alkaline soils west of the Mississippi, but Austin, Texas, landscape designer Sheryl McLaughlin has the solution: vinegar. Sheryl recommends regular additions of ordinary white distilled vinegar, 5 percent acidity, to soil around plants or in containers to lower the pH. She says vinegar applications help plants through stress, particularly after blooming, when they sometimes look chlorotic, and she notes fewer problems with thrips and whiteflies on the vinegar-fed plants.

Ingredients and Supplies

1 pint white distilled vinegar, 5% acidity
2 gallons water

Directions

1. Mix vinegar and water well.
2. Pour the mixture directly on the ground around a 3- to 4-foot shrub.
3. Repeat every 3 months while the plant is actively growing.

Yield: 2⅛ gallons of vinegar mixture

ACID-LOVING PLANTS

Many garden plants, both ornamentals and food-producing crops, grow best in acid soils with a pH below 6.5. They often struggle in alkaline soils, where they have trouble absorbing nutrients.

Common acid-loving plants include:
Azaleas
Blueberries
Butterfly weed
Camellias
Cardinal flowers
Cranberries
Ferns
Gardenias
Heathers
Heaths
Lupines
Mountain laurels
Oaks
Pecans
Rhododendrons
Spruces
Yews

A Quick Pick-Me-Up for Plants

The caffeine in coffee gives us a quick pick-me-up, but coffee and coffee grounds contain nutrients that can give plants a gentle jolt. They're a rich source of nitrogen, tannic acids, and other nutrients. Acid-loving plants, especially, respond to coffee grounds and leftover coffee. (For a list of plants that will benefit from a coffee pick-me-up, see "Acid-Loving Plants" on the facing page.)

Ingredients and Supplies

> Coffee grounds
> Newspaper

Directions

1. Air-dry coffee grounds in a thin layer on newspaper outdoors.
2. Work the grounds directly around the base of acid-loving plants, or, for container plants, sprinkle the surface of the soil lightly with grounds.
3. Repeat monthly.

Note: You can skip the drying step by putting wet grounds directly into your compost pile. If you don't have enough coffee grounds to go around, stop by the local coffee shop or diner and load up. Most are happy to let you take all you can carry. You can also water plants with diluted leftover coffee in water for a quick green-up. For outdoor garden plants, use a 1:2 dilution of coffee in water. For tender or indoor plants, use a 1:4 dilution.

Coffee grounds

Don't throw away those coffee grounds! Instead, spread them out in a ¼" layer on a metal tray to dry. They'll make excellent fertilizer for your acid-loving plants.

Save Your Eggshells Too

When you set aside the coffee grounds from your morning coffee, make sure you save the eggshells from your breakfast eggs as well. Sprinkle the eggshells in your compost pile. Eggshells supply calcium, and the beneficial microbes that break down organic material in your compost pile will work faster and better if you put a little calcium in their diet.

Medicine Cabinet Micronutrients

If your plants are displaying thin yellow leaves, they may be suffering from a magnesium deficiency. But don't despair—chances are good that you have the cure right in your medicine cabinet: Epsom salts. They're composed of magnesium sulfates, so they're beneficial in soil where magnesium or sulfur is deficient.

"Epsom salts make an excellent foliar (leaf) spray to encourage foliage and flower production," says Austin, Texas, landscape designer Sheryl McLaughlin. "Roses love it." You'll find Epsom salts in your pharmacy or grocery store, where a 4-pound box usually costs less than two dollars. And after you finish your yard chores, add a cup of Epsom salts to your bath to help soothe tired muscles, aches, and pains.

Ingredients and Supplies

1 tablespoon Epsom salts
1 gallon water

Directions

1. Add Epsom salts to water.
2. Stir or shake the mixture well.
3. Apply the mixture as a foliar spray or a soil drench.

Yield: 1 gallon of magnesium-rich fertilizer

Note: If you're not sure that a shortage of magnesium is the source of your plants' woes, see "Solving Nutrient Deficiency Problems" on page 26 for help in getting to the root of the problem. If you're still uncertain, try a soil test to learn just what your soil lacks. (See "Organic Soil Testing" on page 57.)

A Sweet Substitute

Epsom salts are a great source of magnesium, but applying Epsom salts to soil will lower the soil pH. If you garden in acidic soil (pH under 6), use dolomitic limestone instead. It's calcium magnesium carbonate, a form of limestone that provides magnesium while neutralizing soil acidity. You'll find it at most garden centers. You can also use dolomitic limestone in place of Epsom salts if you need to meet the standards of an organic certification program that doesn't allow use of Epsom salts.

Fruitful Fruit Tree Fertilizer

With plant food—as with people food—moderation is the key. Fruit trees need nitrogen to bear good crops, but too much nitrogen makes them grow too many leaves at the expense of flowers and fruit. Fish emulsion is an excellent source of nitrogen for fruit trees. By following a three-times-a-year fertilization program, you can bring young fruit trees to bear without a hitch.

Ingredients and Supplies

    1 teaspoon fish emulsion
    5 gallons water
    5-gallon bucket

Directions

1. To fertilize newly planted fruit trees, mix the fish emulsion and water in the bucket and apply. Soak the feeder root area (see the illustration at the right) with the full 5 gallons of formula 3 times: once in early spring while trees are still dormant, once after blossoms fall, and again in early summer.

2. Every year after the first year, increase the concentration of fish emulsion by 1 teaspoon, until the trees reach maturity. Apply the full 5 gallons to the feeder root area 3 times per year, just as described above. By the time the tree is full-size, you'll probably be using 10 teaspoons of concentrated liquid fish fertilizer with every 5 gallons of water for a semi-dwarf (12- to 15-foot-tall) tree.

Yield: 5 gallons of fruit tree fertilizer

Variation: Another good way to fertilize is to mulch your fruit trees early in the spring with 2 or 3 inches of compost or hay that's

When you fertilize young fruit trees, pour the mix around each tree in a band that extends 1' inside the drip line to 3' outside the drip line. This way, you'll reach most of the young tree's feeder roots.

been fortified with a high-nitrogen organic material like manure. Simply sprinkle 2 shovelfuls of dried manure over the ground before you apply the mulch.

All-Purpose Ornamental Tree Fertilizer

Out in the forest, Mother Nature feeds trees and shrubs with a yearly dose of fallen leaves. The leaves decompose to form a nutrient-rich leaf mold mulch for woody plants. Since gardeners usually rake up their leaves so that the leaves won't smother lawn grass, yard trees rarely get to enjoy this natural food. To make up for the loss of food, and to promote good growth and disease resistance, fertilize your trees with compost and this fertilizer formula each summer.

Ingredients and Supplies

> 3 parts cottonseed meal, soy meal, or blood meal
> 2 parts finely ground rock phosphate or steamed bonemeal
> 3 parts wood ashes, granite dust, or greensand
> 1 part calcitic limestone
> Respirator or dust mask
> Gloves
> Safety goggles
> Shovel
> Bucket or plastic drop cloth

Directions

1. Mix all ingredients together in the bucket or on the drop cloth. Be sure to wear the respirator or dust mask, gloves, and goggles when you mix.

2. If you're fertilizing a young tree, apply the fertilizer mix to the soil beneath the tree, starting 1 foot from the trunk and working outward, to about a foot beyond the drip line. (For older trees, see "Find the Feeder Roots" at right.) Use about a pound of fertilizer for every foot in diameter of the crown, as measured at the drip line.

FIND THE FEEDER ROOTS

For the best results when you're fertilizing large trees, apply fertilizer in a band above the feeder roots. Gardeners used to think of trees as plants with long taproots that anchored them to the ground. Some trees have taproots, but all trees have feeder roots—extensive networks of shallow roots that gather nutrients and water from the upper layers of the soil.

As a general rule, most tree roots are located within a circle that has a radius (in feet) that equals the diameter (in inches) of the tree's trunk at a point 1 foot above the ground. The feeder roots are concentrated in a band that takes up the outer two-thirds of this circle.

For example, a tree with a trunk diameter of 12 inches will have most of its roots lying within a circle with a 12-foot radius. Its feeder roots will be concentrated in the outer 8-foot-wide band of this circle ($\frac{2}{3} \times 12 = 8$).

3. Top the fertilizer mix with 1 to 2 inches of compost to act as mulch and help enrich the soil.

When you fertilize a mature tree, spread the fertilizer widely to reach all of the tree's roots. For instance, if your tree has a 12"-diameter trunk, spread fertilizer in a ring around the tree, starting 4' away from the trunk and extending out to 12' away.

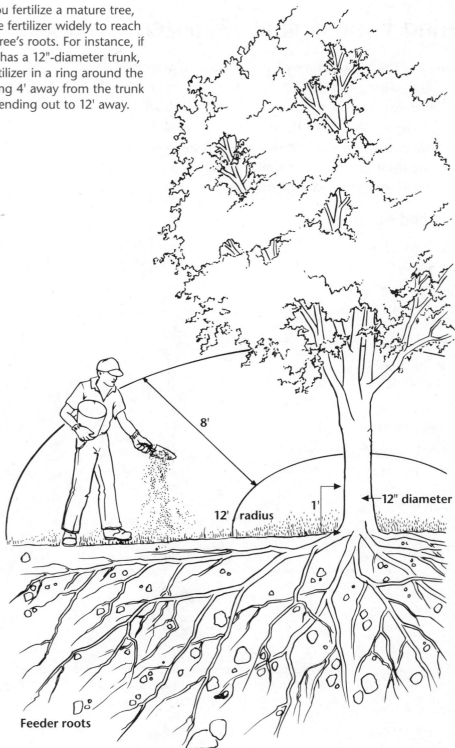

8'

12' radius

1'

12" diameter

Feeder roots

Flowering Houseplant Fertilizer

Foliage plants will put on plenty of leaf growth if you feed them with a high-nitrogen fertilizer, like fish emulsion. But flowering houseplants need more potassium and phosphorus to put on a blooming big show. Go ahead and give flowering plants fish emulsion when you fertilize your foliage plants, but supplement their diet with this mix, which has an NPK (nitrogen–phosphorus–potassium) ratio of 5–6–4.

Ingredients and Supplies

2 parts cottonseed meal
2 parts bonemeal
2 parts wood ashes
Bowl or bucket for mixing

Directions

1. Mix all ingredients together in a bowl.
2. Using a fork, work the fertilizer into the top layer of soil, applying every 6 to 8 weeks at a rate of 1 teaspoon per 6-inch pot.
3. Store unused fertilizer in a sealed, labeled container for future feedings.

Be gentle when you work fertilizer into houseplants' soil—you don't want to tear up the plant's roots. Use an old fork or a chopstick to mix the fertilizer into the soil without injuring the plant.

Vinegar Tonic Tea for Houseplants

Do your houseplants look pale and undernourished despite regular feedings? Maybe your water is to blame. Nutrients are less available in hard (alkaline) water, but you're sure to have a simple solution at hand. Just a little bit of vinegar, diluted in water, can help make vital nutrients more available to the plants by shifting the water's pH into the neutral range. And because it's loaded with up to 50 trace minerals, vinegar may be just the thing to perk up your plants. Raw, unpasteurized apple cider vinegar, when used with every watering, works especially well to green up sallow houseplants.

Ingredients and Supplies

1 tablespoon apple cider vinegar,
   5% acidity
1 gallon water

Directions

1. Mix vinegar and water.
2. Use the mixture every time you water your houseplants.

Yield: About 1 gallon of vinegar tonic

If you know the volume of your watering can, simply fill the container with water, add the correct amount of apple cider vinegar, and spruce up lackluster houseplants with a dose of vinegar water.

A Variety of Vinegar Cures

Vinegar has many beneficial uses in the garden, from acidifying the soil to killing insects and weeds to keeping bugs from bugging you. For a sampling of other formulas that call for vinegar, turn to:

"Paralyzing Pest Salsa," a fiery mix that stops pests cold, page 85

"Deluxe Baking Soda Spray," a one-shot spray for diseases and insect pests, page 133

"A Shot of Vinegar," a weed killer, page 152

"Invincible Herbal Insect Repellent," to keep bugs from bugging you, page 259

Chapter 3

SOIL IMPROVEMENT AND SOIL MIX FORMULAS

Soil: The Heart of Your Garden

Fertile soil is the heart of every great garden. In the woods or a wetland, the Deep South or the desert—no matter where your garden grows—you can use the recipes in this chapter to create rich, well-balanced garden soil and special soil mixes for seed-starting, container planting, and more. We've even included recipes that let you tap the remarkable soil-building powers of earthworms. The more you build up your soil, the better your plants will grow, and the fewer pest and disease problems you'll have. Even watering is easier because rich, organic soils absorb water quickly and then hold it in the root zone.

Regular use of compost improves almost any soil, and compost is a key ingredient in most of the recipes in this chapter. But in addition to plenty of organic matter from compost or other sources, healthy garden soil also needs to have a balance of the various minerals that are vital for good plant growth.

Since soils vary widely in their natural content of potassium, phosphorus, calcium, and other mineral nutrients, the only way to detect an imbalance is to have your soil tested. To locate soil testing services in your area, ask your garden center or Cooperative Extension Service. And before you send a soil sample to a testing facility, ask if they will provide you with *organic* soil amendment recommendations along with the test results. The companies listed in "Organic Soil Testing" at right will provide organic recommendations based on your soil test results.

Organic Soil Testing

Many soils are naturally deficient in one or more important minerals. Or the minerals may be plentiful but not in correct balance with one another. The only way to know if your soil is well-balanced and nutrient-rich is to have it tested every few years. And to get good, organic advice on how to correct any imbalances the test may reveal, we recommend the following testing services:

Cook's Consulting
R.D. 2, Box 13
Lowville, NY 13367
(315) 376-3002

I. F. M.
333 Ohme Garden Road
Wenatchee, WA 98801
(800) 332-3179

Peaceful Valley Farm Supply
Box 2209
Grass Valley, CA 95945
(916) 272-4769

Timberleaf Soil Testing Services
26489 Ynez Road, Suite C-197
Temecula, CA 92591
(909) 677-7510

Wallace Labs
365 Coral Circle
El Segundo, CA 90245
(310) 615-0116

Woods End Research Laboratory
P.O. Box 297
Mt. Vernon, ME 04352
(207) 293-2457

Building Perfect, Fertile Soil

Regular use of compost has produced a totally sustainable and remarkably healthy garden at the Rodale Institute headquarters near Kutztown, Pennsylvania. Head gardener Eileen Weinsteiger has been tending the 40,000-square-foot demonstration garden for almost 25 years (and the Institute has been studying compost for over 50 years!). The garden's remarkable fertility is the result of Eileen's three-part annual soil fertility plan.

Ingredients and Supplies

Compost (enough to cover each garden
   bed to a depth of ½–1 inch)
Grass clippings
Cover crop seed

Directions

1. In the spring, before you cultivate and plant your garden, spread ½ to 1 inch of the compost over your garden. Or apply the compost as a mulch after your crops are up and growing. To cover a 10 × 10-foot (100 square feet) garden with ½ to 1 inch of compost, you'll need about 8 cubic feet, or 320 pounds, of compost. "Here at the Institute, we make enough compost just from our garden weeds and spent plants each fall to give our beds an inch or so of compost every spring," Eileen says.

2. Mulch your garden with grass clippings during the summer to prevent weeds and conserve moisture. The grass mulch protects soil organisms from the hot sun *and* releases a nice, steady dose of nitrogen as it decomposes.

3. Once every 5 years, grow a full-season "green manure" cover crop on each bed to supplement the annual applications of compost and mulch. Eileen usually uses crimson clover on the Rodale Institute beds. To get an idea of how much cover crop seed you'll need, Eileen suggests doubling the recommended field-seeding rate. Turn the cover crop under in the fall or early spring.

Note: Whenever there's time in late summer for a quick soil-builder after an early crop is finished, Eileen also recommends sowing a fast-growing fall or winter cover crop such as crimson clover or spring oats, then turning it under in the spring a few weeks before planting. These green manure crops produce large amounts of organic matter that decomposes and releases nutrients when the crop is turned under. (You'll find seeds for the cover crops best suited to your region at farm supply stores or garden centers.)

Don't Bankrupt Your Garden

Growing vegetable crops and harvesting their nutrient-rich roots, seeds, and fruits without returning any organic matter to the soil is like withdrawing money from your bank account without making corresponding deposits—eventually the reserves are depleted. Soil minerals are used up, and the microorganisms that help to build and maintain healthy, fertile soil starve. But Eileen Weinsteiger's program of applying compost, mulch, and cover crops keeps the soil rich and healthy by making regular deposits to balance her crops' withdrawals. She does this by recycling organic material in the same way that Mother Nature does when plants die, fall to the ground, and decompose. In addition to putting in as much as you take out—just like a bank!—Eileen recommends that you get your soil tested from time to time, just to be sure you don't need to add lime or other mineral dusts to correct the pH or any natural mineral deficiencies that might exist in your region's soils.

One look at the Rodale Institute's bountiful gardens and at the birds, butterflies, and beneficial insects that abound among the lush vegetables and flowers will tell you that all the inhabitants are very happy! You can see this model organic garden in person— Eileen and her crew would love to have you stop by anytime. Under the leadership of Rodale Institute vice president Anthony Rodale, grandson of Rodale Press founder J. I. Rodale, the garden is being expanded. For a free brochure about tours and special programs, write to the Rodale Institute Experimental Farm, 611 Siegfriedale Road, Kutztown, PA 19530.

Keep your soil producing by replacing the nutrients that your plants take out. On the left, the soil wasn't replenished, making the plant miserable. On the right, the plant is thriving because the soil was cared for.

Healthy, vigorous growth resists disease.

Moisture stress increases disease susceptibility.

Weeds compete for water and nutrients.

Compacted soil limits root growth.

Roots spread easily in loose, rich soil.

Organic matter increases soil moisture and nutrients.

Customize Compost Use to Your Climate

The farther south you live, the more compost you should use, according to Eric Evans, director of the Woods End Research Laboratory in Mt. Vernon, Maine. Warmer temperatures in southern regions (USDA Hardiness Zones 8 and warmer) mean longer growing seasons and greater annual nutrient needs.

Ingredients and Supplies

Pencil and paper or calculator
Compost

Directions

1. Find the USDA Plant Hardiness Zone for your area in "'Zone In' on Your Garden's Compost Needs" below.

2. Choose the amount of compost in inches to apply to your garden each year, based on your climate and whether you're starting a new garden or maintaining exisiting beds.

3. Multiply the area of your garden in square inches by the recommended amount of compost to find how many cubic inches of compost to apply.

4. If desired, divide the number of cubic inches of compost by 1,728 cubic inches per cubic foot to find the cubic feet of compost you need to cover your garden.

Note: "If you can apply these amounts of compost to your crops each year, you usually don't need any additional fertilizers," Eric explains, although he recommends that you have your soil tested every few years to be sure that its overall mineral balance is correct.

"ZONE IN" ON YOUR GARDEN'S COMPOST NEEDS

Here are Eric Evans's guidelines for the right amount of compost to apply annually to new beds or to established gardens, tailored for hot, moderate, and cold climates. Use the USDA Plant Hardiness Zone you live in to find your garden's general climate conditions. (If you garden in very sandy soil or where there's high annual rainfall, use the higher recommended amounts of compost.)

HARDINESS ZONES	CLIMATE	INCHES OF COMPOST PER YEAR	
		NEW BEDS	ESTABLISHED BEDS
8 and warmer	Hot	2–4	1
5, 6, and 7	Moderate	1–2	½
4 and colder	Cold	1	½

Slow and Steady Wins the Race

It's tempting to think about giving your garden a *real* boost with an application of one of those fertilizers with the big numbers on the bag. Lots of nitrogen (N, the first number), lots of phosphorus (P, the second number), and lots of potassium (K, the third number). After all, if a little bit of nutrients is good, a lot is better, right?

Not in this case. For fertilizing, the big numbers don't translate into big benefits over the life of your garden. And the numbers on the bag don't tell the whole story when it comes to organic materials, because not all of the N, P, and K in composts is in a soluble—or "available"—form. And that's a *good* thing, because even though the available NPK rating of compost is usually less than 1%–1%–1%, compost actually feeds soil microbes that produce more *total* amounts of N, P, and K that are released over the course of several growing seasons. So with compost, your plants get a slow, *steady* dose of nutrients as microbes break down the compost ingredients. And the release of nutrients speeds up when the soil gets warmer (because the microbes reproduce faster)—just when your plants are also growing faster and need more food. Synthetic fertilizers—the ones with higher levels of available nutrients—give your crops only a temporary fix, without feeding those vital soil microbes.

Those microbes you feed with compost and protect with mulch will produce more than just plant nutrients. Scientific studies have confirmed that soil bacteria and fungi also secrete compounds that improve soil structure and even make "antibiotics" that destroy harmful plant disease organisms. Some of these "microbial fungicides" are now being produced commercially as a safer alternative to toxic chemical fungicides.

> In order to thrive, your plants need a balanced "diet" of five critical nutrients: the N, P, and K of fertilizer bags, plus magnesium and calcium. A lack of any one of these macronutrients usually first appears as a deficiency symptom on the part of the plant that uses that nutrient.

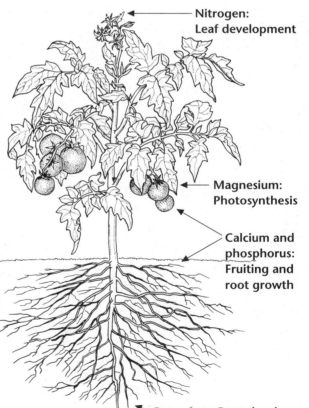

Nitrogen: Leaf development

Magnesium: Photosynthesis

Calcium and phosphorus: Fruiting and root growth

Potassium: Root development and disease resistance

Summer Sorghum Soil-Builder

Growing cover crops is a great way to build soil fertility. This summertime soil-building formula uses grain sorghum, a fast-growing plant that's easy to use, according to Niles Kinerk, president of the Gardens Alive! mail-order company in Lawrenceburg, Indiana. While there are types of sorghum that are specifically bred for use as cover crops, Niles says that he sows just a grain sorghum from seed that he buys at his local feed store.

Ingredients and Supplies

Sorghum seed
Mower

Directions

1. After spring garden crops, like peas and broccoli, finish up, sow sorghum in their place. Just scatter the seed thickly and rake it in. Sorghum loves heat and is very drought-tolerant. Niles predicts that you'll be astounded by the results: "In just 4 short weeks, the fast-growing sorghum will be knee high!"

2. Mow down the sorghum and till it in. "It quickly produces even more biomass than buckwheat, and its stems and roots are brittle, so it's easy to till in," Niles explains. "And it doesn't resprout like clover and rye sometimes do."

Use fast-growing sorghum as a cover crop. In 4 short weeks, it grows knee high and is ready to cut down and till in for a great soil-builder.

Note: If you let it continue to grow, the sorghum would grow tall and become difficult to mow or turn under. But for a quick, midsummer soil-improver, a 4-week sorghum patch is just the ticket.

OTHER QUICK COVER CROPS

When it comes to speedy soil-builders, you can sow other seeds besides sorghum. Here are some other cover crops that produce a lot of organic matter to help pump up your garden soil in a relatively short time:

Buckwheat is a quick-growing summer annual that flowers in 4 to 6 weeks and grows 2 to 5 feet tall. Turn buckwheat under about a week after it blooms. Plant several successive crops of buckwheat to smother serious weed problems. Buckwheat reseeds readily if it's not cut before seedheads form.

Cowpea is an annual legume that grows quickly in hot, dry weather. Cowpea's long taproots pull moisture and minerals from deep in the soil and make the plants more drought-tolerant than many cover crops. And cowpea also tolerates a wide range of soil texture and pH. Plant it between spring and fall vegetable crops. Treat the seed with "cowpea"-type inoculant before sowing. Incorporate plants into the soil while they're still green.

Fava bean is an annual legume that grows quickly in cool, damp weather. In northern areas, plant fava bean in early spring before your summer crops. In warm areas, use it as a winter annual. Fava bean is a tremendous soil improver. The deep roots of fava bean plants bring minerals and trace elements to the soil's surface, and they fix more nitrogen than most legumes. Dig it into the soil when it blooms, 42 to 63 days after it's sown.

Field pea is an annual legume that likes cool, moist weather. Use it as a spring cover crop or as a winter annual in Maryland and south. You can sow the seeds of sturdier cover crops, like barley, rye, or wheat, with field pea seeds, so that as they mature, the other plants will support the weak, vining stems of the field peas. Sow field pea with oats to effectively smother weeds. Treat the seed with "pea"-type inoculant before sowing. Incorporate field pea into the soil at bloom time.

Hairy vetch is a cold-hardy annual legume that overwinters in the Northeast. Sow the seed in any well-drained soil in the fall. It grows slowly over winter and very fast in spring, for excellent weed suppression and lots of organic matter. Mow hairy vetch in spring and leave the cuttings as a mulch around your garden transplants. It may inhibit seedling germination.

Oats grow quickly in cool weather. Use them as a quick fall cover crop that will be killed by cold weather to form a ready-made spring mulch.

Annual ryegrass is a rapid grower that's good for suppressing weeds. Plant it as a summer cover crop between spring and fall crops. Till annual ryegrass into the soil several weeks before planting the next crop, because the ryegrass will tie up nitrogen as it decomposes. Be sure to ask for annual ryegrass when buying seed, because perennial ryegrass and cereal rye are also used as cover crops.

Create a Desert Worm Oasis

Earthworms are the stars in this dryland soil-building technique recommended by soil conservation specialist Jim Brooks of Tijeras, New Mexico. Jim uses straw bales to create the perfect environment for moisture-loving worms to thrive even in the desert.

Ingredients and Supplies

> 1 straw bale (or more)
> Worm food (any available organic matter, like coffee grounds, manure, food scraps, and leaves; see "Foods Worms Love" on page 21 for more ideas)
> 1 handful worms

Straw bales covered by organic matter

You can improve even poor desert soil with the aid of worms, a sunken straw bale or two to hold moisture, and a heap of organic matter to keep the worms fat and happy.

Directions

1. "Plant" the straw bale a few inches into the ground. If possible, locate the bale in a low spot where rainwater will collect.
2. Water the bale with a hose or wait for rain to moisten the straw.
3. "Next, add the redworms and whatever worm food you have," Jim recommends. Redworms are the kind of worm that's usually sold as fish bait. "It's also helpful to add an inoculant made up of compost, soil, and duff (decomposing plant matter) collected from as many different locations as possible where plants are thriving," Jim says. "Just a couple handfuls from each

location will contain vital, site-specific bacteria and fungi that the worms will then distribute in the area you're improving," he explains. Place the worms and their food on top of the moistened bale or on the soil next to it.
4. Keep adding organic matter of all kinds to maintain a layer that is at least 6 inches thick around and atop the bale. "Pretty soon the redworms (which will thrive only in the rich organic waste layer) will be joined by soil-dwelling earthworms," Jim predicts. "You can continue expanding the worm-food mulched area indefinitely."

HOW COMPOST IMPROVES SANDY SOILS

Compost holds moisture, so it improves sandy soil just by helping it hold onto some of the water that plants need to grow. But compost also feeds soil-dwelling microbes, which produce sugar and starch compounds that actually cause tiny soil particles to stick together, creating clusters of particles that scientists call aggregates. These aggregates improve the texture of the soil, allowing it to hold optimal amounts of air and water for healthy root growth. Worked into the soil, light, crumbly compost adds air spaces and drainage, correcting the sticky, water-holding texture of clay soils.

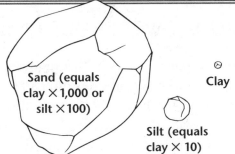

Sand (equals clay × 1,000 or silt × 100)

Clay

Silt (equals clay × 10)

Soil particle sizes affect your soil's drainage. The large spaces between sand grains frequently cause water to drain too quickly for roots to take up. Clay particles, however, hold water tightly, often preventing enough oxygen from reaching plant roots.

SOIL TEXTURE TIPS

Improving the texture of your soil is easy: Just add sand or organic material to increase soil drainage or retain moisture. But first, you need to know what you're working with.

Here's a simple test that will tell you which type of soil you have. All you need to do is to take a handful of soil and moisten it with enough water so that you can squeeze it into a ball, then feel the results.

Sandy soil. Squeeze the moist soil into a ball. Open your hand and look at it. If the ball breaks apart, you have sandy soil.

Loamy sand soil. If you can squeeze the moist soil into a ball without its breaking apart, try to push some of the soil out of the ball with your thumb to form a ribbon. If you can't make a ribbon, you have loamy sand soil.

Other types of soil. If you can push the soil into a ribbon, make it as long as you can, and then measure it. Next take a small piece of soil and add enough water to make mud in the palm of your hand. Rub a finger into the mud to find out if it feels gritty and sandy or smooth and sticky like clay. Now match the results to the following soil types:

Gritty ribbons shorter than 1 inch are *sandy loam* soil; smooth and equally short ribbons are *silty loam*. Short ribbons that feel both gritty and smooth are *loam*.

Ribbons of soil between 1 and 2 inches long that feel gritty are *sandy clay loam*; those that feel smooth are *silty clay loam*; those that feel both gritty and smooth are *clay loam*.

If the ribbon of soil is more than 2 inches long and feels gritty, it's *sandy clay*; if it feels smooth, it's *silty clay*, and if it feels both smooth and gritty, it's *clay*.

Raise Your Beds and Lower Your Labor

Improve your soil with NO digging, using this nifty raised bed recipe from landscape designer Pat Lanza of Wurtsboro, New York. You just layer the ingredients for these "lasagna" beds right on top of the existing sod or soil. Pat says that her recipe will give you a raised garden bed "in half the time and with a third the work" of conventional bed-preparation methods! Pat's "lasagna" recipe is for a 4 × 12-foot garden bed.

Ingredients and Supplies

Newspapers, wet (no glossy colored sections)

4-cubic-foot bale peat moss, moistened

3 bushels grass clippings

3 bushels shredded leaves

3 bushels compost

4 bags dehydrated manure or 4 wheel-barrows full of aged barnyard manure

1 bucket wood ashes or 4 cups limestone

Plastic sheet (to cover bed)

Stones or bricks

Directions

1. Measure the bed and mark the corners, then stomp down any tall weeds or grass.

2. Lay wet newspaper—about 10 to 12 sheets thick—over the sod, overlapping the edges.

3. Now make your "lasagna": Cover the paper with a 2-inch layer of moistened peat moss, then 4 inches of grass clippings, 2 more inches of peat, then 4 inches of shredded leaves, 2 inches of peat, 4 inches of compost, 2 inches of peat, and 4 inches of manure. (You can substitute other organic materials, such as hay or straw, for the peat moss, grass, leaves, compost, and manure.)

4. Moisten each layer thoroughly as you go, repeating the layers until all the ingredients are used. Sprinkle the ashes or lime over the top of the bed.

5. Cover this "lasagna" with plastic, using rocks or bricks to secure the edges, and let it "bake" for at least a few weeks—the longer the better.

6. When you're ready to start planting, re-move the plastic, and stir all the ingredients together with a garden fork. Then pop in your plants, water, and mulch.

Yield: One 4 × 12-foot raised bed that can provide fresh herbs, vegetables, and flowers for 1 to 4 people all season

Note: Pat says this recipe gives you a rich, raised bed with delicious soil and without any digging. "It's so easy, and it takes little time and little money," she adds. And, just one season after you build your bed, you'll find that even the hardest clay soil under it will be looser due to the magic worked by the composted materials in the bed (and the earthworms they attract).

(Learn more about Pat's time-saving gardening techniques in her book, *Lasagna Gardening*, due out in bookstores in 1998.)

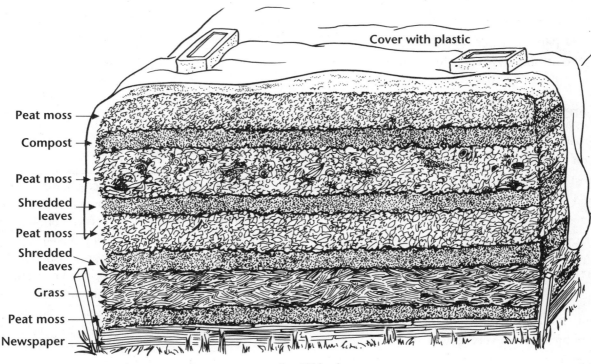

Cover with plastic

Peat moss
Compost
Peat moss
Shredded leaves
Peat moss
Shredded leaves
Grass
Peat moss
Newspaper

4' × 12' bed

Create the perfect soil for raised beds! After covering the top of the pile with plastic, sun-bake lasagna-like layers of organic ingredients for a few weeks. The materials will break down over time to create rich, crumbly compost you can grow your plants in.

Boost Your Beds with Bark

In warm, southern regions, soil microbes are so active that they use up compost *very* fast. This simple recipe from Mississippi extension horticulturist Felder Rushing will make your compost's soil-improving benefits last longer.

Ingredients and Supplies

1 part compost
1 part small bark chips
Cottonseed meal (a few pounds, at most)
Tiller or garden fork

Directions

1. Add the bark chips to your compost pile as you make it, or mix the chips into the compost before you spread it on a new garden bed. Garden centers sell bark mulch of various sizes; for this recipe, you want chips about the size of your fingernail (not the big nuggets or shredded bark, which may be too coarse).

2. Dig the mixture of bark chips and compost thoroughly into the soil, as deeply as you can with a tiller or a garden fork. "The bark chips will break down very slowly, so they help to keep the soil loose even after the rest of the compost is used up," explains Felder.

3. To be sure your soil has enough nitrogen for the microbes that are breaking down the bark chips *and* for your plants, sprinkle a little cottonseed meal (which contains about 6 percent nitrogen in a slow-release form) over the beds each spring. Felder says it doesn't take much—"just a light dusting."

A Menu for Microbes

The soil microorganisms—bacteria, fungi, and protozoa—that break down compost materials into humus need certain conditions and materials to do their job well. They like warm soils, moist-but-not-soggy conditions, and oxygen. They need carbon for energy and nitrogen for growth. In your compost pile, or in the soil, a ratio of 25 to 30 parts carbon to every 1 part nitrogen helps to ensure a healthy, sustained population of these beneficial organisms.

In southern regions, where warm temperatures speed up the composting process, adding wood chips (carbon) and a dusting of cottonseed meal (nitrogen) to your garden beds supplies hungry soil microbes with the foods they need and helps them produce a steady supply of nutrients for your plants.

Earthworm Playground

You can easily harvest nutrient-rich earthworm droppings—called castings—with this clever technique from Betty Mackey, author of *The Gardener's Home Companion*. Use the castings like well-aged manure, applying them anyplace where you want to enrich and condition the soil.

Ingredients and Supplies

Compost pile
Fresh grass
    clippings,
      supplied weekly
Leaves and/or pine needles
Rake, trowel, and bucket

Earthworm "playground"

Castings harvested from under mulch

Each week, add an inch-deep layer of leaves, grass clippings, and pine needles next to your compost pile for worms to enjoy. The rich castings the wigglers leave behind are excellent plant food.

Directions

1. Spread a layer of leaves, pine needles, and fresh grass clippings over an area of about 2 square yards on the ground at one side of your compost pile. The clippings are especially attractive to earthworms feeding in the compost pile, and the leaves and pine needles maintain the moist environment that the worms need.

2. Each week, add about an inch of fresh clippings to the playground and more mulch as needed.

3. Whenever you need a batch of worm manure to feed your plants, just rake back the mulch and wait a few minutes as the worms dive for cover. Then use your trowel to scoop the rich layer of castings they've left into a bucket. Rake the clippings and mulch back over the area. You can repeat this process as often as once a week.

Note: Betty says this technique would probably work even without the nearby compost pile, but she feels that you'll get more worms and more rich worm manure if you feed your wiggly herd beside a compost pile.

Ultra-Light Potting Mix

You can still move even really big containers if you fill them with this ultra-light mix developed by New Yorker Linda Yang, author of *The City and Town Gardener*. The mix's lightness comes from the large proportion of perlite, a porous, very lightweight soil amendment.

Ingredients and Supplies

    5 parts perlite
    1 part soil
    5 parts peat or compost
    Organic fertilizer or dehydrated
        cow manure

Directions

1. Moisten the perlite to reduce the dust, and then mix all the ingredients together.
2. Add a handful of granular organic fertilizer or a trowelful of dehydrated cow manure to each 3 gallons of mix.
3. Use this light mix to fill hanging baskets, windowboxes, and balcony or rooftop garden containers. Keep an eye on moisture—this mix drains quickly.

Empty plastic bottles

Potting mix

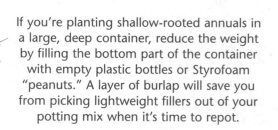

If you're planting shallow-rooted annuals in a large, deep container, reduce the weight by filling the bottom part of the container with empty plastic bottles or Styrofoam "peanuts." A layer of burlap will save you from picking lightweight fillers out of your potting mix when it's time to repot.

Super-Simple Potting Mix

What could possibly be simpler than this two-ingredient container mix recipe from Connie Beck, who teaches vocational horticulture in San Diego County, California. You can buy perlite—a very lightweight natural mineral—at garden centers.

Ingredients and Supplies

> 1 part perlite
> 1 part compost (sifted)

Directions

1. Moisten the perlite before you start mixing—it's usually very dusty.
2. Mix the perlite into the compost, and you're ready to plant!

Note: Connie says that this mix is *so* good at preventing diseases that she lacks examples of plant problems to show her students.

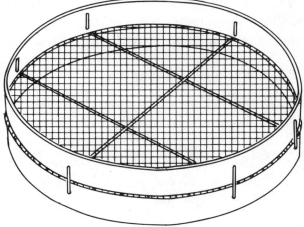

Use a compost sifter to filter out lumps, sticks, and other debris from your compost, leaving fine-textured organic matter to add to your potting mix.

Super-Simple Seed-Starting Mix

This variation on Connie Beck's mix (above) substitutes vermiculite (moisture-holding bits of expanded mica), guaranteeing that transplants get off to a good start.

Ingredients and Supplies

> 1 part vermiculite
> 1 part compost (sifted)
> Milled sphagnum peat moss, or clean, fine sand

Directions

1. Blend vermiculite into compost and fill flats or small (4-inch) pots with the mix.
2. Sow your seeds as directed on the package.
3. Sprinkle a fine dusting of moss or sand on the surface of the mix to discourage the fatal disease called "damping-off" that can infect seedlings at ground level in moist conditions.

Essential Outdoor Container Mix

Plants growing outdoors in containers need a rich soil mix, since their roots have a limited amount of soil to draw nutrients from. They also need a mix that holds plenty of moisture without becoming so soggy that their roots rot. Soil expert Garn Wallace, Ph.D., of Wallace Laboratories in El Segundo, California, suggests filling your planters with this soil mix that's formulated to provide both these essential features.

Ingredients and Supplies

2½ gallons loam soil (not too sandy and not heavy clay)

2½ gallons compost

1 teaspoon Sul-Po-Mag (for eastern soils) or ½ teaspoon sulfate of potash (for western soils)

¾ tablespoon gypsum (calcium sulfate)

2–4 tablespoons blood meal

Wheelbarrow (optional)

Directions

1. Mix the first 4 ingredients plus half of the blood meal thoroughly in a wheelbarrow or on a driveway. The blood meal breaks down quickly and releases nitrogen, which leaches easily from the soil. To assure ample nitrogen for the entire season, Garn suggests adding only half of the blood meal when you make the mix then applying the second half after planting.

2. About 6 weeks after planting, apply the remaining blood meal to the soil in your containers.

Yield: 5 gallons of mix

Note: More is not better when it comes to the Sul-Po-Mag or sulfate of potash and the gypsum in this recipe. Do not use more than the suggested amounts of these natural mineral powders—they are very concentrated! And Garn cautions that you should water your containers carefully: "Try not to apply excess water that would leach away nutrients as it runs out the bottom of the pot."

Variation: Make It Last Longer

For long-term container plantings or for potted perennials, fruit trees, or shrubs, adjust the recipe above by adding 1 or 2 gallons of composted bark chips to the 5 gallons of soil and compost. Each year, mix up the appropriate mineral powders and blood meal with a little fresh compost and add them as a topdressing to the container. The bark pieces will decompose slowly, helping to maintain good soil structure for several years.

Variation: A BIG Batch of Mix

If you need a large amount of mix to fill several really big containers or raised beds, this recipe will make a whopping 200 gallons (27 cubic feet, or 1 cubic yard) of mix.

    20 5-gallon buckets loam soil

    20 5-gallon buckets compost

⅔ pound of Sul-Po-Mag (for eastern soils) or ⅓ pound of sulfate of potash (for western soils)

1 pound gypsum

2–4 pounds blood meal

Use sulphate of potash.

Use Sul-Po-Mag.

Magnesium is an essential ingredient for plant growth. Most eastern soils are deficient in this nutrient, whereas most western soils have enough or too much. When you combine garden soil with other soil amendments, make sure that you have the proper amount of magnesium in your mix.

Zephyr Farm's High Fertility Seed-Starting Mix

This deluxe seed-starting mix gives consistently great results, reports its developer, John Greenler of Zephyr Community Farm in Stoughton, Wisconsin. It includes compost and an organic "fertility mix" that provides just the right amounts of nutrients to get your seedlings off to a strong start.

John uses mature compost that has aged in a pile for at least one year. He recommends sheep, horse, or cow straw bedding to make the compost, and cautions against using poultry-based compost and manures mixed with slow-decomposing wood chips.

Ingredients and Supplies

¼ cup ground limestone
1½ cups Fertility Mix (see the recipe on the facing page)
3-gallon bucket (for measuring)

2 buckets sphagnum peat moss
1½ buckets vermiculite
1½ buckets compost, shredded and sifted (see "Note" below)

Directions

1. Sprinkle the ground limestone and Fertility Mix over the peat and mix them thoroughly.

2. Add the vermiculite and compost and continue mixing until all ingredients are evenly distributed.

Yield: 15 gallons of seed-starting mix

Note: To fill your seedling containers, moisten the mix so that you can feel just a little moisture when you touch it. Spread the mix into the containers without pressure and lightly tap them to settle it. Then add more mix to the top of the containers. John says this mix is very fertile and you shouldn't need to provide seedlings with any additional fertilizer as long as you avoid excess watering that could leach out nutrients.

To prepare the compost for the seedling mix, spread it out on a large tarp to dry, then shred it, if possible, and sift it through ¼-inch hardware cloth. "Compost provides nutrients and beneficial disease-preventing microbes, plus it makes it easier to keep the mix evenly moist," John explains.

Rock 'n Roll Sifter

Sift your compost to gather fine-textured material for seed starting. You can purchase compost sifters at garden centers or through mail order catalogs, or make your own. Here's one that fits over your wheelbarrow.

Simply screw two 24-inch-long 2 × 4s to two 48-inch-long 2 × 4s to form a 24-inch-wide square with handles. Use two 3-inch screws at each corner. Then attach a piece of ¼-inch wire mesh large enough to cover the bottom of the square with enough overlap to run up the sides of each board an inch or so; staple the mesh to the boards with a staple gun to form the sieve.

To use, place the sifter over your wheelbarrow and shovel compost onto it. Then rock or roll the wheelbarrow to help sift the compost through the mesh. Any big pieces

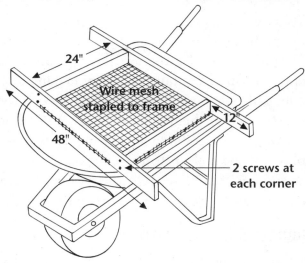

of compost materials that don't sift through the mesh are great for using when you start a new compost pile—they add lots of beneficial microorganisms to get things off to a good start.

Zephyr Farm's Original Organic Fertility Mix

Use this booster mix to add essential nutrients, like nitrogen, phosphorus, and magnesium, to any seed-starting mix or potting soil.

Ingredients and Supplies

2 cups rock phosphate
2 cups greensand
2 cups blood meal
½ cup bonemeal
¼ cup kelp (seaweed) meal

Directions

1. Mix all ingredients together.
2. Sprinkle the Fertility Mix over 15 gallons of commercial potting soil, or stir it into the seed-starting formula on the facing page as described in the directions.

Yield: 6¾ cups of Fertility Mix

Deluxe Seed-Starting and Soil-Block Mix

Your seedlings will get off to a great start in a loose, light planting mix like this recipe from Maine's master organic grower Eliot Coleman, author of *The New Organic Grower*. Use the mix in traditional plastic seedling flats, recycled yogurt cups, or other containers, or try making soil blocks—lightly compressed cubes of potting soil made with a special tool called a soil block-maker (see "Sources," beginning on page 308). Eliot says that the advantage of starting your seedlings in soil blocks is that "roots grow throughout the block of the soil up to the edges and then wait, poised to continue growing as soon as they're set into the garden, instead of circling around the walls and becoming rootbound as they do if grown in regular containers."

Ingredients and Supplies

10-quart bucket (for measuring)
½ cup lime
40 quarts peat moss
Dust mask
Wheelbarrow
2 buckets coarse sand or perlite

1 cup colloidal phosphate
1 cup greensand
1 cup blood meal (if you plan to use the mix for growing larger transplants)
1 bucket soil
2 buckets very well-aged compost, sifted

Directions

1. Mix the lime into the peat moss. Wear a dust mask to avoid breathing dust from dry ingredients. A wheelbarrow is a good mixing container.

2. Combine the peat-lime mixture with the coarse sand or perlite, the colloidal phosphate, and the greensand, which provides potassium and trace elements. If you're making this mix for growing larger transplants, add the blood meal, too. Leave out the blood meal if you're making small soil blocks for germinating seeds—they don't need the extra nourishment.

3. Mix in the soil and the compost and stir all ingredients together thoroughly.

4. Fill your containers with the mix and tap them to eliminate any large air pockets. Then plant your seeds according to the packet directions and loosely cover the containers with plastic to keep the mix moist until they sprout.

Yield: About 2 bushels of planting mix

Note: To make soil blocks, Eliot recommends moistening the mix with about 1 part water to 3 parts mix. Spread the moistened mix on a hard surface at a depth that is thicker than the blocks you're making. Press the block-maker into the mix with a quick push, followed by a twisting motion when it hits the table surface. Then lift the block-maker, set it into your tray and eject the blocks with the plunger. You can set your finished soil blocks in regular plastic seedling flats or, Eliot suggests, try using plastic bread trays from a commercial bakery.

For large potting jobs, you'll need to mix *a lot* of soil. A wheelbarrow is the perfect container for combining ingredients to make planting mixes.

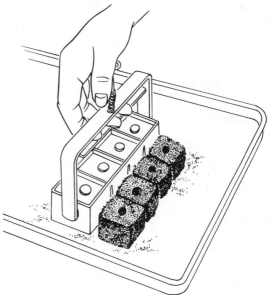

Moisten your planting mix before using a soil block maker—moist mix makes it easier to form blocks that will hold together.

Ward Off Damping-Off

The compost in Eliot Coleman's seed-starting mix will help prevent damping-off, a fungal disease that infects seedling stems and causes the young plants to fall over and die. Other steps to prevent damping-off include:

- Providing good air circulation. Run a small fan near the pots and don't plant seeds too thickly.
- Cover seeds with a layer of milled light sphagnum moss (often sold as "No Damp Off"). Studies have shown the moss contains compounds that inhibit damping-off.
- Give seedlings the brightest light you can. If you don't have a greenhouse or large south-facing window, use fluorescent shop lights and keep your plants just an inch or so below the tubes. 🌿

Oyster Shells for Alkaline-Loving Plants

To increase the pH of naturally acidic soils (pH under 7; most common in the East) so that you can grow plants such as rosemary or lavender that prefer alkaline conditions (pH over 7), try this potting mix recipe from Massachusetts herb specialist Pamela D. Jacobsen.

Ingredients and Supplies

1 part oyster shells (sold at feed stores as a supplement for laying hens)

½ part coarse sand (builder's sand)

½ part perlite

1 part compost

1 part packaged houseplant soil mix

Directions

1. Moisten perlite slightly to control dust, then combine all ingredients.

2. Use this mix to fill containers for growing rosemary or other tender alkaline-loving plants so that you can easily move them inside when cold weather threatens.

Yield: 4 parts of potting mix

Variation: Pamela also uses oyster shells in outdoor beds for plants like hardy lavender.

She amends the soil in a new planting site with up to 25 percent oyster shells, then mulches the plants with a 1-inch layer of the crushed shells. "The oyster shells really serve two purposes," Pamela explains. "They raise the soil pH, and they also improve the drainage, which is very important for herbs like rosemary and lavender, especially in Massachusetts's long, hard winters."

OTHER WAYS TO PUMP UP SOIL pH

Other readily available and inexpensive amendments can raise your soil's pH. It takes 1 or 2 seasons for soil organisms to release the nutrients in these slow-acting additives, so apply them in the fall to give them time to work before you plant. Increase application rates from light in sandy soils to heavier applications in clay soils. Be sure to start with a simple soil test before trying to raise or lower your soil's pH.

SOIL AMENDMENT	APPLICATION RATE (LBS. PER 100 SQ. FT.)
Calcitic lime	2–9
Dolomitic lime	2–7.75
Wood ashes	2

Bring On the Oyster Shells!

The plants listed below will appreciate Pamela Jacobsen's oyster shell treatments if your soil tends to have a low pH. And of course, they're great for garden soil that's naturally alkaline (above pH 7).

Flowers

Ageratum (*Ageratum houstonianum*)
Japanese anemone (*Anemone × hybrida*)
Avens (*Geum* spp.)
Baby's-breath (*Gypsophila paniculata*)
Bergenias (*Bergenia* spp.)
Coral bells (*Heuchera* spp.)
Cosmos (*Cosmos* spp.)
Irises (*Iris* spp.)
Mignonette (*Reseda odorata*)
Mulleins (*Verbascum* spp.)
Nasturtium (*Tropaeolum majus*)
Sweet pea (*Lathyrus odoratus*)
Peonies (*Paeonia* spp.)
Phlox (*Phlox* spp.)
Pinks (*Dianthus* spp.)
Snapdragon (*Antirrhinum majus*)
Zinnias (*Zinnia* spp.)

Herbs

Lavenders (*Lavandula* spp.)
Rosemary (*Rosmarinus officinalis*)
Rue (*Ruta graveolens*)
Thyme (*Thymus vulgaris*)

Trees and Shrubs

Carob (*Ceratonia siliqua*)
Catalpas (*Catalpa* spp.)
Kentucky coffee tree (*Gymnocladus dioica*)
American elm (*Ulmus americana*)
Euonymus (*Euonymus* spp.)
Hackberries (*Celtis* spp.)
Hawthorns (*Crataegus* spp.)
Black locust (*Robinia pseudoacacia*)
Honey locust (*Gleditisia triacanthos*)
Black maple (*Acer saccharum* subsp. *nigrum*)
Bur oak (*Quercus macrocarpa*)
Sycamores (*Platanus* spp.)

Vegetables

Asparagus
Beets
Broccoli
Cabbage
Chinese cabbage
Cauliflower
Celery
Swiss chard
Leeks
Muskmelons
Okra
Onions
Parsnips
Salsify
Spinach
Watercress

Vines

Clematis (*Clematis* spp.)
Virgina creeper (*Parthenocissus quinquefolia*)
Boston ivy (*Parthenocissus tricuspidata*)
Passionflowers (*Passiflora* spp.)

Satisfy Acid-Loving Plants with Sulfur

Even if your soil isn't naturally acidic, you can grow acid-loving plants like azaleas, rhododendrons, or blueberries, says Dan Hartmann, general manager of Hartmann's Plantation in Grand Junction, Michigan. The secret is to add the right amount of sulfur to the soil to lower the pH. Dan explains how to figure out "the right amount."

Ingredients and Supplies

Soil pH test results
Granular or powdered sulfur
Peat moss or acidic compost

Directions

1. Before you can determine how much sulfur to add, you need to get your soil tested to find out the pH. Check with your garden center or local extension office for information on testing services; home test kits are also available.

2. Use the chart on the facing page to determine how much sulfur to add to lower the pH to about 5.5, which is low enough for blueberries and many other acid-lovers.

3. "If possible, apply the sulfur to the planting area in the fall," Dan advises, "or at the very least 1 month before you plant in the spring."

4. If you absolutely have to plant immediately, amend the soil *in the planting hole* with up to 50 percent peat moss. Then apply the sulfur to the top of the soil just beyond the planting hole. The naturally acidic peat

Dormant blueberry bush

Add sulfur to surrounding soil.

Half peat/ half soil

3 × rootball diameter

Appease your acid-loving transplant in less-than-acidic conditions by mixing 1 part peat moss (which is naturally acidic) to 1 part garden soil in the planting hole, then applying sulfur to the top of the soil just beyond the hole.

moss will get the plants started and by the time their roots reach into the soil outside the peaty area, the sulfur will have had time to lower the pH.

5. Dan says you'll also need to add more sulfur in the future. "Probably every year if you started with a pH 7 soil; every other year for pH 6.5; and every 3 to 4 years if your soil was pH 6." He cautions that you should apply sulfur only in the winter when the plants are dormant.

HOW MUCH SULFUR TO ADD

The amount of sulfur you need to add to your soil to keep acid-loving plants like blueberries happy depends on the type of soil in your garden, as well as the pH you start with. Sandy soils typically need less sulfur to lower pH levels, while loam and clay soils take more sulfur to change their pH. If you're not sure what kind of soil you have, see "Soil Texture Tips" on page 65. Then use the results of a soil pH test to find your soil's current pH and the pounds of sulfur you need to add, per 100 square feet of garden space, to acidify the soil to a pH of about 5.5.

CURRENT pH	SANDY SOIL (LBS.)	LOAMY SOIL (LBS.)	CLAY SOIL (LBS.)
6.0	0.4	1.2	1.4
6.5	0.8	2.4	2.6
7.0	1.2	3.5	3.7
7.5	1.5	4.6	4.9

PLANTS THAT PREFER A LOW pH

The plants listed below will thrive in soil acidified with Dan Hartmann's methods, as well as in naturally acidic soil (below pH 7). Most acid-loving plants, including many of these, will also tolerate neutral soil.

Flowers
Bleeding hearts (*Dicentra* spp.)
Butterfly weed (*Asclepias tuberosa*)
Candytufts (*Iberis* spp.)
Cardinal flower (*Lobelia cardinalis*)
Creeping phlox (*Phlox stolonifera*)
Euphorbias (*Euphorbia* spp.)
Heather (*Calluna vulgaris*)
Japanese iris (*Iris ensata*)
Lilies (*Lilium* spp.)
Lupines (*Lupinus* spp.)

Trees and Shrubs
Azaleas (*Rhododendron* spp.)
Birches (*Betula* spp.)
Camellia (*Camellia japonica*)
Dogwoods (*Cornus* spp.)
Gardenia (*Gardenia jasminoides*)
Hollies (*Ilex* spp.)

Hydrangeas (*Hydrangea* spp.)
Junipers (*Juniperus* spp.)
Magnolias (*Magnolia* spp.)
Mountain ash (*Sorbus* spp.)
Mountain laurel (*Kalmia latifolia*)
Pines (*Pinus* spp.)
Rhododendrons (*Rhododendron* spp.)

Herbs
Parsley (*Petroselinum crispum*)

Fruits and Vegetables
Apples
Blackberries and raspberries
Blueberries
Carrots
Eggplant
Gooseberries
Huckleberries
Lima beans
Potatoes
Pumpkins
Strawberries
Sweet potatoes
Tomatoes

Chapter 4

PEST CONTROL FORMULAS

Potions and Practices for Organic Pest Control

On any warm summer day, your garden is filled with flying, crawling, and jumping insects. But very few of these creatures are plant pests. Most of them—including spiders, lady beetles, and many wasps and flies—are more interested in capturing other insects than in aggravating gardeners. So controlling the few insects that are pests really isn't hard. Organic gardeners have devised lots of useful sprays, barriers, and traps for controlling pests without chemical pesticides.

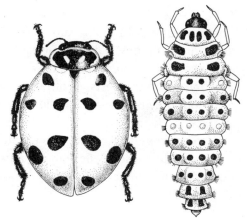

Ladybug　　**Ladybug larva**
Ladybugs, lacewings, ichneumon wasps, and many other beneficial insects are hard at work in your garden destroying plant-eating pests.

Pest insects usually have specific food requirements. Many of the pest control formulas in this chapter work by tricking pests into thinking that they are on the wrong plant or making them eat something that they can't digest.

You'll also find formulas in this chapter for bigger pests, like squirrels, deer, cats, and dogs. These pesky animals can frustrate gardeners by eating or trampling plants. But, although we don't want animals to hurt our gardens, we also don't want to hurt the animals, so all of the formulas you'll find here are strictly nonpoisonous. They work by conditioning animals to look elsewhere for dinner.

Ichneumon wasp

Use these same approaches when developing your own formulas to solve unusual pest problems in your garden. For example, if you have a problem with an insect that eats one type of plant but is never seen on another, try planting the two types of plants close to each other to confuse the pest and lessen the damage. Or you might brew a tea from leaves of the plant the pest ignores and use it to drench the plant that the pest likes. It just might fool them!

Your First Defense Against Pests

If you spot insect pests on a plant, simply pick them off! Then dispense with the pests using two flat rocks or whatever squashing method you can think up.

If the pests are too small, fast, or numerous for hand-picking, take action right away with an appropriate pest control formula. Pest populations tend to build up very quickly, and it's always easier to control a pest problem the day you discover it than to wait for another day—by then, you may face double the problem.

Pest Patrol Bucket Blend

No insect prisoners can escape when you hand-pick pests and toss them into this easy-to-mix blend of soap, oil, and water. In her garden near Fenelon Falls, Ontario, Mary Perlmutter, author of *How Does Your Garden Grow...Organically?*, takes this blend along on pest patrol every morning to dispatch any pesky insects like Japanese beetles, Colorado potato beetles, and tomato hornworms that she finds attacking her plants.

Ingredients and Supplies

> 1 quart water (approximately)
> 1 small bucket or pail
> 1 teaspoon dishwashing liquid
> 2 tablespoons cooking oil (any type)

Directions

1. Put 2 to 3 inches of water in the bucket or pail.

2. Add dishwashing liquid and oil and mix. The oil will float to the top, where it will remain as small droplets.

3. Gather unwanted insects from your garden, tossing the pests into the mixture as you go.

Yield: About 1 quart of pest-killing mixture

Note: "The oil means they have no hope of being able to crawl back out," Mary reports. Caterpillars quickly sink to the bottom of the soap-oil mix, and Colorado potato beetles swim for only a few seconds. The dishwashing liquid in this blend helps keep the oil mixed into the water. By breaking down an insect's outer covering, or cuticle, it also speeds the demise of the pests you toss into your bucket.

Mary often uses the same mixture for several days. When she's finished with the liquid, she pours it onto her slow compost pile (where she puts tree prunings and other organic materials that break down slowly).

HATE TO HAND-PICK?

Many gardeners are squeamish about handling insects with their bare hands. If you're averse to plucking pests with your fingers, try using disposable latex gloves when you go on pest patrol. Your hands will stay clean, and you'll still have enough dexterity to nab the pests. Another option when your prey is slow-moving, like slugs, is to pick up the pests with chopsticks. You can also shake pests like Colorado potato beetles and Japanese beetles off of plants and directly into your bucket of oily soap mixture.

Paralyzing Pest Salsa

Paralyze pests with salsa that's only a little stronger than you might eat on your chips. The creator of this formula, Santa Barbara gardener and author Kathleen Yeomans, uses it to control pests ranging from ants to black widow spiders.

"This is my favorite all-purpose insect spray," Kathleen says. According to Kathleen, the spray will make ants pass out cold, and it has actually killed a black widow spider.

Ingredients and Supplies

2 pounds ripe, blemished tomatoes
1 large onion
1 pound fresh chili peppers
2 cloves garlic
Food processor or blender
1 cup vinegar
½ teaspoon pepper
Cheesecloth or coffee filter
Pump spray bottle

Directions

1. Roughly chop the tomatoes, onion, peppers, and garlic.
2. Place the chopped vegetables in a food processor or blender and blend until liquefied.
3. Add vinegar and pepper to the mixture.
4. Strain the mixture through several layers of cheesecloth or a disposable coffee filter.
5. Pour the strained liquid into the pump spray bottle.
6. Spray the liquid directly on pests that you spot in your garden.

Yield: About 3 cups of insect-knockout salsa

Garlic

Chili Pepper

Onion

Tomato

Get rid of pests fast by spraying your plants with this wicked salsa! Combine tomatoes, onions, chili peppers, and garlic with vinegar and black pepper to make the spray.

Note: Crushed garlic contains allicin, the smelly compound that confounds the sensory receptors of insects in search of a tasty plant feast. Hot peppers are loaded with fiery capsaicin, which gives a chemical burn to marauding mammals and some soft-bodied insects. Onions help give the salsa an extra aromatic kick, and the sulfur in them may suppress some fungal diseases. Many pests avoid tomatoes, so the unmistakable tomato odor signals them to look elsewhere.

Caution: This salsa can be highly irritating if it gets in your eyes or mouth, so spray it only on a windless day.

Pest-Puzzling Garlic Extract

Garlic has a perplexing effect on a wide range of garden pests, from aphids to Mexican bean beetles. This formula for garlic extract comes from David Stern, an organic farmer and director of the Garlic Seed Foundation in Rose, New York. Garlic extract probably works by confusing insects in search of their favorite host plants, so for maximum effectiveness, spray before any pests have become a serious problem.

Ingredients and Supplies

¼ pound garlic (2–3 whole garlic bulbs)
1 quart water
4–5 drops dishwashing liquid
Blender or food processor
Cheesecloth
1-quart glass jar

Directions

1. Separate the garlic bulbs into cloves but do not peel them.

2. Place the whole garlic cloves in a blender or food processor with 1 cup of the water. Chop well. If you have lots of garlic plants, you can use garlic leaves instead of cloves. The chopped leaves also contain allicin, one of the pest-repelling ingredients in garlic.

3. Add the rest of the water and the dishwashing liquid. Blend until liquefied. (This usually takes several minutes.)

4. Strain the mixture through cheesecloth to remove bits of garlic that might clog the sprayer. It's a good idea to strain a second time if any debris remains in the concentrate.

5. Store the strained concentrate in a glass jar with a tight fitting lid until you are ready to use it.

GOOD BUGS DON'T LIKE GARLIC

Be selective when you spray your plants with garlic extract. Even though it's organic, it can disrupt or even kill helpful insects like syrphid flies and lacewings which prey on pest insects. 🐞

Yield: About 1 quart of concentrated garlic extract

Note: To make a spray from the concentrated extract, dilute 1 part extract with 10 parts water (¼ cup concentrate to 2½ cups water). Put the diluted extract in a pump spray bottle or pressure sprayer and apply to plants that are under pest attack or that you suspect are likely targets, like young bean and potato plants. David points out that you can also apply the garlic extract to the soil to discourage nematodes.

Citrus Killer for Aphids

Pesky insects go into convulsions when doused with citrus oil extract. This mixture quickly neutralizes aphids and other soft-bodied insects in the California garden of Kathleen Yeomans, author of *The Able Gardener*. She also uses it to deter ants. "The spray will keep ants away for a while, but they may come back," Kathleen observes. But since this mixture has such a refreshing smell, you'll probably enjoy using it often.

Ingredients and Supplies

> 1 pint water
> Rind from 1 lemon, grated
> Cheesecloth
> Pump spray bottle

Directions

1. Bring the water to a boil. Remove from heat and add the grated lemon rind.
2. Allow the mixture to steep overnight.
3. Strain the mixture through cheesecloth, and pour into the pump spray bottle.
4. Apply the mixture to plant leaves that are under attack by aphids or other soft-bodied insects. The mixture must come in contact with the insects' bodies to be effective.

Yield: About 1 pint of citrus oil extract

Adult aphid

Aphids will suck your plant's juices and can cause considerable damage if you don't control them. A safe and simple spray, made with lemon rind and water, is all you need to stop aphids in their tracks.

Citrus Substitutes

Lemon isn't the only source for a citrus spray. You can make a similar spray using orange or grapefruit rinds. Richard Merrill, Director of Horticulture at Cabrillo Community College in Santa Cruz, California, has tried several kinds of citrus sprays on aphids. "Citrus fruits with pungent rinds work best, since they probably include more limonene and linalool, which are the active ingredients," he says. For example, a navel orange with a mild, sweet rind would probably not carry the punch of a spray made from the rind of a sour orange, grapefruit, or lemon. 🐛

Hot Spray for Flea Beetles

Shoo away pesky flea beetles by dousing plants with a potent mixture of garlic and hot pepper. Pennsylvania market gardener Cass Peterson uses this mixture to keep flea beetles from feeding on her spring broccoli and cabbage.

Ingredients and Supplies

>   6 cloves garlic
>   Hammer
>   1-quart glass jar with lid
>   1 tablespoon powdered or crushed hot
>   pepper
>   1 quart warm water
>   Cheesecloth
>   Pump spray bottle

Directions

1. Smash unpeeled garlic cloves with a hammer.
2. Put the crushed garlic in the glass jar.
3. Add the hot pepper and warm water. Screw on the lid.
4. Shake up the mixture.
5. Set the jar in the sun to steep for 2 days or longer. "If you pop off the lid to take a sniff and your eyes water, it's ready," Cass says.
6. Strain the mixture through the cheesecloth and pour the liquid into a pump spray bottle.

Yield: About 1 quart of garlic pepper spray

Note: Apply the garlic pepper spray as soon as you see flea beetles, and reapply it after rains or heavy dew. Since flea beetles feed on both sides of plant leaves, make sure that the plants are thoroughly drenched. As with any water-based spray, this mixture can damage plant leaves if applied in the middle of a hot, sunny day.

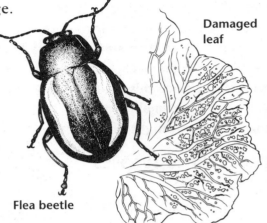

Damaged leaf

Flea beetle

Hungry flea beetles will eat hundreds of holes in your cabbage leaves if you let them. Shoo them away with a spicy garlic pepper spray.

Cass suggests starting a new batch of spray every few days in late spring, when flea beetles are at their worst. Work outdoors, where you won't mind the mess and smell. If a hammer isn't handy, Cass smashes the garlic with a brick, piece of wood, or the palm of her hand.

Variation: You can use any type of pepper for this mix as long as it's really hot. Since Cass grows a variety of hot peppers, she picks whatever type is plentiful. Cayenne pepper or crushed pepper flakes, available on the spice shelf at the supermarket, work equally well and make a convenient substitute for crushed whole pepper.

New York-Style Slug Bait

Stop slugs dead with a do-it-yourself slug saloon. At Cornell University in Ithaca, New York, Dr. Marvin Pritts has studied beers, nonalcoholic beers, and various yeast-sugar mixtures to trap slugs in strawberries. In the strawberry fields where he conducted his research, beer attracted many more slugs than the other mixtures did. The slugs didn't care for plain sugar and water; they wanted beer—nonalcoholic as well as regular beer—and they weren't fussy about the brand! "We looked at many different brands, and there really wasn't much difference," Marvin says.

Ingredients and Supplies

- 2 roofing shingles
- 1 heavy knife or utility shears
- 6 shallow containers such as quart jar lids
- 1 can or bottle of any brand of beer, nonalcoholic or regular
- 1 pail or bucket

Directions

1. Cut roofing shingles into 3 1-foot-square pieces.

2. Fold the squares in half to form covers for your slug traps.

3. Settle the edges of the covers into the mulch or soil near plants that are being damaged by slugs.

4. Fill containers to the rim with beer. Slide the containers under the covers and leave them in place.

5. After 1 or 2 days, empty the trapped slugs and old beer into a pail or bucket.

6. Refill the traps with more beer.

Yield: 6 slug traps

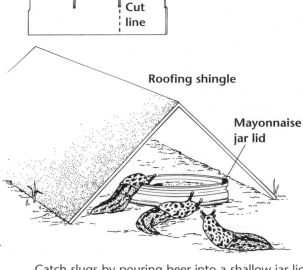

Cut line

Roofing shingle

Mayonnaise jar lid

Catch slugs by pouring beer into a shallow jar lid and setting it near your slug-infested plants. Slugs love beer, so the critters will crawl into the cap and drown. A folded roofing shingle over the lid makes a shady retreat to further entice them.

Note: Marvin says to check the undersides of the covers, too. Slugs may be hiding there, waiting for their chance at the beer. All of the slugs that actually make it into the traps will be dead, but the late arrivals may still be alive.

Ailing Slug "Ale"

If there's one pest that every gardener loves to hate, it's a slug. Slugs can ruin tender young vegetables and beautiful flower gardens in just a few nights' feedings. But slimy slugs will drink themselves to death when you offer them this aromatic brew concocted by Carl Elliot, garden coordinator for Seattle Tilth's demonstration garden.

Any time is a good time to get rid of garden slugs, but Carl says to be especially vigilant in the fall. That way, there will be fewer slugs around in the spring, when your garden is brimming with the young, tender plants that slugs like best.

Ingredients and Supplies

1 quart unpasteurized beer
1 tablespoon sugar
1 teaspoon baking yeast
Plastic milk jug or large glass jar
15 1-quart plastic yogurt containers

Directions

1. Mix ingredients together in the milk jug or jar. If you're not sure whether the beer you have is unpasteurized, check the bottle label.
2. Let the mixture sit in a warm (70°F) place for a few days, until you see bubbles form.
3. While the mixture is brewing, make some of Carl's Seattle-style slug traps by cutting openings 1 inch high × 2 inches wide in the sides of the yogurt containers, as shown in the illustration at right.
4. Pour the beery brew about ½ inch deep into the yogurt containers and replace the lids.
5. Bury the yogurt containers around your garden so that the openings in the sides are about ¼ inch above the soil line.

Yield: Enough brew to fill about 15 slug traps

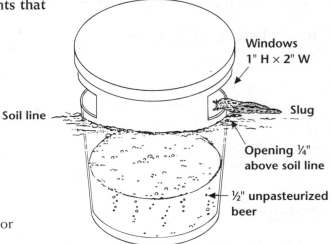

Windows
1" H × 2" W

Soil line

Slug

Opening ¼"
above soil line

½" unpasteurized
beer

To make a slug trap, take a 1-quart yogurt container and cut entrance holes near the rim. Bury the container in your garden so that the holes are ¼" above the ground, pour in ½" of beer, then replace the lid.

Note: When setting the traps, make sure that the windows in the traps are just a little higher than ground level to keep ground beetles from falling in. Ground beetles eat slug eggs, so the more of them you have, the better. Empty, clean, and refill the traps every 3 days, Carl advises. "Slugs like fresh beer. They won't go in there if it smells like bacteria," he says.

A Low-Profile Slug Trap

Here's an inconspicuous beer-baited slug trap that's perfect for high-visibility flower beds. Save some 1-liter soda bottles. Cut the bottles in half, and insert the top half of the bottle upside down into the bottom half. This will create a funnel effect. Pour ½ cup of beer into each funnel and sink the bottles partway into the soil. The slugs will crawl in and drown. To clean out the traps, remove the funnel part, and pour the contents of the traps on your compost pile. Then you can add fresh beer, put the funnels in place again, and put the traps back in the garden.

A 1-liter plastic soda bottle makes a cheap, effective slug trap that practically disappears amid your flowers. Just add beer—a slug favorite—and watch the slimy pests slide down the funnel to meet their fate.

Slug-Dissolving Spray

Fry baby slugs alive when they're hiding in the crowns of daylilies and other perennials in the spring. For slugs that are too small to handpick or be attracted to traps, Marianne Binetti uses this recipe in her Washington State garden.

Ingredients and Supplies

1½ cups nonsudsing ammonia
1½ cups water
1-quart pump spray bottle

Directions

1. Pour the ammonia and water into the spray bottle.
2. Shake gently to mix.

3. Spray the mixture in areas where small slugs appear to be active.

Note: "It fries the skin off the slugs, but it doesn't hurt the plants, and the ammonia breaks down into nitrogen," Marianne says. She keeps a spray bottle filled with this solution by the back door so that it's always ready to use when she discovers slimy slugs slinking around in her garden.

Flower Pot Death Traps for Slugs

Some people eat snails, but nothing eats slugs except other slugs. All slugs are cannibals, so you can trap them using fellow slugs as bait. Marianne Binetti, a garden columnist and television personality from Enumclaw, Washington, came up with an attractive but deadly way to deal with slugs that reside near her raised beds.

Ingredients and Supplies

Clay pots of various sizes

Directions

1. Put clay pots on the frame of your raised beds, upside down, with ½ inch of the lip extending out from the frame.
2. After a few days, check each of the pots for slugs.
3. Knock any slugs that you find out of the pots. Smash the slugs on the top of bed frame, and rearrange the pots so that they cover the dead slugs. The dead slugs attract more slugs to the pots, so you can kill more slugs every few days. "I know it sounds horrible, but it works," Marianne says.

Attract slugs to your raised bed? Yes! But only to collect and destroy them. Set a line of flowerpots upside down on the raised bed frames, placing them so that there is a ½" opening on the outer edge for slugs to crawl in. Simply uncover the critters, smash them, replace the pot, and more will come crawling.

BURLAP BAG BOOBY TRAP

Slay slippery little milk slugs before they shred young lettuce or other spring seedlings. Seattle Tilth demonstration garden coordinator Carl Elliot lays down old burlap bags all around his lettuce bed.

In the morning, when the slugs have retreated under the bags to hide for the day, Carl crushes them with his feet. He leaves the dead slugs under the bags to lure more slugs.

Mealybug Death Drench

Melt mealybugs from the stems of orchids and sensitive tropical houseplants with this cheap and easy spray. Bob Thompson, an orchid hobbyist who lives near Daytona Beach, Florida, says this formula will control mealybugs on any plant, including citrus and poinsettias. The soap kills some of the mealybugs right away as it penetrates their protective coating, Bob says. Survivors are then suffocated by the thin coating of corn oil. "It's horribly effective," Bob reports. "Within days, every mealybug is gone."

Ingredients and Supplies

> 1 gallon water
> Pressure sprayer
> 2 tablespoons corn oil
> 2 tablespoons dishwashing liquid

Directions

1. Place the water in a clean pressure sprayer.
2. Mix in oil and dishwashing liquid.
3. Apply thoroughly to plants infested with mealybugs. Make sure the mixture coats the insects well. The mixture will not harm sensitive orchid foliage, but to be effective, it must contact the insects directly.

Yield: 1 gallon of mealybug-killing drench

Note: Bob usually makes a gallon-size batch of drench for his greenhouse full of orchids. For smaller jobs, just make a quart of drench and use a pump spray bottle.

Recheck your plants about 2 weeks after treatment because some mealybug eggs may have survived. If you find only a few mealybugs, either repeat the treatment or follow up with an alcohol spray (see "Massacre Mealybugs with Rubbing Alcohol" at right).

MASSACRE MEALYBUGS WITH RUBBING ALCOHOL

If you have only one plant infested with mealybugs, don't mess with a soap spray. Just spritz the mealybugs with rubbing alcohol. Bob Thompson keeps a small spray bottle filled with alcohol in his orchid greenhouse and uses it to neutralize any mealybugs he finds on isolated plants. Bob uses rubbing alcohol straight from the bottle (it's usually a mixture of 70 percent alcohol and 30 percent water).

Get rid of sap-sucking mealybugs by spraying them with rubbing alcohol. Your houseplants will thank you!

Steam Treatment for Fire Ants

If you share your garden space with fire ants, you know how painful their stings can be. Gwen Snyder and Phil Strniste, owners of Bee Natural Farm in Fairhope, Alabama, keep fire ants at bay by steaming the mounds with hot water to kill the queen ants and disperse the colonies.

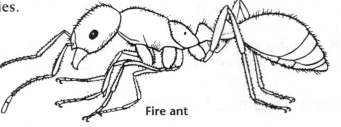

Fire ant

Ingredients and Supplies

    1–2 gallons water
    Large pot (such as a canner)
    Cooking thermometer

Directions

1. Put the water into the pot. Be sure that you can carry the pot comfortably. If a large pot filled with water is too heavy, use smaller pots. (The last thing you want to do is burn yourself by spilling the hot water.)
2. On the stove, heat the water to between 160° and 170°F. Gwen and Phil find that this temperature is hot enough to kill fire ants and safer to handle than boiling water.
3. Quietly carry your pot or pots of water outdoors and set them near the fire ant mound.
4. Douse the mound quickly with 1 to 2 gallons of hot water. Your objective is to kill the queen, so don't disturb the colony before pouring on the water. The worker ants will quickly spirit the queen away when the mound is disturbed. The queen is most likely to be active on a warm day between 11:00 A.M. and 2:00 P.M.

Note: By the time you return to the ant colony on the second day, the surviving ants will have built a new home. To really be effective against large colonies, the treatment

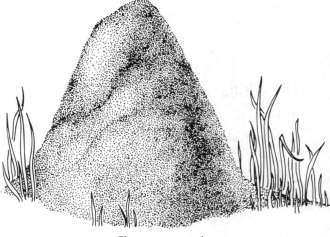

Fire ant mound
Fire ants inflict venomous stings, and they're quick to attack at the slightest provocation. They form tall earth mounds, where they live in large colonies.

may need to be repeated for 3 consecutive days, Gwen and Phil say. If the colony disappears after 1 or 2 applications, look around to see if the ants have moved to a new spot. Continue to steam out any small colonies as soon as they appear, provided that they are far enough away from plants that the hot water will not injure the plants' roots.

Fire Ant Sticky Traps

In their garden, Gwen Snyder and Phil Strniste find that hot water never gets rid of every last fire ant. They use a different method for keeping ants from chewing on okra flowers and pods, which fire ants are especially fond of. Phil paints the main stems of his okra plants with a sticky substance used to trap insects, such as Stickem or Tangle-Trap. The fire ants either get stuck or won't try to cross the sticky barrier, so they never reach the flowers and pods.

You can also use a band of sticky goo to protect citrus trees from fire ant feeding. Fire ants chew on the bark and growing tips of citrus trees and also feed on the fruit.

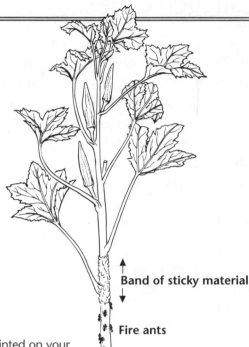

Band of sticky material

Fire ants

A barrier of sticky goo, like Tangle-Trap or Stickem, painted on your okra stems prevents hungry fire ants from reaching flowers and pods.

Try a Dusty Fire Ant Deterrent

Disturbing an active fire ant mound is certainly no picnic for you or your pets, and it's all too easy to do in an area infested with these pests. Although they're small—⅛- to ¼-inch long—fire ants inflict a painful sting, and they often attack by the hundreds when their territory is invaded.

Fire ants are pests in the garden, where they may damage eggplant, corn, okra, strawberries, and potatoes. They can also become household pests, entering through small cracks near the soil line and building nests inside walls, around plumbing, and under carpeting.

If you live in an area where fire ants are active, use a dusty barrier of diatomaceous earth (DE) to help keep these pests from moving into your garden or your home. DE is a natural material made from the fossilized remains of diatoms. When insects come in contact with DE, it damages and dries their waxy outer skeleton, and they die of dehydration.

To keep fire ants out of your house, caulk openings, especially near the soil level. Then apply a 2- to 3-inch band of DE around the foundation. Use a similar DE band around your garden to exclude fire ants from your crops. Wear a dust mask and goggles when applying DE to avoid inhaling the dust or getting it in your eyes.

Chigger-Chasing Sulfur

If you live in the Southeast, you probably know the unpleasant aftereffects of an encounter with chiggers. Take heart! You can conquer the chiggers lurking in your lawn with two well-timed applications of soil sulfur, a concentrated sulfur product available at some garden centers that is used to lower soil pH. Trisha Shirey, grounds manager at Lake Austin Spa Resort in Austin, Texas, says this remedy is especially effective in soft swaths of Bermuda grass.

Ingredients and Supplies

5 pounds powdered soil sulfur
Drop or broadcast spreader
Rubber gloves
Dust mask
Oscillating sprinkler

Directions

1. Early in the morning when the grass is wet with dew, use the drop or broadcast spreader to apply the sulfur, taking care to apply it as evenly as possible. Sulfur is a natural chemical dust, so wear rubber gloves and a dust mask to protect your hands and lungs while you work.

2. Immediately water the area for about 20 minutes using an oscillating sprinkler. Be sure that the sulfur is completely washed down into the grass.

Yield: Enough sulfur to treat 100 square feet of lawn

SULFUR SIDE EFFECTS

Sulfur not only chases chiggers away but it also tends to lower soil pH (makes the soil more acidic). So if you're applying sulfur on soils that tend to be alkaline, you're probably doing yourself a double favor. But if your soil is naturally acidic, check the pH in the fall if you used soil sulfur during the summer. If the pH has fallen below 5.3, you'll need to apply lime to raise the pH. Ask your local Cooperative Extension Service for recommendations on how much lime to apply, or see "Other Ways to Pump Up Soil pH" on page 78.

Note: For best results, Trisha suggests following this procedure twice each summer—once in late spring and again in late summer. Tricia thinks that the sulfur treatment can also help control fleas in the lawn.

Rub Out Pests with Rubbing Alcohol

Houseplants bothered by pests? Rub them out with rubbing alcohol. Gardener Dominique Inge of Granbury, Texas, finds this recipe effective against mealybugs, whiteflies, red spider mites, aphids, fungus gnats, and scale. She cautions that it may cause leaf burn on some plants and doesn't recommend it for African violets.

Ingredients and Supplies

½–1 cup rubbing alcohol
1 quart water
Pump spray bottle

Directions

1. Mix ingredients in a pump spray bottle.
2. Test spray on a leaf to check for burning.
3. Wait 1 day and check for damage before treating the entire plant.
4. Treat at 3-day intervals for 10 days or as needed. Don't use this in the heat of the day.

Yield: 4½–5 cups of alcohol spray

WASH AND VACUUM PESTS AWAY

Ordinary water is a great weapon for dispatching houseplant pests. If your houseplants are infested with spider mites or aphids, try putting the plants in your kitchen sink and running a strong stream or spray of cool water over the foliage and stems. The force of the water can literally wash whiteflies, mites, and aphids right off the plants. Check the plants a few days later. If you find pesky pests that survived the treatment, wash the plants again. (Note that African violets dislike having their foliage washed, so don't try this technique on your violets.)

For plants that you can't wash, try vacuuming instead! Get out your handheld vacuum cleaner. With one hand, move the vacuum lightly over the plants, and with the other hand, support or hold the foliage so that the suction of the vaccuum won't tear the leaves. Keep in mind that the insects you vacuum up may be only stunned, not killed. When you're finished pest-vacuuming, move away from your plants before you open the vacuum. Dump the pests into soapy water to kill them. This treatment works well for whiteflies, but may not be strong enough to suck off aphids or all spider mites.

Tomato Stake Whitefly Trap

Trick whiteflies with the color yellow. Whiteflies are attracted to yellow surfaces, and you can buy commercially produced traps that have sticky yellow surfaces where whiteflies land and get fatally stuck. In Brooklyn, Ohio, tomato lover Katherine Jarmusik came up with a nifty way to recycle some household items into a sticky whitefly trap at a cost that is much lower than the price of commercial traps.

Adult whitefly

Ingredients and Supplies

4 6-foot-long tomato stakes
4 48-ounce juice cans, each with 1 end
    removed
Yellow paint
Paintbrush
12 yellow or clear plastic bags
    (like the ones used to cover
    newspapers on rainy days)
Petroleum jelly

Directions

1. Use the stakes to support growing tomatoes. Or, if you're already using another type of support for your tomatoes, pound in the stakes alongside the plants. Four stakes set every 2 feet will protect a row of 10 tomatoes.

2. Paint the juice cans yellow.

3. Place the painted cans over the tops of the tomato stakes.

4. Cover each can with a yellow or clear plastic bag.

5. Smear petroleum jelly on the outside of the bags.

Yield: 4 super-sticky whitefly traps

A whitefly looks just like its name suggests—a flying white blur. These pests feed on sap, gathering in large swarms on leaf undersides. If you shake an infested plant, a cloud of tiny whiteflies will take to the air.

Can covered with plastic bag

Trap whiteflies by placing a plastic bag over an inverted can and coating the bag with petroleum jelly. Put the can on top of a stake in the midst of your tomatoes.

DEALING WITH DEAD WHITEFLIES

Whiteflies are so attracted to her yellow traps that the whole bag is soon covered, Katherine Jarmusik says. When the whiteflies get too thick on the bags, she removes the old bags, throws them away, and replaces them with new ones that are coated with fresh petroleum jelly.

Katherine finds that 4 cans, with 2 or 3 bag replacements per can, are enough to protect her 20 × 30-foot garden plot from whitefly damage. Yellow is the key to success with these traps, Katherine points out. "If you have enough yellow plastic bags, you can skip the step of painting the cans." 🐞

Vinegar Foils Fungus Gnats

Lure fungus gnats and fruit flies to a watery death with a simple cider vinegar trap. Christine Haugen, director of Green Horizons International who specializes in earth-safe pest control, uses this formula when fungus gnats or fruit flies invade her Virginia home. "The gnats will find the jar within a few minutes and land on the rim to investigate," Christine says. "Then they will continue on in and drown."

Ingredients and Supplies

1 small wide-mouth jar (a baby food or bouillon jar works well)
1 tablespoon cider vinegar

Directions

1. Fill the jar about ⅞ full with water.
2. Add the vinegar.
3. Place the jar on a kitchen counter or table, especially near ripening fruit. You can also place the traps near houseplants if they're infested with fungus gnats. Leave the trap undisturbed.

Yield: About ⅔ cup of fungus gnat attractant

Note: In most situations, all the fungus gnats and fruit flies in your house will die in the

FIGHTING FUNGUS GNAT LARVAE

Fungus gnats look like tiny fruit flies with beige wings. The gnats may lay eggs in the soil of houseplants, and their larvae may suck juices from the roots of the plants. Since the cider vinegar traps attract only adult fungus gnats, Christine Haugen suggests using neem to control the larvae in the soil. Neem is an organic pest control product extracted from the neem tree; it's available at garden centers and from mail-order garden suppliers. 🐞

trap within a few days. If you have a severe problem, you may need to replace the mixture in the jar after a week or so.

Confuse Cuke Beetles with Rattails

Confuse cucumber beetles and other garden pests by planting rattail radishes in and around your vegetables. After Master Gardener Carol Kelly of Saltsburg, Pennsylvania, heard other gardeners talking about interplanting radishes with pest-plagued crops, she decided to try rattail radishes, a special variety of radishes that have edible pods. She especially recommends planting this tasty deterrent around your summer squash plants to repel cucumber beetles.

Carol thinks that regular radishes will discourage cucumber beetles, too, but the rattail radish plants grow bigger—often 18 inches tall—and she likes the flavor of the edible pods, which appear after the flowers. "I pick them when they're still young and tender and chop them into salads," Carol says. Rattail radishes develop a thick taproot, but it's not edible like other kinds of radishes.

Striped cucumber beetles often eat squash family crops, beans, peas, and other plants. Besides consuming your crops, they can also transmit plant diseases.

Ingredients and Supplies

    1 packet summer squash seeds
    1 packet rattail radish seeds

Directions

1. After danger of frost has passed, plant squash seeds or transplants directly in the garden.

2. Sow a few rattail radish seeds in between the rows or around the hills of squash and at the ends of the rows. Rattail radish seeds are available in seed catalogs—check the listings for oriental vegetables. (One source is Pine-tree Garden Seeds; see "Sources," beginning on page 308.)

If you're planting different types of summer squash together, such as pattypan squash and zucchini, plant extra rattail radishes between them. The radishes will confuse pests and serve as row markers at the same time.

Onion Rings for Cabbage Loopers

Confuse cabbage loopers and cabbageworms by surrounding your broccoli, cabbage, and cauliflower plants with onions. In both spring and fall, Charlotte, North Carolina, gardener Jeff Davis sees very few loopers when he uses this easy companion planting method.

Ingredients and Supplies

> 20 assorted cabbage, cauliflower, broccoli, kohlrabi, or brussels sprout seedlings
> 100 onion sets

Directions

1. In the spring, set out the seedlings in the normal manner, spacing them at least 18 inches apart.

2. As you settle in each plant, surround it with a ring of onion sets, spacing them 4 inches apart. The idea, Jeff says, is to encircle the cabbage family plants so that they're hidden by a screen of onions.

Note: Jeff inspects his plants often in search of cabbage loopers, but rarely finds one of the leaf-eating visitors. On 20 cabbage plants surrounded by onions, he may find 3 loopers at the peak of their season.

Some of the onions eventually grow into bulbs, but Jeff harvests most of them for use as green onions.

Cabbage looper

Imported cabbageworm

Imported cabbageworms and cabbage loopers feed on leaves in the cabbage family. Imported cabbageworm adults are white butterflies, whereas cabbage looper adults are gray mottled moths.

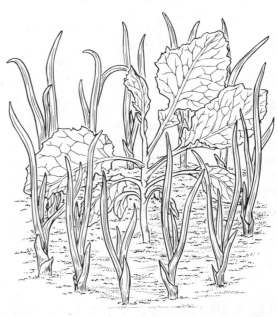

Discourage the adult moths of cabbageworms and cabbage loopers from laying eggs on cabbage-family plants by planting a ring of onion sets around each seedling.

Beetle-Busting Potato Planting

Outsmart Colorado potato beetles before they stage a feast in your potato patch. Cynthia Connolly, an organic market gardener in Monticello, Florida, uses a companion planting plan to confound the beetles. Her not-so-secret weapons are garlic and onions. "The year we first tried this, Colorado potato beetles devastated our other potatoes, but the ones grown with the garlic had hardly any damage at all," Cynthia explains. Potato beetle adults looking for host plants upon which to lay eggs apparently are confused by the barrier of onions and garlic that guards the spuds.

Adult Colorado potato beetle

Larva

You can identify a Colorado potato beetle adult by the striking black and yellow stripes along the wing covers. These plump beetles develop from blimplike larvae, which are orange with black spots on each side.

Ingredients and Supplies

30 garlic cloves or plants

40 onion plants or sets

Seed potatoes for a 20-foot-long row
(about 5 pounds)

Directions

1. In the fall, dig or till a garden bed or row in an area of your garden where potatoes have not been grown for 2 years.

2. Plant sprouting garlic cloves (or set out garlic plants) in a line down the outside of one side of the row or bed.

3. In early spring, plant seed potatoes down the middle of the prepared row or bed.

4. Plant onion plants or sets down the side of the row or bed opposite from the garlic, so that the potatoes are surrounded on all sides with garlic and onions.

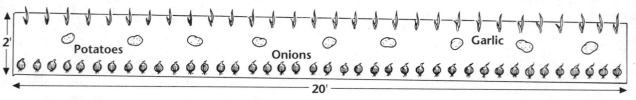

A planting of garlic and onions around vulnerable potatoes will help confuse Colorado potato beetles and keep them from locating their favorite food.

1 teaspoon chili powder

Gummy Grasshopper Flour Formula

Stop grasshoppers from eating your plants by making them eat all-purpose flour. When you use this simple flour dust, grasshoppers, blister beetles, and other chewing insects will end up with their mouthparts so gummed up that they can't eat another thing, reports Trisha Shirey, grounds manager at Lake Austin Spa Resort in Austin, Texas.

Ingredients and Supplies

3 cups plain all-purpose flour
Garden duster or salt shaker
Ice pick or carving fork
Garden hose with spray nozzle

Directions

1. Put the flour in the garden duster. (If you're treating only a small area, use less flour and put the flour in a salt shaker.)
2. Go out in your garden and jiggle the plants upon which grasshoppers or blister beetles are feeding (this gets the insects moving).
3. Dust the insects and the leaves with flour.
4. After 2 days, rinse off the flour using a fine spray from a hose. On plants with hairy leaves, such as tomatoes, you may need to rinse twice to clean off the flour.

Note: When the grasshoppers eat dusted leaves, they ingest so much flour that they become sick and stop eating, Trisha says. Since the success of the method hinges on getting plenty of flour on the leaves that the bugs are eating, it's best to apply the

dust in the morning, while the plants are damp with dew.

As long as you rinse off the flour after 2 days, you won't harm your plants. But don't use self-rising flour, because the salts in that type of flour may injure plant leaves and aren't good for your soil.

PAPER BAG DUSTER

If you don't have a commercial garden duster, save yourself the investment by improvising a duster using a simple brown paper lunch bag. With an ice pick or carving fork, punch about a dozen small holes in the bottom and lower sides of the bag. Put flour in the bag. Then, when you want to apply the dust, hold the bag closed with one hand and tap the bottom of the bag with your other hand to release a cloud of floury dust. Empty powder containers, grated cheese jars, or discarded spice jars with shaker lids are other good prospects for recycling into a duster. Anything with a shaker top works well for this type of nonmeasured application.

Skip-a-Season Planting

To whip chronic pest problems, starve them out. Dr. Judy Hough-Goldstein, a professor of entomology and applied ecology at the University of Delaware, recommends a special strategy that discourages pests by denying them their favorite foods. With this technique, you'll have to forego planting certain crops for a season, but you'll reduce pest problems without the expense and trouble of buying or making barriers, traps, sprays, or dusts.

Ingredients and Supplies

An established vegetable garden
2 crops that have chronic pest problems
Notebook (for keeping garden records)

Directions

1. Choose 2 crops that have suffered from pest problems in your garden in the past. Judy suggests 2 likely subjects: potatoes (subject to attack by Colorado potato beetles) and onions (which can be seriously damaged by onion root maggots). Designate one of your problem crops as crop #1 and the other as crop #2.

2. Plant your garden as you usually would, with one exception. Don't plant any seeds, sets, or plants of crop #1. (It's okay to plant crop #2.)

3. The following year when you plant your garden, plant crop #1, but don't plant any seeds, sets, or plants of crop #2, the second pest-troubled crop.

4. During the season, keep records of the number of pests on crop #1 and the severity of damage they cause.

5. The third year, plant crop #2, and skip crop #1. Keep notes again on damage.
6. For the fourth year, start again with step #3.

Note: "Many people have the experience of starting a new garden and having no pest problems, and then insects get worse and worse every year," Judy observes. That's because the insects become established local residents when they are provided with their favorite foods year after year. The starvation strategy will be most effective if your garden is isolated from others, so that the pests can't find an alternate source of food easily. It also works best for pests that feed on only one type of crop, such as Mexican bean beetles and squash bugs.

Skip-a-season planting may not reduce pest problems in an area where there are a lot of gardens or in a community garden setting.

Another Starvation Strategy

There is a way to plant your crop and keep pests from eating it, too. Cover the crops with row covers—lightweight synthetic fabric that lets air and water through but keeps pests out. When properly used, row covers are an impenetrable barrier between insects and the crops they seek. To protect crops from pests, you need to cover the crop as soon as you plant it and securely weigh down the sides of the row covers by covering them with boards or burying them in the soil. Check under row covers from time to time to make sure that no insects have sneaked inside. Otherwise, they'll be free to feast to their heart's content.

There's another special barrier that's useful for starving cutworms, a pest that isn't stopped by row covers. Cutworms are soil-dwelling insect larvae that like to chew on the stems of plants. Cutworms travel just below the surface of the soil searching for tender transplant stems. When they find a tasty stem, they dig in, sometimes cutting right through the stem and killing the plant.

To foil cutworms, just collect the cardboard tubes from rolls of toilet paper or paper towels and cut the tubes into 2-inch sections. Nestle one "cutworm collar" around the stem of each young vegetable and flower transplant (cutworms will attack a wide variety of plants) right after planting, pushing the collar about 1 inch into the soil. The collar will block the traveling pests and save your plants' stems from becoming cutworm snacks.

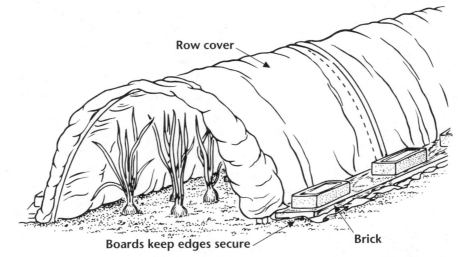

Row cover

Boards keep edges secure

Brick

You can protect crops like broccoli, cabbage, and cauliflower that don't need insect pollination by keeping them under a row cover from planting until harvest. This is a great way to prevent problems with imported cabbageworms or cabbage loopers that often plague these cabbage family crops. For crops like squash and melons that need insect pollination to produce a harvest, remove row covers when the flowers open.

Cover-Crop Knockout for Nematodes

Root knot nematodes can sap the life out of your vegetable crops. "These microscopic worms pierce the roots of plants and parasitize the plants, causing knots along the roots," explains Malcolm Beck, founder of Garden-Ville and author of *The Secret Life of Compost.* "Eventually the parasitized plants just wither and die."

Malcolm has discovered that growing a season-long cover crop of a special type of rye and vetch can remedy nematode problems and improve your soil at the same time. The massive shallow root system of elbon ryegrass or cereal rye destroys the root knot nematodes and adds loads of organic matter to the soil. Deep-rooted lana vetch is a legume, a special type of plant that can change nitrogen from the air into nitrogen compounds that plant roots can absorb.

Ingredients and Supplies

½ pound lana or hairy vetch seed
½–¾ pound elbon or cereal rye seed
Scythe or lawn mower

Directions

1. Mix the vetch and rye seed together and scatter it over a garden bed. (Aim for seeds to end up 1 to 4 inches apart.)
2. Water the seed well.
3. Watch the crop for several weeks. When the rye is 2 to 3 feet tall, but before it blooms, cut it down with a scythe or mower.
4. Leave the rye cuttings in place to decompose, or add them to your compost pile for a rich nitrogen boost.
5. Allow the vetch and rye to grow for the rest of the season. Note: If the rye regrows vigorously, you may need to mow or cut it a second and even a third time.
6. In the fall, till the cover crop into the soil. The following spring, the bed will be ready for a garden crop.

Yield: Enough seed mix to plant 1,000 square feet of garden

MORE NEMATODE KNOCKOUTS

There are two other simple techniques for reducing root-knot nematode problems. One approach is simply to increase the organic matter content of the soil by adding compost. The other is to apply molasses or sugar to the soil at a rate of 20 pounds per 1,000 square feet.

Spicy Squirrel and Mouse Stopper

Give squirrels a hot foot before they dig up bulbs or turn away mice before they nibble at tender tree trunks. Mary Perlmutter, author of *How Does Your Garden Grow…Organically?* and a past president of the Canadian Organic Growers Association, says this mixture will help keep squirrels gathering acorns instead of tulip bulbs and will stop mice from girdling young trees.

Ingredients and Supplies

½ ounce Tabasco sauce

1 pint water

½ teaspoon dishwashing liquid

1 teaspoon chili powder

1 plastic squirt bottle

Directions

1. Mix all ingredients together.

2. Pour the mixture into the squirt bottle.

Yield: About 1 pint of squirrel-and-mouse deterring sauce

Note: After planting bulbs in late summer or fall, squirt the mixture into the soil around the bulbs. As fall turns to winter, dribble some of the mix around the base of young trees that may be attractive to nibbling mice. These pests are especially fond of the thin bark of fruit trees. When winter turns to spring, mix a new batch and spray it around the edges of your tulip beds to bring squirrel problems to a standstill. It works for mischievous chipmunks, too!

3"

2'

Tail mark

Mouse tracks

If you see squirrel or mouse tracks leading away from your damaged bulbs or trees, you'll know who's responsible for the mischief.

Squirrel tracks

Squirrel Solution

Stop squirrels from decapitating tulips or chewing up other flower buds with this spicy mixture invented by Diana Jones of Baltimore, Maryland. Diana's neighbor has used it to protect her rhododendron buds from squirrels, too.

Ingredients and Supplies

2 tablespoons cayenne pepper
1 quart very hot water
Cheesecloth
Pump spray bottle
1 teaspoon horticultural oil

Directions

1. Mix the cayenne pepper with very hot water.

2. Allow the mixture to steep until cool.

3. Strain the mixture through cheesecloth and pour it into a pump spray bottle.

4. Add the horticultural oil and shake well to mix.

5. Spray the mixture on tulips as soon as the plants begin producing buds in the spring.

Yield: 1 quart of squirrel-stopping solution

Note: "The squirrels used to decapitate my tulips as soon as the buds began to color up and then leave them lying on the ground," Diana says. As long as she sprays the tulips well when the buds are still green, the squirrels leave them alone. Unless the season is unusually rainy, Diana finds that spraying only one time usually does the trick.

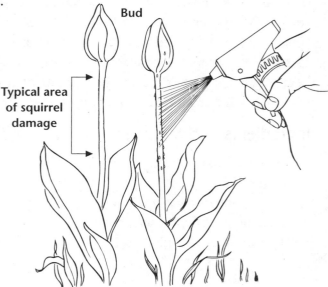

Bud

Typical area of squirrel damage

Imagine a squirrel's surprise when it bites down on a tulip bud sprayed with a hot cayenne pepper solution! It'll think twice before nibbling another bud.

Another Way to Ward Off Squirrels

If squirrels—or chipmunks—use blooming tulip tops as a way to find the tasty bulbs belowground, turn them away with this simple trick: Apply a light sprinkling (about 1 tablespoon) of used cat box litter around the base of your flower plants (don't use the litter for food crops). It takes only a little bit of litter to convince squirrels that a hungry cat is lurking nearby and that they should look elsewhere for their meal.

Fishy Deer Deterrent

When deer come after his flowers, Frank Arnosky frustrates them with this aromatic recipe made with ingredients that are good for his plants' health. Halfway between San Antonio and Austin, Texas, Frank and Pamela Arnosky battle deer all year on their 5-acre cut-flower farm.

Ingredients and Supplies

3 tablespoons kelp
1 cup fish emulsion
3 tablespoons liquid hand soap
3-gallon backpack or pump sprayer

Directions

1. Mix ingredients together in the sprayer tank. Frank uses liquid Dial and notes that he doesn't always measure the liquid soap—he just adds "one good squirt."
2. Fill the sprayer to the fill line with water.
3. Apply the spray to any plant that is being eaten by deer. Spray until the mixture drips off the leaves.
4. Reapply every 7 to 10 days or following any heavy rain that washes the mixture off plant leaves.

Yield: 3 gallons of deer deterrent spray

Note: Frank thinks that deer are repelled by the smell of the fish emulsion, and if they do take a bite, they don't like the taste of the soap. To further offend the deer, Frank hangs his dirty work shirt on a pitchfork at the end of a row and leaves it there for a couple of days. Pamela thinks that a smelly blanket from the doghouse is a good addition to the deer war aroma arsenal. The occasional presence of a dog in and around the garden also helps keep pesky deer at bay.

Caution: Limit the use of this smelly spray to the ornamental plants in your garden to avoid getting a mouthful of fishy-soapy flavor in your next salad!

What's That Smell?

In addition to soap and fish, the stench of rotten eggs disgusts deer. Dr. Larry Clark, project leader for repellents at the National Wildlife Research Center in Fort Collins, Colorado, says that his father tried to cook up a rotten egg deer deterrent in his garage, "but it was really potent—and it really stinks." Dr. Clark thinks that gardeners with deer problems are better off using Deer-Away, a commercial product that contains the sulfurous compounds that give putrefied eggs their deer-deterring punch. Unlike rotten eggs, which wash away quickly when it rains, Deer-Away is effective for several weeks.

Castor Oil Mole Repellent

Moles make a U-turn when they encounter the smell of castor oil, the magic ingredient in this formula. Seattle area gardener Don North tried many other mole remedies and finally got great results with this mixture.

Ingredients and Supplies

> 1 cup warm water, divided in half
> 4 tablespoons dishwashing liquid
> Blender
> 3 ounces castor oil
> 1-quart glass jar with lid (for storage)
> Rubber spatula

Although moles eat grubs and other insects, they can ruin a lawn's looks and damage young plant roots with their tunneling.

Directions

1. Place ½ cup warm water and dishwashing liquid in a blender.
2. Blend on low speed a few seconds.
3. With blender on, pour castor oil into the foamy mixture, and blend for 30 seconds or until well mixed.
4. Pour mixture into the glass jar.
5. Place remaining ½ cup warm water into the empty blender, scrape castor oil mixture from the sides of the blender with a rubber spatula, and blend again for 30 seconds.
6. Pour second mixture into the jar, screw on the lid, and shake to mix.

Yield: About 12 ounces of mole repellent

Note: To use the mole repellent, mix 2 tablespoons in a gallon of warm water. If you have a severe mole problem, you can spray the diluted mixture all over your yard.

"Instead of spraying it, I find a mole mound or tunnel, make an opening in it with a stick, and pour in about a cup of the diluted mixture," Don says. Then he stomps on the mound or tunnel. With over an acre of yard to keep mole-free, Don's seek-and-pour method is much quicker and easier than spraying.

If you'd rather not make up your own mixture, Don has also gotten excellent results with a commercial product called Mole-Med, which is made from ingredients similar to the ones in this homemade formula. Mole-Med is available from mail-order garden suppliers. You may also find castor oil sprays useful in chasing away chipmunks, squirrels, and gophers that are damaging your garden with their digging. For these pests, spray castor oil solution directly on the areas where damage occurs.

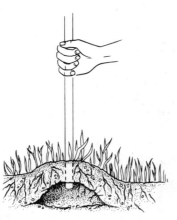

Step 1: To discourage moles from ruining your yard with their tunnels, first poke a hole into a tunnel with a stick.

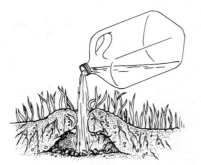

Step 2: Next, pour in a cup of diluted mole repellent made from castor oil, water, and dishwashing liquid.

Step 3: Finally, stomp on the treated tunnel to collapse it.

STOP GIVING MOLES FREE GRUB(S)

Moles don't harm plants by eating them because moles are insect eaters. But if you have moles, you probably also have pests like Japanese beetles, which eat plant leaves and then lay eggs that hatch into root-eating grubs—a favorite snack for tunnel-building moles.

You'll be doing your plants a double favor when you get rid of beetles and grubs, because your moles will move to where the pickings are easier. You can defeat beetles and grubs and say good-bye to moles several ways.

- Pick beetles by hand in the morning, when they're cool and sluggish, and drop them into a container of soapy water. Dump the deceased beetles on your compost pile or toss 'em—container and all—into the trash.
- Place an old sheet, a piece of plastic, or an opened newspaper under plants and shake beetles onto it. Toss out both sheet and beetles.
- Defeat grubs by spraying your lawn and garden with milky disease spore. Milky spore, sold at garden centers, combines spores of *Bacillus popilliae* and *Bacillus lentimorbus*. Grubs eat the spores and die.
- Place valued plants where they're in partial or full shade in the afternoon. Since Japanese beetles like to bask in sun as they eat, shade-tolerant plants will be spared.

Scented Soap Deer Deterrent

Disgust deer with the flowery scent of soap. Like many wild animals, deer have a highly developed sense of smell. Eric Sideman, director of technical services for the Maine Organic Farmers and Gardeners Association, recommends using scented deodorant soap to keep deer from bothering your garden. Any brand of soap will do, but the smellier the soap, the better it seems to work, Eric says.

Ingredients and Supplies

Several small bars scented soap
An ice pick
String, cut into 14-inch pieces

Directions

1. Unwrap the bars of soap.
2. Use the ice pick to bore a small hole in the middle of each bar. Watch your fingers!
3. Run a string through the hole.
4. Tie the ends together securely.
5. Hang the soap at waist level from trees and bushes outside your garden, spacing them 20 to 25 feet apart.

Note: Eric emphasizes the importance of hanging your scented soap barrier long before you actually need the protection. Put the soap up when you first plant your crop. If you wait until deer damage has already started, the soap bars may not do much good.

Variation: If you need to protect several plants for just a few weeks when deer browsing is severe, or if your plants are so large that they'll require many bars of soap, commercial repellent sprays are a good alternative. Products that have soaps or rotted egg solids as their active ingredients are very effective when applied according to label instructions.

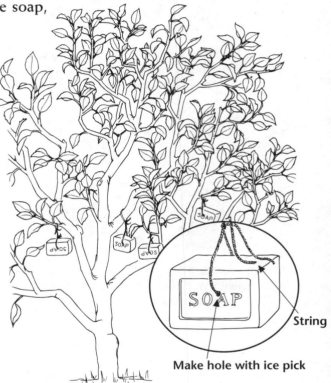

String

Make hole with ice pick

Keep deer from munching your plants by hanging a few deodorant soap bars in your bushes and trees at waist height. Deer will wrinkle their noses at the perfumed soap and search elsewhere for food.

Deter Deer with Smelly Plants

Deer delight in devouring a wide range of garden plants, from vegetables to shrubs. Deer favorites seem to vary from region to region, but there are some plants that deer dislike fairly reliably. Patti Simons, a former deer rehabilitator in Austin, Texas, suggests that you protect your garden from deer damage by interplanting these strongly scented herbs and other deer-discouraging plants throughout your garden.

Ingredients and Supplies

Highly aromatic herbs
Strongly scented, poisonous, prickly, or unappetizing (to deer) plants
Rampantly spreading plants
Vining plants

Directions

1. Plant a generous mix of the 4 types of plants listed above around the boundaries of your yard. When deer brush against these aromatic plants, the scent rubs off on their fur. The deer end up enveloped in a cloud of strong scents that confuses their senses and tends to discourage them from eating.

2. As you notice plants that deer seem to prefer, try hiding them from the deer by planting a nonpreferred plant very close by.

Create a "deer-stopper" garden of strong-scented and prickly plants around the area where deer enter your yard. With no tasty morsels to draw them into your garden, deer are likely to bypass your yard in search of plants they prefer. This plan shows one example of an attractive combination of plants that deer find unappealing and even repellent. The numbers in parentheses show the quantity of each plant used in this plan.

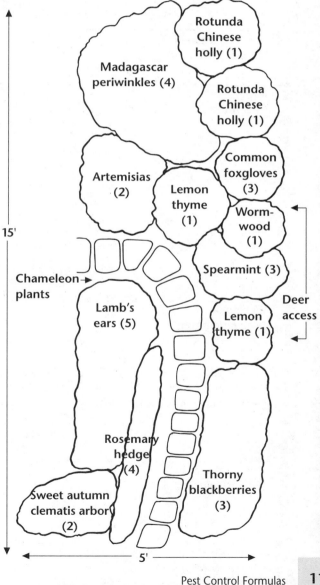

Rotunda Chinese holly (1)

Madagascar periwinkles (4)

Rotunda Chinese holly (1)

Artemisias (2)

Lemon thyme (1)

Common foxgloves (3)

Worm-wood (1)

Spearmint (3)

Chameleon plants

Lamb's ears (5)

Lemon thyme (1)

Deer access

Rosemary hedge (4)

Thorny blackberries (3)

Sweet autumn clematis arbor (2)

15'

5'

PLANTS THAT DEER DON'T DESIRE

While deer's tastes for your landscape plants may vary, depending on where you live and how hungry the deer are, there are some plants that Bambi is less likely to eat. The plants in this table are among those that deer rarely—if ever—dine on; you may discover others that are effective in your area.

PLANT	🌿 DESCRIPTION ☀ HARDINESS ZONES
HIGHLY AROMATIC HERBS	
Artemisias (*Artemisia* **spp.**)	🌿 Gray to silvery gray plants grown for their attractive foliage rather than their flowers; most species are perennial, from 1 to 3 feet tall ☀ Zones 3 to 9
Mexican oregano (*Lippia graveolens*)	🌿 3- to 6-foot-tall shrub with dark green leaves and small pale flowers ☀ Hardy to Zone 8
Mints (*Mentha* **spp.**)	🌿 Up to 30-inch-tall perennials with small purple or pink spike flowers in midsummer; may spread rampantly ☀ Zones 5 to 9
Rosemary (*Rosmarinus officinalis*)	🌿 2- to 6-foot-tall upright tender perennial with needlelike leaves and small blue, lilac, or pink flowers; also prostrate and creeping forms ☀ Zones 8 to 10
Lemon thyme (*Thymus* × *citriodorus*)	🌿 6 to 12 inches tall and 18 to 24 inches wide with dark green or variegated foliage with lemony scent; purple flowers in early summer (but doesn't set seed) ☀ Zones 5 to 9
Wormwood (*Artemisia absinthium*)	🌿 3- to 5-foot-tall bushy perennial with 2- to 5-inch-long gray-green leaves; small yellow flowers in summer ☀ Zones 5 to 9
RAMPANT SPREADERS	
Chameleon plant (*Houttuynia cordata* 'Chameleon')	🌿 Perennial groundcover with showy green, red, and yellow 2- to 3-inch heart shaped leaves and small white flowers in summer; likes moist soil conditions ☀ Zones 5 to 8
Obedient plant (*Physostegia virginiana*)	🌿 Also called Virginia false dragonhead; 3- to 4-foot-tall perennial with 5-inch-long leaves and spikes of 1- to 1½-inch purple, pink, or white flowers that bloom in summer ☀ Zones 3 to 9
Queen-Anne's-lace (*Daucus carota*)	🌿 Biennial; 1 to 3 feet tall with ferny foliage and clusters of tiny lacy white flowers in midsummer ☀ Zones 2 to 9

PLANT	🌿 DESCRIPTION 🌻 HARDINESS ZONES
VINING PLANTS	
Sweet autumn clematis (*Clematis maximowicziana*)	🌿 Vigorous perennial vine with dark green 4-inch-long leaves, covered with small white blooms in late summer and fall 🌻 Zones 5 to 9
Wisterias (*Wisteria* spp.)	🌿 Very vigorous woody vines, can grow over 10 feet a year; drooping clusters of fragrant violet flowers bloom in spring 🌻 Zones 4 or 5 to 10
POISONOUS, PRICKLY, UNAPPETIZING PLANTS	
Blackberries (*Rubus* spp.)	🌿 Perennial vines with luscious black berries form an inpenetrable hedge; choose a thorny variety that is best suited for your area; plant 3 to 4 feet apart 🌻 Zones 5 to 9
Butterfly weed (*Asclepias tuberosa*)	🌿 1- to 3-foot-tall perennial with 2- to 5-inch clusters of waxy bright orange, red, or yellow ½-inch flowers in midsummer 🌻 Zones 3 to 9
Foxgloves (*Digitalis* spp.)	🌿 2- to 5-feet tall biennial or short-lived perennials with tall spikes of pink, white, yellow, or brown flowers 🌻 Zones 4 to 8
'Rotunda' Chinese holly (*Ilex cornuta* 'Rotunda')	🌿 Compact, dense, spiny-leaved shrub that does not fruit; 3 to 4 feet tall and 6 to 8 feet wide; can be grown as a thick dense hedge 🌻 Zones 7 to 9
Lamb's-ears (*Stachys byzantina*)	🌿 Perennial with soft, wooly gray-white leaves and fuzzy 6- to 15-inch-long spikes of purple blossoms 🌻 Zones 4 to 8
Madagascar periwinkle (*Catharanthus roseus*)	🌿 Also called annual vinca; annual with dark green leaves with white central veins and 2-inch, 5-petaled white, rose, or pink flowers; 12 to 18 inches tall 🌻 Annual
Spurge (*Euphorbia* spp.)	🌿 Most species are 1 to 3 feet tall and bloom in spring, with 2- to 3-inch flower clusters surrounded by showy yellow bracts (modified leaves) 🌻 Perennial, hardiness varies with species

Dog-Gone Potion

Deter digging dogs by dousing their favorite digging holes with this pungent potion. Toronto gardener Mary Perlmutter also recommends this mixture for treating the soil where you don't want dogs to nap.

Ingredients and Supplies

- 1 clove garlic, chopped
- 1 pungent onion, chopped
- 1 quart warm water
- 1 teaspoon Tabasco sauce
- 1 tablespoon cayenne pepper
- 1 large plastic or metal pail

Directions

1. Mix all ingredients together in the pail.

2. Allow to steep overnight.

3. Use a metal can to scoop up the mix and dribble it onto soil where dogs are likely to dig or lie. You can also use this formula to discourage dogs that are intent on rearranging your compost heap. When the compost is turned and you want it left alone, sprinkle it thoroughly with Dog-Gone Potion.

Yield: About 1 quart of Dog-Gone Potion

SNEAKY SCAT TACTICS

Nobody wants to hurt a pet, but when pets are pestering the plants in your garden, it's time to show them the door. Here are some sneaky ways to lure them away from your garden and keep them otherwise occupied.

- Kitties love catnip (*Nepeta cataria*)—they'll frazzle themselves and the plant by eating it, batting it around, and rolling on it. You can capitalize on their catnip compulsion by planting kitty "trap crops" of catnip to keep them out of your garden. Simply dig up a small plot at the edge of your property, far away from your garden and your bird feeders. Plant a patch of catnip, and nearby, dig up the soil and mix in some sand, so they'll have a place where they can dig, roll, and munch catnip to their heart's content. They'll never give your garden a second thought.

- If your dog is digging in your garden, you may not be able to change its pesky habit, but you can redirect it! Give the dog its own sandbox—you can make an inexpensive one by filling a kiddy swimming pool with sand. Put the sandbox far away from your garden and bury treats, like dog biscuits and chew toys, in the sand for Fido to dig up. Pretty soon, your pooch will look forward to digging for buried treasures in its sandbox and will forget all about digging in your garden. 🐾

Cat-Away Solution

Cats generally don't eat garden plants (except catnip), but they can be a problem when they dig into the soft soil of garden beds. To discourage them before they get in the habit, try this peppery mixture. Toronto master gardener and author of *How Does Your Garden Grow…Organically?* Mary Perlmutter suggests using this soupy repellent outside on freshly cultivated beds or along fences that surround the garden.

Ingredients and Supplies

2 tablespoons cayenne pepper
3 tablespoons powdered mustard
5 tablespoons plain flour
Large bowl (for mixing)
2 quarts water
Funnel
Plastic squirt bottle

Directions

1. Mix pepper, mustard, and flour together in a large bowl.
2. Add the water gradually, mixing all ingredients thoroughly as you go.
3. Pour the mixture through the funnel into the plastic squirt bottle.
4. Squirt the mixture where cats are likely to walk on their way to garden beds.

Yield: About 2 quarts of cat-repelling solution

Vinegar Spray Keeps Cats Away

Use vinegar to chase away wandering tomcats and neutralize the smell that they leave behind. "The cats can smell the vinegar but I can't," says Victoria Price of Silver Spring, Maryland. She puts vinegar around the base of her birdbath, on her patio wall, and on the trunk of a cedar tree that's a popular gathering place for cats. As long as the cats can smell the vinegar, it works like a scent fence to keep them away.

Ingredients and Supplies

White vinegar
Small plastic squirt bottle

Directions

1. Fill the bottle with the vinegar.
2. Squirt 1 to 2 ounces of vinegar where cats have sprayed and onto stone or concrete surfaces where they are likely to visit.

FORMULAS FOR DISEASE CONTROL

Defeating Plant Diseases the Organic Way

Whether it's rust on your roses or powdery mildew on your pumpkins, the ugly symptoms and disappointing crops caused by plant diseases have no doubt resulted in suffering for you (or rather, your plants). All kinds of plants, from mighty oaks to dainty annual flowers, are susceptible to the bacteria, fungi, and viruses that cause plant diseases. But that doesn't mean that you're doomed to diseased plants. You have lots of solutions, from disease-prevention planting plans to homemade remedies that can help you keep your vegetables, flowers, lawn, trees, and shrubs healthy.

Prevention is the best defense. It's easier to keep your plants disease-free than to try to cure them once they're infected. The best way to ensure your plants' health is to provide a healthy, fast-draining soil and appropriate growing conditions. Organic matter is the key to soil health and good drainage, so make sure that your soil has plenty. (See "Soil Improvement and Soil Mix Formulas," beginning on page 56, for recipes for building healthy soil.)

The right plants can make disease prevention much easier. Choose disease resistant varieties whenever possible and match plants to the conditions in your garden.

Adopt a disease prevention routine. When you walk through your garden, always be on the lookout for discolored leaves or other symptoms that just don't look right. If you see diseased leaves, pluck them off of your plants to prevent the disease from spreading. If necessary, remove a sickly plant before it infects its neighbors.

If you're growing fruits and vegetables, be sure to clear out plant debris after your harvest so that you don't give diseases a place to camp out, waiting for spring to strike again. (Don't work in the garden when plants are wet because water is a great disease conductor.) Compost any healthy material you remove from your plants, but be sure to throw any diseased leaves or stems into the garbage.

Doctor plants with care. In some cases, you can use sprays, powders, and other treatments to discourage disease or prevent it from spreading. When treating plants with a spray or powder, keep these simple rules in mind:

- **Test your treatments.** Try both homemade and store-bought cures on one leaf first to test your plant's sensitivity. It's like trying out a stain removal product on a small area before going whole hog. Wait a day to see if any problems turn up before you treat the entire plant.

Proceed with caution: Before treating a whole plant, apply a disease-fighting spray or powder to just one leaf to gauge a plant's sensitivity. If you see signs of damage after a day, dilute the spray and test again or find an alternative method.

- **Stick sprays in place.** If your spray rolls off your plants' leaves, it isn't going to do much good. Try adding a drop of liquid soap (with as few additives as possible) to your sprays to break up surface tension on leaves and help the mix stay in place.
- **Get started early.** First thing in the morning is the best time to spray. Don't use sprays late in the day when humidity is building up or dew is settling since these are prime conditions for some diseases to spread.
- **Watch the weather.** Don't apply treatments in windy or rainy weather. If it rains after an application, plan to reapply.

- **Keep cool.** Don't treat plants when temperatures are above 90°F. Some sprays can burn leaves at high temperatures.
- **Cover up.** Remember to use any spray or powder with caution, no matter how harmless it may seem. Wear long sleeves, goggles, gloves, and long pants. Use a dust mask with powders and a respirator with sprays that may irritate your throat or lungs.
- **Store disease-control products carefully.** Always label containers and keep them out of the reach of children and pets. Do not expose sprays or powders to light or heat.

Plant Disease Primer

How can you tell when your plants are sick? Common symptoms include yellow or blotchy leaves, distorted growth, patches of mold, and dying leaves or plants. But other problems, like a nutrient deficiency or lack of water, may cause these symptoms too. Making the right diagnosis can be tricky.

If you think your plants are diseased, compare their symptoms to those described below for some common plant diseases. Then, check the symptoms caused by lack of nutrients in "Solving Nutrient Deficiency Problems" on page 26. Chances are, you'll figure out what's troubling your plants. If you're stumped, take a sample of the plant to your local Cooperative Extension office and ask for help in diagnosing the problem.

Blights. Spreading brown spots or patches on leaves can be a clue that your plants have a fungal blight. The fruits may shrivel and rot. Other types of blight may look like a white or gray growth on the flowers.

Downy or powdery mildew. If your plants have a white powdery coating on the leaves, the problem is powdery mildew. If the fuzzy coating is on the undersides of the leaves, downy mildew may be the cause. Various fungi cause these diseases, which can affect a wide range of plants.

Mosaic. Mosaic is a viral disease that causes a range of symptoms including mottled leaves, twisted growth, and stunted plants.

Rust. If your plants look as if they're covered with rust, the cause is rust fungi.

Stem, root, and crown rots. These fungal diseases cause stems, crowns, and/or roots to become soft. Affected parts often turn brown or black or look water-soaked. Plants may be stunted or wilted.

Wilts. Both bacteria and fungi can cause wilt diseases. The common symptoms are yellow leaves and wilted plants. Suspect wilt diseases especially if plants wilt suddenly even when the soil is fairly moist.

Compost Tea Cure-All for Plants

To blast away blight in the vegetable garden, start your plants off with a few sips of compost tea. That's the advice of Steve Peters, agricultural planning associate for Seeds of Change, an organic seed company. "I have used compost tea as a preventive measure—it's pretty remarkable," says Steve, who says he's been pleased with the success even with plants like tomatoes and potatoes that are susceptible to the fungal diseases early blight and late blight.

Ingredients and Supplies

5-gallon bucket
Good-quality, finished compost
Fine-screened strainer
Backpack or pump sprayer

Directions

1. Fill the bucket halfway with compost, then add an equal amount of water, and stir.

2. Continue to stir the mix every other day with a large stick or branch, letting the stuff steep for about 1 week or until the liquid is mahogany colored.

3. Let the solid material settle to the bottom of the bucket and run the liquid through a fine screen. "You're basically decanting it," Steve says. "You've got a lot of solid material in there and if you're not careful, it can clog your sprayer. With careful pouring, it should be okay."

4. Pour the strained mixture into a backpack sprayer. Or pour it into a spray bottle and store the remainder in the bucket. Make sure that you label the bucket.

PLAY IT SAFE

Before you make compost tea, be sure that your compost is completely finished. The original ingredients should be unrecognizable, and the odor should be clean and earthy.

Steve Peters points out that the tea is benign as long as it's made from a completely finished compost. But he recommends that you avoid spraying plants like leafy greens with the tea as an added health safety precaution. "You don't want to be putting semi-raw material on something you're going to eat directly," Steve explains. He adds that compost tea spray works particularly well for fruiting crops, like cucumbers or watermelons, since the fruits don't come in contact with the spray.

5. Spray young plants about once a week. The tea has a double benefit, Steve says. "It also acts as a foliar (leaf) fertilizer."

Yield: About 2½ gallons of compost tea

Seedling-Ease Chamomile Tea

It's sad to watch beautiful little seedlings suddenly wilt and die—cut down before their time by a disease called damping-off. There is no cure for this soil-dwelling fungal disease, but according to Penny King, an herbal educator, you can prevent damping-off with chamomile tea. Penny saw her share of damping-off when she grew herbs commercially as the owner of Pennyroyal Herbs in Georgetown, Texas. She found that she could prevent damping-off losses simply by watering her seedlings with chamomile tea.

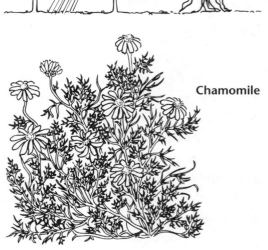

Damping-off

Ingredients and Supplies

1 cup water
2 teaspoons dried chamomile flowers
Strainer

Directions

1. Bring the water to a boil, then remove from heat and stir in the chamomile flowers. Cover and allow the mixture to come to room temperature.

2. Strain the liquid and use full strength. Dampen potting soil mixtures with the tea before you plant your seeds. And then water with the tea blend, spraying the soil lightly each day with the chamomile tea instead of water.

Chamomile

Yield: About 1 cup of Seedling-Ease tea

Note: You can also use chamomile tea to water cuttings and to soak seeds prior to planting.

Variations: For a slightly stronger antifungal tea, add 2 teaspoons of dried horsetail (*Equisetum arvense*) to the water and chamomile flowers. (You can buy dried horsetail from many mail-order herb suppliers.)

Chamomile's daisies hold health benefits for people *and* plants! Long hailed for its soothing effects on humans, a simple chamomile tea solution is also an effective way to protect seedlings from damping-off disease.

Use this stronger tea solution on established plants that exhibit signs of fungal disease. Repeated applications of the tea can cure many fungal problems. Be sure to spray both sides of the leaves thoroughly.

"Hot" Compost Helps, Too

Adding "hot" compost to your seed-starting mix also helps protect your seedlings from disease, says compost-and-disease expert Harry Hoitink, Ph.D., professor of plant pathology at The Ohio State University. Just amend a standard peat/vermiculite starting mix with at least 5 percent mature compost, preferably from a pile that has recently been heated. Any disease organisms in the compost materials are killed in the hot pile. Then, as the compost cools, beneficial disease-preventing microbes reproduce quickly and get the upper hand. 🐾

More Chamomile Tea for Seedlings

"Chamomile tea definitely works," says Steve Peters, an agricultural planning associate for Seeds of Change, an organic seed company. Even broccoli and other brassica seedlings, which often fall prey to the low light and lack of air circulation in greenhouses, will survive with a dousing of strong chamomile tea.

Steve mixes 1 cup of dried chamomile flowers with 1 quart of water to make his tea. He suggests steeping the brew for at least an hour, explaining that "the stronger it is, the more effective it is." He adds that the taste of this strong tea, should you try it, would probably be too bitter to drink.

Spray the seedlings as soon as they appear. Continue spraying daily until the seedlings are past the danger point (about two weeks).

Using sterile soil for seed-starting, rather than garden soil or potting soil that has already been used, should be your first step in preventing the damping-off fungus, Steve advises. And keeping soil moist, rather than soaked, is also important. For more tips on how to keep your seedlings healthy, see "Ward Off Damping-Off" on page 77. 🐾

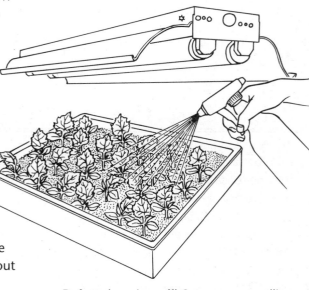

Defeat damping-off! Spray your seedlings with chamomile tea as soon as they pop up, and continue daily for about 2 weeks. A daily spray will combat the dreaded damping-off fungus that makes tender seedlings topple over and die.

Andy's Simple Alfalfa Solution

Try giving your flowers and vegetables a shot of alfalfa for a nutritional boost that makes plants stronger and more able to fight off diseases. You can prevent most types of fungal diseases if you spray your plants with alfalfa tea early in the season, says Andy Lopez, founder of the Invisible Gardeners of America. And what if you don't have a field of alfalfa growing nearby? Don't worry— alfalfa is available as a powdery meal that you can buy from farm or organic garden suppliers. (See "Sources," beginning on page 308.)

Ingredients and Supplies

1 cup alfalfa meal
1-gallon bucket
Cheesecloth
Biodegradable dishwashing liquid
Backpack or pump sprayer

Directions

1. Add the alfalfa meal to a bucket of water. Let it sit for a few hours, then strain the mixture through cheesecloth.
2. Add a dash of biodegradable dishwashing liquid to help the tea stick to plant leaves.
3. Fill the spray bottle with the mixture and spray plants.

Yield: About 1 gallon of alfalfa solution

WELL-FED LEAVES RESIST DISEASE

Just as people take a daily vitamin to keep from getting sick, plants stay healthier when they get occasional doses of nutrient-rich organic sprays like Andy Lopez's alfalfa solution. Applying foliar (leaf) sprays may not prevent disease organisms from attacking your plants. But well-nourished plants are more likely to keep growing and producing even if they are suffering from disease. You may not notice the disease symptoms until very late in the season.

To learn the best technique for foliar feeding, turn to "The Fine Art of Foliar (Leaf) Feeding" on page 27. When you spray nutrient solutions to help prevent disease, it's best to spray in the early morning, especially if you live in a humid climate.

Other formulas for foliar feeding include "Seedling Starter Solution" on page 32, "Give Your Plants a Weed Feed" on page 34, "Hay Gives Plants Horsepower" on page 40, "Compost Is His Plants' Cup of Tea" on page 41, and "Medicine Cabinet Micronutrients" on page 50. You'll find nutrient solutions that gardeners use to fight diseases in "Fishy Foliar Spray" on page 139, "Stick It to 'Em Molasses Spray" on page 140, and "Wash Away Fungi with Garrett's Spray" on page 141.

Rhubarb Spray to the Rescue

For a garden rescue straight from the garden, try Mary Perlmutter's recipe for a rhubarb spray that destroys fungal diseases as well as aphids and June bugs. "If I see signs of a disease that's just starting, I give it a shot of the rhubarb mixture," says author and organic gardener Mary, who has experimented for years with using plants like rhubarb and garlic for solving disease problems in her rural Canadian garden.

Ingredients and Supplies

½ cup rhubarb leaves (about 6 leaves), crushed
3 quarts water
Pot (for boiling)

Blender (optional)
Cheesecloth or fine-mesh sieve
Pump spray bottle

Directions

1. Cut or tear rhubarb leaves into small pieces. Mary uses rhubarb from her garden, but if you need to buy some, you may find rhubarb with its leaves intact at a farmer's market. Most supermarkets sell it with the leaves removed.

2. Place the leaves in the water and bring it to a rolling boil.

3. Steep the leaves for at least an hour. Mary says she likes to steep them overnight.

4. Shred the boiled leaves further in a blender, if desired. Strain the solution through the cheesecloth or sieve and pour it into a spray bottle. Add the leaf residue to your compost pile.

5. Spray affected plants thoroughly.

Yield: About 3 quarts of rhubarb-leaf spray

Note: Mary suggests making a new batch of rhubarb spray each time you want to spray. "I have been known to strain it and put it in the freezer," she says, "but I prefer a fresh mixture." She adds that you can also keep leftover spray—carefully labeled—in the refrigerator; for a freshness check, be sure that it doesn't have an off odor. Or, if you have a spot where you'd like to lower the pH in your garden, just pour the excess rhubarb spray into your compost or soil for a slightly acidic boost.

Hello Jell-O Seed Starter

To get her flower and vegetable seeds off to a disease-free start, organic gardener Marion Hess of Northville, Michigan, believes in a sweet approach. She sprinkles her seeds with Jell-O powder. She also feeds her young plants with Jell-O as they grow.

Ingredients and Supplies

Peat pots
Potting soil
Seeds
1 package Jell-O powder, any flavor
    with sugar
Powdered skim milk, in amount equal to
    Jell-O (optional)
Salt shaker or other sprinkling device
Newspaper

Sprinkle seeds or seedlings with flavored gelatin powder. The nitrogen in the gelatin speeds sprouting and boosts plant growth, and the sugar feeds beneficial soil microbes.

Directions

1. Fill the peat pots with potting soil and place 2 seeds in each pot.
2. Fill the salt shaker with the Jell-O powder (and powdered skim milk, if desired, for extra calcium) and sprinkle the powder lightly on top. Gently press down the powder and cover lightly with soil.
3. Moisten the soil and cover it with damp newspaper.
4. After 4 days, remove the newspaper and keep the seeds in a warm area with temperatures of 55° to 65°F.

Note: Should your friends snicker about your plant's snacking habits, just tell them that it makes sense when you think about what's in Jell-O, Marion says. "The gelatin helps the plant hold water, and the sugar feeds the organisms in the soil."

JELL-O DIET PLAN FOR PLANTS

Even after your plants are up and running, Jell-O can still help keep them healthy, Marion Hess says. "In any organic, liquid fertilizer, such as compost tea, I always add Jell-O," she reveals. Add ½ to 1 teaspoon of Jell-O powder to 1 gallon of fertilizer in a bucket. Mix well and use the mixture immediately to prevent thickening. Pour directly on the soil. Because of possible thickening, you don't want to use a spray bottle with this mixture, Marion warns.

Many adventurous gardeners use Jell-O for their houseplants, but Marion says it's just as great at fighting off fungal diseases in outdoor plants. And, she adds, while any flavor will do, lemon's her top choice, because she thinks the citrusy odor repels some bugs. 🌿

Compost Your Lawn Problems

Looking for a magic pill to cure all your lawn ills? Compost comes mighty close—it will feed your lawn, improve the soil structure, *and* prevent diseases! And it doesn't take very much compost to do all this, according to Cornell University plant pathologist Eric Nelson, Ph.D., who has been researching compost's ability to prevent lawn diseases. Here's his recommendation, based on the latest research.

Ingredients and Supplies

Composted poultry manure
Cyclone or drop-type fertilizer spreader

Directions

1. If you have chickens, you can make your own poultry compost. If a flock of hens isn't for you, buy composted poultry manure bagged at nurseries and garden centers. Why poultry manure? Eric says that of all the composts Cornell has tested on lawns, composted poultry manure seems to work best for suppressing diseases.

2. Apply 10 pounds of compost per 1,000 square feet of lawn about once a month during the growing season. Regular applications of this "black gold" can prevent a whole host of diseases that strike both cool and warm season grasses, including snow mold, brown patch, dollar spot, pythium blight, necrotic ring spot, red thread, and summer patch.

Note: If you use homemade compost, screen it to remove any chunks before applying it with the spreader. The compost will go through the screen and the spreader best if you let it dry out a little before you try to screen it.

Before applying compost to your lawn with a spreader, use a screen to filter out larger chunks, sticks, and other debris that might clog the spreader.

Disease-Proof Your Garden with a Dose of Compost

Lawn grass isn't the only plant that gets healthier when you treat it with compost. According to renowned compost-and-disease expert Harry Hoitink, professor of plant pathology at The Ohio State University, extensive international research has now proven that you can protect your garden crops from diseases by applying compost regularly. To get maximum disease-preventing power, Harry says to "use a *surface* mulch of *slightly immature* compost in your garden beds."

Spicy Garlic Garden Spray

Get the best results from garden sprays by catching problems right away, advises Mary Perlmutter, author of *How Does Your Garden Grow...Organically?* Mary vigilantly patrols her garden each morning for signs of distress. If she spies any trace of fungal disease (rust on a hollyhock or blackspot on a rose, for instance), she prepares this potent garlic cure, applies it, and sees improvement almost immediately.

Ingredients and Supplies

3 cloves garlic, crushed
1 onion, peeled and minced
1 teaspoon Jalapeno pepper, crushed
Fine-meshed sieve or cheesecloth
Pump spray bottle
1 drop dishwashing liquid or 2 table-
    spoons vegetable or horticultural oil
    (optional)

Directions

1. Steep garlic, onion, and pepper in 1 quart of warm water for 1 hour or longer.
2. Strain the mix through a sieve or piece of cheesecloth and retain the liquid.
3. In the spray bottle, dilute 1 part of the strained liquid in 4 parts warm water and add the soap or oil, if desired. (Adding oil will help the mixture remain on the plants longer; adding soap will improve spray coverage on leaves and stems.)
4. Mist plants lightly.

Yield: About 1 quart of spicy spray concentrate

Be Wary, Says Mary

You may not have five hours each morning to survey your vegetables, flowers, perennial plants, and fruit trees, as Mary Perlmutter does. But, she points out, it would be a shame not to take a quick walk through your yard at least once a day to find out how your crop is growing. That way, you can nip problems in the bud before diseases turn into death sentences.

"I check the plants," Mary explains. "I don't touch every single plant; but if I see a plant that's looking sad, I will examine it. Usually, it's from lack of water." Mary's biggest problem may be summer drought, but she keeps an eye out for other problems too. She looks for yellowing, white powder, strange patterns on leaves, dull leaves that should be shiny, curling leaves, and any other symptoms that suggest illness or other problems.

Early action, whether it's spraying to stop disease from spreading or careful pruning of diseased leaves, can keep small problems small. "You have to be in touch with all parts of the garden," Mary says.

More Great Garlic Ideas

If the idea of garlic in the garden grabs your interest, try these variations. Horticulturist and organic gardener Howard Garrett recommends the first two sprays for fighting diseases and insects.

Garrett's garlic/pepper blend. Liquefy two garlic cloves and two hot peppers in a blender that is half-filled with water. Strain out the garlic and pepper bits, then mix the remaining liquid with enough water to make 1 gallon of spicy concentrate. For the final spray, use ¼ cup of the concentrate for each gallon of water. Two tablespoons of molasses will help the mixture adhere to leaves.

Plain and simple garlic juice. For a plain garlic juice, use three garlic cloves and follow the directions above—it makes a great additive for any garden-disease or insect-pest spray.

For extra garlic power in his garden, Andy Lopez goes a different route. Andy is the founder of the Invisible Gardeners of America, an organization which provides education on organic gardening techniques to its 6,000 members. Here's his recipe for a fungus-free garden.

Get growing to fight fungus. Andy *grows* the pungent herb around vulnerable plants, explaining that the garlic aroma provides a fungus-free environment. Andy adds that "garlic has been around for centuries as a fungal control."

Garlic has so many uses that you'll want to have lots of it around. Growing your own garlic is an easy and economical way to keep a steady supply of this useful bulb on

hand, and it lets you try different kinds of garlic for cooking and for pest and disease control.

Start with whole bulbs from a local grower. Separate the individual cloves and plant them in mid-fall in full sun and well-drained soil. Set the cloves 1 to 2 inches deep and 6 to 8 inches apart. Harvest in early July when most of the leaves have turned brown, and lay the plants in a dark, dry spot to cure for several weeks. Trim leaves and roots and brush away excess soil, then store in cool, dry conditions. 🍂

Help protect your rose bushes from fungal diseases by encircling each bush with 4 garlic bulbs. Plant the bulbs 6" away from the rose, being careful not to disturb its roots. Two bulbs are plenty for younger roses.

Mighty-Milk Tomato Blight Cure

To ward off common tomato diseases, like early blight, try a sprinkling of powdered milk when you set out the tomato transplants. This simple suggestion comes from organic gardener Marion Hess, who is a special contributor for Prodigy's on-line gardening newsletter *Prodigy Gardens Newsletter*. Marion credits milk with her amazing tomato track record of no diseases, ever. "I have never even had to rotate my crop," she marvels. And the technique is gentle, Marion assures. "It won't hurt anything in your yard."

Ingredients and Supplies

¼ cup plus 2 tablespoons powdered nonfat milk
¼ cup Epsom salts (optional)
1 shovelful of compost (optional)
Salt shaker or other sprinkling device
Hand trowel

Directions

1. Prepare your garden site or planting container for planting by digging a hole.
2. Use the shaker or your hand to sprinkle the powdered nonfat milk into the planting hole. Add the Epsom salts and compost or composted manure, if desired. The Epsom salts and compost will boost your plant's overall growth and disease resistance, Marion says.
3. Mix the ingredients into the soil with the hand trowel.
4. Set your tomato plant in place and refill the hole with soil.
5. Sprinkle about 2 tablespoons additional powdered nonfat milk around the plant, then mix the milk into the soil with the trowel.

MULCH TOMATOES IN TO KEEP DISEASE OUT

A layer of mulch doesn't just keep moisture in the soil; it also can protect your tomatoes from diseases, says Dr. Frank Killebrew, extension plant pathologist at Mississippi State University. "The mulch provides a physical barrier between soil and plant surfaces and reduces the amount of disease inoculum that is splashed onto foliage, stems, and fruits during rainy periods," explains Dr. Killebrew. Mulching can prevent tomato (and cucumber) rot diseases. He suggests using black plastic or organic materials such as bark, composted sawdust, oat straw, or pine needles for mulch. 🦋

6. Add more powdered milk every few weeks throughout the growing season by sprinkling about 2 tablespoons of the powder on top of the soil. When you use your trowel (or a spade or garden fork) to mix the powder into the soil, take care not to damage roots that are growing near the soil surface.

Wipe Out Black Spot
with Tomato Leaf Tonic

When black spot attacks her roses, organic gardener and author Mary Perlmutter uses ingredients that are plentiful all summer long: tomato leaves and onions! Mary steeps the leaves and onion in alcohol. The sharp-smelling solution not only discourages the black spot fungus but aphids, asparagus beetles, and scale insects as well.

Ingredients and Supplies

10 tomato leaves
1 medium-size onion, finely chopped
½ cup rubbing alcohol
Cotton batting
Stick, about the size of a chopstick

Directions

1. Pick 10 tomato leaves from a healthy tomato plant and chop them into small pieces.

2. Combine the onion with the tomato leaves in the rubbing alcohol. Steep the mixture overnight.

3. Make a cotton swab by wrapping a piece of the cotton batting around the stick. The idea is to make a swab that is large enough to let you apply the mixture easily.

4. In the morning, remove any diseased leaves from your roses. Dip the swab in the tomato-onion solution and wipe the entire plant, including the tops and undersides of all the leaves.

Yield: About ½ cup of black spot-stopping Tomato Leaf Tonic

BEATING BLACK SPOT

Black spot (*Diplocarpon rosae*) is a disfiguring fungal disease that infects roses during warm, wet weather. The disease causes black spots ringed with yellow on rose leaves. While black spot is rarely fatal, a severely infected plant may drop all of its leaves.

Luckily, you can thwart black spot with good gardening practices. Every time you visit your garden, clean up fallen leaves and organic debris to remove places where black spot spores collect. While you're there, prune off and destroy infected leaves and seriously infected canes.

You can also keep black spot off plants by being careful not to splash spore-laden, muddy water on them when watering. A mulch of disease-fighting compost actually kills spores in the soil and keeps them from splashing onto plants.

Good air circulation also prevents black spot spores from taking hold. To open the center of rose bushes to air and sun, carry pruners on garden visits and cut out any inward-growing shoots. Growing roses in full sun and spacing them far enough apart for adequate air circulation can stop black spot troubles before they start.

Baking Soda Blitz

For a disease fighter that's cheap, easy, and proven effective, look no further than your kitchen cabinet. This recipe, offered by Dr. Thomas A. Zitter, a professor in the Cornell University Department of Plant Pathology, includes lightweight oil that acts as a spreader-sticker to help the baking soda stay on leaves. By keeping the baking soda on the leaves, the oil makes the spray more effective.

Use this recipe when you have to spray only occasionally—some plants may be injured by repeated applications of oil.

Ingredients and Supplies

1 tablespoon baking soda
1 tablespoon horticultural oil
1 gallon water
1-gallon backpack or pump sprayer

Directions

1. Mix the baking soda, oil, and water in the sprayer.
2. Spray each plant completely, including the tough-to-reach spots like the undersides of leaves, says Dr. Zitter. "Some of these things (fungi) do very well on the underside of a leaf. If you spray only the top, you will reduce the population by half—if you're lucky—and you will have a new set of spores."
Yield: About 1 gallon of fungus-fighting spray

Fight fungal diseases like black spot and powdery mildew with baking soda spray—it's cheap and effective! Be sure to spray the undersides of leaves as well as the tops.

Variation: Dr. Zitter points out that while baking soda is great, its near relation, potassium bicarbonate, performed even better in studies and the Environmental Protection Agency (EPA) has approved it as a commercial home and garden product. (Look for potassium bicarbonate at garden centers.)

Deluxe Baking Soda Spray

Instead of mixing separate sprays for diseases and insects, consider using Dennis Glowniak's deluxe combo spray, which works for both. Spray weekly and it's "good-bye pests!" promises Dennis, president of the California Organic Garden Club.

Ingredients and Supplies

1½ tablespoons baking soda
1 tablespoon insecticidal soap
1 tablespoon canola oil
1 cup plus 1 gallon water
1 tablespoon vinegar
Backpack or pump sprayer

Directions

1. Mix the baking soda, soap, and oil with 1 cup of water.
2. Add the vinegar. Don't mix the vinegar in until last or the mixture may bubble over.
3. Pour the mixture into the sprayer and add 1 gallon of water. Shake or stir to combine the ingredients.
4. Spray plants, covering the tops and bottoms of the leaves.

Yield: About 1 gallon of baking soda spray

Baking Soda's Best as a Problem Preventer

You should always keep a simple solution of 1 teaspoon baking soda to a quart of water mixed and ready for action in your garden, states Dorothy Read, editor of *The Garden Sampler* magazine, which is based in Peru, Vermont. The spray stops fungal diseases on everything from roses to pumpkins, Dorothy claims.

Dorothy's recipe is simple and effective at combating fungal diseases such as black spot and powdery mildew, but there are other versions you can try as well. No matter which recipe you use, be snappy about it, Dorothy urges, because while bicarbonates stop the spread of fungi, they can't clean up a diseased mess. Dorothy explains that baking soda works best as a preventive—if you've had trouble with fungal diseases in the past, start spraying susceptible plants before disease symptoms start and continue at weekly intervals to prevent the problem.

Powdery Mildew Solution

Here's a new twist on the popular baking soda-and-oil mix for controlling powdery mildew. Iowa-based garden writer Veronica Fowler offers this version that uses Murphy's Oil Soap. "The baking soda alters the pH of the leaf, making it more difficult for powdery mildew to form," Veronica explains. "The oil soap serves as a spreader-sticker, so that the mix spreads more evenly and doesn't wash off as readily."

Ingredients and Supplies

1 gallon warm water
3 tablespoons baking soda
1 tablespoon Murphy's Oil Soap

Directions

1. Mix all ingredients well.

2. Spray plants when you spot the very first sign of powdery mildew—a grayish coating on leaves. Coat both sides of leaves thoroughly. Spray every 7 to 10 days until daytime temperatures start getting into the 70s.

Yield: About 1 gallon of Powdery Mildew Solution

Note: On plants with chronic powdery mildew problems, use this spray as a preventive. Spray once or twice in very early spring before any sign of disease appears. If you notice powdery mildew, take action to stop its spread. Remove all affected leaves and spray with a baking soda solution. Prune or thin to improve air movement around the foliage. Finally, make sure the plant isn't stressed by drought or other problems; stressed plants seem more susceptible to infection.

PLANTS PESTERED BY POWDERY MILDEW

The fungal disease powdery mildew is ugly but it seldom does serious harm. If you're growing a plant that's susceptible to the fungus—check the list below—and don't like how it looks, keep baking soda and Murphy's Oil Soap handy for a quick preventive spray.

Trees and Shrubs
Crabapples (*Malus* spp.)
Crape myrtle (*Lagerstroemia indica*)
English oak (*Quercus robur*)
Euonymous (*Euonymous* spp.)
Hackberries (*Celtis* spp.)
Honeysuckles (*Lonicera* spp.)
Lilac (*Syringa vulgaris*)
Privets (*Ligustrum* spp.)
Roses (*Rosa* spp.)

Flowers
Bee balm (*Monarda didyma*)
Dahlias (*Dahlia* hybrids)
Delphinium (*Delphinium* × *elatum*)
Phlox (*Phlox paniculata*)
Zinnia (*Zinnia elegans*)

Spray Away Brown Patch in Lawns

If your lovely green lawn develops brown or yellow rings or patches that die out, brown patch may be the culprit. A variety of Rhizoctonia fungi causes this disease; some species thrive in cool weather, while others affect grasses in warm weather.

If brown patch plagues your lawn, fight back with this formula from John Dromgoole, owner of Garden-Ville in Austin, Texas. Follow up with John's suggestions for correcting water and fertilizer problems or the disease will return.

Ingredients and Supplies

1 rounded tablespoon baking soda or
    potassium bicarbonate
1 tablespoon horticultural oil
1 gallon water

Directions

1. Mix all ingredients thoroughly.

2. Spray lightly on your lawn. Avoid over-use or drenching the soil with baking soda.

Yield: About 1 gallon of spray for battling brown patch

Note: John says potassium bicarbonate, available in garden centers, is the best choice for this spray. Unlike baking soda, potassium bicarbonate leaves no salt residue in the soil.

COMPOST STOPS BROWN PATCH COLD

How can you tell if your lawn has brown patch? Take a look at your lawn care techniques. John Dromgoole says, "the disease is generally caused by poor drainage, too much rain or irrigation, and/or too much nitrogen fertilizer. Another symptom is that the leaves easily pull loose from the runners."

Aerate to improve the movement of air, nutrients, and water through the soil. And fix drainage problems by filling in low spots or installing drain tiles in your yard. To permanently solve brown patch problems, John suggests applying a half-inch layer of finished compost to your lawn. The microbe trichoderma, which exists in compost, is a powerful deterrent to brown patch.

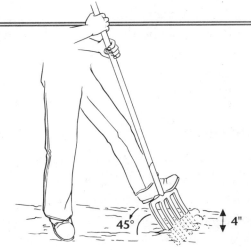

You can aerate your lawn with a spading fork. Insert the tines about 4" into the ground at a 45° angle. Press down lightly to loosen the soil, then pull out the fork. Repeat at 1' intervals.

Lawn Fungus Fighter

If your lawn develops 2- to 6-inch-diameter reddish-brown spots during the hot, sticky days of summer, it may have a fungal disease called Fusarium blight. Rather than watch those spots turn tan and then yellow as the grass roots die, follow the lead of Robert Redmon, a director of grounds management for the University of Alabama in Huntsville.

When part of the lawn Robert tends became diseased and developed unstoppable brown patches, he made a concoction with two fungus-busting agents: bleach and oil. This mix will help you get temporary control of a fungus-infested lawn during high stress periods. Then you can use cultural controls (see "Lawn Care Prescription" on the facing page) for a long-term solution. Robert says that he has used this spray primarily for fescues, but adds that it should work equally well for other cool-season grasses.

Ingredients and Supplies

1 ounce household bleach
2 ounces horticultural oil or a surfactant (the amount according to the label)
4 gallons water
Pump spray bottle or hose-end sprayer
White Dutch clover seed
Goggles
Rubber gloves

Directions

1. Mix the bleach and oil with water in the sprayer. (This mix will cover about 1,000 square feet of lawn.) Be very careful when you handle bleach. Wear goggles, rubber gloves, and long sleeves and take care to avoid splashing when you pour the bleach.
2. Spray the mix on affected areas starting when temperatures consistently reach the mid-60s at night.

3. Fusarium blight is a disease that migrates from the soil to plant parts and then spreads as the temperature and humidity increase. You'll need to reapply the spray monthly to keep the blight under control.
4. When you reseed the area in the fall with fescue or other grass seed, include some clover—¼ to ⅓ pound of clover per 50 pounds of fescue seed, Robert says. That's enough for approximately ½ acre of overseeding.

Note: This recipe should work where fungicides have failed, Robert claims. "I had used a fungicide in another spot that didn't seem to be doing the job, but the bleach-and-oil mixture seemed to take care of it," he states.

Variation: If you want a bleachless control for fusarium blight and other diseases, use compost. Adding compost to your lawn may control some diseases because organic matter increases the number of beneficial

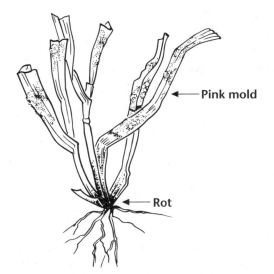

Pink mold

Rot

The most stressed areas of your lawn—the parts along walkways and driveways—are usually the first to show symptoms of Fusarium blight. You'll see a dark rot at the crown and roots of the grass plants, and the leaves may have a fuzzy, pink mold coating.

microorganisms in the soil. A healthy population of beneficial microorganisms can crowd out disease microorganisms or, in some cases, even kill them.

To add compost to your lawn, screen it first to remove any large pieces, then apply it using a cyclone or drop-type spreader. (See "Compost Your Lawn Problems" on page 127.) If you prefer to use a sprayer, mix up a hearty compost tea solution (see "Compost Tea Cure-All for Plants" on page 121) and spray it on.

Lawn Care Prescription

Robert Redmon has more advice for a healthy lawn. Follow these tips and you won't have to worry about finding cures for fungal diseases.

- Plant resistant grass varieties.
- Once your grass is growing, make sure that it gets enough water (1 inch per week).
- Don't water your lawn at night, when it is sure to stay damp, because wet conditions help fungi spread.
- Mow your lawn when it's dry, and leave it alone when it's wet to avoid spreading fungi.

- Fertilize with an organic fertilizer.
- Aerate your lawn so that water and air can move easily through the soil.

Dr. H. Arthur Lamey, a plant pathologist at North Dakota State University Extension Service in Fargo, also suggests that you avoid evening watering. He adds these precautions to ward off the fungal spores that, he says, plant themselves almost like seeds.

- Don't mow grass too short.
- Remove excess thatch. 🦋

Dual-Purpose Garden Spray

A garden product that you may already have can help your plants fight off fungal diseases. Antidesiccants (or antitranspirants) are best known as the stuff you spray on Christmas trees or wreaths to hold in moisture and make them last longer. But studies show that the sprays can also fight off rust and powdery mildew, says landscape consultant Mark Whitelaw, a consulting rosarian for the American Rose Society.

Ingredients and Supplies

> Antitranspirant or antidesiccant
> Backpack or pump sprayer

Directions

1. Antitranspirants are sold at nurseries under various commercial names as a ready-to-use spray or as a concentrate that you'll need to mix up. Buy whichever is most useful to you. And don't let those long words scare you off—antitranspirants are virtually nontoxic and biodegradable. They work by creating a film on a plant's leaves.

2. When you spray, be sure to coat the tops and bottoms of leaves. Application techniques depend on which form you buy, Mark says, so read and follow label directions. By coating the leaves and stems, you block fungi from the leaves and/or give any fungal spores that are already there a coat, which prevents them from spreading. The film will not protect new growth, so reapply as needed, according to the label.

Water First

Whether you're feeding your plants, using a foliar (leaf) spray, insecticidal soap, or any other man-made interference, getting out your hose or watering can should always be step number one. "Always, always irrigate before applying any chemical, of any sort, for any purpose!" Mark Whitelaw insists. "This puts less stress on the roots and foliage of the plant." If you don't water, you'll create conditions that can injure the leaves.

Note: Gardeners in cool, humid climates, like the Pacific Northwest and New England, boast success with antidesiccants in fighting the dreaded rose rust which thrives in their area, Mark says. At the same time, antidesiccants are popular with some in southern California's dry inland areas. "Antitranspirants are particularly effective against powdery mildew in areas where hot, dry conditions prevail during the day, but high humidity conditions exist at night and early morning," he explains.

Fishy Foliar Spray

You can feed your plants and slow the spread of fungal diseases at the same time when you combine two ocean-going ingredients in a foliar (leaf) spray. Rick Estes, president of the New Hampshire chapter of the Northeast Organic Farming Association, uses this nutrient-rich seaweed and fish emulsion "soup" when plants show the first symptom of disease. He also uses it during the growing season and at transplanting time to give plants an energy boost.

Ingredients and Supplies

- 2–4 tablespoons liquid seaweed
- 2–4 tablespoons liquid fish emulsion (sold at most garden centers and some discount chain stores)
- 1 gallon water
- Backpack, pump, or hose-end sprayer

Directions

1. Before you get started, take note: You may have to set your alarm clock. "You should get up before the sun hits the leaves to foliar-feed," Rick says. "Then the stomata (pore-like openings) of the leaves are open, taking in their moisture" for the day ahead.
2. Mix the liquids with 1 gallon of water in the sprayer and shake to blend thoroughly.
3. Spray generously, coating tops and bottoms of leaves. Stretch out your treatments. Don't spray more often than every 5 days, Rick suggests, even if plants show symptoms of a fungus or other ailment. "Always give the plants time to put the extra nutrients to work,"

SEAWEED STRAIGHT

For a last-ditch effort, when a treasured plant is nearly dead, Rose Marie Nichols McGee reaches for the liquid seaweed—a magical tip that she cherishes but hesitates to share. "I love liquid seaweed, but I'm always nervous about making too many claims for something. It's a tip we kind of pass on to friends," says the president of Nichols Garden Nursery.

So consider this a tip from a friend: To try to save a dying plant, make a circle of liquid seaweed around the trunk or stem and water it in. "If there's still something there, the seaweed gives it a booster."

he says. Rick recommends a dose of "nutrient and mineral soup" at transplanting time to help reduce shock and give plants a boost. For the squeamish (or those with curious cats): You can buy odorless fish emulsion.

Yield: About 1 gallon of Fishy Foliar Spray

Stick It to 'Em Molasses Spray

Molasses is anything but slow in fighting fungal disease in the garden, says organic gardener Andy Lopez, founder of the Invisible Gardeners of America. Don't worry about bugs, he says. "The plants absorb the molasses instantly. There's nothing left for the bugs!" Andy often mixes sulfured molasses with other organic garden sprays because, he says, the sugar feeds the plants and the sulfur is a natural fungicide.

Ingredients and Supplies

    1 cup molasses
    1 cup seaweed powder (optional)
    1 cup powdered milk (optional)
    1 cup rock powder (optional)
    1 gallon warm water
    Backpack or pump sprayer
    Old panty hose
    Fine-meshed strainer

Directions

1. If you are using only molasses, stir thoroughly into warm water, and spray (skip steps 2 and 3). If you have any or all of the optional ingredients, mix the molasses and powders into a thick paste and follow steps 2 and 3.

2. Wrap about 1 cup of the paste in the panty hose and tie it into a ball. Place the ball in water and let it sit for 2 to 4 hours.

3. Strain the liquid and mist plants every few weeks. You can use it to stop the spread of fungal diseases or as a preventive.

Yield: About 1 gallon of molasses spray

Note: Pick the right sprayer for your garden's size. For a few plants or a small garden, a hand-held pump spray bottle will do the job. For a medium-size garden, a 1½-gallon pump sprayer will speed up the application. For bigger gardens, a backpack model not only holds more spray, but is easier to haul around.

Whether you're applying an organic foliar (leaf) fertilizer or an organic spray to control diseases or pests, start with the right size sprayer. Spraying is most efficient when you mix up only as much spray as you need and you use all of the spray that you make. That way there are no leftovers to store or dispose of and you can clean your sprayer when the job's done.

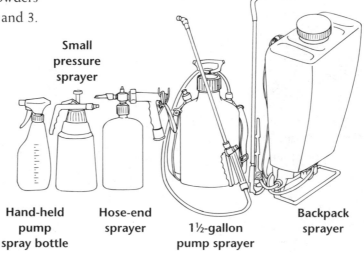

Small pressure sprayer

Hand-held pump spray bottle

Hose-end sprayer

1½-gallon pump sprayer

Backpack sprayer

Wash Away Fungi with Garrett's Spray

For a natural fungicide for ornamental plants, horticulturist and organic gardener Howard Garrett recommends his own homemade spray. Garrett spray packs a punch because it contains four fungus-fighting ingredients. You can add even more antifungal power with additives like baking soda (see the variations below).

Ingredients and Supplies

1–2 cups compost tea (see "Compost Tea Cure-All for Plants" on page 121)
1 tablespoon liquid seaweed
1 tablespoon blackstrap molasses
1 tablespoon apple cider vinegar
1 gallon water
Backpack or pump sprayer

Directions

1. Mix the ingredients in the sprayer. The acidity of the vinegar helps to kill black spot on roses, powdery mildew, brown patch, and other nasty fungi, Howard says. And the manure-based compost tea has natural fungus-fighting abilities.

2. Spray during the cool part of the day. As tempting as it is to blast away, don't overdo it, Howard cautions. To avoid damage to leaves, mist plant lightly and be sure not to drip vinegar on the soil.

3. Clean your sprayer thoroughly after use.

Variations: To give your fungus-fighting spray even more "umph," add baking soda, potassium bicarbonate, or ¼ cup garlic tea. To make garlic tea, liquefy 3 bulbs of garlic in a blender and strain out the solids. Pour the garlic juice into a 1-gallon container and fill with water. Shake the garlic juice well before using.

COMPOST TEA KEEPS ORNAMENTALS FUNGUS FREE

Compost is an effective fungus fighter that can help control any fungal problems that your ornamental plants might have. Compost teas made from manure are more effective at fighting fungi than compost teas made from only vegetable matter. But don't use compost teas made from manure on edible plants. Animal manure may contain E. coli bacteria which could be transferred to your fruits, vegetables, and herbs if you spray them with the tea.

Making compost for compost tea is easy. Any mix of vegetable matter and animal manure (from herbivores or poultry) will do, but for the best results, make a compost pile that's about 80 percent plant matter and 20 percent chicken, cow, goat, horse, or sheep manure. Use whatever materials you have available for the plant matter, including leaves, hay, grass clippings, tree trimmings, food scraps, bark, sawdust, rice hulls, and weeds (before they set seed).

For information on getting your compost cooking, turn to "Compost Formulas," starting on page 1. Tips for turning compost into nourishing, disease-fighting compost teas appear in "Compost Is His Plants' Cup of Tea" on page 41 and "Compost Tea Cure-All for Plants" on page 121.

Oil on the Offense Spray

To prevent fungal diseases from taking hold in late winter and early spring when wet, rainy weather can mean trouble, spray your plants with diluted oil, suggests Andy Lopez, founder of the Invisible Gardeners of America. Andy uses oil on fruit trees, vegetables, roses, and most flowers. However, he cautions, oil benefits only shiny-leaf plants. Do not spray oil on fuzzy-leaf plants, which are vulnerable to burning.

Ingredients and Supplies

1 teaspoon oil (plant-based oil such as castor, coconut, or a light salad oil)

1 teaspoon liquid soap (any biodegradable dishwashing liquid or Dr. Bronner's Peppermint 18-in-1 Soap)

1 gallon water (with chamomile tea or compost tea, optional)

Backpack or pump sprayer

Directions

1. Mix the oil, soap, and water in the sprayer. Water is easiest, but if you've got it, substitute a few cups of chamomile tea or compost tea, both of which help inhibit disease, Andy suggests.

2. Spray a fine mist on plants as often as needed, "usually daily the first week, then weekly, and, if it holds out, then monthly."

Yield: About 1 gallon of preventive oil spray

Note: Andy is picky about the types of oil he will use in the garden. Plant-based oils, such as castor oil or coconut oil, are his favorites, but he is also fond of fish oils, which have minerals that can help strengthen plants against disease. Because it contains peppermint oil (which acts as an insect repellent), he likes to use Dr. Bronner's peppermint soap when mixing any garden spray with a liquid soap.

Variation: Because it's a cheap, easy, and effective alternative, many gardeners prefer plain old salad oil for disease prevention, says Marion Hess, special contributor for Prodigy's on-line gardening newsletter, *Prodigy Gardens Newsletter.* "You mix 1 teaspoon of a light salad oil, like canola or safflower, and 1 teaspoon of liquid soap in 1 gallon of water. It seems to prevent disease."

Even when they're made with vegetable oil instead of petroleum oil, oil sprays can injure your plants if you don't apply them properly. Avoid using an oil spray when temperatures are expected to go above 85°F or below freezing. It's always best to test an oil spray on a few leaves and then wait and watch for a few days before dousing an entire plant.

Fire-Away Rust Removal

If you're fond of old-fashioned hollyhocks, odds are that you're familiar with rust, the ugly orange fungus that can quickly disfigure an entire garden. "Even if you stayed on it every single day with a chemical, you would not get all of the spores," says Mary Lou Heard, owner of Heard's Country Gardens in Westminster, California. So she devised the "fire method." She just makes a tiny fire beneath the hollyhock (with safety precautions!) to kill spores. It works for roses and snapdragons, too.

Ingredients and Supplies

¼ cup shredded paper or paper scraps
Matches
Jug of water and/or fire extinguisher

Directions

1. First, remember that you are lighting a fire; although it's small, use precautions. Have a jug of water or a fire extinguisher nearby. Make sure that there is no dry material nearby that could catch a flame and be sure to completely extinguish any remaining sparks.

2. Begin by placing a thin layer of the paper at the base of the plant. "You make a little circle of fire around the stem," Mary Lou says. She explains that the fire makes an instant flash of heat in a full circle around the base of the plant. Mary Lou emphasizes that you want to make sure that the area of heat extends to the outermost leaf, however far away that farthest leaf is. That way, you can be sure that you're hitting all the rust spores.

3. Light the fire. Expect a quick flame for 5 to 10 seconds. It should extinguish on its

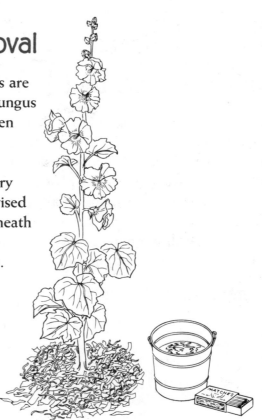

The heat from a small flash fire will help kill the rust spores that often plague hollyhocks. Use a thin layer of paper to encircle the plant stem without touching it, fill a bucket of water and place nearby, then light the paper and fire away.

own; if not, use the water to douse it. You may lose some lower leaves in the process, Mary Lou cautions. But she adds, "When the plant recovers from this little bitty heat, it comes back so gorgeous."

Note: If more than one plant shows symptoms of rust, repeat the process individually, for each plant. In 2 weeks, check to be sure that the plant is clean. If there are any diseased leaves, remove them. If the fungus reappears, treat that plant again. Mary Lou says she's never had any problems past that point.

Deter Disease with Disinfectant Dips for Tools

Clean your tools! You've heard that advice before, but now it's time to take it seriously. Using bleach or another disinfectant for tools is a must, says Dr. Cheryl Smith, a specialist in plant health with the University of New Hampshire Cooperative Extension. "If you're going to do pruning or any type of cutting, cut diseased areas of a plant last, and make sure that cutting tools, even scissors, get thoroughly cleaned prior to next use," Cheryl says. Otherwise, an isolated problem could become a full-scale plague.

Ingredients and Supplies

1½ cups household bleach
1 gallon water
Clean bucket
New steel wool pad
Motor oil or other oil used to condition
    tools

Directions

1. Mix the bleach and water to produce a 10 percent solution. This works fine for most cleaning.

2. Dip tools in the disinfectant after each use. For plants or trees that are already suffering symptoms, dip tools as you go along, cautions landscape consultant Mark Whitelaw. "If you are pruning severely diseased shrubs, or shrubs with highly infectious diseases, I recommend dipping the 'business end' of the pruners between making each cut."

3. After disinfecting, your tools need tender loving care to prevent discoloration or corrosion. Rinse thoroughly, then rub them lightly with a clean steel wool pad.

Wash Up

Don't forget to clean your shovel, hand tools, gloves, and even gardening shoes to prevent diseases from spreading, especially if you suspect a soil-borne disease. After you are finished working in the garden, wash your gloves and shoe soles in warm, soapy water and hang them out to dry.

4. Sharpen the edges if you'd like, and oil the tools before storing them for the next outing.

Yield: About 1 gallon of tool-disinfecting dip

Variation: To destroy fire blight bacteria that afflicts apple and crabapple trees, use 3 cups of bleach in 1 gallon of water (a 20 percent solution), says Dr. H. Arthur Lamey, a plant pathologist with the North Dakota State University Extension Service in Fargo. Or you may use pine cleaner at full strength, he says; just be sure that the label lists 19.9 percent pine oil.

CUT OUT DISEASE PROBLEMS WITH PROPER PRUNING

To prevent diseases on fruit and other trees, start with sharp shears, says landscape consultant Mark Whitelaw. "Clean cuts reduce the likelihood of rot and disease." Never leave a stump or stub. Cut limbs close to, but not flush with, the trunk—where the branch and branch collar (swollen area) meet. Prune so that branches grow outward; inward growth reduces air circulation, which helps diseases grow. Prune when leaves are dry.

Branch collar

When you remove dead, broken, or diseased limbs from trees, cut close and clean so you don't give diseases a chance to invade the wounds. Pruning off limbs where the branch and branch collar meet helps the tree quickly heal over and protect the openings.

Foiled Again

As a shimmery mulch, aluminum foil can help foil viruses that afflict your vegetables, says Dr. Frank Killebrew, extension plant pathologist at Mississippi State University. And if you wrap it around plant stems, foil can also deter fungal diseases.

Ingredients and Supplies

Aluminum foil or other light-reflective material

Directions

1. For a mulch, spread a 30-inch-wide light-reflective material on the soil surrounding squash or tomatoes, Dr. Killebrew suggests. The shimmer scares away aphids and thrips, which carry disfiguring, crop-reducing viruses.

2. To deter southern blight on tomatoes and peppers, wrap aluminum foil around plant stems, from 2 inches below the soil surface to 2 inches above the soil surface. The foil serves as a physical barrier against the fungus.

Herbal Soap Spray

Keeping plants clean and disease-free is the backbone of Donna Carrier's job as owner of Organic Plant Care, an interior landscaping company based in East Swanzey, New Hampshire. Soap sprays are a crucial part of her strictly organic regimen, but they don't have to smell bad to work, she says. Donna concocted her own soap spray that's scented with fragrant herbs.

Ingredients and Supplies

- 1 cup wormwood or tansy
- 1 cup lavender
- 1 cup sage
- 1-quart heat-resistant canning jar
- 2 cups water
- 1 teaspoon liquid, nondetergent soap, like castile soap or Murphy's Oil Soap
- Pump spray bottle

Directions

1. Place the wormwood or tansy, lavender, and sage in the canning jar and fill the jar with boiling water.

2. Let the mix sit until it cools to room temperature. Then drain off and reserve the liquid.

3. Combine ⅛ cup of the herbal liquid with 2 cups water and 1 teaspoon liquid nondetergent soap.

4. Fill the pump spray bottle and spray the mixture on plants. Repeat once a month.

Yield: About 2 cups of herbal soap spray

Note: If your plants are very dirty or dusty, saturate a cotton cloth with the liquid and wipe the leaves clean.

Soapy Indoor Plant Spray

For indoor plants that are exposed to pollutants from heaters or stoves, a cleaning spray can boost health and deter diseases, says Donna Carrier, owner of Organic Plant Care, East Swanzey, New Hampshire. This gentle spray cleans dust and dirt from plants and does not pose any risks to plants or animals, she adds. You can use it in your outdoor garden, too.

Ingredients and Supplies

- 1 tablespoon liquid, nondetergent soap
- 1 tablespoon liquid seaweed (optional)
- 1 quart lukewarm water
- Pump spray bottle
- Clean cloth

Directions

1. Mix soap, seaweed, and water together in the spray bottle.

2. Spray plants liberally and wipe off excess moisture with a clean cloth. Use monthly.

Yield: About 1 quart of soapy plant spray

Plant Mixing Plan

To save cucumbers and squash from one of their greatest enemies—bacterial wilt—try companion planting, suggests Dennis Glowniak, president of the California Organic Garden Club. Dennis says you can't beat this combination of tansy and radishes for a healthy summer-long feast of cucumbers and squash.

Like many bacterial diseases, wilt is carried by an insect pest. In this case, it's the cucumber beetle, which injects the wilt disease as it feeds. In this planting plan, the pungent aroma of tansy confuses and repels the beetles, while the radishes lure them away from the vine crops.

Ingredients and Supplies

Squash or cucumber transplants
Radish seeds
Tansy plants

Directions

1. Plant the squash or cucumber transplants in your garden, and tuck radish seeds into the soil in a circle around each transplant. The radishes should pop up within a day or two.
2. Check the radishes daily for cucumber beetles and squish any that you find. If you're squeamish about squishing them, drop the beetles into a jar or bag and throw it into the trash.
3. Plant the tansy the same day you plant your vegetable transplants. Tansy can be invasive, so set it in a plastic pot with the bottom cut out and set the plant in the soil, pot and all, to contain it. If you plant tansy directly into the soil, check it regularly and pull up any underground shoots that wander away from the planting area. Plant a 4-inch

clump of tansy for every 2 vegetable plants. Anecdotal evidence suggests that the tansy encourages overall healthy growth in cucumbers, Dennis says.
4. Divide unpotted tansy with a shovel at least annually. "You don't walk away from tansy," Dennis warns.

ANOTHER FRIENDLY MIX

Some herbs have a reputation for helping their neighbors fight off disease. "Try basil, for tomatoes," for instance, Dennis Glowniak recommends. "People think of basil and tomato as going well together in sauces, but actually a number of tests have shown that when they're planted together, both plants are more vigorous." Dennis explains that a vigorous plant repels diseases and insects more easily than one that's unthrifty. To give your tomatoes the benefits of basil (and vice versa), simply plant one basil plant inside each tomato cage, on the sunny side.

Keep 'Em Moving

To give your vegetable plants an added edge against diseases, enter them in a witness relocation program of sorts. That is, move them around each season so that the diseases are less likely to find them. If you always plant in the same spot, "it's inevitable that you're going to build up disease-causing microbes in the soil," says Dr. Frank Killebrew, extension plant pathologist at Mississippi State University. "Sooner or later, you're going to get zapped."

Ingredients and Supplies

Notebook (for keeping garden records)
Chart (for reference)
Disease-resistant vegetable seeds or plants

Directions

1. "Crop rotation does require some record keeping," Dr. Killebrew says. If you've kept a garden diary in the past few years, all the better. If not, now's the time to start. Begin by making a record of what you grow where.

2. Rotate your crops as best you can, for a minimum of 3 years. If you have a small garden, you may not be able to rotate crops effectively. In that case, consider moving the location of your garden every few years.

Note: For an easy rotation, group members of the same plant family together so that you can move them together. If you have plenty of space, split family members apart to confuse insects in addition to disrupting diseases. Then make sure that you rotate all of the individuals to new locations where no members of the same family have grown in the previous 2 years. Ideally, you should move crops to new ground after just 1 season, but certainly after 2 seasons, Dr. Killebrew says.

MORE DISEASE-STOPPING METHODS

Crop rotation goes a long way toward reducing disease (and insect) problems, but like any other garden technique, it's not a complete solution. "Crop rotation in itself does not mean that you've walked away from the problem," Dr. Frank Killebrew says. You still need to take other steps, like mulching and planting disease-resistant vegetable varieties. Mulch helps tomatoes and other vegetables avoid being splashed by rain or irrigation water—on its own, the water is harmless, but it gives diseases a medium for spreading. Planting disease-resistant varieties is a great way to combat wilts and other diseases which are willing to wait in the soil. Fusarium wilt, for instance, will not disappear from the soil just because you've moved its favorite meal away for a few years.

FAMILY-STYLE CROP ROTATION

Group related vegetables (crops that are in the same plant family) together in garden beds or an area of your garden to set up a simple crop rotation system. Move each family group to a different bed or planting area each year to disrupt attacks by diseases and insects.

YEAR 1

Squash Family
Cantaloupe Squash
Cucumbers Watermelon
Pumpkins

Onion Family
Garlic
Leeks
Onions
Shallots

Cabbage Family
Broccoli Cauliflower
Brussels Collards
sprouts Mustard
Cabbage Turnips

Grass Family
Corn

Pea Family
Beans
Peas

Tomato Family
Eggplant
Peppers
Potatoes
Tomatoes

Beet Family
Beets
Spinach
Swiss chard

Carrot Family
Carrots
Celery
Parsnips

YEAR 2

Pea Family
Beans
Peas

Grass Family
Corn

Squash Family
Cantaloupe Squash
Cucumbers Watermelon
Pumpkins

Tomato Family
Eggplant
Peppers
Potatoes
Tomatoes

Beet Family
Beets
Spinach
Swiss chard

Carrot Family
Carrots
Celery
Parsnips

Cabbage Family
Broccoli Cauliflower
Brussels Collards
sprouts Mustard
Cabbage Turnips

Onion Family
Garlic
Leeks
Onions
Shallots

YEAR 3

Beet Family
Beets
Spinach
Swiss chard

Carrot Family
Carrots
Celery
Parsnips

Tomato Family
Eggplant
Peppers
Potatoes
Tomatoes

Pea Family
Beans
Peas

Grass Family
Corn

Cabbage Family
Broccoli Cauliflower
Brussels Collards
sprouts Mustard
Cabbage Turnips

Onion Family
Garlic
Leeks
Onions
Shallots

Squash Family
Cantaloupe Squash
Cucumbers Watermelon
Pumpkins

Chapter 6

FORMULAS FOR WEED CONTROL

Weed-Busters

Anyone who plants a garden enlists in a never-ending battle with weeds. Some gardeners take the quick-fix, shotgun approach and blast them with chemicals. In fact, home gardeners spend more than $200 million a year on herbicides. But that's only part of the cost. Chemical herbicides have been implicated in groundwater pollution, soil degradation, and even serious human health problems. In the end, it's a bad bargain, because the weeds keep coming back.

But many enlightened gardeners take a more holistic approach. They say that a weed is just a plant out of place. And, in fact, one person's weed may be another person's flower or even salad green. While one gardener struggles to eliminate violets from a lawn, another will cultivate them in the flower bed, and still others may enjoy their foliage and flowers in salads.

That's not to say that every weed has a good side. Or that we have to learn to live with them. In fact, you can have a weed-free lawn and garden without resorting to dangerous chemicals or spending hours on the back-breaking labor of hoeing or chopping or pulling weeds.

There's a whole slew of natural products that will kill weeds if applied correctly. In fact, you'll be surprised at the number of potent—but safe and environmentally sound—natural weed killers that are already in your cupboard or medicine cabinet.

In this chapter, you'll find some of the best homemade weed-killing recipes from organic gardeners around the country. But that's not all. You can enlist the power of the sun to burn out weeds. All it takes is a little bit of plastic and a little time. Or you can elbow them out with cover crops—and we've got a list of some surprising, versatile, and good-looking crops that you can use. And, of course, there's mulch. We've got that covered, too, well beyond the common grass clippings and straw. You'll learn how to manage your mulch materials so that they do a good job of smothering weeds and building the soil, while looking good all through the season.

When you put these weed-busting formulas to work in your garden, you'll find that it's not difficult at all to put weeds in their place.

Weeds at Work

Many gardeners say that having a few weeds in the garden isn't such a bad thing. Linda Anne LeBoutillier of Waterloo Gardens in Devon, Pennsylvania, always leaves a few weeds growing so that rabbits can eat their fill of clover and lamb's quarters rather than garden plants. Other weeds, such as Queen-Anne's-lace, serve as a magnet for beneficial bugs. Besides, Linda Anne figures, keeping some areas untouched grants a peaceful, natural touch to her gardening. "I have so many birds and butterflies here," she says. "For the balance of nature, I can live with some weeds."

151

A Shot of Vinegar

If you're tired of hand-pulling broad-leaved weeds, like henbit and dandelion, from your lawn, you can thwart them with a well-placed shot of vinegar, says Texas landscape consultant Mark Whitelaw. Take care not to splash it on the turf or any plants you'd like to keep, though, because vinegar will kill grassy plants as well. "I've even used it to kill Bermuda grass in the cracks and crevices of sidewalks," says Mark. It seems to have a residual effect in the soil, as well, "because it keeps the Bermuda grass from coming back for up to an entire year," he says.

Ingredients and Supplies

Vinegar (as close to 10% acidity
    as possible)
Dishwashing liquid (optional)
Pump spray bottle

Directions

1. Fill the spray bottle with undiluted vinegar (or mix 3 parts vinegar to 1 part dishwashing liquid).

2. Spray in a narrow stream, dousing the weed's leaves and crown (the area at the base of the plant).

3. Rinse the sprayer well with water, especially if it has metal parts, because vinegar is corrosive.

Yield: 1 bottleful of weed-pickling spray

Note: Carry a section of newspaper or a piece of cardboard with you when you're dousing weeds with vinegar. Use it to shield

To kill broad-leaved weeds in sidewalk cracks or other places, a simple spray of vinegar on their leaves and crowns should do the trick. Be careful not to splash any vinegar on plants that you want to keep.

desirable plants when you need to spray weeds growing near them. And don't get carried away with this weed treatment—repeated applications of vinegar will acidify the soil so that nothing will grow in it.

BEATING BROAD-LEAVED WEEDS

Weeds can be either grass plants, like crabgrass, or broadleaf plants, like dandelions. Broadleaf weeds can be annual, biennial, or perennial. You can kill off many broadleaf weeds, including the ones shown below, by applying some type of weed-killing formula to the leaves (try "A Shot of Vinegar" on the facing page or "Win the Weed War with Gin" on page 156). Annuals like henbit will die after you spray them, but perennials like plantain may resprout from the roots.

Plantain

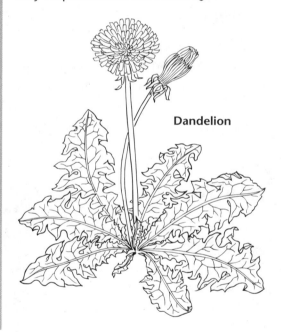

Dandelion

Henbit

Mullein

Weeds in Hot Water

Instead of scratching and digging and pulling weeds from sidewalk or driveway cracks, you can use boiling water to eliminate them quickly and safely. Boiling water will kill any plant or seed it touches, says Michigan organic gardener Marion Hess, a special contributor to Prodigy's on-line gardening newsletter, *Prodigy Gardens Newsletter*. So be careful not to splash any of it on neighboring garden plants or turf. Though this hot bath will destroy weed seeds that are already in the soil, seeds can be blown or carried in again, so Marion always leaves the dead weeds in place to mulch the soil and discourage germination of more weed seeds.

Ingredients and Supplies

Tea kettle or pan

Directions

1. Boil a full kettle of water.
2. Pour slowly and carefully, dousing both the weeds and the soil immediately surrounding them.

Yield: 1 kettleful of weed-whacking water

Bubble Trouble Soap Spray

A strong dose of soap can kill weeds by burning their leaves and roots, says California gardener Andy Lopez, founder of the Invisible Gardeners of America. "Different weeds require different strengths of soap," Andy says. You'll have to experiment to see how tough your weeds are.

Ingredients and Supplies

5 tablespoons natural liquid soap
1 quart water
Pump spray bottle

Directions

1. Mix the soap and water.
2. Spray leaves and the root area of weeds during the hottest time of day.
3. Check in 24 hours. The weed should appear burned and nearly dead. If not, double the concentration and spray again.

Yield: About a quart of soap solution

PARK THAT TILLER

The wise gardener trying to eradicate an aggressive weed follows one commandment, says Seattle gardener Barbara Donnette: "Thou shalt not till!" Tilling to remove persistent and perennial weeds or herbs like the ones shown below will produce the opposite effect. It breaks the plant and its roots and rhizomes into tiny stubs that can multiply into monster plants. At the Seattle P-Patch Community Gardens, where Barbara is program manager, a patch of comfrey that was mistakenly tilled proceeded to infest the entire acre. "Twice a year, for 10 years, we did comfrey combat," she says. "But more comfrey always came up the next spring." 🐛

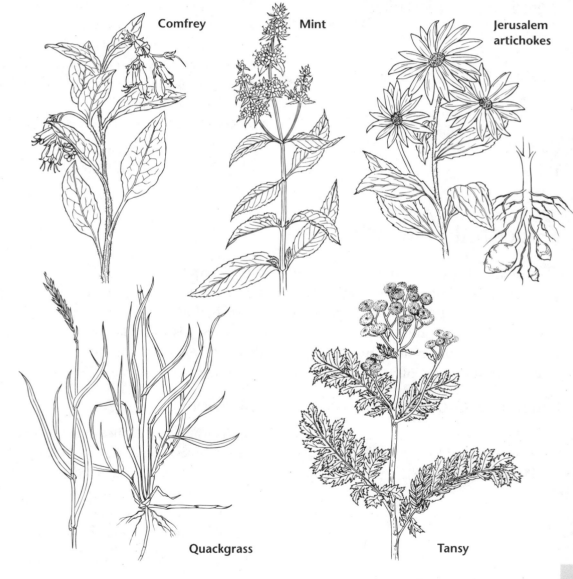

Comfrey

Mint

Jerusalem artichokes

Quackgrass

Tansy

Win the Weed War with Gin

Like most organic gardeners, Marion Hess of Northville, Michigan, doesn't demand a completely weed-free lawn. But if dandelions and other tough weeds reach epidemic proportions, she blasts them with this special high-proof concoction. One application kills just about any weed, but it's intended for spot use only. Apply it carefully and accurately to single weeds because it can harm grass blades as well.

Ingredients and Supplies

1 ounce gin
1 ounce apple cider vinegar
1 tablespoon baby shampoo
1 quart water
Pump spray bottle

Directions

1. Combine all ingredients in the spray bottle.

2. Adjust your sprayer to a stream setting.
3. Spray on a hot, sunny day, wetting all leaves and dousing the plant.
4. Repeat the dose if the weed is not dead the following day, or use a weeding tool to yank it out, root and all.
5. Reseed bare spots with grass to discourage germination of other weed seeds.

Yield: About 1 quart of high-proof weeder

Alcohol Attack

"The simplest way to kill a weed is with alcohol," says California gardener Andy Lopez, founder of the Invisible Gardeners of America. "One or 2 tablespoons in a quart of water will dehydrate almost any plant," he says. Because the strength of weeds varies, his formula may require a little experimentation. Andy says that it takes 5 tablespoons of alcohol in a quart of water to wipe out poison ivy, for example.

Ingredients and Supplies

1 quart water
1 (or more) tablespoons rubbing alcohol
Pump spray bottle

Directions

1. Mix water and alcohol in the spray bottle. (Use 1 tablespoon of alcohol for weed seedlings or thin-leaved weeds and 2 tablespoons or more for tougher weeds.)
2. Spray weed leaves thoroughly but lightly. (Avoid misting surrounding plants.)

Yield: About 1 quart of alcohol solution

Sorry, Charlie

If creeping Charlie catches hold in your lawn, it can be a recurring nightmare. To solve problems with this low-growing, yellow-flowered weed in your lawn, try borax, the same laundry additive that makes your white socks whiter. When Dr. Micheal Owen, an Iowa State University weed scientist, studied the effect of borax in controlling the shade-loving weed, he found that "the results were comparable to those from commercial herbicides." He notes that borax is most effective as a weed-killer in late spring or early summer, when weeds are growing actively. Be warned though: Borax doesn't work on other weeds (like dandelions) and it may cause a temporary yellowing of nearby grass. If you see some yellowing in surrounding grass, just mow frequently and it should color up within six weeks.

Creeping Charlie is a low-growing perennial weed that can wreak havoc with your lawn's good looks. A treatment of water mixed with borax will help keep Charlie's creeping under control.

Ingredients and Supplies

- 5 teaspoons borax, like 20 Mule Team Borax, for every 25 square feet of lawn
- 1 quart water
- Pump spray bottle

Directions

1. Mix borax in water. (Measure exactly: Too little and you won't get the job done; too much and you could kill your grass, too.)

2. Spray to cover a 25-square-foot area.

3. Water and fertilize your turf after the treatment so that it rapidly fills in the space left by the dead weeds.

Yield: About 1 quart of borax solution

Killer Cola

Linda Anne LeBoutillier of Waterloo Gardens in Devon, Pennsylvania, has reached back into her childhood memories to resurrect an old, unconventional weed-killer: Coca-Cola. "My grandfather used Coca-Cola on the weeds between the cracks in the sidewalks," says Linda Anne. He would take a drink from that old green bottle, then pour the rest on the weeds." She swears it works. "Just pour it in the center of the leaves, preferably on a hot day when they'll roast." It may take up to a week for the weed to completely keel over, Linda Anne says.

Gluten for (Weed) Punishment

Want to fertilize your lawn and garden and suppress the growth of new weeds at the same time? Believe it or not, corn gluten meal—a filler in many dog foods—does the trick, says Carolyn Ormsbee, staff horticulturist for Gardener's Supply Company in Burlington, Vermont. Available from mail-order garden suppliers, corn gluten prevents the germination of weed seeds, including lamb's quarters, purslane, and dandelion; it won't kill existing weeds or other plants.

Ingredients and Supplies

> 20 pounds corn gluten meal for every
> 1,000 square feet
> Any garden spreader

Directions

1. Fill spreader with dry gluten meal.
2. Apply evenly at about the time weeds start germinating in your area and again in late summer or early fall. (You can also apply the meal by hand.)
3. In a vegetable garden or flower bed, work the meal into the top 3 inches of soil.
4. Water thoroughly. This starts weed seeds germinating and also activates the gluten.
5. Adjust your fertilizer program. Since corn gluten provides a good dose of nitrogen, be sure to hold off on fertilizing for 2 to 4 weeks.
6. Refrain from sowing seed in the area for 6 months. Though existing flowers, turf, or vegetables won't be affected, corn gluten prevents all seed germination for several months after it's applied.

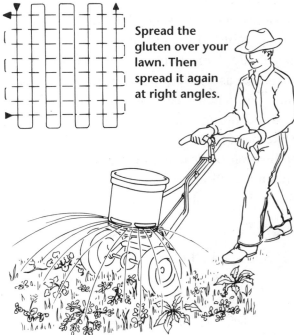

Spread the gluten over your lawn. Then spread it again at right angles.

Prevent weed seeds from sprouting in your lawn by applying corn gluten meal, a by-product from milling corn. Spread the meal in a crisscross pattern for best coverage.

7. Reapply every year.
8. Be patient. Weed populations should decrease dramatically over 2 to 3 years.

Bake 'Em in Plastic

To get rid of lingering weeds and their seeds in a new flower or vegetable bed, try trapping the sun's heat to burn them to death. All you need is clear plastic to cover the area and the patience (and space) to leave the area alone while the sun does its work. While this technique, called solarizing, works fastest in hot climates, you can do it during summer's peak heat in northern states, says Michigan organic gardener Marion Hess, a special contributor to Prodigy's on-line gardening newsletter, *Prodigy Gardens Newsletter*.

Ingredients and Supplies

Tiller or hand shovel
Enough clear plastic to cover an
    entire plot
Rocks
Clear plastic tape (optional)

Directions

1. Till the soil 5 inches deep.
2. Water soil well, soaking it to a depth of 6 to 12 inches.
3. Cover the area tightly and completely with the plastic sheets, making sure that all the soil is well covered and there are no gaps.
4. Tuck the edges of the plastic into the soil and weigh them down with rocks.
5. Wait. In hot climates, solarization can take as little as 3 weeks or up to 2 months. In cooler climates, leave the plastic cover on for at least 2 months.
6. Inspect the cover frequently for holes. If any develop, patch them with tape.

To use the sun's heat to kill weeds and weed seed in a new garden, rake the bed smooth, water it well, and cover it tightly with clear plastic for up to 2 months during the summer.

7. Remove plastic, and pull any remaining weeds from the bed.
8. Plant your garden or take other measures to cover the soil to keep weed seeds from entering this weed-free zone.

Covering the Uglies

Mulching is probably the most common form of weed control—except for yanking! But while everybody does it, no two people seem to do it the same way. Gardeners show their creativity and resourcefulness by recycling all sorts of waste material as mulch. Most of it works to smother weeds, hold moisture, and even improve the soil. But a lot of these materials aren't especially attractive. If you use cardboard, newspaper, or old plastic bags as your mulching medium, you may merit a gold medal for recycling, but you won't win any garden beauty contests. Don't let that stop you from using these materials, though. It's easy to cover them up with more attractive mulch materials, from wood chips to shredded leaves.

Shredded leaves

Newspaper

Ingredients and Supplies

Cardboard, plastic, or newspaper (for the base layer)

Wood chips, shredded leaves, grass clippings, cocoa mulch, small stones, or gravel (for the top layer)

Directions

1. Lay single sheets of cardboard or plastic, or ½- to 1-inch-thick sections of newspaper, across garden paths or rows.

2. Cover with the top layer of your choice.

A thick layer of newspaper is a great weed-stopping mulch for vegetable beds. To plant through the mulch, just cut a small hole in the paper for each transplant. To make the bed look nicer, top the paper with shredded leaves or grass clippings.

Note: Water your garden well before you mulch. If you poke holes through the mulch for putting in transplants, water them right at their planting holes. Otherwise, your weed-blocking mulch may keep water from reaching your transplants' roots.

CARDBOARD WITH CHIPS

At the Seattle P-Patch Community Gardens, program manager Barbara Donnette has mulching down to a science. "We spread a layer of cardboard between raised beds and cover it with wood chips," she says. Cardboard is her favorite bottom layer because it comes in large pieces that slowly deteriorate after they've done their job of smothering weeds. As the cardboard deteriorates, simply add wood chips to the top to keep new weeds from sprouting, Barbara suggests. Plastic works well, too, but it tears frequently, and pieces work their way to the surface, giving the garden a junky look.

Cardboard is also an excellent base mulch for a garden bed that's infested with tough weeds like thistles, which can sometimes push their way through light mulches like leaves or straw. It's also a good weapon for reclaiming a bed that's too weed-filled to till or even hand-dig.

Just cover the entire bed with sturdy corrugated cardboard and top the cardboard with a more decorative mulch like grass clippings or cocoa mulch. After mulching the bed, let it sit for two weeks or longer. The weeds will begin to die off and decompose under the cardboard. When you plant the bed, simply use a trowel to cut through the mulch and cardboard wherever you want to insert a plant. Set the plant in place, and then push the mulch close to, but not touching, the plant stem.

As the garden grows, check frequently for weeds near your plants' stems. A few may still be alive and find their way through the hole in the cardboard layer. It's easy to pull these escapees. By the following season, the cardboard will have decomposed, and you should have a nearly weed-free garden bed.

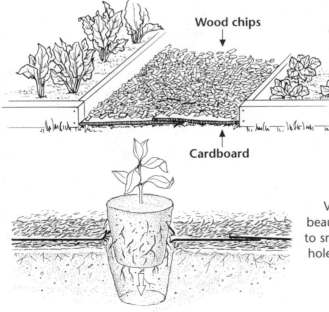

Wood chips

Cardboard

If your garden paths are weedy, just chop down the weedy tops and cover the paths with cardboard. Top off things with wood chips for prettier paths.

Vegetable and flower transplants grow beautifully in a bed mulched with cardboard to smother out competing weeds. Just punch holes in the cardboard and slip the rootballs of the transplants through into the soil underneath.

Basic Spread-It-On-Thick Mulch

You can use a wide variety of organic materials as mulch to smother weeds and improve the soil in the process. Whatever you use, make sure to spread it at least 3 inches thick to prevent sunlight from reaching the soil surface, says Margaret Sharpe, editor of *The Old Texas Rose* newsletter. She often mulches in the fall to prevent late-season weed growth, then tills the mulch under in spring at planting time.

Ingredients and Supplies

Wood chips, shredded bark, grass clippings, shredded leaves, cocoa mulch, compost, straw or hay, coffee chaff, seaweed (rinsed completely to remove salt), and much more!

Directions

Spread mulch ingredients in a 3- to 4-inch-deep layer around plants or on garden paths.

Note: Nearly any organic material can be used as a mulch, but some can have an impact on soil pH and fertility. Leaves, for example, can be either acid or alkaline. Margaret has a good supply of pecan leaves on hand, but she knows that they're alkaline, so she mixes in acidic pine needles to balance the pH. Some mulches are high in carbon and low in nitrogen. Sawdust, for example, will use up nitrogen as it decomposes, so it's a good idea to mix it with a nitrogen-rich material such as grass clippings.

Variations: Rose Marie Nichols McGee, president of Nichols Garden Nursery in Albany,

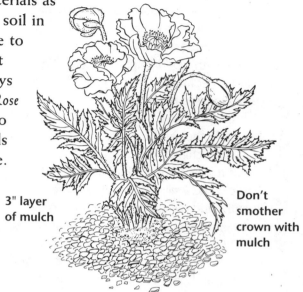

3" layer of mulch

Don't smother crown with mulch

Stop weeds with mulch! A 3"-thick layer of mulch around your plants keeps the soil too cool for many weed seeds to sprout. It's also a tough barrier for delicate weed seedlings to push through.

Oregon, collects "mint straw" from local mint-oil producers to use as a mulch in the nursery's herb and vegetable gardens. "It holds down the weeds and improves the tilth of our soil," she says. In Seattle, Barbara Donnette turned to local coffee roasters for free coffee chaff, which is produced in the roasting process. "It's acidic and provides a little bit of nitrogen," she says. Mary Lou Heard, owner of Heard's Country Gardens in Westminster, California, likes to mulch with cocoa shells. They're attractive, nicely scented, and they seem to discourage cats from digging in her garden.

Sprout 'n' Hoe Is the Way to Go

To protect young seedlings from weed competition, change your timing a tad. When you carefully work up a fine seedbed for sowing seeds, you usually bring weed seeds to the surface as well. You also may be cutting perennial weed roots into small pieces that look harmless but are still capable of resprouting. All too often, a crop of weeds springs up more quickly and aggressively than your precious plants.

Rodale garden book editor Fern Bradley outwits weeds by letting them sprout *before* she plants her seeds. "I welcome weeds to grow in my garden—for a week or two," Fern says. "Then I hoe them down to make way for the seeds I want to grow."

Ingredients and Supplies

Digging fork or tiller
Hand cultivator or trowel (optional)
Soil amendments (optional)
Rake
Sprinkler
Oscillating or scuffle hoe
Seeds (of your choice)

Directions

1. Use a digging fork or tiller to cultivate the soil in the bed you want to plant.

2. If necessary, work over the bed by hand, using a hand cultivator or trowel to dig out tough perennial weeds and weed roots.

3. Dig or till the bed again, adding any soil amendments (such as compost or bonemeal) that are needed, and rake it smooth.

To get the jump on weeds in empty garden beds, prepare the bed just as you would for planting—but don't plant it right away! Instead, water it gently for a week or so to encourage weeds to sprout. Then, hoe the weed seedlings and pull perennial weeds by hand. The result: A nearly weed-free, ready-to-plant garden bed.

4. Water the bed as needed to keep it moist for 7 to 10 days. Weeds should sprout in the bed.

5. When the bed is covered with weeds that are 1 to 2 inches tall, carefully pull out any perennial weeds by hand.

6. Work the bed lightly with an oscillating or scuffle hoe to cut off weed seedlings just below the soil surface. This will kill the weed seedlings, leaving you a weed-free bed.

7. Carefully plant the bed with seeds of garden plants. Disturb the soil as little as possible to avoid bringing up any new weed seeds.

Try a Rye Bed

To make a weed-free garden bed from scratch, try smothering the weeds in winter rye, suggests Julie Berbiglia, author of *The Lazy Gardener's Guide to Organic Gardening*. Julie says that she and her coworkers kept an 11 × 11-foot plot in rye all summer at the organic demonstration gardens of the Scarritt-Bennett Center's Organic Garden and Arboretum in Nashville, Tennessee. "By July, the rye was completely dried, and it had smothered out every kind of weed," says Julie. "The roots went down several inches and aerated the soil. When we pulled them up, the soil was very soft, without any digging."

Ingredients and Supplies

About 1 pound winter ryegrass seed for 500 feet

A dense crop of winter rye chokes out competing weeds and improves the soil. To kill the rye before it goes to seed, break the crop stems and lay flattened cardboard boxes on top. Cover the cardboard with an inch of compost. Let the rye decompose for several weeks and then plant straight into the compost.

Directions

1. Sow winter rye in the fall.

2. Till it under in the spring, or let it grow out over the summer and till it under in fall.

Variation: You can save yourself a lot of time tilling down rye if you follow Julie's no-dig cover crop technique. When the rye reaches about 3 feet tall, lay cardboard over the rye, breaking and flattening the ryegrass beneath it. Then cover the cardboard with a 1-inch-thick layer of compost. In 1 to 2 months, the rye and cardboard should be decomposed. "That created some of our richest plots," Julie says. "We planted our tomatoes in them, and we had tomatoes like I've never seen before."

"Using cover crops is probably the most important single aspect of our weed control," says Alan Kapuler, research director for Seeds of Change, an organic seed company in Santa Fe, New Mexico. You can sow seeds of traditional cover crops such as rye, hairy vetch, clovers, and buckwheat to add green matter to your soil and smother weeds. Or you can use your imagination to find other plants to fill space before weeds do. That's the key: no bare ground, Alan says. Along with traditional cover crops, Alan plants flowers, herbs, and even vegetables as cover crops to keep ground covered with desirable rather than pest plants. Here are some of the more unusual (and effective) cover crops used by Alan.

Anise hyssop provides shelter and nectar for bees.

Bronze fennel offers shelter for beneficial insects.

Lettuce grows quickly and provides green matter that can be turned under the soil.

Marigolds discourage nematodes in the soil.

Peas add nitrogen to the soil.

Poppies provide beauty as well as weed control.

Sunflowers can be cut and left to decompose on the ground, where they act as a mulch and add carbon to the soil.

Compost Your Weeds Away

If you don't want to dig out a weed patch to make way for a garden patch, take a lesson from California organic gardener Carrie Teasdale. She makes an on-site compost pile that not only provides humus for her garden but smothers weeds as well. Choosing a site where weeds are growing makes sense, Carrie says. "If there are weeds growing, that's a good place for a garden." She lets her on-site compost cook for several months, noting that the hotter the weather, the quicker it will break down.

Ingredients and Supplies

Horse manure
Dried leaves, shredded, or straw
Grass clippings
Fish meal or alfalfa meal (optional)

Directions

1. Cut weeds and let them fall in place.
2. Cover weeds with 4-inch-deep layers of horse manure and leaves or straw. If desired, sprinkle fish meal or alfalfa meal between layers to speed the process a bit.
3. Cover with a 2-inch-deep layer of grass clippings.
4. Allow to decompose in place.

Weed-Free Lawn Formula

A thick lawn is a weed-free lawn, says Michael Kaufman, owner of Kaufman Lawn Care, an organic lawn service company in Michigan. "You can't have two plants in the same place. So if you have a nice thick lawn, there's no room for weeds," says Michael. Fertilizing, reseeding (if necessary), and reducing thatch are among the basics of Michael's weed-busting formula. His special fertilizer mix also helps grasses survive drought.

Ingredients and Supplies

2 cups fish emulsion
2 cups seaweed extract
5 gallons water
Hose-end sprayer

Directions

1. Evaluate the condition of your lawn. If it's relatively weed-free and doesn't have a thatch problem (see "How Thick Is Your Thatch?" on the facing page to learn about thatch), proceed to step 2. If your lawn contains more than 25 percent weeds or has more than ½-inch-deep buildup of thatch, you'll need to reseed or dethatch and reseed before proceeding to step 2.
2. Mix fish emulsion, seaweed extract, and water in the hose-end sprayer. You can also use just one of the fertilizers instead of both of them. In that case, use 2½ cups of fish emulsion, or 4½ to 5 cups of seaweed extract, with the 5 gallons of water.

3. In the spring, apply the fertilizer mixture to your lawn.
4. Repeat the application in fall.

Yield: Enough lawn rejuvenating formula to treat 5,000 square feet of lawn

Note: Especially weedy lawns require more drastic action. If your lawn is more than half weeds, your best bet is to till it under and start from scratch, Michael says. You don't have to sow the same type of grass that was growing there previously. Just ask your local seed supplier for the best types for your area, and make sure that you use disease-resistant hybrid seed.

All lawns have some thatch—a ground-level layer of dried, undecomposed grass stems and roots. A little bit of thatch actually helps your lawn. It protects the roots from damage and regulates soil temperature and moisture. But when thatch gets too thick, it becomes a problem. A layer of thatch that's more than ½ inch thick can block air, water, and fertilizer from penetrating into the soil. Thick thatch is also a good hiding place for grass-eating insect pests like chinch bugs.

To check your lawn for thatch, get down on your hands and knees and take a good look at your lawn. You should be able to spot the soil surface here and there among the grass blades. If you don't see soil, but instead see tan material that looks like dead grass or straw, that's thatch. Pick a spot and push through the thatch to the soil below. Then use a small ruler to measure the thickness. Do this in a few different spots around your lawn.

If your lawn has too much thatch—more than ½ inch—you'll need to remove it and re-seed, says Michael Kaufman. To dethatch the lawn, use a core cultivator to aerate, then rake the lawn vigorously with a metal rake or special cavex rake. For areas over 1,000 square feet, it might be easier to rent a dethatching machine. These machines are available from many local equipment rental companies.

After you remove the thatch, your grass may look thinner, and some areas of bare soil could be exposed. It's important to spread seed over all the areas you dethatched, other-wise weeds may just spring up in the bare areas. Consult your local seed supplier for rec-ommendations of the best type of seed to overseed your existing lawn. You can use a hand-crank spreader to sow the seed, or just spread it by hand. Water thoroughly and

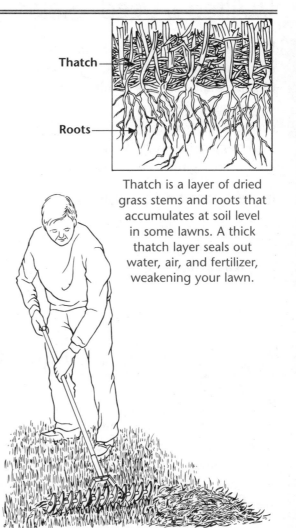

Thatch is a layer of dried grass stems and roots that accumulates at soil level in some lawns. A thick thatch layer seals out water, air, and fertilizer, weakening your lawn.

To remove thatch buildup in your lawn, rake the grass vigorously with a cavex rake (also called a dethatching rake). Its special wide tines cut through thatch and pull it loose, allowing more water and air to reach grass roots.

deeply after overseeding, just as you would if you were seeding a lawn from scratch, and keep the soil moist until the grass comes up (usually two to four weeks). You may even need to water it every day. 🦫

Wilted Weed Salad

If you can't beat 'em, eat 'em. That's Tennessee gardener Julie Berbiglia's novel approach to weeds. Julie, author of *The Lazy Gardener's Guide to Organic Gardening*, has found that weeds—from violets to dandelions—can be as tasty as traditional greens. And they usually appear earlier in the season. Ironically, she's found that increasing demand has the effect of reducing the supply. "As I continually harvest dandelions as a cut-and-come-again lettuce, they die out," Julie says with a laugh.

Ingredients and Supplies

Young dandelion greens
Wild mustard greens
Herbal vinegar

Directions

1. Steam dandelion and mustard greens together.
2. Serve with herbal vinegar.

Caution: Don't collect plants that may have been treated with pest- or weed-killing sprays.

No Shrinking Violet Salad

Besides containing a healthy dose of vitamin C, the deep green leaves of violets have a very mild, lettucy flavor, says Tennessee gardener Julie Berbiglia. As opposed to expensive greens, violets are free (and often are so numerous as to be considered weeds), and they withstand the summer's heat and the winter's cold. "My boyfriend thinks that potatoes are the only real vegetable, but even he likes violet leaves," Julie says.

Ingredients and Supplies

Dandelion greens
Flowerpots
Violet leaves and flowers
Lettuce
Purslane
Chickweed greens
Lamb's-quarters
Herbal vinegar

Directions

1. Blanch dandelion greens by covering them for about a week with the flowerpots.
2. Wash all greens and toss together.
3. Dress with herbal vinegar.

Caution: Don't gather your salad weeds from roadsides (or neighbors' yards) where they may have been treated with pest- or weed-killing sprays. Even organic sprays might leave a bad taste in your mouth.

Weeds You Can Eat

One way to put weeds to good use is to eat them! Several types of common garden weeds, including the ones shown below, are edible. Always be very careful when harvesting and eating weeds or any other wild plants. Use a detailed identification guide or get advice from an expert plantsperson. You can use tender greens of weeds like dandelion and purslane in tasty, healthful salads.

Put weeds to good use—in your salad bowl! Edible weeds add variety and nutrition to salads, and they'll liven up the lettuce with a burst of flavor.

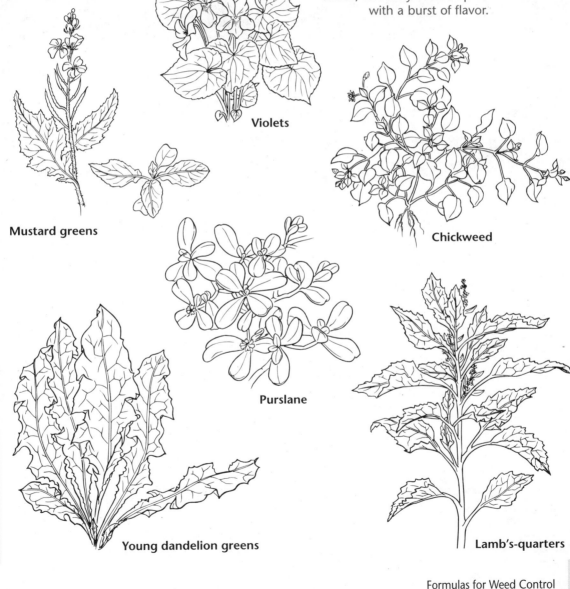

Violets

Mustard greens

Chickweed

Purslane

Young dandelion greens

Lamb's-quarters

Chapter 7

Bird, Butterfly, and Beneficial Insect Formulas

Lady beetle

Bringing in the Beautiful Beneficials

Want a garden that's colorful, healthy, and free of major pest problems? Just make sure that your yard is inviting to insect-eating birds, pest-destroying beneficial insects, and pollinating bees and butterflies.

The recipes in this chapter provide food for your invited guests. But birds, butterflies, and beneficial insects have some other needs too—specifically, water, shelter, and living space. These essential items are easy to provide, and because water and sheltering plants are attractive, you'll enjoy them as much as the beneficials.

Start with water. Birds, butterflies, and beneficial insects can't survive or thrive without it. A birdbath works great for your feathered friends.

Mud puddles and a shallow pan of water that's filled with small stones will give butterflies and beneficial insects a place to land and drink. Change the water in containers frequently—daily if possible—so that birds, butterflies, and beneficial insects can always get a fresh, clean drink.

Food, water, shelter, and nest sites are the keys to inviting birds, butterflies, and beneficial insects into your yard.

A hungry bird, like this wood thrush, is an excellent ally against insect pests in the garden. While you may notice birds most often when they're eating seeds at your feeders, they're great bug-catchers, too, especially when they have hungry nestlings to feed.

Give them shelter. Birds, butterflies, and beneficial insects need places where they can hide from predators, as well as sites where they can lay their eggs or raise their young. Planting a mix of trees, shrubs, herbs, and flowers is a great way to provide homes and food for both birds and beneficial insects.

Evergreens, like pines, are good choices for attracting birds, since they supply both seeds and shelter. Combine them with dogwoods and other fruit-producing plants to make excellent feeding and nesting sites.

Beneficial insects, like hover flies and lacewings, are always on the lookout for plants like dill and yarrow that provide them with pollen- and nectar-rich flowers. And butterfly caterpillars enjoy the leaves of a variety of plants, including milkweed and parsley.

Don't worry if birds think that your garden fruits look attractive or if butterfly caterpillars start munching on herb leaves—just set out more of their favorites so that there's plenty for everybody. You can also put a floating row cover over specific plants that you want to save for your use only.

As soon as brightly colored birds and butterflies start visiting your yard and beneficial insects start pollinating flowers and patrolling for pests, you'll see that they give a *lot* more than they take. See "Recommended Reading" beginning on page 318 for books with more details on gardening to attract birds and beneficial insects to your yard.

Migratory monarchs are almost certain to visit your garden if it contains milkweed or its ornamental cousin, butterfly weed. Alkaloids in milkweed sap give monarch butterflies a bad flavor. Predators quickly learn to recognize monarchs' distinctive orange-and-black colors and to leave them alone in favor of tastier prey.

"Orange" You Fond of Hummingbirds?

This simple formula lures hordes of hummingbirds—especially Anna's and black-chinned types—to Charity Hagen's yard in Wildomar, California. "If you want to *really* attract a lot of hummingbirds," Charity says, "add orange extract to the hummingbird nectar." She explains that you can buy orange extract at the grocery store or just squeeze orange juice into the hummingbird feed mixture.

Ingredients and Supplies

1 part sugar

3 parts water

A few drops of
   orange extract
   or orange juice

Directions

1. Dissolve the sugar in the water.

2. Add the orange extract or orange juice and stir a few times. (Don't add red food coloring, since it's bad for the birds' health.)

3. Pour the mix into a hummingbird feeder, or store it in the refrigerator for up to 2 weeks.

Note: You probably won't have to worry about leftover nectar, since, according to Charity, "it keeps the hummingbirds coming back for more—they just can't resist it, and

Look for ruby-throated hummingbirds (*right*) in the eastern half of the United States and in southeastern and south central Canada. Keep an eye out for black-chinned hummingbirds (*left*) and other species in the western states.

the orioles love it too!" But if any mix remains in the feeder after a week, discard it and replace it with fresh formula. Wash out the feeder before adding the fresh mix.

Birdsong Granola

This recipe is a "natural" for health-conscious birds! "I always make granola for my family," explains Diane Winslow, an avid birder and the owner of It's About Thyme herb nursery in Austin, Texas. "And as I read about what nutrients birds need, it seemed like a granola-like mix would be good for them, too." Your birds will love it!

Ingredients and Supplies

- 1 cup corn oil or peanut oil
- 1 cup honey
- 2 cups chopped nuts
- 2 cups millet
- 1 cup wheat germ
- 2 cups raisins or other dried fruit, except coconut
- 2 cups hulled sunflower seeds
- 2 cups crumbled dog biscuits

Directions

1. Mix the oil and honey, then heat gently just until they blend together.

2. Mix the other ingredients in a large bowl. Add the warm honey and oil, and stir to combine.

3. Press the mix into a shallow baking pan.

4. Bake at 375°F for 10 minutes.

5. Let cool, then crumble and serve to birds.

Yield: 11 cups of granola

Variations: You can using this recipe as a starting point, then add other ingredients as they become available. Diane adds crumbs from bread, cake, or crackers. "You can use any dried fruit except coconut, which swells in the bird's stomach," Diane cautions. In the winter, combine the granola with suet to supply the extra fat birds need to keep warm.

SERVING SUGGESTIONS

Scatter some Birdsong Granola on the ground and birds will come. But for a really good response from your feathered friends, follow the example of Charity Hagen of Wildomar, California. Charity says that the key to attracting lots of birds is the placement of the feeders.

To attract the greatest variety of birds, place your feeders at different sites and arrange them at different heights. Place several feeding trays or platforms on the ground, then set up one or two feeders a few inches above ground level. Arrange some feeders a foot or two off the ground, and hang other feeders higher up in trees. (Place the ground-feeders in an open area away from bushes and plants so that predators can't sneak up on the birds.)

When you use multiple feeding stations, you give ground-feeding birds all the room they need to eat in comfort. And by adding feeders at several different heights, you provide feeding options for birds that are too shy to feed directly on the ground.

Make dining convenient for your feathered friends.
A ground feeder makes eating easy for cardinals, while
nuthatches prefer raised platform feeders. Titmice like
any feeder that's set off the ground, and chickadees
visit all kinds of feeders, including hanging types.

Bird, Butterfly, and Beneficial Insect Formulas

175

Bird, Butterfly, & Beneficial Insect Formulas

Christmas Cookies for the Birds

This Christmas, decorate the leafless trees around your home, not with lights and tinsel, but with suet cakes cut into festive shapes. That's how Barbara Lucich of Pleasanton, California, and her siblings decorate around their mother's home for the holidays.

Ingredients and Supplies

Cookie cutters
Waxed paper
1 cup lard
1 cup crunchy peanut butter
2 cups rolled oats
2 cups cornmeal
1 cup flour
½ cup sugar
Makeshift hole puncher, such as a chopstick, skewer, or awl
Ribbon or yarn

Directions

1. Place the cookie cutters on a tray covered with waxed paper.

2. Melt the lard and peanut butter in a saucepan at low heat. Add the remaining ingredients and stir well to form a thick mixture.

3. Pour or spoon the mix into the cookie cutters to a depth of about 1 inch.

4. Poke a hole in the suet near the top of each cutter. Make the hole large enough to thread ribbon or yarn through.

5. Put the tray of filled cookie cutters into the freezer for at least 1 week.

6. Remove the cookies from the cutters and peel off the waxed paper. Thread ribbon or yarn through each and hang them outside.

Yield: Approximately 8 cookies

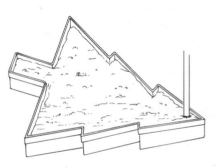

A

B

C

Make sure that your holidays are for the birds with peanut-oat freezer cookies! Pour or spoon the cookie mix into cookie cutters (*A*), then poke a hole in one end of each cookie ornament (*B*). String a ribbon or yarn through each hole once the cookies are frozen so that you can hang the ornaments in a tree (*C*).

Suet Smorgasbord

Bird enthusiast Robin Guy feeds birds all year long at her home in Lake Forest, Illinois. The birds appreciate her offerings in spring, summer, and fall, but particularly enjoy a special treat she cooks up for them when cold winds blow. "In winter, once we've had a few hard freezes, we give the birds some extra fat in their feed in the form of suet," she says. Cherries and seeds make this mix particularly palatable to birds.

Ingredients and Supplies

  1–1½ pounds beef fat
  ¼ cup millet (red and white mixed, if possible)
  ⅓ cup cracked corn
  ⅛–¼ cup safflower seeds
  ¾ cup chopped dried cherries
  Small containers, like plastic margarine or cottage cheese tubs
  Waxed paper

Directions

1. Warm the beef fat in a saucepan until it melts. Pour off the liquid as the fat melts to prevent it from burning.

2. Let the liquid fat cool slightly, then stir in the other ingredients. Robin notes, "All measurements are approximate. I never measure—I just add whatever is needed to make it look right!" It looks right, Robin says, when the seeds and fruit are almost touching each other, with the fat acting as a binder.

3. Line the containers with waxed paper and pour in the mix.

4. Refrigerate until cool, then store in the freezer until ready for use. You can put a suet cake out for the birds without thawing it.

Free Ingredients for Your Suet Smorgasbord

You can get fruit and fat for suet mixes without spending a dime! Robin Guy gets the fruit for cherry suet from her cherry trees. She collects imperfect cherries with insect holes or bird damage, cuts up the fruit in halves or quarters, and dries them in her dehydrator. Then Robin stores the dried cherries in the freezer until winter when she makes suet. If you eat meat, follow Robin's example and cut the beef fat from your steaks. Freeze it in labeled packages until you're ready to make suet. Otherwise, you can get fat inexpensively or free from a butcher.

Pop a suet cake out of its container and hang it in a mesh bag or wire suet cage.

Yield: About 4 cups of suet

Variation: Cracked Corn Suet

Increase cracked corn to 1 cup. Replace cherries with ¼ cup black oil sunflower seeds.

Variation: Sunflower Suet

Decrease cracked corn to ¼ cup. Replace cherries with 1 cup black oil sunflower seeds.

Beat-the-Heat Bird Treat

It's a challenge finding suet-type bird feeds that don't melt down in hot climates. Just ask Paul Reinartz, a gardener and bird lover from Austin, Texas. When his suet mixes became rancid thanks to hot Texas temperatures, Paul started looking for alternatives. He found a way to beat the heat when his sister-in-law shared this peanut-butter–based recipe with him.

Ingredients and Supplies

1½ cups water
1 cup uncooked oatmeal
¾ cup lard or bacon grease, melted
1 cup Cream of Wheat or Wheatina
1 cup hominy grits or corn meal
½ cup raisins or dried currants
1½ cups creamy peanut butter (chunky is
    acceptable if that's all you have)
2 handfuls birdseed or chicken scratch
Waxed paper
Zipper-closing plastic storage bag

Directions

1. Bring the water to a boil and add the oatmeal. Turn down the heat and let simmer for 1 minute.

2. Remove the oatmeal from the heat and stir in the remaining ingredients in the order listed above.

3. When the mixture is cool enough to handle—without sticking to your hands like glue—mold it into round cakes that are about the size of a tennis ball (2½ to 3 inches in diameter).

4. Set aside any cakes that you plan to use immediately. Place the rest on a waxed-paper–lined cookie sheet and put them in the freezer.

5. When the cakes are frozen, store them in a plastic storage bag in the freezer.

6. When you're ready to serve a cake to the birds, let it thaw until it's soft. Then you can set the cake in a birdfeeder, hang it in a mesh bag, or press it onto the surface of a pine cone. Paul recommends placing the cakes in a shaded area so they'll keep longer.

Yield: 6 to 8 cakes

A Sampling of Suet-Lovers

Birds large and small love suet. When you hang suet treats in your yard, you may have bird visitors ranging from wily woodpeckers to cheerful chickadees. Titmice, mockingbirds, and jays belong to the suet-loving crowd, too.

Gardeners in the Southeast and Texas who put out Beat-the-Heat Bird Treats may spot downy and red-bellied woodpeckers, white-breasted and brown-headed nuthatches, Carolina chickadees, blue jays, and summer tanagers enjoying the suety mixture.

CATER TO SMALL BIRDS WITH A COCONUT FEEDER

To keep large birds from eating his peanut butter suet cakes, Paul Reinartz devised this coconut feeder. Small birds, like chickadees, can light on it, but larger birds set it rocking.

You'll need one small coconut that is about 5 inches in diameter, one small piece of scrap wood about the size of a thumbnail (about ¾ inch square and thick), and one small eyehook. You'll also need one dowel rod that's about the diameter of a pencil and about 8 inches long—the length depends on the size of the coconut.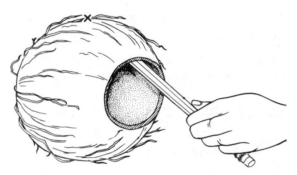

2½" diameter

Step 1. Use a fine-bladed saw, like a hacksaw or keyhole saw, to cut a round hole about 2½"–3" in diameter in the top of a coconut—the end that has indentations. (Paul cautions that coconuts crack easily, so handle them gently.) Then scrape out the contents of the coconut.

Step 2. Balance the coconut on the tip of a pencil inserted through the hole. When you find the spot where the pencil must rest to balance the coconut, mark the location of the pencil tip on the outside of the shell. Carefully drill a hole in the top of the coconut using a small drill bit. Move the bit around so that the hole is bigger than the threaded end of the eye hook.

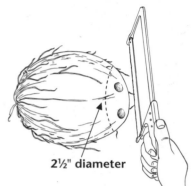

Eye hook

Scrap wood with drilled hole

Step 3. Drill a hole in the center of a small piece of scrap wood. Then place the scrap wood inside the top of the coconut, aligning the drilled holes. Put the eye hook through the coconut and thread it into the wood.

Glue

Notch

Step 4. Cut a notch in the bottom of the large opening, then glue a dowel to the back of the coconut and into the notch. Pack a softened peanut butter suet cake into the back of a coconut feeder and hang the feeder from a tree.

A Bee-ootiful Garden

Be a friend to bees by growing plants that will attract them to your garden. A mixture of perennial herbs and self-sowing annuals attracts bees and adds beauty to your garden too, says Rose Marie Nichols McGee, president of Nichols Garden Nursery in Albany, Oregon. The plants in this mix are so easy to grow that "it's hard to go really wrong with it," she adds. (See "Flowers That Attract Beneficial Insects" on the facing page for plant descriptions.)

Ingredients and Supplies

- 1 seed packet sweet alyssum
- 1 seed packet catmint (or buy small transplants)
- 1 seed packet coriander
- 1 seed packet dill
- 1 seed packet tansy phacelia
- 1 seed packet poached egg flower or meadow foam
- 1 seed packet corn poppies
- 1 seed packet single-flowered sunflowers
- 1 seed packet white yarrow (or buy small transplants)
- Organic fertilizer (optional)

Directions

1. In early spring, prepare planting areas on the borders of your garden. A band of flowers 1 foot wide will bring bees and all kinds of other beneficial insects. Depending on the amount of seed per packet, this mix covers between 100 and 200 feet of border.

2. Sow small amounts of each type of seed on prepared ground that's moderately fertile

How can you tell if your black-and-yellow-striped visitor is a honeybee? Honeybees are hairy and about ⅝" long, with black and yellow stripes on their abdomens. When you see them in your yard, you know that they're hard at work pollinating your plants.

and free of weeds. (In areas with mild winters, you can plant seed in the fall if you prefer.) For more on growing plants from seed, see page 267.

3. Gently water the seeds in and keep the ground evenly moist while the flowers are getting established (the first month or so after planting).

4. Once the seeds are up, water them with a diluted organic fertilizer, such as a weak solution of fish emulsion or liquid seaweed. If your soil is good and fertile, you can skip the additional fertilizer.

FLOWERS THAT ATTRACT BENEFICIAL INSECTS

When you plant this mix of annual and perennial flowers in your yard, you'll provide food for hungry bees who will repay you by pollinating the plants in your garden. These blooms will also attract other beneficial insects, including hover- or syrphid flies, lacewings, lady beetles, and parasitic wasps.

PLANT	🐛 DESCRIPTION ☀ HARDINESS ZONES
Sweet alyssum (*Lobularia maritima*)	🐛 Clusters of ¼-inch-wide pink, purple, or white flowers on 4- to 8-inch-tall mounded plants ☀ Annual
Catmint (*Nepeta* × *faassenii*)	🐛 Perennial with ½-inch-wide blue-violet flowers on long stems; plants grow 1½ to 2 feet tall ☀ Zones 3 to 8
Coriander (*Coriandrum sativum*)	🐛 Herb with tiny white flowers on 1- to 3-foot tall plants ☀ Annual
Dill (*Anethum graveolens*)	🐛 Herb with yellow-green flower heads and feathery foliage; plants grow to 3 feet tall ☀ Annual
Tansy phacelia (*Phacelia tanacetifolium*)	🐛 Bell-shaped blue to lavender flowers on 1- to 4-foot-tall plants; wear gloves when handling this plant, since it causes some gardeners to break out in a rash ☀ Annual
Poached egg flower or meadow foam (*Limnanthes douglasii*)	🐛 Flowers that have yellow centers and white edges; spreading plants grow to 1 foot tall ☀ Annual
Corn poppy, Shirley poppy (*Papaver rhoeas*)	🐛 3- to 4-inch-wide pink, purple, red, or white flowers; plants grow 2 to 3 feet tall ☀ Annual
Single-flowered sunflower (*Helianthus annuus*)	🐛 Yellow, orange, or maroon flowers with dark centers; flowers are up to 1 foot wide on 1- to 12-foot-tall stems (size depends on variety) ☀ Annual
White yarrow (*Achillea millefolium*)	🐛 Perennial with 2- to 3-inch-wide flowers on 1- to 2½-foot-tall plants ☀ Zones 3 to 9

Blooms for the Birds

Are you too busy to fill the bird feeder? With this mix of plants, you can still feed the birds all summer. That's because the plants all have bird-attracting seeds. "Because these are annual plants, you can grow them in any region," explains horticulturist Linda Harris of Ferry-Morse Seeds. (See "Annual Flowers for the Birds" on page 184 for plant descriptions.)

Ingredients and Supplies

Metal garden rake
1 seed packet sweet alyssum
1 seed packet grain amaranth
1 seed packet China aster
1 seed packet bachelor's buttons
1 seed packet black-eyed Susan

1 seed packet cosmos
1 seed packet flax
1 seed packet pincushion flower
1 seed packet corn poppy or Shirley poppy
1 seed packet sunflower

Directions

1. Prepare the site by digging or tilling to loosen the soil if needed. If you're planting on a site that has had weed problems in the past, check "Sprout 'n' Hoe Is the Way to Go" on page 163 for a simple technique for reducing weed problems before you plant.
2. Scratch the soil surface about 1 inch deep with a metal garden rake. Then use the back of the rake to smooth the soil.
3. After your area's last spring frost date, mix the seeds together. Each seed packet contains about 100 seeds, which will cover a bed that's about 10 × 20 feet (200 square feet). You may need to combine only a portion of the seed in each packet. You can save the leftover seed or share it with your friends.

4. Broadcast the seed over the bed by hand. You may want to add some sand or potting soil to the seeds first to make the mix easier to distribute evenly.
5. Press the seed into the soil surface by walking gently on the bed or by dragging a board over the bed.
6. Keep the seeds moist until the seedlings are about 2 inches tall.

Note: Linda points out that most of the plants will reseed, so you don't have to re-plant every year. But if you want to make sure that a particular flower always appears, scatter more of those seeds over your planting area each spring.

Site Your Bird Garden Right

This planting has a very informal, wildflower-meadow look, according to Linda Harris, so choose a site that's not too close to the house but still close enough to enjoy. To make the planting look less wild and more gardenlike, she suggests growing three different sunflower varieties of different heights. The similar flowers will help tie the planting together for a more coordinated look.

Grow bird-attracting plants like corn poppies, flax, and pincushion flowers. Mix them all together like a wildflower meadow, or group each type individually for a more traditional bed or border.

ANNUAL FLOWERS FOR THE BIRDS

These annuals produce seeds that birds like to eat. All of these flowers thrive in full sun, so choose an open spot for your bird-garden planting.

PLANT	DESCRIPTION
Sweet alyssum (*Lobularia maritima*)	Pink, purple, or white blooms appear in ¾-inch-wide clusters on 6- to 12-inch-tall mounds of foliage
Grain amaranth (*Amaranthus hypochondriacus*)	Spiked flower heads grow 1 foot tall and are red, green, or marbled red and green; the seed heads are beautiful; plants grow 6 feet tall
China aster (*Callistephus chinensis*)	Blue, rose, or white blooms are 2½ inches wide; plants grow 2 feet tall
Bachelor's buttons (*Centaurea cyanus*)	Blue, pink, purple, red, or white blooms grow 1 to 2 inches wide on 12- to 30-inch-tall plants
Black-eyed Susan (*Rudbeckia hirta*)	Daisylike yellow blooms have brown centers and grow 2 to 3 inches wide; plants grow 1 to 3 feet tall
Cosmos (*Cosmos bipinnatus* and *C. sulphureus*)	Blooms are 1 to 2 inches wide; *C. bipinnatus* has pink, white, or crimson ray flowers with a yellow center; plants grow 4 to 6 feet tall; *C. sulphureus* has yellow, red, or orange daisylike blooms on 2- to 3-foot-tall stems
Flax (*Linum usitatissimum*)	Blue or white delicate ½-inch-wide blooms grow on 3- to 4-foot-long stems
Larkspur (*Consolida orientalis*)	Blue, rose, violet, or white blooms are 1¼ inches long and grow on long spikes; plants grow 1 to 2 feet tall
Pincushion flower (*Scabiosa atropurpurea*)	Rounded 2-inch-wide blooms come in blue, cream, lavender, maroon, pink, and white; plants grow 2 to 3 feet tall
Corn poppy, Shirley poppy (*Papaver rhoeas*)	Four-petaled 2-inch-wide blooms come in deep purple, red, or white; plants grow 2 to 3 feet tall
Sunflower (*Helianthus annuus*)	Yellow, red, and rust-colored blooms grow 3 to 12 inches wide on plants that are 1 to 12 feet tall (size depends on the variety)

A Fluttery Butterfly Garden

Butterflies can't live on nectar alone. If you want to attract lots of butterflies and get them to stick around, try this three-part recipe from LuAnn Craighton, a naturalist with the education department at Callaway Gardens in Pine Mountain, Georgia. LuAnn says the first step is to pick a place with the right living conditions. Next, grow a variety of plants. And third, care for the plants organically.

Ingredients and Supplies

10 nectar-producing flowers for adult butterflies (see "Pick the Right Nectar Plants" on page 186)

10 host plants for butterfly caterpillars (see "Pick the Right Caterpillar Host Plants" on page 188)

1 (or more) 3 × 3-foot sunny garden spots sheltered from strong winds

1 or 2 flat stones (for warming spots)

Shallow puddle or terra-cotta saucer filled with wet sand and laced with a few dashes of Epsom salts

1 seat (for butterfly watching)

Directions

1. In a spot that gets at least 6 hours of sun each day, plant a variety of plants that attract butterflies and provide food for their young.

2. Add 1 or 2 flat stones where the butterflies can warm themselves.

3. Provide a puddle or other shallow water source so that your butterflies can drink or search for salts.

4. Site a bench where you can enjoy the show!

Protect the caterpillars that have yellow, black, and white stripes when you see them on your milkweeds! They'll munch on the milkweed plants, then turn into majestic monarch butterflies.

Fluttery Facts

- Butterflies are cold-blooded and don't get moving until their body temperature reaches about 80°F.
- When butterflies gather in groups around puddles, they're after salts in the mud, not just the water.
- Larvae chew holes in the leaves of host plants, but seldom harm the plant.
- The organic caterpillar killer BT (*Bacillus thuringiensis*) controls cabbage loopers and other vegetable-eating larvae. But it will also kill butterfly larvae if it drifts to their host plants. Avoid BT and hand-pick problem caterpillars, or be *extremely* careful if you use BT.
- In hot, dry climates, butterflies appreciate dappled shade in the heat of the day.

PICK THE RIGHT NECTAR PLANTS

You don't have to resort to trial-and-error to find out which plants attract butterflies. Ann Swengel, a vice president of the North American Butterfly Association (NABA), suggests growing some of these nectar and host plants as a starting point for attracting a variety of butterflies. For a much longer list, write to NABA at 4 Delaware Road, Morristown, NJ 07960.

| PLANT | ❧ DESCRIPTION |
	☀ HARDINESS ZONES
Black-eyed Susan (*Rudbeckia hirta*)	❧ Yellow and brown daisylike blooms; 2- to 3-foot-tall hairy-leaved plant ☀ Annual
Purple coneflower (*Echinacea purpurea*)	❧ Rose-pink daisylike blooms; 2- to 4-foot-tall perennial ☀ Zones 3 to 8
Yellow cosmos (*Cosmos sulphureus*)	❧ Yellow, orange, or red daisylike blooms; 2- to 3-foot-tall bushy plants ☀ Annual
Goldenrods (*Solidago* spp.)	❧ Plumelike clusters of golden or yellow blooms; 1- to 5-foot-tall perennial ☀ Zones 3 to 9
Impatiens (*Impatiens wallerana*)	❧ Flat, spurred blooms in lavender, pink, red, orange, or white; 6- to 24-inch-tall, neatly mounded plants ☀ Annual
Joe-Pye weeds (*Eupatorium* spp.)	❧ Substantial clusters of fuzzy rose-purple flowers; bold 3- to 12-foot-tall perennials ☀ Zones 3 to 8
Lantanas (*Lantana* spp.)	❧ Flat-topped clusters of red and yellow or pink blooms; 18-inch- to 4-foot-tall shrubby plant ☀ Zones 8 to 10 (treat as an annual farther north)
Lupines (*Lupinus* spp.)	❧ Dense 2-foot-long spikes of pealike flowers in shades of pink, white, blue, purple; bushy perennials grow 2½ to 3½ feet tall ☀ Zones 3 to 6
French marigold (*Tagetes patula*)	❧ Daisylike to rounded red and yellow blooms (choose single-flowered cultivars instead of doubles—butterflies can reach the nectar more easily); 6- to 20-inch-tall plant with strongly scented leaves ☀ Annual

FLOWERS

PLANT	🌿 DESCRIPTION ☀ HARDINESS ZONES
FLOWERS	
Mints (*Mentha* spp.)	🌿 Spikes of small, 2-lipped purple, pink, or white flowers bloom at top of plants; bushy, spreading perennials grow to 2 feet tall ☀ Zones 5 to 9
Pineapple sage (*Salvia elegans*)	🌿 Small bright red 2-lipped blooms; 2- to 3-foot-tall herb with fragrant leaves ☀ Annual
Rose verbena (*Verbena canadensis*)	🌿 Rounded clusters of purple, rose, or white blooms; 8- to 18-inch-tall perennial ☀ Zones 4 to 10 (treat as an annual farther north)
Brazilian vervain (*Verbena bonariensis*)	🌿 Rounded clusters of tiny violet blooms; 3- to 4-foot-tall perennial ☀ Zones 7 to 9
Zinnia (*Zinnia elegans*)	🌿 Round, flat, or mounded blooms in every color but blue; 6- to 36-inch-tall plants grow low and mounded or upright and bushy ☀ Annual
SHRUBS	
Glossy abelia (*Abelia* × *grandiflora*)	🌿 Clusters of small pinkish purple or white blooms; 3 to 6 feet tall and wide; rounded, semi-evergreen shrub ☀ Zones 6 to 10
Azaleas (*Rhododendron* spp.)	🌿 Lavender, orange, pink, red, white, or yellow funnel-shaped blooms; 1 to 20 feet tall (depending on species); evergreen and deciduous shrubs ☀ Zones 4 to 9
Orange-eye butterfly bush (*Buddleia davidii*)	🌿 Pink, purple, red, or white fragrant lilaclike blooms; 5- to 15-foot-tall arching plant that flowers best if cut back to the ground each spring ☀ Zones 5 to 10
Lilacs (*Syringa* spp.)	🌿 Large, very fragrant blue, lavender, pink, or white bloom clusters; 4- to 20-foot-tall upright plants look loosely rounded over time ☀ Zones 3 to 7

PICK THE RIGHT CATERPILLAR HOST PLANTS

Butterflies typically lay their eggs on the plants that their caterpillars feed on. If you want to attract a specific butterfly, provide the food plant or plants that it needs to survive. Caterpillars are always hungry, so don't be surprised when they munch the plant leaves to pieces!

PLANT	🌿 DESCRIPTION / ☀ HARDINESS ZONES / 🦋 BUTTERFLIES ATTRACTED
Asters (*Aster* spp.)	🌿 Mounds of purple, pink, red, or white daisylike blooms; 1- to 8-foot-tall bushy plants ☀ Zones 2 to 8, depending on the species 🦋 Pearl and northern crescents
Clovers (*Trifolium* spp.)	🌿 White, red, or pink ball-like flowers; plants range from low creeping forms to 2 feet tall ☀ Annual, biennial, or perennial, depending on the species 🦋 Clouded sulphurs and acmon blues
Herbs (dill, carrots, fennel, and parsley)	🌿 Yellow, greenish, or white flat-topped or ball-like clusters (called umbels); fragrant feathery foliage for all but parsley, which has flat or curled leaves ☀ Annuals or biennials 🦋 Black and anise swallowtails
Hollyhock (*Alcea rosea*)	🌿 Large white, pink, red, or yellow bowl-shaped blooms; 3- to 6-foot-tall flower stems ☀ Biennial grown as an annual 🦋 Painted and west coast ladies and common checkered skippers
Milkweeds (*Asclepias* spp.)	🌿 Clusters of green, orange, yellow, pink, or purple blooms; 1- to 5-foot-tall flower stems ☀ Zones 3 to 9 🦋 Monarchs
Wild petunias (*Ruellia* spp.)	🌿 Solitary or loose clusters of trumpet-shaped blooms in red, pink, or blue; 1- to 3-foot-tall perennials ☀ Zone 10 🦋 White peacocks
Snapdragon (*Antirrhinum majus*)	🌿 Spikes of tubular 2-lipped flowers in every color but blue; 1- to 4-foot-tall low mounded or tall spiky plants ☀ Annual 🦋 Common buckeyes

HERBACEOUS PLANTS

PLANT	❦ DESCRIPTION ☀ HARDINESS ZONES 🦋 BUTTERFLIES ATTRACTED
HERBACEOUS PLANTS	
Sunflower (*Helianthus annuus*)	❦ Large yellow daisylike blooms; sturdy 2- to 12-foot-tall flower stalks (size depends on the cultivar) ☀ Annual 🦋 Gorgone checkerspots (these butterflies are found only in and near the Great Plains, so don't expect to attract them elsewhere)
Violets (*Viola* spp.)	❦ Blue, violet, white, red, orange, or yellow blooms; 1- to 12-inch-tall plants ☀ Zones 3 to 9, depending on the species 🦋 Some fritillaries
TREES	
Cherries (*Prunus* spp.)	❦ Large group of trees and shrubs, many ornamental and others popular for their stone fruits; clusters of white to pink single or double flowers ☀ Zones 2 to 10, depending on the species 🦋 Some tiger swallowtails, coral hairstreak, Lorquin's admiral
Citrus (*Citrus* spp.)	❦ Evergreen shrubs to small trees, several popular for their fruits; white or purple flowers produced singly or in clusters ☀ Zones 8 to 10, depending on the species 🦋 Some swallowtails
Oaks (*Quercus* spp.)	❦ Large group of deciduous or evergreen trees and some shrubs, with acorn fruit; greenish male flowers in drooping catkins, female flowers single or in small spikes at base of leaves, both male and female on same plant ☀ Zones 3 to 10, depending on the species 🦋 Some hairstreaks, some duskywings
Willows (*Salix* spp.)	❦ Large group of shrubs and trees, many grown as ornamentals; tiny yellow or green flowers in catkins, male and female on separate plants ☀ Zones 2 to 9, depending on the species 🦋 Some fritillaries, some swallowtails, some tortoiseshells, some admirals, some hairstreaks, faunus anglewing, viceroy, mourning cloak, red-spotted purple

Chapter 8

HERBAL FORMULAS FOR COOKING AND CRAFTS

The Pleasures of Herbs

Herbs may be the most versatile plants on earth. Of course, they're unsurpassed for spicing up virtually any dish, but herbs offer much more than seasoning. The seeds, leaves, and even roots of culinary herb plants are power-packed ingredients outside the kitchen, too. Hard-working herbs can be used as natural cleansers and disinfectants. Some herbs can brighten a room with their scent. Others add natural beauty to crafts and gifts.

Part of the appeal of herbs is their intense fragrance and flavor. In many of the formulas in this chapter, a spoonful or two of concentrated herb oil is all that's required. You'll find a rich choice of formulas that will help you get the most from your herb garden. But before you can use them to their best potential, you need to know how to harvest and store herbs.

Harvesting Fresh Herbs

There's nothing like the luxury of knowing that you have a supply of fresh herbs growing just steps away from the kitchen. Because nothing beats the flavor of just-picked herbs, the best time to harvest herbs is when you need them! However, if it's more convenient to plan ahead, early in the day is the best time for harvesting. Head out to the garden with sharp scissors or clippers just after the morning dew has evaporated.

Unless it's time to harvest the whole plant, think of harvesting as pruning the plant for continued growth. Clip off up to one-fourth of the plant by pruning the tips or cutting off whole stalks that detract from the plant's appearance.

If you won't be using the herbs right away, shake off any surface dirt and submerge the stalks upright in a glass of water. To store for longer than a day, place the glass in a plastic bag, tie it loosely with a twist-tie, and refrigerate. Alternately, you can wrap the cuttings in a damp paper towel and enclose the bundle in a plastic bag. Either way, most herbs will stay fresh for up to three days when refrigerated.

To prepare fresh herbs for cooking, snip the leaves from the stalk with scissors, allowing the leaves to fall onto a cutting board. Then mince the leaves with a sharp knife. You can also roll a small handful of the herb into a ball and use sharp scissors to cut the herbs into fine pieces. You can use a food processor to chop large amounts of herbs, but if you try this method, take care not to over-process the herbs or you'll end up with green mush.

You can use fresh herbs in place of dried herbs in any recipe. Simply increase the amount of dried herb that's called for with two- to three-fold that amount of fresh herb. This takes into consideration the loss of water in dried herbs: As herbs dry, their flavor becomes concentrated. In most recipes, it's best to add either fresh or dried herbs in the last 15 minutes of cooking to retain the most delicate flavor.

Drying Herbs

You can dry herbs throughout the growing season as time allows. For best results, harvest them on a sunny day during a dry spell, and wait until the morning dew has evaporated before harvesting. If evening is the best time for you, harvest before the dew forms again. Harvest the herbs with scissors as described on page 191, and shake off any surface dirt. Then cover the cuttings with a towel as you work to protect them from shriveling in the burning sun.

Don't bother to wash the herbs unless they are very muddy. Just begin drying them as soon as possible using one of the following techniques:

To hang-dry herbs, first lay stalks on a counter and sort by size. Bunch four or five stem ends together and fasten tightly with wet twine, rubber bands, or twist-ties. Hang the herbs out of direct sunlight in a dry area with good air circulation. You can string a clothesline in an unused room of your home and use clothespins to secure bunches of herbs to the line. If there is no available space out of direct sunlight, put the herbs in paper bags with the stem ends coming out of the top of the bag. Cut several holes in the bags to allow for air circulation, and hang them.

For screen drying, set up screens on wood blocks to provide air space. Set them out of direct sunlight. The herbs can be just touching each other, as they'll shrink. Lay herbs in a single layer on each screen. If you don't have a good supply of screen, you can spread out the herbs in a single layer in wicker baskets for drying.

To prepare a cup of chopped herbs quickly, place the leaves in a teacup and snip with scissors until the herbs are uniformly minced.

For quick salad garnishes, roll a handful of fresh herbs into a ball and snip them with scissors, letting the pieces fall into your salad.

Probably the easiest way to dry herbs is with a food dehydrator. Just follow the instructions that come with the dehydrator.

You can also dry herbs in a microwave oven. Spread a cup of herbs in a single layer between paper towels. Microwave on high for 30 seconds. Turn the herbs over and microwave on high for another 30 seconds. Repeat this process until the herbs feel brittle and rattle when you shake the paper towels. Total drying time is about 3 minutes. Take care not to overcook or the herbs will taste scorched.

To dry herbs in direct sunlight, place them stem side up in a paper bag that has several holes cut out for air circulation. Attach the bag to a string or clothesline using clothespins.

Storing Herbs

Although herbs hanging in the kitchen add a homey touch, leaving them exposed to moisture in the air for too long will eventually degrade their flavor. Therefore, as soon as the herbs are crackly dry, remove the leaves from the stalks. Be careful not to crumble the leaves or you'll lose some of the aromatic oils. Place the leaves in airtight containers. Glass or ceramic containers are your best choice because metal and plastic can affect the flavor of delicate herbs. Store the containers in a cool, dark place away from heat for up to a year.

To use home-dried herbs in recipes, crumble the leaves when measuring to get an accurate measure and then proceed as directed. If you need to buy dried herbs, check for a fresh smell and bright color.

Once herbs are harvested or safely stored, you're ready to unleash their power in our homemade formulas for savory seasonings, like vinegars and herb-flavored oils, in refreshing teas, or in many of their useful guises in cleansers, potpourris, or candles.

Herbal Cubes

Herbs like parsley and basil have a lot of moisture in their leaves. Although hang drying will work, freezing often gives more flavorful results. To prepare, place 2 cups of herbs in the blender with 4 cups of water, and blend until herbs are well distributed in the water. Then freeze the herbal water in ice cube trays. When frozen, unmold and place in plastic zipper bags, then label. To use, drop an herb cube into sauces, soups, or stews during the last 15 minutes of cooking. If you don't want added water in the recipe, defrost the cubes in a small container and strain out the water.

It's also easy to freeze herbs in oil for recipes such as pesto. To prepare, chop the basil (or other herb of your choice) in a food processor, add just enough olive oil to make a paste, and then freeze in yogurt cups.

Warm and Spicy Tea

Although delicate leaves and flowers are the most common herb tea ingredients, pungent roots, barks, and spicy seeds also make tasty brews. But these tougher plant components need a little boiling for best flavor. "This is my husband's favorite tea," says Mindy Toomay, cookbook writer and author of *A Cozy Book of Herbal Teas*. "This blend is also good iced, but you must double the strength as the melting ice cubes will dilute it."

Ingredients and Supplies

3 cups water
Stainless steel, enamel, or glass saucepan
2 slices fresh ginger root, each slice
   ¼ inch thick
2 teaspoons dried rose hips, crushed
1 teaspoon dried aniseed
   (*Pimpinella anisum*), crushed
Strainer

Directions

1. Bring water to a boil in the saucepan.
2. Pound ginger slices gently with the broad side of a knife to break up the pulp.
3. Place the ginger, rose hips, and aniseed in the boiling water, reduce the heat to medium, and simmer, uncovered, for 5 minutes.
4. Strain and pour the mixture into a warmed teacups.
5. Sweeten with honey, if desired.

Yield: 2 cups of root seed tea

Brewing the Best Tea

Most commonly, tea is made by the process of "infusion," which involves pouring boiling water over herbs and allowing the brew to steep before drinking. The French term "tisane" is also used to describe this process. This method is the best for making tea from herb leaves and flowers. "Decoction" is the technical term for boiling plant materials in water to make tea. This is the preferred method for brewing tough plant parts, like barks, seeds, and roots, and coarse leaves, like bay leaves. Some herbal tea recipes combine both delicate and coarse materials. In this case, boil the tough parts first, strain, and pour the liquid over the remaining herbs in a teapot.

Fancy Ice Cubes Dress Up Cold Drinks

For that special touch when serving iced tea or other cold beverages, pour them over floral ice cubes. To create the colorful cubes, just add whole blossoms or individual petals of any edible flower, such as calendula or violets, to ice cube trays. The floral ice is perfect for chilling drinks, including herbal teas, at a summer garden party.

Ingredients and Supplies

Blossoms or petals of borage, calendula, pansies, roses, thyme, or violets

Ice cube trays

Directions

1. Gather edible flower blossoms and rinse them in cold water to remove garden dust or bits of soil. Gather only blossoms from plants that have never been sprayed or treated with any type of insect- or disease-killing sprays.

2. Fill ice cube trays half-full with water.

3. Put 1 blossom (for small-petaled flowers) or 1 individual petal (of large-petaled flowers) in each compartment of the tray.

4. Put the trays in the freezer and freeze the cubes until set.

5. Remove the trays from the freezer and fill them to the top with water.

6. Return the trays to the freezer and let the cubes freeze solid.

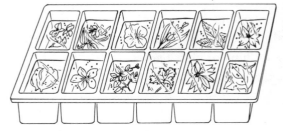

The secret to making ice cubes with flower and herb blossoms in the center is to fill ice cube trays only halfway with water and flowers at first. Freeze the partially-filled trays enough to set, then top the trays with more water and freeze them solid.

Caution: Before using any type of flower to make floral ice cubes, be sure that you've verified that the flower is edible and that you've identified the flower correctly. If you're in doubt, contact your local Cooperative Extension Service for information on edible flowers and for help in identifying particular flowers. Don't use flowers from plants that have been fertilized with manure or manure tea. Also, never make floral ice cubes with flowers that you've bought from a florist or supermarket—the flowers may have been treated with chemical sprays.

A Perfect Pot of Herbal Tea

"Preparing a cup of tea with care is part of the pleasure of drinking it," says Mindy Toomay, author of *A Cozy Book of Herbal Teas*. Follow these simple steps and sample one of Mindy's favorite herb tea blends to "ease the mind and lift the spirits." Double the quantities if you're using fresh herbs.

Ingredients and Supplies

2¼ cups water
Stainless steel, enamel, or glass saucepan
China or glass teapot
2 teaspoons dried chamomile flowers
1½ teaspoons dried lavender flowers
1 teaspoon dried elder flowers
    (*Sambucus canadensis* or *S. nigra*)
⅛ teaspoon powdered cloves
Bamboo or wire mesh strainer
Teacups
Honey (optional)

Directions

1. Bring the water to a boil in the saucepan and pour a little (about ¼ cup) into the teapot to warm it.
2. Swirl the water, then empty it from the teapot and replace it with the herbs.
3. Pour the remaining 2 cups of boiling water over herbs and cloves.
4. Cover the teapot and let it steep for 5 minutes.
5. Pour the tea through a strainer directly into warmed teacups.
6. Sweeten with honey, if desired.

Yield: 2 cups of herbal tea

Herbal Tea to the Rescue

Many herbalists maintain that herb teas can offer more than refreshment; they can also help you feel better. Jane Boyle, a clinical herbalist and teacher in Arnold, Maryland, recommends these herb teas to help you deal with minor health problems. Make sure that you use herbs that haven't been sprayed with chemicals or grown near the roadside. Use 2 to 3 teaspoons of dried herbs per cup of boiling water. Add lemon or honey, if desired.

Chills and fever: boneset leaf (*Eupatorium perfoliatum*)
Diuretic: dandelion leaves and roots or chickweed (*Stellaria media*)
First sign of cold: lemon balm leaf
Headache: lavender buds or basil leaf
Indigestion or gas: fennel seed
Insomnia: chamomile flowers or catnip leaves
Lung congestion: mullein leaf (*Verbascum thapsus*)
Nausea: peppermint leaf or dillweed
Sore throat: thyme leaf

Terrific Tonic Tea

In addition to treating specific complaints, herbs can serve as an integral part of a health maintenance program. Tonic teas are simply strong infusions of herbs that have been brewed for a longer period than regular tea to extract all the nutrients. "I drink 2 quarts of this tea every day to ensure that I get plenty of minerals, like calcium, iron, silica, and magnesium," says herbalist Kathleen Maier, who runs a clinical and teaching practice in Flint Hill, Virginia.

To extract all the goodness from the herbs in this tonic, cap the brewing container tightly and let the herbs steep for at least two hours. Kathleen lets hers sit overnight. Use either all dried or all fresh herbs.

Ingredients and Supplies

- 2 parts oatstraw (*Avena sativa*)
- 2 parts stinging nettles (*Urtica dioica*)
- 2 parts chickweed (*Stellaria media*)
- 2 parts red clover (*Trifolium pratense*)
- 1 part peppermint
- 2-quart Pyrex container with lid

Directions

1. Mix all of the herbs together. Place 2 heaping tablespoons of dried herb mix (or 4 tablespoons of fresh herbs) in the Pyrex container.

2. Fill the container with boiling water.

3. Cap the container tightly, and let it sit at least 2 hours before drinking. (No need to strain out the herbs.)

4. Refrigerate any of the mixture that isn't consumed within 8 hours.

Yield: 2 quarts of tonic tea

Variation: Kathleen also suggests substituting or adding 1 part red raspberry leaves (*Rubus idaeus*), 1 part rose hips, and 1 part alfalfa leaves (*Medico sativa*) in the formula for Terrific Tonic Tea for a slightly different flavor mix.

All-In-One Herbal Vinegar

Pat Reppert, owner of Shale Hill Farm and Herb Gardens in Saugerties, New York, hosts a daily radio cooking show and makes gourmet herbal specialties, including single-ingredient and combination herbal vinegars. She finds that single-herb vinegars sell best because they're more versatile in cooking and because they add zip to salads and sauces without fat, sugar, or salt.

Ingredients and Supplies

> 1 quart white wine vinegar (5% acidity)
> Stainless steel saucepan
>   (don't use aluminum or cast iron)
> 1-quart glass jar with tight-fitting lid
> Fresh herbs (like tarragon, basil, salad
>   burnet, dill, or mint)
> Strainer
> Coffee filter
> Funnel
> Glass bottles with caps (vinegar will rust
>   metal caps and lids)

Directions

1. Heat the vinegar in the saucepan until it's almost ready to bubble, but don't let it boil. Meanwhile, wash and rinse the glass jar and fill it with boiling water.

2. Let the jar sit for a minute or two, then pour out the water, and loosely fill the jar ⅓ full with herbs. (Pat doesn't wash the herbs unless they're dirty.)

3. Pour the hot vinegar over the herbs, filling the jar to the top.

4. Cap the jar and store the mixture in a cool, dark place.

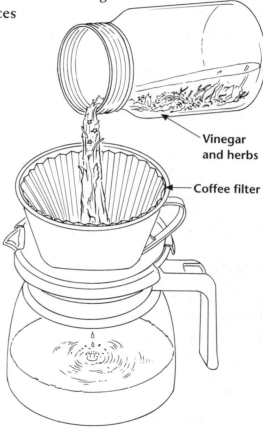

Vinegar and herbs

Coffee filter

A coffee filter is perfect for straining out herbs when you make herbal vinegar.

5. After 1 month, strain the plant material out of the vinegar.

6. Line the funnel with a coffee filter and pour the vinegar through the filter to strain again.

7. Pour the vinegar into a saucepan and heat it to the simmer stage. (Again, don't let it boil.) Skip this step if you used basil, because basil loses its delicate flavor with heat.

8. Pour the hot vinegar into sterile hot bottles.

9. If desired, add a sprig of the fresh herb for decoration.

10. Cap the bottles with sterile caps.

Yield: 1 quart of herb vinegar

Note: Substitute herbal vinegar for all or part of the vinegar in recipes for salad dressings, marinades, sauces, mustards, baked beans, pickles, and chutney. Also try adding a splash to soups (especially bean), stir-fries, cooked greens, gravies, and sauces.

Variation: Herbalist Julie Manchester of Woodsong Herbals in Randolph, Vermont, who makes and markets gallons of herbal vinegar each year, says that her best-selling combination is rosemary, shallots, and tarragon in red wine vinegar. A close runner-up, and personal favorite, is opal basil, garlic, and thyme in white wine vinegar. "The color from the opal basil is fabulous!" she says.

Multi-Herb Vinegars

When making flavored vinegars, your recipe is limited only by your imagination. In fact, the possible combinations sometimes seem overwhelming. Maggie Oster, author of *Herbal Vinegar*, grows herbs in Louisville, Kentucky, and has experimented with hundreds of flavored vinegars.

Maggie suggests that if you're using spicy ingredients, like hot peppers, garlic, or herb seeds, you should start with 1 scant tablespoon per cup of vinegar. "Check the flavor every week," she advises, "and feel free to make adjustments." For the freshest flavor, use flavored vinegars within 6 months after opening. Unopened, most vinegars will last at least 1 year. Store flavored vinegars in a cool, dark place.

Apple cider vinegar. Try dill, bay, and garlic; horseradish, shallot, and hot red pepper; or dill, mustard seeds, lemon balm, and garlic.

Champagne or rice vinegar. Flavor with lemon balm, lemon verbena, lemon thyme, lemongrass (*Cymbopogon citratus*), and lemon zest.

Red wine vinegar. Select sage, parsley, and shallots; marjoram, salad burnet (*Sanguisorba minor*), and lemon balm; or cilantro, garlic, and fresh ginger root.

White wine vinegar. Choose tarragon, elder flowers (*Sambucus canadensis* or *S. nigra*), spearmint, lemon balm, shallot, garlic, whole cloves, and peppercorns; orange mint, coriander seeds, garlic, and orange zest; or rosemary, thyme, marjoram, savory (*Satureja* spp.), lavender, bay, garlic, and hot red pepper.

Invigorating Vinegar Tonic

Herbalist Susun Weed, author of *Wise Woman Herbal* and founder of the Wise Woman Center in Woodstock, New York, uses herbal vinegars to boost the mineral count in her diet. "Many herbs and weeds are extremely high in minerals," she says. "And ordinary apple cider vinegar dissolves the minerals from plant tissues and puts them into a form that your body can assimilate. Many of these plants have excellent nutritive qualities beyond adding minerals to the diet," Susun adds. "For example, purslane contains more omega-3 fatty acids than any other known plant."

Ingredients and Supplies

> 1-quart glass bottle with nonmetal lid
> 1 quart pasteurized apple cider vinegar
>   (5% acidity)
> Fresh herbs and wild plants
> Waxed paper and rubber band (optional)

Directions

1. Fill the jar loosely with any 1 fresh plant material, cut small.

2. Pour vinegar over the herb, filling the jar to the top.

3. Label the jar and cap, or cover with waxed paper attached with a rubber band.

4. Let the vinegar stand in a cool, dark place for at least 6 weeks. "Sometimes I don't bother to strain it," confesses Susun. "I just eat the pickled plant material as well as putting the vinegar on salads, in marinades, and in lentil and bean soups."

Yield: 1 quart of vinegar tonic

Because vinegar will rust metal, it's best to store herbal vinegars in jars with plastic or other nonmetal lids. If you use a metal lid, cover the mouth of the jar with waxed paper before screwing on the lid.

For a zesty way to add bone-building calcium to your diet, herbalist Rosemary Gladstar, author of *Herbal Healing for Women* and founder of Sage Herbal Retreat Center in East Barre, Vermont, recommends a vinegar blend using equal parts of alfalfa, nettle, oat straw, and raspberry leaves.

Herbalist Susun Weed uses a variety of cultivated and wild herbs to make her Invigorating Vinegar Tonic. Here are some of Susun's recommendations:

Cultivated herbs: thyme, catnip, bee balm (also known as bergamot), lemon balm, sage, lavender, and horseradish root

Wild herbs: dandelion root or leaf (*Taraxacum officinale*), chickweed (*Stellaria media*), yarrow, goldenrod flowers (*Solidago* spp.), bugleweed (*Lycopus* sp.), purslane (*Portulaca oleracea*), self-heal (*Prunella vulgaris*), burdock root (*Arctium minus*), and wintergreen (*Gaultheria procumbens*)

Salt-Free Herbal Seasoning

Herbalist Kathy Lee, founder of Walk in Beauty, a retail herb shop and mail-order supplier in Colfax, California, really enjoys creating recipes that combine high nutrition with good flavor. She says that it's easy because "all of the Mediterranean herbs are high in healthful antioxidants." This tasty seasoning mix adds great flavor to food without adding salt. Toasted sesame seeds add beneficial calcium to this mix.

Ingredients and Supplies

1 cup sesame seeds
Small cast-iron frying pan
2 tablespoons garlic powder
1 tablespoon dried rosemary
1 tablespoon dried marjoram
1 tablespoon dried thyme
1 tablespoon dried lemon zest
Blender or food processor
Airtight storage container

Directions

1. Toast sesame seeds in a cast-iron pan over medium heat until brown, but not burned.
2. Cool toasted seeds slightly, then blend them with remaining ingredients.
3. Store the mixture in an airtight container.

Yield: About 1⅓ cups of herbal seasoning

Herbes de Provence

Getting into the low-salt, low-fat healthy habit is a lot easier when your pantry is stocked with gourmet herb seasoning blends. Marge Clark of Oak Hill Farm in West Lebanon, Indiana, and author of *The Best of Thymes* has been teaching gourmet herb workshops for 15 years. Marge gathered this recipe on a trip to Provence. "There are many versions of this formula," she reports, "but all of them feature lavender and thyme."

You can use this classic blend on cheese, poultry, meat, fish, and vegetables. For the freshest flavor, keep herb leaves whole until you're ready to cook because crumbling them releases volatile essential oils. Most chefs prefer to use glass or ceramic containers for mixing and storing dried herbs.

Ingredients and Supplies

Equal parts dried thyme, lavender buds,
    rosemary, savory, marjoram, basil,
    and fennel seeds or aniseed
Mixing bowl or brown paper bag
Airtight glass or ceramic storage containers

Directions

1. Mix herbs well in the mixing bowl or shake in the paper bag.
2. Store the herb mix in tightly covered containers.
3. When you're ready to use the mix, shake the container to blend the herbs well. Pour some into your hand and crumble the leaves between your fingers before adding them to a recipe or sprinkling them over your food.

GOAT CHEESE À LA PROVENCE

Creating marinated goat cheese is a snap when you use this ready-mixed herbal blend. Combine ½ cup extra-virgin olive oil with 1 tablespoon Herbes de Provence, and pour over a block or log of goat cheese in a dish. Cover the dish and let the cheese marinate in the refrigerator for several days. Serve at room temperature with crusty French bread.

Bouquet Garni

A bouquet garni is an ancient method of adding flavor to soups, stews, and other hearty dishes. And Marge Clark, author of *The Best of Thymes*, has found a simple way to make these little bundles of flavor. "I used to tie up the seasonings in a little square of cheesecloth—but then I discovered coffee filters!" says Marge.

Ingredients and Supplies

1 bay leaf
1 tablespoon dried tarragon
1 teaspoon dried parsley
1 teaspoon dried rosemary
1 teaspoon dried thyme
6–8 whole black peppercorns
1 small coffee filter
White kitchen string

Directions

1. Mix the herbs in the coffee filter and tie the filter closed with string.
2. Drop the bundle into the pot during the last half-hour of cooking. Remove the bundle before serving.

Yield: 1 bouquet garni

Note: You may find it more efficient to prepare several bouquets garnis at one time in assembly-line fashion. Then they'll be right at hand when you're preparing that special soup or stew. Just store the bundles in airtight containers until you're ready to use them.

Cook-by-the-Numbers Herbal Blends

Ever find yourself wondering, "What herb goes with what?" Barbara Steele and Marlene Lufriu, co-owners of Alloway Gardens in Littlestown, Pennsylvania, came up with this handy list of common dishes, and the herbs that suit them, to answer that perennial question.

Beef: equal parts of savory, basil, marjoram, thyme, and parsley
Chicken: equal parts of parsley, tarragon, marjoram, and basil
Fish: equal parts of marjoram, thyme, parsley, and basil
Italian: 2 parts of basil, 1 part each of rosemary, parsley, and oregano, ½ part of thyme
Lamb: equal parts of parsley, marjoram, and rosemary
Soups: equal parts of parsley, thyme, and marjoram
Vegetables: equal parts of savory, parsley, marjoram, and basil

Powerhouse Herbal Blend

This unusual blend of kitchen herbs and wild greens is a satisfying salt substitute that's rich in minerals. "My family loves this mix," says herbalist Julie Manchester of Woodsong Herbals in Randolph, Vermont. "Just don't mention that you're seasoning dinner with weeds!"

Ingredients and Supplies

2 parts dried dandelion leaf
  (*Taraxacum officinale*)
2 parts dried stinging nettle leaf
  (*Urtica dioica*)
2 parts dried plantain leaf
  (*Plantago major* or *P. lanceolata*)
2 parts dried cabbage leaf
1 part dried chives or scallion greens
1 part dried parsley
1 part dried watercress leaves

1 part dried field mustard leaves
  (*Brassica rapa*)
Blender or food processor
Airtight storage container

Directions

1. Combine ingredients in blender.
2. Process until mixture is finely ground (in blender, pulse on "chop" setting).
3. Store in a labeled airtight container.

Perfect Pizza Seasoning

Homemade pizza is a quick-and-easy meal when you use ready-made pizza crust from the store. You can buy premade pizza sauce too, but for a more authentic flavor, try using plain tomato sauce (perhaps you have canned or frozen sauce made from your garden tomatoes!) and this mix of dried herbs and vegetables.

Ingredients and Supplies

¼ cup dried oregano
2 tablespoons dried basil
2 teaspoons onion powder
1½ teaspoons garlic powder
¼ teaspoon crushed red pepper
  flakes
Small bowl
Glass jar with airtight lid

Directions

1. Mix ingredients in the bowl.
2. Pour the mixture into the jar, seal it, and store it in a cool, dry place.
3. Sprinkle the mix on top of pizza as desired before baking, or mix 1 tablespoon into 1 quart of sauce before spreading the sauce on the pizza dough.

Yield: 7 tablespoons of pizza seasoning

Basil-Garlic Herbal Oil

Pat Reppert, owner of Shale Hill Farm and Herb Gardens in Saugerties, New York, teaches herb cookery on her daily radio show in Kingston, New York. She reports that herbal oils are the latest trend for dressing up simple dishes, especially vegetables. Use this oil in stir-fries or to baste vegetables before roasting, broiling, or grilling. Just a thin coating imparts a rich flavor while keeping the calories down.

Ingredients and Supplies

½ cup basil leaves or other herbs (use ⅓ cup if using stronger flavored herbs, like rosemary, thyme, and oregano)
1 cup extra-virgin olive oil
Stainless steel skillet

3 cloves garlic, peeled and cut into matchstick-size pieces
1 teaspoon lemon juice
Strainer (optional)
Sterilized bottle and cap

Directions

1. Swish the basil leaves briefly in cold water to clean them.
2. Spread basil on towels and pat gently to dry them.
3. Remove stems and measure out ½ cup of loosely packed leaves.
4. Heat the olive oil in a skillet.
5. When the oil is hot but not smoking, stir in the garlic and sauté it until the garlic barely begins to brown (stir frequently).
6. Remove the garlic from the heat and stir in the herbs and lemon juice.
7. Let the mixture cool for 1 hour at room temperature.
8. Strain out plant material (or leave it in for stronger flavored oil) and pour the cooled oil into a sterilized bottle. Cap the jar and label it, including the exact date of preparation.
9. Keep the oil refrigerated and discard any that's unused after 2 weeks.

Yield: Approximately 1 cup of herb-garlic flavored oil

Note: Olive oil congeals in the refrigerator, but you can let the oil stand at room temperature for an hour or so to let it clear before using it. Just make sure to keep it refrigerated at all other times.

Caution: Because oil is highly perishable once it's infused with plant material, make flavored oils in small batches and always keep them refrigerated. Discard any leftover flavored oil after 2 weeks.

One-Pot Roasted Garlic and Garlic Oil

If you love garlic, don't use it just as a seasoning. Roasted whole garlic is a delicious hot side dish. Roasting mellows garlic flavor and brings out a delicious sweetness. You can also mash roasted garlic and use it as a spread on crackers or bread. Roasted garlic oil is a mouth-watering topping for meat or vegetables.

Ingredients and Supplies

> 6–8 garlic bulbs
> Knife
> Small ovenproof baking dish
> 1 cup good-quality olive oil
> Glass bottle
> Funnel
> Small container

Directions

1. Preheat oven (or toaster oven) to 375°F.

2. Slice the tops off of the garlic bulbs.

3. Arrange the garlic in the baking dish and add the olive oil.

4. Cover and bake for 1 hour.

5. Remove the cover and bake for an additional 15 minutes.

6. While the garlic finishes cooking, sterilize the glass bottle.

7. If you're serving the garlic as a side dish, remove it to a serving plate. If you want to save the garlic paste, let the dish and garlic cool first. Then squeeze the garlic paste into a container and cover it with a thin layer of the garlic-flavored oil.

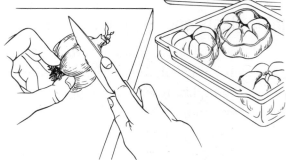

To make delicious roasted garlic, cut the tops off the bulbs, arrange the garlic in a baking dish, and bake it with olive oil.

Roasted garlic oil

After baking garlic in olive oil, let the oil cool and pour it into a sterilized jar. You can keep the refrigerated oil for 2 weeks and use it as a dressing for meat or vegetables.

8. Make sure that the oil is cool enough to handle safely. Put the funnel in the mouth of the bottle and pour the oil into the funnel.

Yield: 6 to 8 bulbs of roasted garlic and about ¾ cup of roasted garlic oil

Note: You can store garlic paste and garlic oil in the refrigerator for up to 2 weeks.

Discard any paste and oil that is unused after that time.

Caution: When you first remove the baking dish from the oven, handle it with great care. Hot oil can cause serious burns. Always let the oil cool before you try to pour it into a storage bottle.

Double-Roasted Rosemary Vegetables

Hearty roasted vegetables transform root-cellar pickings like potatoes and winter squash into sublime winter treats. Try serving these roasted vegetables as an appetizer or over dressed salad greens as a change of pace.

Ingredients and Supplies

12 baby potatoes, scrubbed (cut larger potatoes into 2-inch chunks)

1 large sweet potato or peeled winter squash, scrubbed and cut into 2-inch chunks

4 small beets, scrubbed (don't cut or they'll bleed)

Roasted garlic oil (see recipe on the facing page)

Casserole dish with lid or aluminum foil

Rosemary sprigs

Sea salt (optional)

Directions

1. Preheat oven to 375°F.
2. In the casserole dish, toss vegetables with enough roasted garlic oil to coat lightly.
3. Arrange vegetables in a single layer.
4. Place several sprigs of rosemary between and on top of vegetables; add salt, if desired.

HEALTHY HERBAL SEASONING

Instead of using butter on steamed vegetables or rice, try this quick no-cholesterol seasoning. Mix 2 tablespoons of canola, sunflower, or olive oil with 1 teaspoon of dried crumbled herbs, like marjoram or thyme, in a small microwave-safe container. Microwave on high for 30 seconds or until oil is hot. Let the mixture stand for 15 minutes before using. You can also use this healthy topping to baste fish or chicken before baking or broiling.

5. Cover and bake for 1 hour.
6. Remove lid and bake another 15 minutes until vegetables are fork-tender.
7. Serve hot or at room temperature.

Yield: Serves 4

Tina's Super-Crisp Herbal Salad

Use your yard as well as your garden as a source for the herbs and greens in this tasty and colorful salad. "I can find at least a cupful of wild greens every day of the year unless there's deep snow," claims veteran kitchen gardener and horticulture teacher Tina James of Reisterstown, Maryland. In addition to cultivated herbs and greens, Tina includes dandelions, chickweed, and violet leaves in her salads. She says, "They're infinitely more nutritious than lettuce!"

Ingredients and Supplies

3 parts mild seasonal greens, like lettuce, mâche, spinach, and tatsoi (an oriental mustard)

1 part spicy seasonal greens, like arugula, watercress, sorrel, 'Red Giant' mustard, and mizuna

½ part seasonal edible weeds, like chickweed, dandelion greens, and purslane

Signature Salad Dressing (see recipe on page 212)

¼ part fresh snipped herbs

Seasonal flower and herb blossoms, like calendula, pansy, violet, thyme, red clover, chive, and borage

Freshly ground black pepper to taste

Directions

1. Wash the greens and the edible weeds.

2. Tear the greens into fork-size pieces and use scissors to finely snip the edible weeds.

3. Dry the salad greens and edible weeds, using one of the methods described in "Spin Dry Your Salad" on the facing page.

4. Place the greens in a covered bowl or wrap them in a towel.

5. Chill until serving time. Ideally, the greens should chill for an hour. If you're in a rush, place them in the freezer for 3 to 5 minutes—no more! Set the timer so that they don't freeze.

6. While the salad chills, make the Signature Salad Dressing. Tina likes to use nasturtium

blossom rice vinegar and extra-virgin olive oil when making the dressing for this salad.

7. Mix the herbs into the salad greens immediately before serving. Use sharp scissors and snip the herbs directly into the bowl.

8. Distribute the salad dressing evenly over the greens. Use less dressing than you think you will need. You can always add more.

9. Lightly toss the salad mix. The dressing should coat the salad without any excess dripping into the bottom of the bowl. Experiment until you have a feel for just the right amount of dressing to use.

10. Sprinkle the flower garnish on top of the salad. Use small flowers like violets whole, but separate larger flowers like pansies into separate petals. Also pull apart flower heads like chives and clover. Serve on chilled plates. Season with freshly ground pepper to taste.

Note: Tina's favorite herb blend for this salad is 2 parts garlic chives, 1 part basil, and ½ part marjoram. In winter, forage for wild garlic mustard as a substitute for garlic chives—the garlic mustard tastes best once the weather gets really cold. And buy Italian flat leaf parsley as a replacement for the basil.

Caution: Don't gather edible weeds that may have been treated with weed- or pest-killing sprays. Even organic sprays can leave behind a bad-tasting residue.

Spin Dry Your Salad

For truly crispy salad, your salad greens must be free of surface water. If the lettuce or other greens are even a little wet, your salad is likely to turn limp and mushy, especially when you add salad dressing.

To dry salad greens well after washing them with water, use a salad spinner if you have one. But check the greens after you spin them. They may still be slightly wet. If they are, spread them out on a clean towel or paper towels to finish drying.

If you don't have a salad spinner, you can wrap washed salad greens in a large towel and shake them until they're dry.

To dry large amounts of washed salad greens quickly, try the "human salad spinner" method. Put washed greens in a clean pillowcase. Hold the pillowcase closed and twirl it vigorously.

When using the towel or pillowcase methods, you can leave the greens inside their fabric wrapping while they chill for an hour. Then shake them out into your salad serving bowl, and they're ready for dressing.

Salad greens inside pillowcase

Savory Winter Greens Salad

When the temperature drops, herbalist and garden writer Tina James of Reisterstown, Maryland, switches from salads of crisp greens to cooked green salads. "In summer, lettuce seems very cooling," explains Tina. "But cooked greens, like kale and collards, bring a sense of warmth to the table."

Ingredients and Supplies

6-quart stockpot
1 tablespoon apple cider vinegar
2 pounds collard or kale greens
Colander
Garlic chives or garlic mustard
Signature Salad Dressing
    (see page 212)
1 tablespoon tamari soy sauce
1 tablespoon toasted sesame oil
1 package prepared sauerkraut
Sliced red radishes, grated daikon radish,
    or grated apple

Directions

1. Fill stockpot with water.
2. Add the vinegar and bring the mixture to a vigorous boil.
3. While water is heating, wash greens and cut into julienne strips (see the illustration at the right).
4. Boil greens for 5 minutes or until tender.
5. Strain greens through a colander, then run cold water over them until they are cool. Let drain.
6. Place a layer of cooked greens on a salad dish. Snip a thin layer of garlic chives or garlic mustard over the greens and dress with salad dressing. Dribble a little tamari soy sauce over

To cut greens into julienne strips, first arrange a few leaves in layers, then roll them up together.

Using a chef's knife, make thin slices from one end of the roll to the other. Each slice will produce one long julienne strip.

the greens, and sprinkle with toasted sesame oil. Add a ½ inch layer of sauerkraut. Garnish with radishes or apples, if desired.

Yield: Serves 6

Go Wild with Herbal Salads

Garden herbs like thyme, tarragon, and borage will liven up a conventional garden salad, but wild herbs can add an unexpected highlight. Wild herbs like garlic mustard (*Alliaria petiolata*) add spicy flavor and an interesting texture to salads. Plus, wild herbs can be quite nutritious! The leaves and flowers of blue violet (*Viola papilionacea*) are rich in vitamin A, while purslane (*Portulaca oleracea*) leaves and

stems score high in omega-3 fatty acids. Dandelion (*Taraxacum officinale*) leaves are highly nutritious, and chickweed (*Stellaria media*) leaves are rich in minerals. Before you harvest any wild plants for salads, be sure you've identified the plant correctly and that it is safe to eat. If you're in doubt, consult your local Cooperative Extension office for recommendations on edible wild plants and for help in identifying plants.

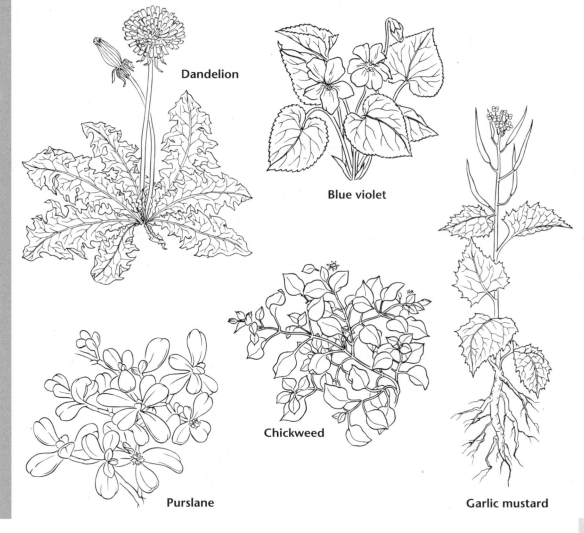

Dandelion

Blue violet

Chickweed

Purslane

Garlic mustard

Signature Salad Dressing

Season your salad with homemade herbal vinegars and oils for fresh flavor that can't be beat. Horticulture teacher and herbalist Tina James of Reisterstown, Maryland, recommends using this basic recipe to create your own signature blend, featuring the herbs you like best. You can use any flavor of oil and vinegar, but Tina says a combination of tarragon-flavored vinegar with extra-virgin olive oil is a perennial favorite.

Ingredients and Supplies

> 1 part herb-flavored vinegar
> 3 parts herb-flavored olive oil
> Glass jar
> 2 teaspoons dried herbs per 1 cup
> of salad dressing*

Directions

1. Place the oil and vinegar in a glass jar.

2. Add the dried herbs.

3. Shake before using.

4. Use a light touch when adding dressing to your salad—drizzle on less than you think you'll need. You can always add more.

5. Lightly toss your dressed salad. The dressing should coat the salad without any excess dripping into the bottom of the bowl.

Variation: You can also use fresh herbs for your Signature Salad Dressing. If you do,

FRENCH-STYLE HERB SALAD

Can't get enough of the flavors of herbs? You can take them beyond seasoning to create a satisfying salad made entirely of fresh herb leaves. Mix equal parts of flat-leaved Italian parsley, onion or garlic chives, dill, tarragon, and mint. Toss lightly with unflavored vinegar and oil salad dressing. Add freshly ground black pepper to taste. Serve as a condiment.

follow the example of professional chefs and mix them into your salad before pouring on the dressing, rather than adding them directly to the oil and vinegar mix as you would dried herbs.

* For suggested herb blends for salads and other foods, see "Cook-by-the-Numbers Herbal Blends" on page 203.

Potpourri of Christmas Legends

Herbalist and floral designer Betsy Williams of Andover, Massachusetts, author of *Potpourri and Fragrant Projects*, uses plant materials linked to Christmas in her potpourri. Betsy suggests using the language of flowers to create a "message mix" for the occasion. For example, thyme represents courage and sweet woodruff means humility. It is said that Joseph gathered these herbs to mix with the straw in the manger.

Ingredients and Supplies

Small glass jar with tight-fitting lid
½ cup frankincense tears
¼ cup orris root, cut and peeled (or buy
 orris root chunks)
20 drops lavender oil
10 drops rosemary oil
4–6 cups Christmas herbs, like thyme and
 sweet woodruff
⅛ cup myrrh powder
½ cup chamomile and lavender flowers
Large ceramic, stainless steel, or glass
 mixing bowl
1-gallon glass jar with tight-fitting lid
Gold metallic ribbon, cut into small snips
Citrus peel, cut into stars and dried

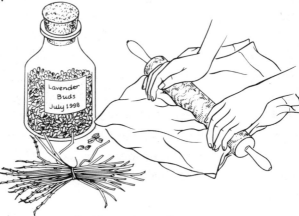

Bundled lavender stalks

To strip lavender flower buds quickly, put the stalks in a pillowcase. Roll the encased lavender with a rolling pin to separate the buds from the stalks. Store the flowers in a jar to use in potpourri. Tie together the bare stalks to make fragrant fire starters.

Directions

1. Measure frankincense (check mail-order herb suppliers) and orris root into small jar.
2. Drip the oils over the mixture, tighten the lid, and shake the jar to distribute the oils.
3. Set aside for at least 3 days to allow the oils to blend with the plant material.
4. Put the mixed Christmas herbs, myrrh powder, and chamomile and lavender flowers into the mixing bowl.

5. Add oil, frankincense, and orris root to the herbs; mix well without crumbling the herbs.
6. Transfer the mix to the 1-gallon jar. Shake the jar gently to blend the ingredients.
7. Allow the mix to age for at least 6 weeks, shaking often.
8. Add the ribbon snips and citrus peel to the potpourri as you package it for gifts.

Yield: 4 to 6 cups of potpourri

Garden Harvest Potpourri

The fragrance of an ideal potpourri is a mix of many scents that's not dominated by any one ingredient. Potpourri blends should also look as nice as they smell, with distinct leaves and flowers. "Fragrance-crafting isn't an exact science," says herbalist and artist Terry Whye of the Whye Clay Works Pottery Studio in Finksburg, Maryland. "Keep playing until you achieve a blend that you really like. And don't forget to take notes so that you can make it again!"

Terry gathers material for her best-selling potpourri blend throughout the year. It includes evergreen needles from the holiday tree, flowers and herbs, and spicy bay leaves and juniper berries. Terry fine-tunes the blend with essential oils and a fixative to preserve the scent. "The mix changes every year because my garden changes," says Terry.

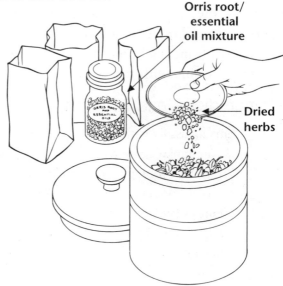

Orris root/essential oil mixture

Dried herbs

For pleasing potpourri, experiment with different blends of herbs, flowers, berries, pods, and other plant material, along with essential oils and a fixative like orris root.

Ingredients and Supplies

1 teaspoon essential oil or oil blend
 (Terry uses rosemary, lavender, geranium, clary sage, and citrus oils)
3 tablespoons orris root pieces per quart
 of plant material
Glass jar with lid
1 quart dried leaves, flowers, bark, and
 berries
Ceramic crock with lid or a large glass
 jar with lid

Directions

1. Mix the essential oil and orris root in the glass jar.
2. Cap the jar and let it mellow in a cool dark place for a day to a week.

3. Mix the dried materials in the crock, stirring gently with your hands. Sprinkle in the orris root mix as you go along.
4. Let it sit overnight, take a whiff, and adjust the formula as desired.
5. Let the potpourri mellow for 2 weeks. Check the scent again, and make any needed adjustments.
6. Allow the mix to sit for 2 more weeks.
7. To use the potpourri, open the lid to perfume a room. Close the container after several hours to preserve the scent.

Yield: 1 quart of colorful potpourri

SEASONAL POTPOURRI INGREDIENTS

The beauty of making your own potpourri mixes is that you can adjust the way they look and the way they smell to match the changing seasons.

In winter. Use bay leaves, sweet birch bark (*Betula lenta*), wild black cherry bark (*Prunus serotina*), dried citrus peel, evergreen needles, small pine cones, sassafras roots (*Sassafras albidum*), and wintergreen leaves (*Gaultheria procumbens*).

For spring and summer. Gather scented flowers, like basil, bee balm (also known as bergamot), borage, burnet (*Sanguisorba minor*), calendula, chamomile, red clover (*Trifolium pratense*), daffodil, honeysuckle, jasmine, lavender, lily-of-the-valley, marjoram, mint, mock orange (*Philadelphus* × *virginalis*), pansy, rose, flowering tobacco (*Nicotiana alata*), violet, wisteria, and sweet woodruff. Add fragrant leaves, like bee balm, citrus, eucalyptus, scented geranium, lemon balm, lemongrass (*Cymbopogon citratus*), lemon verbena, lavender, mints, patchouli (*Pogostemon cablin*), rosemary, sage, sweet grass (*Hierochloe odorata*), thyme, violet, and sweet woodruff. Also use everlasting flowers, such as globe amaranth (*Gomphrena globosa*), bells of Ireland (*Moluccella laevis*), hydrangea, rocket larkspur (*Consolida ambigua*), Lenten rose (*Helleborus orientalis*), red or pink peony petals, poppy flower heads, statice, winged everlasting (*Ammobium alatum*), and yarrow.

In autumn. Include bayberries (*Myrica pensylvanica*), coriander seeds, fennel seeds, hawthorn berries (*Crataegus* spp.), juniper berries, nigella seed pods (*Nigella damascena*), rose hips, and smooth sumac berries (*Rhus glabra*). Terry likes to use seeds and pods that look interesting, like milkweed, acorns, and dried grass seedheads.

Dry ingredients and store in individual airtight containers until ready to prepare the mix. Terry dries her materials on screens and in baskets and paper bags in a warm dry room. "Don't dry or store everything together," she cautions. "You'll lose the individual fragrances."

If your potpourri seems to have lost some fragrance, refresh it by mixing in 1 teaspoon of brandy or essential herbal oil. Experiment with these fragrant formulas to create or refresh potpourri.

Citrus: 1 part each bee balm (also known as bergamot), lemon, and tangerine

Floral: 3 parts rose, 2 parts jasmine, and 1 part carnation

Garden: 2 parts rose and 1 part each thyme, sandalwood, caraway, cloves, and lavender

Herb: 4 parts lavender, 2 parts rosemary, 1 part marjoram, and 1 part bay

Spice: 2 parts allspice and 1 part each cinnamon, clove, and tangerine

Homemade Herbal Beeswax Candles

Beeswax candles decorated with herbs and flowers are a precious commodity. "A bee consumes an average of 17 pounds of honey to make 1 pound of beeswax," says Kathy McQuade-Sedler, herbalist and owner of Sedler's Mother Earth Herbs in Grass Valley, California. "Beeswax has a lovely fragrance all its own and burns much longer than paraffin."

Ingredients and Supplies

    Vegetable grater or heavy flat-bladed
        knife
    1–1½ pounds beeswax (the lightest color
        available)
    Clean recycled metal can
    Double boiler
    30-ply flat braid candle wicking
    Muffin tin
    Nonstick vegetable-oil spray
    Chopsticks
    Dried herbs and flowers, like slivered
        rose petals, calendula petals, and
        lavender buds

To keep candle wicks upright while making molded beeswax candles, drape the wicks over chopsticks laid across the mold— in this case, a muffin tin.

Directions

1. Cover your work area with newspaper, old towels, or plastic.
2. Grate the beeswax, or slice it into thin shavings. Place the wax in the can.
3. Fill the bottom of the double boiler about half full with water. Bring water to a low boil over medium-low heat.
4. Place the metal can in the double boiler and melt the wax slowly.
5. Cut the wicking into 5-inch-long pieces.
6. Coat the muffin tin with the vegetable-oil spray. Dot melted wax into each cup.

7. Lay chopsticks across the muffin tins. Press the wicks into the soft wax, and drape the wicks over the chopsticks.
8. Pour the wax into the cups slowly, filling ¼ full. Allow to set for 10 minutes.
9. Finish filling the muffin cups, sprinkling in the dried herbs and flowers little by little as you pour the wax.
10. Allow the wax to harden. The candles will pull away from the pan the same way a cake does when it's ready.
11. Pop the candles out onto a towel, and let them sit out for at least 24 hours before using.
12. Before burning the candles, trim the wicks to between ¼ and ½ inch.

Yield: 12 herbal beeswax candles

Fancy Herbal-Scented Flames

When making your own candles, you can add excitement with the scents and colors of fragrant oils and herbs. For fragrance, you don't need to use the more expensive pure essential oils; fragrance oils and perfume work well. For natural color, use powdered alkanet root (red), powdered curry, saffron or turmeric (yellow), cinnamon or cosmetic red clay (reddish brown), powdered stinging nettle or parsley leaves (green), or paprika (orange).

Ingredients and Supplies

Vegetable grater or heavy flat-bladed knife
Clean recycled metal can
Double boiler
30-ply flat braid candle wicking
Muffin tin
Nonstick vegetable-oil spray
Chopsticks
1–1½ pounds beeswax
Teabags made of muslin

For fragrant candles
½–1 teaspoon perfume or fragrant oils per pound of wax

For natural color candles
Herbs for natural color (1 teaspoon at a time until desired color is reached)

Directions

1. Follow steps 1 through 5 from "Homemade Herbal Beeswax Candles" on the facing page.
2. For fragrance: Add perfume or fragrant oil to the melted beeswax. Mix well and stir as you pour to keep the oils in suspension. You can also dip the wicks into the oils.

For natural color: Enclose 1 teaspoon of coloring herbs in a muslin teabag and steep in wax for 10 minutes; remove bag and mix wax well. To test color, pour a drop onto white paper. Repeat the process with a new muslin teabag of herbs until you reach the desired color.
3. Continue with steps 6 through 12 from "Homemade Herbal Beeswax Candles." (In step 9, add decorative dried herbs to the candles, if desired.)

Custom Candle Shortcut

Even if you feel that you're not ready to make your own candles from scratch, you can create beautiful, personalized candles for gifts or holiday decorations. It's easy to decorate store-bought candles with homemade potpourri.

Ingredients and Supplies

Vegetable grater or heavy flat-bladed knife

Beeswax (enough, when melted, to submerge your candles in)

2 clean recycled metal cans (wide and tall enough to contain sufficient liquid to submerge your candles)

Double boiler

Candles, at least 2½ inches in diameter and up to 6 inches in length

Clear hair spray or spray paint

Thick white glue

Potpourri mix

Directions

1. Cover your work area with newspaper, old towels, or plastic.

2. Grate the beeswax, or use a heavy flat-bladed knife to slice the wax into thin shavings. Then place beeswax in one metal can.

3. Fill the bottom of the double boiler about half full with water. Bring water to a low boil over medium-low heat.

4. Place the metal can with the beeswax in the double boiler and melt the wax slowly. Fill the second can partway with cold water (enough to submerge the candle when it is dipped in, without causing the water to overflow).

5. Spray candle with clear hair spray or spray paint to help the glue adhere.

6. Apply thick white glue to the candle where you want the potpourri to adhere. (For safety, avoid the top and bottom of the candle.)

7. Press potpourri into the glue or roll the candle in potpourri.

8. Hold the candle by the wick and dip it into the beeswax for a few seconds.

9. Remove from wax and immediately lower the candle into the cold water.

10. Repeat steps 8 and 9 once or twice.

11. Let candle dry for at least 24 hours before using.

Pinecone Fire Starters

For a delightful forest fragrance from your home hearth, try pinecone fire starters. Artist JoAnn Stak of Dandelion Designs in Burlington, Vermont, enjoys making these simple, but ingenious crafts. A small basket of pinecone fire starters makes a nice holiday gift.

Ingredients and Supplies

Vegetable grater or heavy flat-bladed knife
Beeswax
Clean recycled metal can (wide enough for
    pinecones to fit into)
Double boiler
Pinecones
Tongs
1-inch pieces of candle wicking

Directions

1. Grate the beeswax or use the flat-bladed knife to slice the wax into thin shavings. Place the beeswax in the metal can.
2. Fill the bottom of the double boiler about half full with water. Bring water to a low boil over medium-high heat.
3. Place the metal can in water in the top of the double boiler and melt the wax slowly.
4. Hold a pinecone with the tongs, and dip it into the melted wax for a few seconds.
5. Lift the pinecone out of the wax, and hold it above the can while excess wax drips off.
6. Let the wax cool partially. Press a piece of candle wicking into the soft wax, and set the cone aside to let the wax harden.

Note: You can add fragrant oil to the beeswax when making these fire starters. See "Fancy Herbal-Scented Flames" on page 217 for directions for adding oil to melted beeswax.

To make a pinecone fire starter, dip one end of a pinecone into a metal can that contains melted beeswax.

Wicking

After the wax cools and hardens partway, press a piece of candle wicking into the soft wax.

Caution: Hot wax can cause serious burns. Wear protective gloves when attaching the wick to the soft, warm wax.

Mullein-Stalk Candlesticks

The stiff, dried flower stalks of mullein (*Verbascum thapsus*) make great natural candlesticks. Mullein produces yellow flowers that are reputed to have medicinal qualities, and you'll often spot the woolly-leaved plant growing as a weed in fencerows and along roadsides. Cut a few flower stalks to dip in wax to make long-burning candles.

Ingredients and Supplies

Mullein flower stalks
Knife or scissors
Vegetable grater or heavy flat-bladed knife
Beeswax
2 clean recycled metal cans (at least 6 inches across)
Double boiler
Tongs
Sand
Ceramic dish

Mullein stalk

To make a natural candlestick from mullein flower stalks, first cut the stalks into 6"-long pieces.

Waxed mullein

After you dip a piece of mullein stalk into melted wax and let it dry, you can plant the waxed stalk in a dish filled with sand and set it aflame— no wick required!

Directions

1. Strip leaves and flowers off mullein stalks.
2. Use a knife or scissors to cut the stalks into 6-inch-long sections.
3. Grate the beeswax or slice it into thin shavings. Place the wax in a can.
4. Fill the bottom of the double boiler about half full with water. Bring water to a low boil over medium-high heat.
5. Place the can in the double boiler and melt the wax slowly. Fill the second can partway with cold water (enough to submerge a section of mullein in without overflowing).
6. Use the tongs to dip a section of mullein stalk in the beeswax for a few seconds.

7. Remove from wax and dip the waxed stalk into the cold water for several seconds.
8. Repeat steps 6 and 7 until you've made as many candles as you want.
9. Dry candles for at least 24 hours before use.
10. Pour sand into the ceramic dish, and firmly set a mullein candle in the sand.

All-Purpose Herbal Soap Concentrate

"The National Research Council has estimated that hypersensitivity to chemicals in common household products results in acute or chronic health problems for about 15 percent of the population," says herbalist and educator Louise Gruenberg of Oak Park, Illinois. She has spent 20 years developing safe and effective natural cleaning formulas. "For the sake of my family's health, I don't mind the extra time it takes to make my own cleaning products," says Louise. This formula is great for tough jobs like vinyl floors, walls, woodwork, and furniture.

Ingredients and Supplies

- ½ cup (or more) concentrated oil soap, such as Murphy's Oil Soap Paste
- Glass measuring cup
- 1 tablespoon orange or lemon essential oil or combination of both
- Wide-mouth glass jar with lid for storage
- 1 cup antibacterial herbs, like lavender, mint, or thyme
- Saucepan

Directions

1. Place the paste in the measuring cup and stir in the essential oils.

2. Tilt the cup to the side. If the oil separates from the mixture around the edges, add more paste and stir.

3. Store the concentrate in a wide-mouth glass jar. (Label it well—it looks like apple jelly!)

4. To use, first make an herbal infusion by placing 1 cup of antibacterial herbs in a saucepan. Pour 4 cups of boiling water over the herbs and let the mixture steep for 2 hours. Then add 1 to 3 teaspoons of concentrate to the 4 cups of herbal infusion. Wipe the cleanser on the surface to be cleaned with a sponge or mop, then rinse quickly. A little vinegar in the rinse water helps remove the soap and also discourages bacterial growth.

Yield: About 1 cup of soap concentrate

Versatile Vinegar

Vinegar is one of the best safe and natural cleansers. You can use it to clean windows, baseboards, wood floors, ceramic tile, plastic, linoleum, and many other surfaces. (Just don't use vinegar on iron or other metal surfaces that rust.) To use, mix 2 cups of vinegar (either white or apple cider) with 2 gallons of hot water in a bucket. Vinegar also has natural antibacterial properties, but for even greater disinfectant power, replace 4 cups of the water with a strong infusion of lavender, rosemary, mint, or thyme. Make the infusion by steeping 1 cup of the herbs in 4 cups of boiling water for two hours.

Refreshing Herbal Spray Disinfectant

Herbalist and artist Terry Whye of Whye Clay Works Pottery Studio in Finksburg, Maryland, uses essential oils to make a stimulating air freshener. She says that it has natural anti-bacterial and antiviral properties, so it's good for general disinfecting and also clears the air around people with colds. Most high-quality essential oils won't stain, but use with care on painted and wooden surfaces as well as on light-colored fabrics.

Ingredients and Supplies

Glass hand-held misting bottle

2 ounces water (distilled or spring water is best)

1 teaspoon each rosemary, eucalyptus, lavender, clary, and lemon essential oils

½ teaspoon peppermint, tea tree, and cedarwood essential oils

⅛ teaspoon (or less) clove bud essential oil

Directions

1. Mix the water and the essential oils in the misting bottle.

2. Shake well.

3. Spray as needed around the perimeter of rooms, in trash cans, closets, drawers, and shoes, under cushions, and inside bedclothes and suitcases.

Yield: About 2 ounces of herbal disinfectant

PUT HERBS IN A VACUUM

Put herbs in a vacuum cleaner, that is! To make vacuuming more of a pleasure than a chore, sprinkle ½ cup of fresh-smelling dried herb leaves, like lemon verbena or rosemary, on the carpet. Run the vacuum over the leaves, and then continue vacuuming the rest of the room. The pleasant fragrance will travel with you as you work.

Lemon verbena

CLEARING THE AIR

Many herbs have natural disinfectant properties. You can custom-blend your own disinfecting air fresheners with any of these essential oils: basil, bay, bee balm (also known as bergamot), camphor, cardamon, chamomile, cinnamon, clary, clove, eucalyptus, fir, ginger, grapefruit, juniper, lavender, lemon balm, meadowsweet, myrrh, myrtle, nutmeg, orange, oregano, patchouli, peppermint, Peru balsam, pine, rose-scented geranium, rosemary, sage, sandalwood, savory, spearmint, spruce, tea tree, and thyme.

When making herbal air fresheners, be sure to handle the essential oils with care. Some, such as Peru balsam, can irritate your skin. Also, test the fragrance of essential oils before you set out air fresheners that contain them. You may not like certain fragrances, or you may find a fragrance irritating when you inhale it.

One easy way to make an herbal air freshener is to dip a cotton ball in one of the essential oils listed above and place the cotton on a saucer.

For a long-lasting bathroom freshener, try custom-made incense. Buy unscented incense sticks (called punks) from a craft supplier. Pour a small amount of essential oil into a dish. Use a small brush to paint the incense sticks with the oil. Apply two or three coats to ensure that the essential oils are absorbed. (It helps to thin the essential oils with a little rubbing alcohol.)

To make a holder for the incense sticks, pour some sand into the opening in a seashell, or put some sand in a decorative dish. Stick the uncoated end of the burning incense stick into the sand. To make the

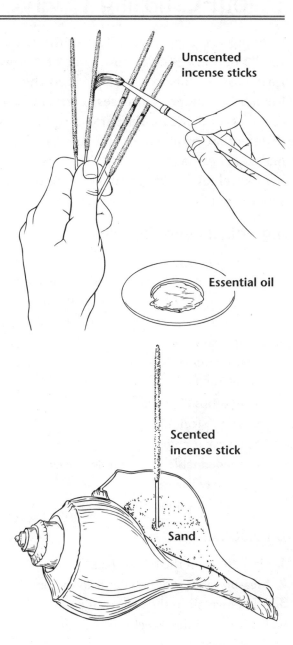

Unscented incense sticks

Essential oil

Scented incense stick

Sand

incense stick last longer, just let it burn for a minute or two, then upend the stick and extinguish the lit portion in the sand. That way, you can reuse each stick several times.

Moth-Chasing Marvels

Looking for a moth-repellent without that horrible mothball smell? Barbara Steele, co-owner of Alloway Gardens in Littlestown, Pennsylvania, created this moth-chasing recipe for her customers' suitcases, garment bags, sweater boxes, drawers, and shoes. Barbara says that this blend also has good disinfectant properties. She suggests "If you don't want to make sachet bags, just stuff the mix in old socks or tie it in a handkerchief." Barbara tucks some of these insect-repellent sachets inside pet beds as well.

Ingredients and Supplies

3 cups herbs (in any proportion, any 4 of these dried herbs: lavender, lavender cotton, mint, rosemary, southernwood, tansy, wormwood, or yarrow)

Large brown bag

4 teaspoons orris root powder

Small mixing bowl

8–10 drops clove oil

Stainless steel fork

1 cup cedar chips

1 rounded tablespoon whole cloves

10–12 bay leaves

2 or 3 clothespins

Directions

1. Place herbs in the brown bag.
2. Measure orris root powder into the bowl.
3. Add clove oil to the orris root and mix well with a stainless steel fork, smoothing out any lumps.
4. Sprinkle the powder over the herbs and shake the bag to mix.
5. Add the remaining ingredients and shake well again.
6. Close the bag tightly and clip with clothespins to hold in place.
7. Let the mix mellow for 2 weeks before you use it.

Yield: About 4 cups of moth-chasing mix

TIME-SAVING SACHET TIP

For no-sew sachet bags for herbal moth repellent or other fragrant herbal mixes, simply stuff the mix into muslin tea bags or recycled paper coin envelopes. To make fun and unusual gift sachets, use "Garden Harvest Potpourri" on page 214 to fill vintage cotton gloves and fancy handkerchiefs tied with a ribbon.

Pantry Protection Herbal Blend

Here's an old-time remedy for roaches and other kitchen pests, from herbalist and garden writer Tina James in Reisterstown, Maryland. "I had never seen a roach until I moved to the city after graduation. Someone told me to sprinkle borax in my cupboards and it really worked!"

Ingredients and Supplies

1 cup borax
¼ cup black pepper
Small glass mixing bowl
¼ cup bay leaves
Scissors

Directions

1. Mix borax and pepper in the bowl.
2. Cut each bay leaf into 4 or 5 pieces and add them to the bowl.
3. Stir to mix.
4. To use, sprinkle a small amount in the corners of cupboards and pantry shelves.

Yield: 1½ cups of pantry-protecting blend

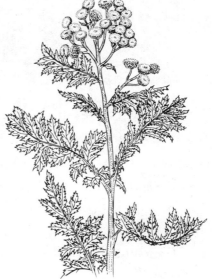

Ants on the march in your home? To repel them, find where they're entering the house and sprinkle the area with fresh or dried tansy.

Repel Them with Candles

Insects bugging you at your picnic? You can make your own bug-repellent candle by placing a few drops of pest-proofing essential oils in the well of a votive candle before lighting it, suggests herbalist Sue-Ryn Burns of Hill Woman Productions on Wellesley Island, New York. Sue-Ryn's favorite insect-repelling combination of essential oils is: 3 parts citronella, 2 parts lavender, 1 part eucalyptus, and 1 part vetiver. Or make some custom-scented incense sticks (see the illustration on page 223), and take them along on your next picnic. 🦋

FORMULAS FOR SALVES, BALMS, AND HOME REMEDIES

Here's to Your Herbal Health

Since the beginning of time, herbalists and physicians have turned to herbs for their almost magical soothing and healing properties. For centuries, herbs were the only medicines available. But the power of herbs is more than the stuff of superstition and old wives' tales. Many of today's prescription drugs are still made from common and not-so-common herbs. Using plants as partners for beauty, comfort, and health is an ancient art now enjoying a much deserved resurgence. And we don't need medical studies to tell us that spending time in a steaming herbal bath refreshes the body as well as the spirit.

Like all work with living things, herb-crafting is an art as well as a science. Although there are standard procedures for making herbal products, you'll find variations among the herbalists who have shared their recipes. One practitioner may like to infuse herbal oils in the sun, another may use a Crock-Pot and achieve equally good results. Similarly, most herbs have a wide range of healing properties. It's not unusual, for example, to find dandelion leaves used as a diuretic as well as a cure for skin blemishes.

Exercise caution when trying an herbal formula, especially if it's meant to be taken internally. If you're pregnant, ingesting some herbs may increase the risk of miscarriage. These include comfrey, feverfew, mugwort, southernwood, tansy, and wormwood. If you're pregnant or undergoing medical treatment, consult a physician before trying any herbal formula.

Keep Things Clean

There is one hard-and-fast rule in making herbal products for both internal and external use: Be sure that all of your equipment and ingredients are *clean*. Sterilize storage containers or wash them well with hot, soapy water. When a recipe calls for cookware, use glass or stainless steel pans. Aluminum can react with some herbs and with ingredients like vinegar.

Most herbalists prefer to use ceramic or glass containers to mix and store herbal products. However, it's fine to put a monthly supply of your homemade cosmetics in plastic containers to avoid the chance of broken glass. Be sure to label your homemade herbal products, including both the date and contents.

Some Herbal Terms

Before you can begin your journey to herbal health, it's important to understand the language of herbal preparations. So here's a thumbnail glossary of important herbal terms.

Infusion. An infusion is simply another word for tea. Herbal infusions are used to enhance body care products and to make healing herbal washes or baths. Infusions are best when prepared fresh for daily use, although they will keep for a few days in the refrigerator.

Tinctures. Also called herbal extracts, tinctures are a concentrated liquid form of herbal medicine made by steeping fresh or dried herbs in a solvent, typically alcohol. Because they are concentrated, tinctures are convenient to use and easy to consume. You'll use them by the drop rather than by the quart or the cup. Tinctures also store well—they'll keep for five years or more in a cool, dark place.

Herb-infused oils. To make an herb-infused oil, you'll steep the herbs in the oil, which imbues the oil with the herbs' healing properties. You can use the resulting oil directly on your skin or combined with other ingredients to make salves and creams. Extra-virgin olive oil is the most commonly used oil for herbal skin preparations because it resists rancidity. The infused herbal oils discussed in this chapter are intended for external use. To learn about herbal oils for cooking, see "Basil-Garlic Herbal Oil" on page 205.

Salves. Salves are a thickened oil usually created by melting beeswax into an infused herbal oil. Used externally to treat skin problems, they keep the healing properties of the herbs in place longer than alcohol or water-based products. Salves can be stored for many years in a cool, dark place. They are quick and easy to make once the herbal oil is prepared.

Essential oils. It takes sophisticated equipment to make essential oils, which are highly concentrated, pure plant distillates extracted from various parts of plants. Also, a huge volume of plant material is required to make even a small amount of pure oil, so it's nearly impossible to make essential oils at home.

However, you can buy herbal oils at herb shops and pharmacies. When shopping

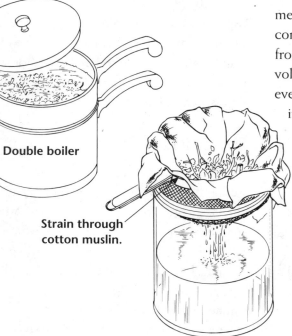

Double boiler

Strain through cotton muslin.

Squeeze muslin to remove excess oil.

Use a double boiler to gently warm extra-virgin olive oil and herbs to make an infused oil. Once the oil has cooled, strain it through a piece of cotton muslin to remove the herbs. Twist the muslin to remove as much oil as possible. See "Basic Herb-Infused Oil" on page 231 for complete instructions.

for essential oils, look for pure essential oils packaged in dark-colored bottles. Synthetic oils, although far less expensive, cannot be safely or effectively used in therapeutic recipes. Due to variations in the oil content of various plants, you'll find a wide range in the cost of essential oils. Pure rose oil, for example, costs $45 for ⅛ ounce, whereas the same amount of lavender oil costs $5.

Essential oils are almost always intended for external use. In addition, most essential oils are too strong to use directly on the skin; they must first be mixed into an oil or cream. Store essential oils in a cool, dark place out of the reach of children. Don't use essential oils if you're pregnant or are undergoing medical treatment. If in doubt, consult with a competent health provider.

It's always a good idea to perform a patch test before using a new essential oil. Dilute a drop or two of the oil in vegetable oil and apply a small amount of the diluted oil to your inner arm. After 30 minutes, remove the test oil and check for any irritation.

To keep essential oils clean, apply with an eyedropper or cotton swab. Also be sure to keep the outside of the bottle clean by wiping the bottom of the bottle after use. Essential oils can mar surfaces, especially plastic ones. Be sure to twist bottle caps on tightly as well.

In addition to using essential oils for creating body care products, you can use the healing power of fragrance in other ways, such as placing a few drops in a scent ring around light bulbs, adding to a diffuser, mixing with potpourri and simmering scents, and adding to cleaning products.

Once you learn how to get the most out of herbs, you'll find that you've opened the door to the time-honored practice of herbal healing and joined centuries of herbalists who have tapped the magic of herbs.

POPULAR ESSENTIAL OILS

Here's a list of the qualities of some of the most useful and enjoyable essential oils for salves, balms, and home remedies.

Bee balm (also known as bergamot): uplifting, clean, antidepressant

Eucalyptus: invigorating, uplifting, antiseptic, decongestant, analgesic

Zonal geranium: uplifting, balancing, relaxing, astringent

Grapefruit: bright, uplifting, clean, cleansing, stimulating

Lavender: antifungal, antiseptic, antidepressant, calming, deodorizing, anti-inflammatory, antibacterial

Lemon: energizing, antiseptic, astringent, antibacterial

Sweet orange: uplifting, antispasmodic, balancing, antiseptic

Peppermint: stimulating, refreshing, uplifting, cooling, antiseptic, expectorant

Rose: sensual, antidepressant, tonic, astringent, antispasmodic, sedative

Rosemary: warming, stimulating, analgesic, antiseptic, antispasmodic, astringent

Sandalwood: soothing, sensual, centering, antiseptic, sedative, warming

Thyme: antibacterial, warming, stimulating, expectorant

Quick and Easy Herbal Soap

Making soap from scratch is a time-consuming challenge, but you don't have to start from scratch to create lovely personalized soap products. Artist JoAnn Stak, owner of Dandelion Designs in Burlington, Vermont, melts bars of purchased glycerin soap, adds her own herbs, and then remolds the soap. Remaking soap is fun and those with sensitive skin can make sure nothing harmful is added. And, as JoAnn points out, cleanup is easy. After all, it's soap!

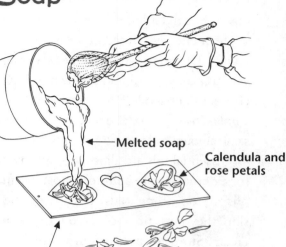

Melted soap

Calendula and rose petals

Mold

Ingredients and Supplies

>   2 cups glycerine soap bars,
>   cut into chunks
>   Double boiler
>   10–20 drops essential oils of herbs or
>   flowers from the list on the facing
>   page (optional)
>   2 tablespoons exfoliating agents from
>   the list (optional)
>   2 teaspoons or 2 gel caps nutritive
>   agents from the list (optional)
>   2 tablespoons dried herbs or flowers
>   from the list (optional)
>   Soap or candy molds (or shallow plastic
>   containers, wider at the top than the
>   bottom)
>   Towel
>   Plastic wrap or plastic zipper bags

Directions

1. Melt soap chunks in a double boiler over medium-low heat.

2. Stir in pure essential oils and/or exfoliating or nutritive agents.

For a designer touch, arrange dried flowers and herbs on melted soap after it has set for a few minutes. Let it set until firm. Pour a thin layer of melted soap over the dried materials, creating a transparent window effect. Allow it to harden again before unmolding.

3. Pour mix into molds. If desired, sprinkle dried herbs and flowers into the mix as you pour so they don't settle to the bottom.

4. Allow to harden for about ½ hour.

5. Pop out soap onto a towel.

6. Let bars sit overnight to harden completely.

7. Wrap bars in plastic or put in plastic zipper bags to preserve scent.

Yield: 2 bars of herbal glycerine soap

HERBAL EXTRAS FOR CUSTOM-MADE SOAP

Add herbs and other ingredients to your homemade soap to create just the type you need—a facial soap, body soap, a gritty soap to help renew your skin, or an enriched soap.

Pure essential oils for facial soap: chamomile, lemon, lavender, neroli, geranium, grapefruit, frankincense, rose attar

Pure essential oils for body soap: rosemary, grapefruit, lavender, bee balm (also known as bergamot), orange, pine, peppermint

Dried herbs and flowers (ground or whole): calendula, rose petal, lavender buds, violet flowers

Exfoliating agents: finely ground oatmeal, finely ground corn meal, finely ground almond kernels, white clay (kaolin), green clay (bentonite)

Nutritive agents: cold-pressed oils, like jojoba, apricot kernel, avocado, evening primrose oil, vitamin E, vitamin A

Test the ingredients on your skin before adding them to soap: Mix a small amount of the herbs and other ingredients in pure vegetable oil and rub the mixture on the inside of your arm. Check in half an hour to make sure that there is no irritation.

Basic Herb-Infused Oil

Many herbal salves and creams start with herb-infused oils. Use this formula from herbalist Pat Carrigan of Shepherdstown, West Virginia, to create herbal oils that you can use directly on your skin or as the basis for other herbal concoctions.

Ingredients and Supplies

Dried or fresh wilted herbs (see page 232 for instructions on wilting fresh herbs)
Double boiler or Crock-Pot
Extra-virgin olive oil
Fine-mesh strainer
Cotton muslin to line strainer
Large glass container or bowl
Sterilized glass jars with lids

Directions

1. Place desired herb or herbs in the double boiler or Crock-Pot. (If you're using roots, chop and infuse them in the oil for at least 2 hours before adding leaves or flowers.)

2. Pour in enough extra-virgin olive oil to cover the herbs with 1 to 2 inches of oil.

3. Gently heat the herbs at about 180°F for 2 to 4 hours. Keep the pot or boiler covered, and stir occasionally.

4. Remove from heat and let the oil cool.

5. Strain the oil through a fine-mesh strainer lined with cotton muslin.

6. Squeeze out any excess oil remaining in the muslin.

7. Pour the oil into sterilized glass jars to store.

Gardeners' Hand Cream

Do your hands throb and ache after a day of weeding? Don't give up on gardening! Instead, try this multipurpose hand cream from herbalist Margi Flint of Earthsong Herbals in Marblehead, Massachusetts. It contains black cohosh to ease arthritic pain, St.-John's-wort to help reconnect nerve tissue, and plantain and calendula to heal nicks and scratches.

Ingredients and Supplies

2 handfuls each of fresh plantain leaf, calendula flowers (*Calendula officinalis*), St.-John's-wort flowers (*Hypericum perforatum*), and black cohosh leaf (*Cimicifuga racemosa*)

Double boiler

Extra-virgin olive oil

Strainer

Linen towel, fine cotton handkerchief, or cheesecloth

Bowl

Glass jar

4-inch piece of Solomon's seal root (*Polygonatum biflorum*) (optional; see "Use Solomon's Seal Sparingly" on the facing page)

1 tablespoon hexane-free castor oil

1 tablespoon coconut oil

½ ounce (or more) beeswax, grated

Blender

¼ cup floral water (lavender, lilac, or rose water)

¼ cup aloe vera gel

Glass wide-mouth jar

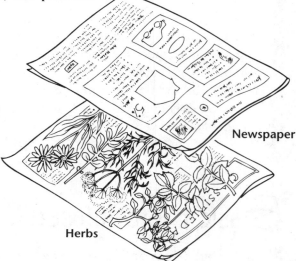

Newspaper

Herbs

Wilt your herbs overnight by spreading them out between sheets of newspaper. The next day, they'll be ready to use in the Gardeners' Hand Cream recipe or in any formula that calls for herb-infused oil.

Directions

1. Let the herbs wilt overnight to reduce their water content.

2. Place the herbs in the double boiler. Pour olive oil over the herbs until there are 2 to 3 inches of oil topping the herbs.

3. Heat the herbs and oil for about 2 hours with the lid of the pot slightly askew.

4. Allow the oil to cool to room temperature.

5. Line the strainer with the towel, handkerchief, or cheesecloth and pour the herb mixture into the strainer.

6. Let the oil drain into a clean bowl for several hours; squeeze out any excess oil.

7. Pour the oil into a glass jar, and label and date it. Set it on a windowsill at eye level.

8. After a day or two, check for any water droplets in the bottom of the jar. If water is evident, pour off the oil into another glass jar, leaving the watery oil at the bottom. "Water will cause the oil to turn rancid, so don't forget this step," cautions Margi. "But don't waste the watery oil. Mix it with some sea salt to make herbal salts for a soothing bath." Margi recommends mixing 3 tablespoons of the oil with 1 cup of sea salt and adding ¼ cup of herbal salt per tubful of bathwater.

9. Place ½ cup of infused oil in the double boiler. (Also include 3 tablespoons of Solomon's seal, if desired.)

10. Add castor and coconut oils and beeswax. Heat just until the wax has melted.

11. Let the wax and oil mixture cool to room temperature. While it cools, put the aloe vera and floral water into a blender.

12. Turn on the blender to its highest speed and slowly pour the oil-wax mixture into the blender.

13. Pour the finished cream into sterile wide-mouth jars.

14. To use the cream, dab some of it onto the backs of your hands and rub it into your hands and fingers until it is well absorbed.

USE SOLOMON'S SEAL SPARINGLY

Another plant with healing qualities is Solomon's seal, says Margi Flint. She also extracts oil from its roots to add to her hand cream, especially for clients with tendon problems.

However, she cautions: "Solomon's seal is abundant where I live but endangered in other areas. Because you destroy the plant by harvesting the root, only harvest from a prolific stand on your own property. And say lots of prayers of gratitude!" When you're gathering herbs for infusions or other formulas, make a habit of taking them only from your own property. That way, you know they're 100 percent organic and you don't deplete wild plant populations.

To infuse oil with Solomon's seal root, repeat steps 2 through 9 of the directions for "Gardeners' Hand Cream," using a 4-inch piece of root, cut into small pieces, and 1 cup of extra-virgin olive oil.

Margi makes the Solomon's seal root oil in a separate batch and uses it in her hand cream only when needed. "Remember to compost any remaining plant material—even the herbs strained from the oil," she adds. "As the Cherokees say, you don't get the medicine until everything goes back to the earth."

Take a Bath with Herbs and Flowers

Herbalist Sue-Ryn Burns of Hill Woman Productions on Wellesley Island, New York, employs the ancient art of salt-drying to preserve the delicate fragrances of herbs and flowers. "Some scents, like lily-of-the-valley and peony, are almost impossible to preserve through any other means," says Sue-Ryn. She prefers to make single-scent salts, but it's fine to mix them if you don't have enough of any one plant. "Moist flowers, like peonies, may cause the salt to cake, so I cover the jar with cheesecloth for a few days to allow some of the moisture to escape before closing it up," says Sue-Ryn. "The extra trouble is worth it for the scent."

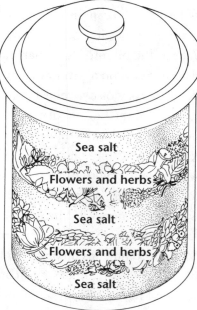

Ingredients and Supplies

Sea salt
Large glass jar or crock with lid
Fragrant flowers and herbs
Large mesh strainer
Wooden spoon

Treat yourself—or a friend—to fragrant bath salts scented with herbs or flowers. This simple and soothing bath additive is easy to make, too—just layer sea salt with fresh-picked flowers or herbs from your garden.

Directions

1. Put an inch of salt in the bottom of the jar.
2. Add a layer of flowers and herbs.
3. Sprinkle salt over the flowers and herbs until they are covered.
4. Add another layer of flowers and herbs, cover with salt, and continue until the jar is full or you run out of blossoms. The last layer should be an inch of salt.
5. Cover the container and let it sit in a cool, dark place until the salt is pleasantly scented—about 3 weeks. It's fine to leave the flowers and herbs in longer, but Sue-Ryn suggests removing them after 3 months to keep the scent fresh.

6. To separate the flowers and herbs from the salt, pour the mix into the strainer gradually and work it through the mesh. Use the spoon to break up any lumps. It won't hurt to leave a few petals in the salt.
7. Store the salt in airtight containers. The salt will keep indefinitely.
8. Put a few petals on top as a decorative identification.
9. To use, add 1 to 2 cups of salt under running water while filling the tub.

FLOWERS AND HERBS FOR SALT-DRYING

Use sea salt to capture the sweet scents of herbs and flowers from your garden. Here are some of the plants Sue-Ryn Burns uses to make soothing bath salts; try these or experiment with your own favorite garden fragrances.

Sweet clover (*Melilotus officinalis*)
Daffodil
Heliotrope (*Heliotropium arborescens*)
Honeysuckle
Hyacinth

Lavender
Lemon balm
Lilac
Lily-of-the-valley
Marjoram
Peonies
Roses
Thyme
Tulip
Violet
Wisteria

Fantastic Fragrant Bath Powder

Make a luxurious yet inexpensive bath powder by combining common pantry ingredients with ground herbs. This recipe is from herbalist Mariam Massaro of Wise Ways Herbals in Worthington, Massachusetts, a mail-order company offering handcrafted natural body care products. A coffee grinder works well to grind the herbs.

Ingredients and Supplies

4 cups arrowroot powder
4 cups cornstarch
2 cups fine sea salt
1 cup powdered white clay (kaolin)
½ cup powdered herbs, like lavender buds, calendula petals (*Calendula officinalis*), orange flower petals, sage leaves, and slippery elm root (*Ulmus rubra*)
Ceramic bowl

Wooden spoon
3 teaspoons essential oils, like lemon, rose, and lavender for a floral scent; peppermint, lavender, and chamomile for a cooling summer powder, or tea tree for antifungal powder
Storage container
Recycled shaker container or powder box

Directions

1. Combine dry ingredients in the bowl and stir well with the wooden spoon.
2. Add the essential oils.
3. Pour the mixture into a storage container and label it. The powder will keep indefinitely.
4. Fill shakers or powder boxes as needed.

Yield: About 3 quarts of herbal body powder

Tension-Taming Bath Tea

Herb tea is good for body and soul—and for a bath! Many of the healing properties of herbs can be absorbed directly through the skin to ease tension, draw out impurities, and stimulate circulation. Herbalist Tina James of Reisterstown, Maryland, says she picks herbs for the evening bath while she's harvesting greens and veggies for dinner. "Regular clipping keeps herbs looking good and growing vigorously," says Tina. "But what to do with all the trimmings? Bath tea is one way to make use of the surplus."

Ingredients and Supplies

4 cups fragrant herbs, coarsely chopped
Large heat-proof glass container
Boiling water (to cover herbs)
Strainer

Directions

1. Place herbs in the glass container.
2. Pour boiling water over the herbs.
3. Cover the brew with a dish or towel to capture the essential oils.
4. Let sit for at least an hour, then strain.
5. To use, draw bath and pour herb tea into the bath water.
6. Relax and enjoy.

Note: Tina recommends turning any of these herbs into tea for your tub: alfalfa, basil, chamomile, comfrey (*Symphytum officinale*), scented geraniums (*Pelargonium* spp.), lavender, lemon balm, mint, mugwort (*Artemisia* spp.), parsley, plantain (*Plantago major*), sage, strawberry, thyme, or violet.

Put a Tea Bag in Your Tub

Make a bath "tea bag" by enclosing dried herbs in a washcloth (a dark-colored washcloth won't show stains). Tie the "tea bag" tightly with string. Hang from the faucet while filling the bath to release the scent and healing properties of the herbs. When bathing, squeeze the bag to release its fragrance. Each bag brews several baths.

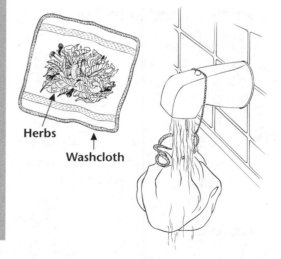

Herbs

Washcloth

Herbal Hair Rinses

"Natural hair care products are a great place to begin an herbal body care program," says herbalist Julie Bailey, owner of Mountain Rose Herbs, a mail-order supplier of herbs and herbal products in North San Juan, California. "They're a snap to make and inexpensive as well," Julie says. The vinegar in this recipe not only smooths out tangles, it also restores your hair's acid balance.

Ingredients and Supplies

Large glass jar with rustproof lid for
   steeping
4 cups raw apple cider vinegar
Plastic squeeze bottle
Distilled or spring water

Herbs for dark hair

2 parts stinging nettle leaves
   (*Urtica dioica*)
1 part chamomile flowers
1 part rosemary leaves

Herbs for light hair

2 parts stinging nettle leaves
1 part chamomile flowers
1 part calendula flowers
   (*Calendula officinalis*)

Herbs for red hair

2 parts stinging nettle leaves
1 part hibiscus flowers
1 part safflower flowers
   (*Carthamus tinctorius*)

Directions

1. Decide which blend of herbs you want to use: herbs for dark hair, light hair, or red hair. Place 1 cup of the appropriate herb blend in the glass jar.

2. Pour enough vinegar over the herbs to cover them completely. (In winter, Julie heats the vinegar in a non-aluminum pan until it's almost ready to boil. Then she pours the hot vinegar over the herbs into a heat-proof glass jar.)

3. Cap the jar.

4. Let the jar sit in the sun for 2 weeks.

5. Strain, label, and date. Store in a cool, dark place. The herbal vinegar will keep at least several years.

6. To use, dilute the herbal vinegar with an equal amount of water to fill the squeeze bottle.

7. After shampooing, squeeze about ½ cup of the vinegar rinse over your hair. Keep your eyes closed as you massage the mixture into your scalp for a few minutes, then rinse.

Yield: 1 quart of herbal hair rinse

Custom-Blended Herbal Shampoo

If you already have a favorite shampoo, you can enhance and personalize it by mixing in a homemade herb infusion. It will also help to stretch your shampoo supply.

Ingredients and Supplies

1 tablespoon dried or 3 tablespoons fresh herbs (use blends specified in "Herbal Hair Rinses" on page 237)

Heat-proof measuring cup

¾ cup boiling water

Tea towel

Strainer

Plastic yogurt cup with lid

Shampoo (try unscented castile or natural baby shampoo)

1 teaspoon jojoba or vitamin E oil

5 drops essential oil, like lavender, rosemary, or basil (optional)

Directions

1. Place herbs in the measuring cup, and pour the boiling water over them.

2. Cover with a tea towel.

3. Cool to room temperature.

4. Strain infusion into the plastic cup.

5. Add 2 tablespoons of shampoo and the jojoba or vitamin E oil to the herbal infusion. Add 5 drops of essential oil, if desired, and shake to mix.

6. To use, shake the mix and shampoo as normal. This diluted shampoo will keep for 2 to 3 days in the shower and up to a week in the refrigerator.

Yield: About 1 cup of herbal shampoo

BAD HAIR DAY? HERBS TO THE RESCUE!

Rosemary will remove that lingering chemical smell from a new perm and fight dandruff as well. Make a cup of strong rosemary tea by pouring 1 cup of boiling water over 1 tablespoon of dried herb. Let the mixture steep until cool. Strain out the herb and rub the tea into your hair or use it as a rinse after shampooing. A few drops of rosemary essential oil mixed into a cup of water to make a rinse will also do the trick.

Essential oils are great for styling and freshening hair as well. Add about 10 drops of lavender, basil, lemon, clary sage, or sandalwood essential oil to 1 cup of distilled or spring water. Shake well, mist your hair, and use your fingers to style your hair. Shake the mister before each use to disperse the oils in the water.

Conditioning Hair Oil

To improve your hair texture and condition your scalp, try this simple herb-infused oil from Mariam Massaro, herbalist and owner of Wise Ways Herbals, a mail-order supplier of natural body care products in Worthington, Massachusetts. "This treatment cleans and stimulates the scalp," she explains. "You'll reap lustrous results after just two or three weeks."

Mariam recommends using dried or wilted herbs when making an infused oil to reduce excess moisture. To wilt fresh herbs, dry them on a screen or between newspaper for a day or two, as shown on page 232. In the summer months, Mariam saves time and energy by using the sun to infuse the oil: Simply pour the oil over the herbs and let it sit outside for two weeks. There's no need to heat the oil first.

Ingredients and Supplies

3 cups good quality olive oil
1 tablespoon dried basil leaf
1 tablespoon dried burdock root
    (*Arctium lappa*)
1 tablespoon dried sage leaf
1 tablespoon dried stinging nettle leaf
    (*Urtica dioica*)
1 tablespoon dried lavender buds

Stainless steel or enamel pan
Heat-proof glass jar with a lid
Strainer lined with muslin
A few drops essential oils, like basil,
    rosemary, and/or lavender (optional)
Glass storage jar with lid
Plastic storage bottle with lid

Directions

1. Heat the olive oil and herbs in the pan until the oil comes to a light simmer and the mix smells nice and strong.

2. Pour oil and herbs in the heat-proof glass jar and cap the jar.

3. Let the mixture sit at room temperature for 4 or 5 days.

4. Strain until the oil is clear.

5. Pour into a glass storage jar and cap tightly. The oil will keep at least a year in a cool, dark place.

6. To use, pour ½ cup of the herb-infused oil into a plastic storage bottle. Add essential oils, if desired. Shake well.

7. Pour a teaspoon or so of the oil in the palms of your hands and massage it into your scalp.

8. Bend over and brush your hair from the nape of your neck to the crown of your head 100 times.

Yield: 3 cups of conditioning hair oil

Corny Cleanser for Oily Skin

Save your face from soap with this herbal cleanser from herbalist Sue-Ryn Burns of Hill Woman Productions on Wellesley Island, New York. Sue-Ryn's mixture of cornmeal, oatmeal, lavender, kelp, and other herbs is great for giving oily skin a deep-yet-gentle cleansing. For a quick face mask, just let the paste dry on your face and then gently brush it off.

Ingredients and Supplies

Blender
6 ounces oatmeal
1½ ounces rose petals
1 ounce lavender buds
Mixing bowl
6 ounces cornmeal
1 ounce Irish moss powder
½ ounce kelp granules
½ ounce comfrey root powder
Storage containers

Directions

1. Blenderize oatmeal with rose petals and lavender buds.

2. Pour the mixture into a clean mixing bowl.

3. Add cornmeal, Irish moss powder, kelp granules, and comfrey root powder, and mix well.

4. Put a small amount into a container for daily use.

5. Store remainder in an airtight container. It will keep indefinitely, although it's best if used within 6 months.

6. To use, rinse your face with water first.

7. Put a small amount of the cleansing powder in your hands and add enough water to make a paste.

Before making an herbal face cleanser, use a blender to chop up ingredients like oatmeal, rose petals, or lavender buds.

8. Rub your face gently, making little circles with your hands.

9. Rinse your face with warm water, ending with a cold splash to close the pores.

Yield: About 1 cup of cleansing grains

Caution: If you are pregnant, consult with a physician before using any formula that contains comfrey root powder.

Corny Cleanser for Dry Skin

If soap makes your skin uncomfortably dry, try this gentle herbal mixture from herbalist Sue-Ryn Burns of Hill Woman Productions on Wellesley Island, New York. Her combination of cornmeal, oatmeal, slippery elm powder, chamomile flowers, and other herbs will leave your skin feeling fresh and smooth. You can use this cleanser as a face mask, too—just leave the paste on your face until it dries, then gently brush it away.

Ingredients and Supplies

Blender
6 ounces oatmeal
1 ounce chamomile flowers
½ ounce elder flowers
½ ounce orange blossoms
Mixing bowl
6 ounces cornmeal
1 ounce Irish moss powder
1 ounce slippery elm powder
½ ounce comfrey root powder
Storage containers

Roman chamomile is an easy-growing perennial herb that makes a great companion for perennial crops such as strawberries. Use the daisy flowers of this handy herb to make homemade chamomile tea, as well as in herbal products like Corny Cleanser for Dry Skin.

Directions

1. Blenderize oatmeal with chamomile flowers, elder flowers, and orange blossoms.
2. Pour the mixture into a clean mixing bowl.
3. Add cornmeal, Irish moss powder, slippery elm powder, and comfrey root powder, and mix well.
4. Put a small amount into a container for daily use.
5. Store remainder in an airtight container. It will keep indefinitely, although it's best if used within 6 months.
6. To use, rinse your face with water first.

7. Put a small amount of the cleansing powder in your hands and add enough water to make a paste.
8. Rub your face gently, making little circles with your hands.
9. Rinse your face with warm water, ending with a cold splash to close the pores.

Yield: About 1 cup of cleansing grains

Caution: If you are pregnant, consult with a physician before using any formula that contains comfrey root powder.

Fluffy Herbal Face Cream

You can make your own luxurious, fluffy, white face cream and customize it with the herbs and essential oils that you like best. Herbalist Rosemary Gladstar, founder of Sage Mountain in East Barre, Vermont, and author of *Herbal Healing for Women*, has trained hundreds of apprentices, many of whom have developed entire natural body care product lines based on her recipes. Here's Rosemary's original face cream recipe:

Ingredients and Supplies

¾ cup grapeseed oil

⅓ cup coconut oil and/or cocoa butter (Rosemary uses both)

1 teaspoon lanolin

½ ounce beeswax, grated

Double boiler

⅔ cup distilled water or rosewater

⅓ cup aloe vera gel (don't use fresh aloe juice, as bacteria can grow in it)

Blender (very clean!)

10,000 units vitamin A (optional)

20,000 units vitamin E (optional)

1 teaspoon black currant seed oil or evening primrose seed oil (optional)

1 tablespoon herbal tinctures from herbs listed in "Steam Your Cares Away" on page 246 (optional) (Note: See "Fight Allergies with Herbs" on page 262 for information on how to make an herbal tincture)

1 teaspoon essential oil of lavender, sandalwood, geranium, chamomile, ylang ylang, or helichrysum (optional)

Wide-mouth jar

Directions

1. Heat the grapeseed and coconut oil, cocoa butter, lanolin, and beeswax in a double boiler until just melted.

2. Remove from heat and let cool to room temperature. (The oils are easier to work with if you do not let them solidify.)

3. Place water and aloe vera gel in the blender.

4. Add optional ingredients to the blender.

5. Turn on the blender to the highest speed and add in the oil mixture in a slow, thin drizzle. ("It's just like making mayonnaise," notes Rosemary.)

6. When the blender starts to cough and choke, turn it off. "Do not overbeat," cautions Rosemary. "Don't give up if it doesn't turn out perfectly the first time," she adds.

"The key is finding the right temperature for the ingredients to blend well."

7. Put a week's supply of face cream in a small clean container for use in the bathroom. Store the remainder in the refrigerator until needed.

8. Apply face cream to the face and neck with clean hands, and smooth the cream into your skin until it's absorbed.

Yield: About 2 cups of herbal face cream

FOR CREAMIER CREAM

Herbalist Terry Whye of Whye Clayworks and Pottery Studio in Finksburg, Maryland, makes Rosemary's herbal face cream for holiday gifts. "I've found that dissolving 1 teaspoon of borax into the water guarantees that the cream sets up for me," Terry says.

Fennel Face Soother

For a refreshing herbal splash, herbalist and licensed aesthetician Stephanie Tourles, author of *The Herbal Body Book* and owner of September's Sun Herbal Soap Company, takes advantage of the skin-softening properties of fennel. "Fennel creates a slipperiness that feels wonderful on the face and body," Stephanie says. "I use this as a hair rinse as well. It restores the natural pH balance of your skin and scalp."

Ingredients and Supplies

2 cups distilled water
1 tablespoon crushed fennel seeds
¼ cup apple cider vinegar

2 teaspoons glycerin (available from a
 pharmacy)
Storage container or pump spray bottle

Directions

1. Boil water.
2. Remove water from heat and add crushed fennel seeds.
3. Cover, steep for 45 minutes, and strain out fennel seeds.
4. Stir vinegar and glycerin into fennel-infused water.

5. Pour into storage container, label and date. Herbal splash will keep for 30 days.
6. Splash or spray on as desired.

Yield: About 2 cups of fennel face soother

Caution: Fennel can cause an allergic reaction in some individuals.

Best-Selling Herbal Massage Oils

Oils infused with healing herbs are among the most versatile homemade body care products. Using an herbal oil as a base, it's easy to create custom-scented massage and bath oils as well as skin softeners for face and body. You can also use the oil as a base for making salves and creams.

This massage oil recipe is a favorite of Julie Bailey, owner of Mountain Rose Herbs, a mail-order supplier of herbs and herbal products in North San Juan, California. Julie makes herbal oil blends for her best-selling massage oils. To reduce the moisture, Julie wilts the herbs for 24 hours by laying them out on screens.

St.-John's-wort

Ingredients and Supplies

2 or 3 clean glass jars
Extra-virgin olive oil
Strainer
Cheesecloth
Glass storage container

Fragrant, relaxing blend
1 part calendula (*Calendula officinalis*)
1 part damiana leaves (*Turnera diffusa*)
1 part lavender buds
1 part red rose petals or rose geranium leaves (*Pelargonium graveolens*)
½ part rosemary leaves
½ part self heal leaves and flowers (*Prunella vulgaris*)

Blend for soothing sore muscles
2 parts calendula petals (*Calendula officinalis*)
1 part chamomile flowers
¾ part ginger root (*Zingiber officinale*)
Rose and lavender essential oils
1 part mugwort leaves and flowers (*Artemisia* spp.)

Directions

1. Decide whether you want to make the fragrant, relaxing oil or the oil to soothe sore muscles. Wilt the appropriate herbs and flowers overnight.
2. Place the wilted herbs and flowers in a glass jar.

3. Cover them with oil and cap tightly.
4. Let sit in the sun for 3 to 4 weeks, shaking every few days.
5. Add more oil as necessary to keep the plant material covered.
6. Line the strainer with cheesecloth.

7. Strain the oil into a clean glass jar, squeezing as much oil out of the cheesecloth as possible.

8. Let the oil sit for 1 to 2 weeks in a cool, dark place.

9. If sediment or water settles to the bottom of the jar, pour off the oil into a clean glass storage jar, being careful not to include the impurities.

10. Store the finished oils in a cool, dark place, where they will keep for at least 1 year.

11. To use, pour a cup of the oil into a small container. Scent with essential oils, if desired.

Note: "I like to pick the plants on the new moon and strain the oil on the next new moon," Julie says. "This gives a natural rhythm to my work."

Variation: To soothe pain, try a massage oil made with St.-John's-wort (*Hypericum perfo-ratum*). "St.-John's-wort oil is a good remedy of choice for inflamed muscle and nerve pain. It's effective for bruises, contusions, in-flamed arthritic joints, and even sunburn," says pharmacist and herbalist Lynn Shumake of Blue Mountain Herbal Apothecary in Glenelg, Maryland.

"The oil is especially fun to make be-cause it turns a beautiful rich burgundy color after 2 to 3 months," Lynn adds. "That's when you know it's ready." Lynn uses sesame oil for his herb-infused oils. "Sesame oil may be more expensive, but it won't turn rancid. In India, where it is considered a sa-cred oil, it's been used for centuries without refrigeration."

QUICK ESSENTIAL MASSAGE OILS

Herbalist Rita C. Karydas, owner of Lunar Farms Herbal Specialist and Learning Center in Gilmer, Texas, makes quick massage oils using grapeseed oil, sweet almond oil, olive oil, and vitamin E oil. "Grapeseed oil is great for massage, since it's absorbed quickly and doesn't leave a sticky film," says Rita. "A combi-nation of sweet almond oil and olive oil has therapeutic properties, soothes, moisturizes, and is good for most skin types. Try 3 parts almond oil to 1 part olive oil. Add ¼ teaspoon of vitamin E as an antioxidant to extend the shelf life of your massage oil blend."

Twenty-five drops of essential oils is enough for a 2-ounce bottle. After you add and mix your essential oils, let the bottle sit for an hour or longer; then smell and adjust the fragrance blend to suit your taste. Try the following essential oils to make special massage blends.

Congestion blend: eucalyptus, lemon, tea tree

Sore muscle blend: lavender, rosemary, peppermint

Sports blend (cooling, stimulating, and relieves muscle pain): sweet birch, pep-permint, spearmint

"Gently massage the oil onto affected areas," Lynn says. "You may apply warm, moist heat with a washcloth. Repeat 2 to 3 times daily." St.-John's-wort may cause sun sensitivity on long exposure. As a precau-tion, use a good sunscreen lotion.

Steam Your Cares Away

For a day of natural pampering, herbalist Shatoiya de la Tour of Dry Creek Herb Farm and Learning Center in Auburn, California, likes to turn fresh herbs into a steaming bowl of fragrance and healing. "Pour boiling water over the herbs and lean over the bowl with a towel draped over your head. The steam opens the pores and the herbs' essential oils treat your skin and offer their healing aroma."

Ingredients and Supplies

Ceramic, stainless steel, or Pyrex bowl
Boiling water
Towel

Relaxing herbs
Catnip (*Nepeta cataria*)
Chamomile flowers
Lavender buds
Lemon balm

Invigorating herbs
Basil
Peppermint
White pine (*Pinus strobus*)
Rosemary
Thyme

Skin-loving herbs
Calendula petals (*Calendula officinalis*)
Elder flower (*Sambucus canadensis*)
Rose petals
Violet leaf and blossom

Skin-healing herbs
Calendula (*Calendula officinalis*)
Oatmeal
Plantain (*Plantago major*)
Red clover flowers

Treat yourself to a relaxing regimen that starts with a 15-minute herbal facial steam, recommends Shatoiya de la Tour. Follow it with an herbal clay mask and a 20- to 30-minute nap on the lawn. Then finish with an herbal splash.

Directions

1. Decide which type of facial steam you want to try: relaxing, invigorating, skin-loving, or skin-healing.
2. Put the appropriate fresh herbs in the bowl and cover with boiling water.
3. With a towel draped over your head, place your face over the bowl. Keep your face a comfortable distance from the heat.
4. Add more boiling water as needed to create more steam.
5. After 15 minutes, rinse your face with cool water and blot dry.

246   Formulas for Salves, Balms, and Home Remedies

Herbal Sleep Pillows

Having trouble sleeping? Maybe you need a soporific pillow. Herbs like hops and mugwort induce sleep; rosemary and lavender are soothing; and thyme is good for the respiratory system. "This pillow works like a charm for my wife, Lucy," claims herbalist Rob Wood of Spoutwood Farm in Glen Rock, Pennsylvania. Rob created this blend from dried herbs, enclosed it in a pillowcase, and then inserted the herbal pillow into another pillowcase. He simply removes the herbal sack and washes the outer pillowcase as needed.

Ingredients and Supplies

- 2 cups lavender buds
- 1 cup hops flowers (*Humulus lupulus*)
- 1 cup oak moss
- ⅔ cup rose geranium leaves (*Pelargonium graveolens*)
- ⅔ cup rosemary leaves
- ⅔ cup lemon balm leaves
- ⅔ cup chamomile flowers
- ⅓ cup thyme leaves and flowers
- ⅓ cup mugwort leaves and flowers (*Artemisia* spp.)
- Large ceramic bowl
- 2 10 × 12-inch pillowcases
- Sewing machine or needle and thread

Directions

1. Mix the herbs in the bowl.

2. Stuff the herbs into one pillowcase and sew it shut.

3. Put the herb pillow inside another pillowcase. Sweet dreams!

Yield: 1 Herbal Sleep Pillow

MAKING YOUR OWN CASES

If you do any home sewing, you may enjoy making your own pillowcases to fill with sleep-enhancing herbs. To make one case, cut two pieces of plain fabric 12 × 14 inches. Put the right sides of the fabric together and sew the two pieces together on three sides, 1 inch from the outside edge. Turn the fabric right-side-out, stuff the pillow with the herbs and sew the remaining edge shut. Follow the same procedure to make the outer case, using decorative fabric. Stuff the plain filled pillow inside the decorative case and sew the decorative case shut.

Simply Wonderful Herbal Cream

This silky smooth cream, created by California herbalist Shatoiya de la Tour of Dry Creek Herb Farm and Learning Center, is a snap to make and very nourishing for all types of skin. Use a very clean food processor or blender to whip up a batch for yourself or as a gift for a friend.

Ingredients and Supplies

> 1 cup grapeseed oil
> 4 ounces grated beeswax
> Double boiler
> 1¼ cup distilled water or rosewater
> ½ cup aloe vera gel
> ¼ cup herb tincture of your choice
>   (calendula is one good choice)
> Food processor or blender (very clean)
> 2 teaspoons lavender essential oil
> Sterilized storage jars

Directions

1. Heat the oil and the beeswax gently in the double boiler just until the beeswax melts.

2. Place the water, aloe vera gel, and herb tincture in the food processor.

3. Process on high speed.

4. Pour the oil mixture in a thin stream through the feeding tube, adding the essential oil last. Stop the machine and scrape the sides as needed.

5. When the cream is smooth, pour it into jars. Stored in a cool, dry place, this cream will keep well for at least 6 months.

Yield: About 2 cups of herbal body cream

A Dandy Dandelion Cure

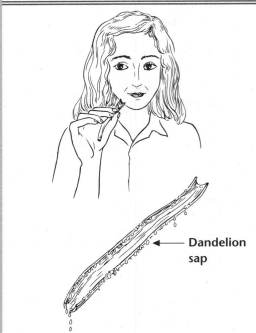

Dandelion sap

You can help pimples clear up with dandelion sap! Slit open the stem of a dandelion flower stalk and dab on some of the sticky white sap. Repeat every several hours. Often, the spots will disappear overnight.

Herbal Cream Aids Aching Feet

When you have tired feet after spending a day touring gardens or plant shopping, try this foot cream formulated to help runners who suffer from tired, sore feet. Created by Aubrey Hampton of Aubrey Organics in Tampa, Florida, this cream softens and soothes the skin and increases circulation. Here's how you can make Feet Relief at home.

Ingredients and Supplies

1 package (10.5 ounces) firm silken tofu
Small mixing bowl
Whisk
3 tablespoons fresh aloe vera flesh or organic aloe vera gel
4 tablespoons shea butter
Blender

3 tablespoons grain alcohol or vodka
3 tablespoons jojoba oil
½ cup olive oil
1 cayenne pepper
2 drops each essential oils of eucalyptus, ginger, peppermint, tea tree, camphor, and wintergreen
Clean storage jar

Directions

1. Place the tofu in a small mixing bowl and whisk until it breaks up.

2. Put the tofu, aloe vera, and shea butter (found in health food stores) in the blender and mix for 1 minute.

3. Turn off blender and stir lightly.

4. Add alcohol and continue to alternate blending with stirring until the mixture is uniform in texture.

5. Add the jojoba oil and blend.

6. Use the cayenne pepper and olive oil to make an infused oil, following the procedure described in "Basic Herb-Infused Oil" on page 231.

7. Add 3 tablespoons of the cayenne pepper oil to the mixture and blend.

8. Add essential oils and continue blending until the cream is smooth.

9. Pour the cream into a clean jar, and store it in the refrigerator for up to 2 weeks.

10. To use, apply the cream to your feet at night after washing them. Be sure to wash your hands after using the cream. Do not get the cream on your face or near your eyes—it will burn. Also avoid getting the cream into any open wounds.

Yield: About 1 pint of foot massage cream

Note: Shea butter is made from the seeds of the shea tree, a tree native to tropical Africa. It is nonallergenic and excellent for dry skin.

Although cayenne pepper oil creates an initial burning sensation, it ultimately relieves pain by blocking the activity of substance P, which is necessary for the transmission of pain impulses to the central nervous system.

Herb-Scented Foot and Body Warmers

What's stuffed with grain, applied hot or cold, and comforts aching muscles and cold feet? A pillow. But not just any pillow! This one is filled with flaxseed and rice and can be heated in the microwave to provide fragrant, warm heat or chilled in the freezer to cool a fever or over-extended muscles.

"I discovered these in a specialty gift shop a few years ago," says Alison Melotti-Cormack, an artist in Chambersburg, Pennsylvania. Alison toyed with the design, creating a prototype that she likes even better than the original inspiration. "It's important to use all-cotton fabrics," cautions Alison. "You don't know what will happen if you heat synthetics in a microwave."

Herb-scented foot and body warmers make the perfect holiday gift for cold winter days.

Ingredients and Supplies

⅓ yard 100% cotton muslin
⅓ yard 100% cotton flannel
9 × 9½ inches paper pattern piece
    (to be cut on the fold)
9½ × 10½ inches paper pattern piece
Thread
Sewing machine
3½ cups long-grain white rice
2 cups flaxseed
Herb sachet (lavender is Alison's
    favorite)

Directions

To make the inner muslin pillow:

1. Using the smaller pattern, cut 2 rectangles, both on the fold of the muslin.
2. Stitch all sides together using ½-inch seam allowances and leaving a 2- to 3-inch opening on one short side. Reinforce the corners by sewing over them several times.

HERBAL EYE PILLOW EASES HEADACHES

To make a soothing eye pillow, make a 7½ × 3½-inch pillowcase from a woven soft fabric such as silk, suede, or flannel. Fill with flaxseed mixed with a few tablespoons of lavender buds and sew shut. To use, chill in the freezer and lay over forehead and eyes for sweet relief. 🎭

3. Turn the muslin sack so that the seam allowances are on the inside.
4. Fill the sack with the rice and flaxseed. (Make a funnel from a piece of paper for easier filling.)
5. Stitch the opening shut.
6. Check for any leaks by tipping the sack from hand to hand, mixing the rice and flaxseed at the same time.

To make the outer flannel pillowcase:

1. Using the smaller pattern, cut 1 rectangle of flannel on the fold.

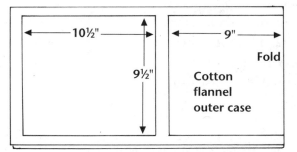

Cut on fold 9" × 9½"

2. Using the larger pattern, cut 2 rectangles of flannel.

3. Hem one of the short seams on each of the 2 flaps of flannel.

4. Lay out the long side of the flannel with right sides up. Overlap the 2 flaps with hemmed sides in the middle and right sides facing downward.

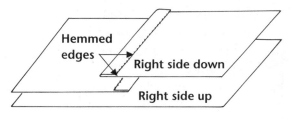

5. Stitch around the periphery of the flannel sack again, reinforcing the corners and double-stitching over the overlaps.

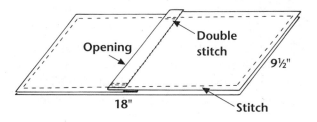

6. Trim seams and corners and turn right sides out. Insert the grain sack through the opening in the middle. Shake and flatten out the grain sack evenly.

7. For warm applications, heat the pillow in the microwave for 2 to 3 minutes. Warm your hands by placing them inside the flap, wrap the pillow around tired shoulders, lay it over cold feet, or place it in the back of your chair or car seat to ease back pain.

For moist heat, place a cup of water in the microwave when heating the pillow. Then lay the pillow over your eyes, nose, and cheeks to ease sinus congestion.

For cold applications, such as reducing swelling, freeze the pillow until it is cold.

8. Be sure to remove the grain sack before washing the flannel pillowcase.

Yield: 1 Herb-Scented Foot and Body Warmer

Note: It's easy to enhance the healing properties of this pillow with herbs. Just drop a small herb sachet into the outer pillow case along with the grain sack. Remove the herbs when heating or chilling the pillow. "I don't add the herbs to the grain sack because they'll need to be refreshed long before the pillow wears out," explains Alison. "And I don't use essential oils, as the scent will remain in the pillow for longer than you may like." By the way, the rice smells wonderful when it's heated.

Herbal Powder Keeps Feet Fresh

Have you been looking for a simple powder to keep feet and footwear fresh? Herbalist Gail Ulrich, author of *Herbs to Enhance Immunity* and founding director of Blazing Star Herbal School in Shelburne Falls, Massachusetts, has this easy recipe to share. "Mix in a few drops of tea tree oil to the powder if foot fungus is a problem," Gail says.

Ingredients and Supplies

½ cup cornstarch
½ cup arrowroot powder
¼ cup powdered calendula petals
      (*Calendula officinalis*)
1 tablespoon black walnut hull or
      chaparral leaf powder
Small mixing bowl
Yogurt cup with lid
½ teaspoon essential oils such as lavender,
      lemon, peppermint, and/or tea tree
Shaker container

Directions

1. Mix together all dry ingredients in a bowl.
2. Put a small amount of the mix in the yogurt cup, and add the essential oils.
3. Shake well to mix.
4. Return the mix to the bowl and mix again.
5. Pour the mix into a shaker container. It will keep indefinitely.

Yield: About 1 cup of herbal foot powder

YARROW FIRST-AID TINCTURE

It's great to feel the warm earth between your toes while you garden. But it's no fun when your bare feet meet with sharp or hard objects in the soil. Keep this simple yarrow tincture on hand for times when your feet (or other parts) need a little first aid.

"Yarrow is my all-purpose remedy for cuts, scrapes, and bruises," says herbalist Margi Flint of Earthsong Herbals in Marblehead, Massachusetts. Margi makes yarrow tincture from the white flowers of the plant and keeps it handy in a plastic spray bottle.

Fill a 1-quart glass jar loosely with fresh yarrow flowers, then add vodka (the cheapest you can buy) to the jar to cover them, allowing for 2 inches of clear alcohol at the top. Let the jar sit for two to three weeks at room temperature, then strain out the yarrow. Fill a quart-size spray bottle with the yarrow tincture and add 20 drops of lavender essential oil. To use, shake the bottle well and spray directly on bruises, cuts, and scrapes. Repeat every several hours until healing is evident. This tincture will keep for at least five years. 🐾

Soak Your Feet in Soothing Herbs

So you think you have tired, aching feet? "This recipe gets a lot of use on the days we're parading around the Sterling Renaissance Festival in period footwear," says Sue-Ryn Burns, herbalist at Hill Woman Productions on Wellesley Island, New York. The herbs in this dried blend are soothing and cleansing and may even help protect your feet against fungal disease.

Ingredients and Supplies

2 parts red clover flowers (*Trifolium pratense*)
2 parts violet leaves and flowers
1 part clary sage leaves (*Salvia sclarea*)
1 part calendula flowers (*Calendula officinalis*)
1 part lavender buds and leaves
1 part thyme leaves
Mixing bowl
Airtight storage container
Nonreactive glass or stainless steel
    saucepan
Strainer
Plastic wash basin or other footbath pan
Essential oils (optional)

Directions

1. Mix all of the herbs together in the mixing bowl.
2. Place the mixture in an airtight container and store it in a cool, dry place—it will stay fresh for up to 1 year.

Nurture your soil and your soles with a garden cover crop of red clover. Sow this clover between the rows of your garden in late summer and let it protect the soil over the winter. When the clover blooms next summer, gather its flowers to use in this soothing foot soak.

3. To use, simmer 3 tablespoons of the herb mix in 2 cups of water in the saucepan for 15 minutes.
4. Strain the mixture into a pan that is big enough to accommodate both feet.
5. Add enough lukewarm water to cover your feet. (Add essential oils, if desired.)
6. Relax for at least 15 minutes.

Refreshing Rosewater

Remember the rosewater your grandmother used? "Although rosewater is usually produced by distilling fresh rose petals," says herbalist Rosemary Gladstar, founder of Sage Mountain in East Barre, Vermont, and author of *Herbal Healing for Women*, "the following recipe is easy to make and just as effective." The more fragrant the petals, the stronger the scent of the lotion.

Ingredients and Supplies

> 3 cups fresh rose petals
> Glass quart jar
> 3 cups distilled witch hazel extract
> 1 cup distilled water
> Strainer
> Linen towel, muslin, or cheesecloth

Directions

1. Place the rose petals in the glass jar, filling it to 3 inches from the top.

2. Mix the witch hazel extract with the distilled water.

3. Fill the jar to the top with the liquid mixture.

4. Cover tightly, label and date, and place in a warm shaded area. Let the mixture sit for 2 to 3 weeks.

5. Strain the rose petals from the liquid by pouring it through linen towel, muslin, or cheesecloth. Wring out the cloth to remove extra rosewater.

6. Store the rosewater in a covered bottle. The rosewater will keep indefinitely, but the fragrance is best within the first year after you make this soothing lotion.

7. To use, apply with a piece of cotton or spray lightly on your face. Rosewater is gentle enough to use around the eyes and can actually be used as a compress to refresh tired eyes.

Yield: 1 quart of rosewater

BLACK EYE BLUES?

Poked your eye on a tomato stake? To soothe a black eye, Matthew Wood, author of *The Book of Herbal Wisdom,* recommends a comfrey poultice. Simply bruise a few comfrey leaves (*Symphytum officinale*) and lay them over the affected area. That ugly bruise will fade in a twinkle. If you're pregnant, don't try this without consulting a doctor first.

Cloves Add Taste to Paste

Brushing your teeth with baking soda or salt still makes for good daily hygiene. Herbalist Stephanie Tourles, author of *The Herbal Body Book* and owner of September's Sun Herbal Soap Company, recommends adding a touch of cloves.

Ingredients and Supplies

- 1 teaspoon baking soda or fine sea salt
- 1 drop peppermint, clove, cinnamon, or spearmint essential oil
- Chopstick or other utensil (for stirring)

Directions

1. Combine the baking soda or salt with the essential oil in a small dish.

2. Use a chopstick or other utensil to mix the ingredients together until they form a smooth, thick paste. If the mixture is runny, add a little more baking soda or salt—a runny powder won't stay on your toothbrush.

3. Put some of the mixture on a toothbrush, and brush your teeth as you would with any commercial toothpaste. Rinse thoroughly.

Spicy Herbal Mouthwash

For naturally fresh breath, use homemade mouthwash with fresh herbs and spices, says herbalist Tina James of Reisterstown, Maryland. If you are using fresh herbs, triple the amount of herbs in the recipe.

Ingredients and Supplies

- 1 tablespoon dried blackberry leaves
- 1 tablespoon dried thyme
- 1 tablespoon dried peppermint
- 1 tablespoon cloves, crushed
- 1 tablespoon nutmeg, freshly grated
- Clean glass jar with lid
- 2 cups vodka (the cheapest you can buy)
- Strainer
- Storage container
- Essential oil of peppermint (optional)

Directions

1. Combine herbs and spices in the jar.

2. Add vodka and stir or shake to make sure that the herbs are covered.

3. Steep at room temperature for 2 weeks.

4. Strain liquid into storage container. It will keep indefinitely.

5. To use, add 2 tablespoons of mouthwash concentrate to ½ cup water. Swish a comfortable amount in your mouth, then spit it out. Repeat until your mouth feels fresh.

Yield: About 2 cups of spicy mouthwash

Comfrey Poultice

Comfrey is a time-honored and effective remedy for bruises, sprains, and even broken bones. "In fact," says herbalist Laurieann Quiry, who practices at Mount Lebanon Herbals in New Lebanon, New York, "comfrey's common name is 'knit bone.'" You can make a poultice from fresh leaves and apply it directly to the affected area.

Whole dried leaves can also be used for poultices. If the leaves are chopped, use warm water to make them into a paste. Wrap the wound with gauze to hold the paste in place.

Ingredients and Supplies

Saucepan
Tongs
Fresh comfrey leaves (*Symphytum officinale*)
Bandage (optional)

Directions

1. Boil water in the saucepan.
2. Using tongs, dip comfrey leaves into the boiling water.
3. Remove the leaves and let them cool until they are cool enough to touch.
4. Wrap the leaves around the wound, holding them in place with a bandage, if necessary.
5. Repeat with freshly heated leaves every 30 minutes.

Note: This poultice is for external use only; do not apply to cuts or open wounds.

GARDENER'S BAND-AID

Lamb's-ears leaf

Blade of grass

"Here's a wonderful remedy I teach all the kids who visit us at Heart's Ease Herb Shop & Gardens in Cambria, California," says Sharon Lovejoy, author of the children's classic *Sunflower Houses*. For minor cuts and scratches, wash the wound, then open an aloe vera leaf and squeeze some of the gel onto the hurt. Next, find a lamb's-ears (*Stachys byzantina*) leaf to wrap around the cut. Tie it in place with a piece of grass. Voilà! An emergency Band-Aid!

Plantain Bath for Poison Ivy

Gardeners who've suffered from an encounter with poison ivy will love this simple and soothing natural bath formula. "Plantain is one of the most useful, yet underused, medicinal herbs," says herbalist Kathleen Maier, who has a clinical and teaching practice in Flint Hill, Virginia. "The leaves can be used both internally and externally to draw out toxins of many kinds, including those of poison ivy." In addition to drinking plantain tea, you can relax in a plantain bath for quick relief.

Ingredients and Supplies

4–5 handfuls fresh plantain leaves
(*Plantago major*)
2 quarts boiling water
Nonreactive glass or stainless steel
saucepan
Strainer
Cheesecloth

Directions

1. Simmer plantain and water in saucepan for 40 minutes to make an infusion.
2. Strain, saving the greens.
3. Add plantain infusion to water in the bathtub. Relax in the water for at least 20 minutes.
4. After bathing, place the cooked plantain greens in the cheesecloth and pat over affected areas.

Yield: 2 quarts of plantain bath infusion

PLANTAIN EASES THE ITCH AND BURN

If you're itching and scratching but just don't have time for a soothing plantain bath, herbalist Carolyn Lee Tubman, who teaches and practices in Milford, Virginia, can recommend a quick fix. Just juice 1 cup of plantain leaves (*Plantago major*) at high speed in a blender or food processor with 3 to 4 cups of water to make a slurry, and dab it on areas affected by poison ivy, stinging nettle, or insect bites. But save a little of the chlorophyll-rich liquid to drink, suggests Carolyn. Rich in bioflavanoids, chlorophyll is an excellent blood purifier and aids digestion as well. Dilute 1 part of the slurry with 3 parts of apple juice or water to make the drink. "Be sure to freeze some plantain juice into ice cubes for emergency use," Carolyn adds.

Poison Ivy Liniment

Herbalist Paul Carmichael, owner of Lily of the Valley Herbs, a retail and mail-order herb shop in Minerva, Ohio, suggests using this goldenseal liniment to soothe not only poison ivy rash, but also clean abrasions, insect bites, ringworm, and other skin rashes. His kids dubbed Paul's best-selling recipe "boo-boo juice."

Ingredients and Supplies

1 tablespoon goldenseal root powder
 (*Hydrastis canadensis*)
1 tablespoon myrrh powder
1 tablespoon white oak bark powder
Glass jar
2 cups isopropyl alcohol
Strainer lined with muslin
16-ounce bottle with cap

Directions

1. Place herbs in the jar and pour in alcohol.
2. Shake well daily.
3. Let the mixture sit for 2 weeks, then strain it into a bottle.
4. To use, dab the liniment on rashes, insect bites, or abrasions.

Yield: 2 cups of "boo-boo juice"

Note: This liniment keeps indefinitely

A Jewel of a Cure

Nature usually offers amends for her plagues. Quite often, the cause and cure are neighbors. Such is the case with jewelweed (*Impatiens capensis*), which grows abundantly at the edges of streams and moist woodlands right alongside that troublesome poison ivy vine. For quick relief from poison ivy, pinch off a piece of jewelweed, slit the stem, and rub the juice on affected areas. To make an emergency stash, cover a pot of jewelweed (leaves, stems, and flowers) with water, simmer until reduced by half, and freeze into cubes. Use the cubes directly on the skin or melt them and make a compress with the liquid. Jewelweed also eases the itch and sting of stinging nettle and insect bites. 🍃

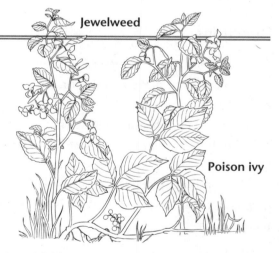

Jewelweed

Poison ivy

When you need relief from the itching caused by poison ivy, jewelweed is a gem. Simply split the stem of the jewelweed and apply the juice to affected areas. As luck would have it, jewelweed often grows right beside the irritating ivy.

Invincible Herbal Insect Repellent

"Gardeners and hikers need powerful insect protection up in these hills," says Tina Wilcox, head gardener at the Ozark Folk Center in Mountain View, Arkansas. "So before heading outdoors, I douse myself with an incredible repellent that my friend Marion Spear and I concocted," Tina says. "It renders me almost invincible to both insects and poison ivy!"

Ingredients and Supplies

Large handful fresh jewelweed
   (*Impatiens capensis*)
Large glass jar with plastic lid (vinegar
   corrodes metal)
Strainer
1 quart apple cider vinegar
½ teaspoon pennyroyal oil
1 teaspoon eucalyptus oil
1 teaspoon orange oil
1 teaspoon citronella oil
Plastic spray bottle

Directions

1. Crush jewelweed in the jar and cover with vinegar.

2. Let steep for several days.

3. Strain out the jewelweed and mix essential oils into the vinegar.

4. Before applying all over, spray a small amount on the inside of your arm and monitor for 15 minutes for any allergic reaction.

5. To use, spray thoroughly on clothing and lightly on any exposed skin except your face. Reapply every ½ hour or so. (To keep insects away from your face, spray your hat or bandanna.)

Yield: About 1 quart of invincible spray

Note: This formula will keep indefinitely.

Caution: If you are pregnant, don't use pennyroyal, even topically, as it may increase the risk of miscarriage.

CHASE AWAY PESTS WITH PENNYROYAL

You can grow your own pest repellent and save a bundle on commercial sprays with a small patch of pennyroyal (either *Mentha pulegium* or *Hedeoma pulegioides*). Plant this pest-repelling herb near your garden or back door. When you head out to do gardening or yard work, grab a handful of leaves, crush them, and rub them on your skin. The oil from the foliage will leave a pleasant minty fragrance on your skin while keeping away flies, mosquitoes, gnats, ticks, and chiggers. It really does work at keeping pests at bay; in fact, many commercial repellents contain pennyroyal oil.

Here's a potpourri of quick herbal fixes for minor health woes ranging from allergies to toothaches. Keep in mind that if you have any injury that's potentially serious, you should seek professional medical assistance.

Allergy attack. Sneezing while you're out walking? "No problem," says Minnesota herbalist Matthew Wood, author of *The Book of Herbal Wisdom*. "Look for some ragweed (*Ambrosia artemisiifolia*) and nibble on the leaf. This can clear up your symptoms, but if it doesn't work instantly, it's not going to help. Ragweed causes allergies because its pollen grains lodge in the nasal passages and irritate the tissues. The leaves are safe. This shows that the plant can cure what it causes!"

Plantain

Echinacea　　**Yarrow**

Bee sting. Grab a plantain leaf (*Plantago major*), chew it up, and smack it on the skin. It offers quick relief that even little kids can use. In fact, herbalist Margi Flint of Earthsong Herbals in Marblehead, Massachusetts, reports that when a visiting friend who is extremely allergic to bee stings was stung, "I gave her a plantain leaf to chew on while I dialed 9-1-1. Before the emergency crew arrived, her symptoms had disappeared. Now she carries plantain with her wherever she goes!" (Note: If you're allergic to bee stings, don't rely on plantain alone to relieve your reaction. Get medical help to be sure you recover safely.)

Bleeding. Apply fresh yarrow flowers or leaves to the wound. Periwinkle leaves (*Vinca major*) are also great styptics—just crush the leaf and press it into the wound (or in your nose for a nosebleed.) To help fend off infection, try chewing on some echinacea root (*Echinacea angustifolia*) or take a dose of echinacea tincture. Herbalist Laurieann Quiry of New Lebanon, New York, says, "Echinacea has powerful antiseptic and antibacterial qualities."

Boils. Use a rolling pin to bruise a cabbage leaf. Tie the cabbage leaf around the boil with a bandage. Change every 30 minutes.

Coughs and colds. "Here's an old-fashioned remedy," says herbalist Tina James of Reisterstown, Maryland. Grate an onion and place it in a heat-proof container with 2 tablespoons of thyme leaves. Add 2 cups of boiling water, cover, and let steep for at least 20 minutes. Strain into a teacup, add lemon and honey, and drink.

Earache. "Chop plantain leaves finely and squeeze out the juice through gauze, or bruise some plantain leaves in your hands until you extract a few drops of juice," advises medical herbalist Claudia Wingo. "Then put a couple of drops in your ear." If you suspect that your eardrum has been perforated, do not use herbal ear drops.

Gas pains. Crush fennel seeds with a mortar and pestle and brew them into a tea. Fennel seed tea also gives quick yet gentle relief to colicky babies. Caution: Some individuals may have an allergic reaction to fennel.

Headache. Simply chew on a leaf of feverfew (*Chrysanthemum parthenium*); some migraine sufferers eat a single feverfew leaf each day to ward off these severe headaches. Feverfew-flower or lavender-flower tea is also effective. (Caution: If you are pregnant, consult with a physician before using any formula that contains feverfew.) Also try rubbing lavender essential oil into the painful areas. (Lavender is one of the few essential oils that can be used directly on the skin.)

Sticker in your finger. Plantain comes to the rescue again. Chew on the leaf and place it on the problem. Tie it in place with a piece of grass or vine, if needed. Replace the leaf every 30 minutes. Within a few hours, you should be able to squeeze the splinter out.

Stomachache. Chew on some mint leaves or make a cup of mint tea. Ginger root (*Zingiber officinale*) tea is also excellent for relieving nausea and motion sickness.

Sunburn. Ouch! Aloe vera soothes the burn. If your aloe vera plant is too small to provide enough to swab all of the affected skin, use purchased aloe vera gel or take the plantain poison ivy bath described on page 257. Or simply add 2 cups of apple cider vinegar to

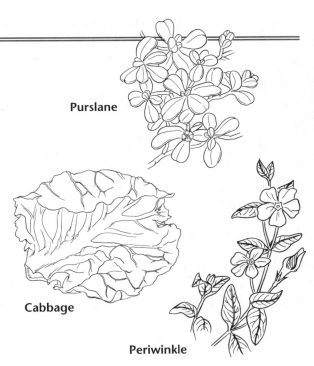

Purslane

Cabbage

Periwinkle

the tub. St.-John's-wort oil applied directly to the skin also gives quick relief for sunburn pain. Avoid additional sun exposure after applying St.-John's-wort oil, as it can make your skin more sensitive to sunlight.

Sun-weary. If too much time in the garden leaves you feeling hot and dry, "Look around for some purslane (*Portulaca oleracea*)," advises Richo Cech of Horizon Herbs in Williams, Oregon. "Munch on the vitamin-rich leaves to rehydrate and re-mineralize your body. You can also chew some of the leaves and lay them over your eyes for quick cooling relief."

Toothache. Essential oil of cloves is an age-old remedy for numbing tooth pain. Put a dab of the oil on a cotton swab and dot the painful area, avoiding the lips and tongue.

Plantain leaf is also great for a toothache. Chew up the leaf and wad it around the painful tooth.

Fight Allergies with Herbs

Are pollen allergies keeping you out of the garden? "When allergy season arrives, we have people standing in line at the shop for this remedy," says Claudia Wingo, a registered nurse and medical herbalist who practices at the Smile Herb Shop in College Park, Maryland. "Start taking this herbal tincture about two weeks before the pollen gets thick," Claudia advises. "The results are truly miraculous."

Ingredients and Supplies

Equal parts fresh leaves of ground ivy (*Glechoma hederacea*), plantain (*Plantago major* or *P. lanceolata*), and stinging nettle (*Urtica dioica*)

Quart glass jar

1 quart vodka

Strainer lined with linen handkerchief or cheesecloth

Eyedropper bottle

Directions

1. Fill jar about ⅓ full with fresh herbs. If you use stinging nettle, be sure to gather the leaves before the plants begin to flower.

2. Fill the jar with vodka.

3. Let the mixture steep for 2 to 3 weeks at room temperature.

4. Strain. Fill an eyedropper bottle with the tincture for daily use.

5. To use, put 20 to 25 drops of the tincture into a small glass of water and drink. Repeat 3 or 4 times a day. For best results, begin

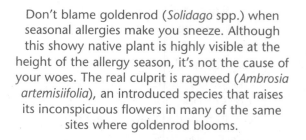

Goldenrod

Ragweed

Don't blame goldenrod (*Solidago* spp.) when seasonal allergies make you sneeze. Although this showy native plant is highly visible at the height of the allergy season, it's not the cause of your woes. The real culprit is ragweed (*Ambrosia artemisiifolia*), an introduced species that raises its inconspicuous flowers in many of the same sites where goldenrod blooms.

taking drops 2 weeks before allergy season and continue until the air clears.

6. Store remainder in a glass jar in a cool, dark place. The tincture will keep for up to 5 years in these conditions.

Yield: About 1 quart of allergy-fighting tincture

Soothing Flea-Bite Wash

To soothe your pet's flea-bitten skin, swab on this herbal infusion created by Maine herbalist Deb Soule of Avena Botanicals, author of *The Roots of Healing: A Woman's Book of Herbs*. Because this formula calls for dried herbs, the mix can be stored for long-term use. If you use fresh herbs, triple the amount of each.

Deb says it helps to apply a healing balm after washing the sore areas. She recommends calendula oil or salve. (Also try "Jack the Dog's Herbal Skin Oil" on page 264.)

Ingredients and Supplies

½ cup dried rosemary leaf
½ cup dried calendula flowers
   (*Calendula officinalis*)
¼ cup dried stinging nettle leaf
   (*Urtica dioica*)
¼ cup dried comfrey leaf
   (*Symphytum officinale*)
¼ cup dried red clover flowers
   (*Trifolium pratense*)
Mixing bowl
Airtight storage container
Non-aluminum saucepan with lid
Strainer

Directions

1. Mix the dried herbs. Store them in an airtight storage container in a cool, dry place for up to 6 months.
2. To make the herbal wash, boil 1 quart of water and stir in 6 tablespoons of the dried herb blend.
3. Turn off heat, cover, and let the infusion steep overnight.
4. The next day, strain the herbs.
5. With a clean cloth, rinse sore areas with the infusion.
6. Repeat several times a day.

Yield: 1¾ cups of dried herb mix (enough to make about 6 quarts of soothing herbal wash)

Note: Comfrey is considered unsafe for internal use by humans. Make sure your pet doesn't lap up this soothing wash while you're applying it.

Give Fleas a Salty Send-Off

After bathing your pet to rid it of fleas, sprinkle salt around areas where animals lie, advises Deb Soule. "Salt dehydrates the fleas and they die."

Piney Flea Shampoo

Here's a safe, effective flea shampoo from herbalist Deb Soule, author of *The Roots of Healing: A Woman's Book of Herbs* and proprietor of Avena Botanicals, an herbal apothecary in Rockport, Maine.

Ingredients and Supplies

1 cup liquid castile soap
⅛ ounce essential oil of pine
Plastic squeeze bottle

Directions

1. Measure soap and pine oil into the plastic bottle and shake well.

2. Add the full amount to your pet's bath water.

Yield: 1 cup of herbal flea shampoo

Jack the Dog's Herbal Skin Oil

To heal sores and "hot spots" that animals can't seem to leave alone, animal herbalist Barb Dawson of Atlanta, Georgia, created this soothing skin oil. "Jack is an Afghan hound I helped rescue," explains Barb. "He was so anxious that he chewed on himself if I left him alone for a minute. That's how this skin oil came about." The story has a happy ending: Jack's sores healed, and he has a wonderful new home.

Ingredients and Supplies

1 part fresh calendula flowers
(*Calendula officinalis*)
1 part fresh sweet fern leaves
(*Comptonia peregrina*)
2 1-pint glass jars with straight sides and tight-fitting lids
1 part fresh comfrey leaves
(*Symphytum officinale*)
Almond oil (the best quality you can afford)

Chopstick
Strainer lined with muslin or linen
Sterilized glass jars for storage
Goldenseal root tincture
(*Hydrastis canadensis*)
Lavender essential oil
Rosemary essential oil
Eyedropper bottle
Gauze

Directions

1. Place equal amounts of calendula flowers and sweet fern leaves in one glass jar.

2. Place comfrey leaves in the other glass jar.

3. Pour enough almond oil in each jar to cover the herbs.

4. Slide a chopstick into the oil to release any air bubbles, then cap jars tightly.

5. Place jars in a sunny window.

6. Wipe the inside of each jar and lid occasionally to remove any moisture.

7. After 2 weeks, strain out plant parts.

8. Store oils in separate sterilized glass jars.

9. Before applying, pour equal amounts of the calendula/sweet fern oil and the comfrey oil into a clean bottle.

10. For each 8 ounces of almond oil, add 4 droppersful of goldenseal tincture and 1 capful of each of the essential oils; shake well.

11. Label and date the bottle. This formula will keep for up to a year if stored in a cool, dark location.

12. To apply, shake the bottle well before each use. Apply liberally to damaged skin using a piece of gauze to dab the oil in place. Try not to rub the sore skin.

Note: Comfrey is considered unsafe for internal use by humans. Make sure your pet doesn't lap up this herbal skin oil while you're applying it.

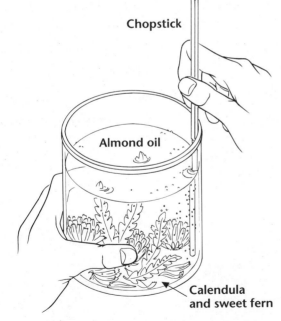

Chopstick

Almond oil

Calendula and sweet fern

It's important to prevent mold from developing while infusing oil with herbs. Air bubbles are possible troublemakers because they can trap water vapors from the herbs and the vapors may promote mold. Get rid of any air bubbles in the herb and oil mixture by occasionally stirring it with a chopstick.

Lid

Moisture under the lid and around the insides of the jar can also encourage mold. Occasionally wipe these areas while the oil-and-herb mixture is setting.

Chapter 10

FANTASTIC YARD AND GARDEN DESIGN FORMULAS

Growing Great Gardens from the Ground Up

The formulas in this chapter make it easy to grow fabulous flower gardens and easy-care lawns. You'll even find a formula for an eye-pleasing mesclun mix that'll fill your salad bowl with tasty, healthful greens. The general information that follows gives you details on preparing the soil for planting seeds or transplants. (See "Seeding a Lawn" on page 305 for lawn seeding instructions and "Growing Wildflowers from Seed" on page 287 for details on sowing wildflower mixes.) Finding and carrying out great yard and garden designs doesn't get much easier than this!

Getting Rid of Weeds and Sod

When you're starting a new garden or lawn, it pays to get rid of competing plants. A slow but easy method is to smother the existing grass or weeds with compost (see "Compost Your Weeds Away" on page 165 for details). Stripping the sod from the soil or rotary tilling the area are faster but more labor-intensive methods.

Strip off the grass. You can use a garden spade to remove sod from your lawn in strips. Slice the edges of a sod strip about 1½ feet wide and 2 to 3 feet long. Then shove the spade under the strip to cut the roots. Roll up the strip so that it's easy to carry away.

Another option is to rent a sod stripper—a gas-powered machine that pushes a blade under the sod to slice the roots. Sod strippers work best on healthy, dense lawns; patchy lawns tend to fall apart.

Turn weeds under. For weedy areas and weak lawns, till the area several times with a rotary tiller or, for large areas, with a tractor-pulled cultivator. Allow a few weeks between tillings for dormant seeds and plant roots to start growing again. It helps to rake the area after each tilling to remove chunks of grass and other plants that could otherwise reroot. Water the tilled area to speed up the regrowth of any remaining weeds and grasses and then repeat the tilling process.

Improving the Soil

Once the soil in your planting area is free of weeds, add fertilizers and soil amendments, such as limestone or sulfur, as recommended by soil test results. (See "Organic Soil Testing" on page 57 for details.)

Most future flower beds and almost all future lawns benefit from having 2 to 4 inches of compost, well-rotted manure, leaf mold, grass clippings, or other fine-textured organic matter worked into the top few inches of soil.

Shortly before you plant, rake or lightly till the soil with a metal rake to smooth it and break up clumps. Loosening the soil lightly encourages better seed-to-soil contact during germination. But tilling too deeply brings weed seeds to the surface, so don't work the soil any deeper than 1 inch.

The Does-Everything Garden

Talk about a hard-working garden! "This planting is easy, self-perpetuating, colorful, edible, and the birds and butterflies like it," claims Jan Johnson of Cathlamet, Washington. She recommends planting this mix of plants and seeds near an area where you often work or relax so that you'll get to watch the birds and butterflies that come to visit.

The amount you plant depends on how much area you'd like to cover—and how much you want to eat! The vegetable quantities listed below are enough for one person. The quantities listed for flowers are minimum amounts.

Ingredients and Supplies

8–10 'Blue Solaise' leeks

6 parsleys (flat or curly)

5 'Red Russian' kales (or curly varieties for colder climates)

3–5 Brazilian vervains (*Verbena bonariensis*)

1 seed packet Iceland poppy (*Papaver nudicaule*)

⅛ pound hairy vetch seed

Directions

1. Choose a sunny spot for your garden. All of these plants thrive in Jan's Zone 8 garden where winters *and* summers are wet, cool, and mild. But you can grow them at least as far north as Zone 4. Brazilian vervain is a perennial in Zones 7 to 10 but can be grown as an annual in colder areas.

2. Plant in spring. (You can plant in fall in regions with mild winters.) Because Jan uses seed she saves, she doesn't have exact quantities, but says, "I broadcast the seed like you'd feed chickens. I call it a liberal sprinkle."

3. Thin if you must. "If everything comes up gangbusters, I thin the kale to about 4 feet and the parsley to 2 feet," Jan says. Thin the leeks to 2 feet, the Brazilian vervain to 3 to 4 feet apart, and the hairy vetch to 2 to 3 feet apart. Do not thin the Iceland poppies.

Note: Add flowers like pot marigold (*Calendula officinalis*), chamomile (*Chamaemelum nobile*), and sweet alyssum (*Lobularia maritima*) to fill in any gaps in your garden that appear in the summer. Annual herbs, such as basil, also make good fillers.

Variation: Replace the 'Blue Solaise' leeks with any other leeks, or plant elephant garlic bulbs instead of leeks.

Why limit your garden to only flowers or vegetables? A mix of both plus herbs makes an attractive planting that you and the birds and butterflies will enjoy.

RECIPE FOR SUCCESS

Jan Johnson offers this potpourri of pointers for continued success with your does-everything garden.

- Replant the bottoms (roots and ¼ inch of stem) of harvested leeks or start new ones from seed in summer. In fall, bury the leeks with leaves to keep them over winter, then uncover and plant around them in spring.
- Plant parsley generously; swallowtail butterflies will lay eggs on the plants. Parsley flowers also attract beneficial insects, so let some plants bloom.
- Sprinkle kale seed sparingly or set out transplants. You can harvest and eat kale all winter and spring, but leave some plants to bolt and set seed in summer.

- Order Brazilian vervain plants from mail-order catalogs or, if you can get mature flower heads from a friend, just drop the dried flowers around the bed. Help seedlings and mature plants overwinter by surrounding them with straw mulch.
- Sow hairy vetch seed sparingly so it doesn't overwhelm the plants it twines around.
- Save seedheads for next year's planting. Gather the seedheads when they are dry and the seeds just begin to fall. Store the seedheads in paper sacks that have been tied shut to keep dust out. Put the bags in a cool, dry place until planting time the following spring.

Easy-Care Annual Bed

You've heard the saying, "The cobbler's children have no shoes." Well, in the gardening version, garden writers (and other busy folks) don't have time to garden! Iowa-based garden writer Veronica Fowler seldom has as much time to garden as she'd like, so she relies on plantings that give lots of impact for little effort.

"This is an easy garden for first-time gardeners," Veronica says, "because these plants thrive with very little care." (See "Easy-Care Annual Flowers" on the facing page for plant descriptions.) The planting is suitable for most areas of the country, but you'll need to irrigate regularly in hot, arid places.

Ingredients and Supplies

The letter in front of each plant name shows the plant's location in the plan on the facing page. The number of plants you'll need to order is in parentheses following the plant name.

- **A** White cleome (1 seed packet)
- **B** 'Versailles Blush Pink' cosmos (1 seed packet)
- **C** 'Zebrina' mallow (1 seed packet)
- **D** 'Lemon Gem' marigold or other small yellow marigold (1 seed packet)
- **E** 'Peter Pan White' zinnia or other dwarf white zinnias (1 seed packet)

Directions

1. Prepare the soil as described in "Getting Rid of Weeds and Sod" and "Improving the Soil" on page 267.

2. Two weeks after the last frost date, sow the seeds directly in the soil, placing them as shown in the plan on the facing page.

3. Keep the soil moist while the seeds germinate and make their first few inches of

This year, decorate your garden with easy-care, brightly flowered annuals. Annuals like cleome and cosmos often reseed, but their seedlings may not match the original varieties. If you want to ensure that you get specific varieties, order and plant the seed again each spring.

growth. When the plants are 1 inch high, thin small plants in front to about 6 inches apart and the taller plants in the middle and back to 1 foot apart.

EASY-CARE ANNUAL FLOWERS

Choose the plants listed here—or similar varieties of these plants—for a stunningly simple, color-filled garden.

PLANT	DESCRIPTION
A **White cleome** (*Cleome hasslerana*, **white cultivars**)	Clusters of 5-petaled flowers are 2 to 3 inches wide and have long stamens; plants reach 3 to 4 feet tall
B **'Versailles Blush Pink' cosmos** (*Cosmos bipinnatus* **'Versailles Blush Pink'**)	The 2½-inch-wide single blooms are pink with gold centers; flower stalks grow 20 to 25 inches tall
C **'Zebrina' mallow** (*Malva sylvestris* **'Zebrina'**)	The 3-inch-wide blooms are purple and white; plants grow 2½ feet tall
D **'Lemon Gem' marigold** (*Tagetes tenuifolia* **'Lemon Gem'**)	Dime-size clear yellow blooms grow on mounded 8- to 10-inch-tall plants
E **'Peter Pan White' zinnia** (*Zinnia elegans* **'Peter Pan White'**)	These 3½-inch-wide double blooms grow on 12-inch-tall flower stems

Easy-Care Annual Bed Plan

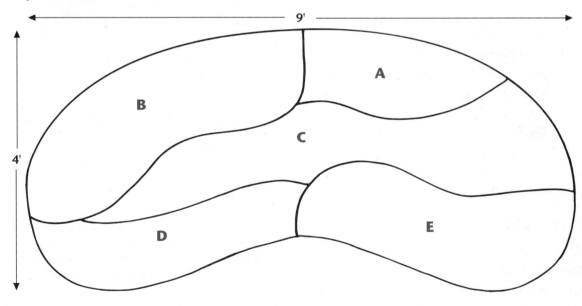

Mix-and-Match Bouquet Garden

Get more bang for your buck by mixing your own seeds together instead of buying premade mixes. You'll get the exact plants you want for less money.

Horticulturist Linda Harris of Ferry-Morse Seeds mixed several different plant varieties to create this beautiful bouquet garden. (See "Mix-and-Match Annual Flowers" on the facing page for plant descriptions.) Linda says she direct-seeded these easy, inexpensive annuals in her garden, "and it was gorgeous! I had plenty of flowers to cut right up until frost."

Ingredients and Supplies

1 seed packet 'Powderpuffs' China aster
1 seed packet 'Covent Garden' baby's-breath
1 seed packet double bachelor's-button
1 seed packet tall crested celosia
1 seed packet 'Sensation' series cosmos
1 seed packet 'Crackerjack' African marigold
1 seed packet dwarf annual phlox
1 seed packet pincushion flower
1 seed packet tall strawflower
1 seed packet 'Whirligig' zinnia

Directions

1. Sow seeds in spring. According to Linda, "You can either plant the seeds in an orderly fashion—in patches, bands, or rows—or mix them all together for more of a wildflower meadow look." If you're planting in bands or rows, follow the planting directions on the seed packet. If you're planting as a wildflower mix, see "Growing Wildflowers from Seed" on page 287 for instructions.

Sow a mix of attractive annuals like asters, celosia, and zinnias together in spring, and you'll have instant flower arrangements to gather in summer and fall.

2. Keep the soil moist for good growth.
3. Cut most flowers just before they open fully (cut celosia after it has opened fully) to use in arrangements.
4. Remove spent flowers to extend your garden's bloom time.

Mix-and-Match Annual Flowers

Whether you like fresh or dried bouquets, you'll find plenty of flowers to choose from in this mix. Plants marked with a single asterisk (*) are attractive when air dried. Plants marked with a double asterisk (**) dry best if you use silica gel (available from craft stores).

Plant	Description
**'Powderpuffs' China aster (*Callistephus chinensis* 'Powderpuffs')	Daisylike blooms are 2½ inches wide and come in a mix of blue, rose, and white; flower stalks grow 2 feet tall
*'Covent Garden' baby's-breath (*Gypsophila elegans* 'Covent Garden')	Airy sprays of white blooms open on 18- to 24-inch-tall flower stalks
*Double bachelor's-button (*Centaurea cyanus*, double cultivars)	Blue, pink, purple, red, and white blooms are 1 to 2 inches wide; flowers stalks grow 12 to 30 inches tall
*Tall crested celosia (*Celosia cristata*)	Blooms are 6 to 12 inches wide and look something like gold or red roosters' combs; flower stems grow 2 to 2½ feet tall
'Sensation' series cosmos (*Cosmos bipinnatus* 'Sensation' series)	Daisylike blooms are 2 inches wide and are crimson, pink, or white with yellow centers; flower stems grow 4 to 6 feet tall
**'Crackerjack' marigold (*Tagetes erecta* 'Crackerjack')	Large double blooms come in yellow, orange, and gold; plants grow 3 feet tall
Dwarf annual phlox (*Phlox drummondii*, dwarf cultivars)	Clusters of ½- to 1-inch-wide blooms are blue, lilac, purple, red, white, or yellow; plants reach 10 inches tall
Pincushion flower (*Scabiosa atropurpurea*)	Rounded 2-inch-wide blooms are blue, cream, lavender, maroon, pink, or white; flower stems reach 2 to 3 feet tall
*Tall strawflower (*Helichrysum bracteatum*, tall cultivars)	Daisylike blooms are 1 to 2 inches wide and come in red, yellow, rose, or orange; flower stems grow 2 to 4 feet tall
**'Whirligig' zinnia (*Zinnia elegans* 'Whirligig')	Double 4-inch-wide bicolored blooms come in combinations of yellow, orange, pink, red, and cream; flower stems grow 24 to 30 inches tall

Four-Season Garden

This nearly circular garden of low-growing heathers, flowering perennials, and small shrubs and trees looks interesting all year— even in winter. (See "Four-Season Plants" on the facing page for plant descriptions.) It was designed for constant color by Ellen Hornig, owner of Seneca Hill Perennials in Oswego, New York.

Ingredients and Supplies

The letter in front of each plant shows the plant's location in the plan on the facing page. The number of plants you'll need to order is in parentheses following the plant name.

A 'Crimson Pygmy' barberries (5 plants)
B Spiny bear's-breech (1)
C Weeping purple beech (1)
D Perennial candytufts (8)
E 'Album' bigroot cranesbills (5)
F 'Biokovo' cranesbills (5)
G Dalmatian cranesbills (7)
H 'Lawrence Flatman' grayleaf cranesbill (1)
I 'Splendens' grayleaf cranesbills (3)
J *Geranium renardii* (4)
K Siberian carpet cypress (4)
L 'Vivelli' heaths (3)
M 'Alba Rigida' heather (1)
N 'Allegro' heathers (4)
O 'Anthony Davis' heathers (3)
P 'Beoley Gold' heathers (3)
Q 'Black Beauty' heather (1)
R 'Caerketton' heathers (3)
S 'H. E. Beale' heathers (4)
T 'Hirsuta Typica' heather (1)
U 'Minima Smith's Variety' heathers (3)
V 'Mrs. R. H. Grey' heathers (2)
W 'Palace Purple' heucheras (5)
X Dwarf Japanese holly (1)
Y Paxistimas (3)
Z Pink tree peonies (2)
AA 'Scarlet Wonder' rhododendron (1)

Directions

In spring or fall, plant in a sunny to partly sunny location with moist, well-drained, acidic soil. For more on soil preparation and planting, see "Getting Rid of Weeds and Sod" and "Improving the Soil" on page 267.

Note: Ellen says that you can use a different cultivar of bigroot cranesbill; there are several excellent selections available. And she somewhat reluctantly adds that you can substitute another dwarf tree for the weeping purple beech, "although I really like the beech's leaf color, branching structure, and slow growth rate."

Variation: "You can substitute different varieties of heathers," Ellen says. She recommends using varieties with colors and textures that contrast in interesting ways. It's easy to get carried away with all the different varieties that are available. That's why Ellen warns you to pay attention to the plants' mature heights and spreads when you're making your selections.

FOUR-SEASON PLANTS

You'll get a delightful mix of flower and leaf colors when you set out this selection of plants. All thrive in full sun, except in southern areas where they prefer light shade.

PLANT	🌿 DESCRIPTION 🌞 HARDINESS ZONES
A 'Crimson Pygmy' barberry (*Berberis thunbergii* var. *atropurpurea* 'Crimson Pygmy')	Purple-leaved shrub has small yellow flowers in spring; plants grow 2 feet tall Zones 4 to 8
B Spiny bear's-breech (*Acanthus spinosus*—may be offered as *A. spinosissimus*)	Perennial with purple and white flowers that grow on 3- to 4-foot-tall spikes Zones 7 to 10
C Weeping purple beech (*Fagus sylvatica* 'Purpurea Pendula')	Weeping purple-leaved tree grows slowly but can reach 40 feet tall Zones 5 to 8
D Perennial candytuft (*Iberis sempervirens*)	Evergreen groundcover with white flowers in spring; grows 6 to 12 inches tall Zones 3 to 9
E 'Album' bigroot cranesbill (*Geranium macrorrhizum* 'Album')	Perennial with white flowers; plants grow 1 to 1½ feet tall Zones 3 to 10
F 'Biokovo' cranesbill (*Geranium* × *cantabrigiense* 'Biokovo')	Perennial that has white flowers with pink centers; plants grow 1 to 1½ feet tall Zones 5 to 10

(continued on page 276)

Four-Season Garden Plan

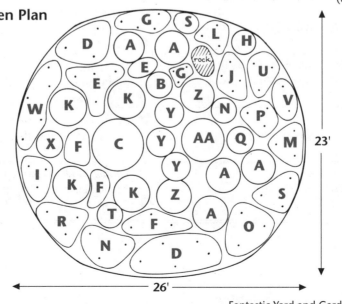

PLANT	DESCRIPTION / HARDINESS ZONES
G **Dalmatian cranesbill** (*Geranium dalmaticum*)	Perennial with mauve flowers; plants grow 4 to 6 inches tall Zones 4 to 8
H **'Lawrence Flatman' grayleaf cranesbill** (*Geranium cinereum* 'Lawrence Flatman')	Perennial with lilac-pink saucer-shaped flowers; plants grow 6 to 12 inches tall Zones 5 to 8
I **'Splendens' grayleaf cranesbill** (*Geranium cinereum* var. *subcaulescens* 'Splendens')	Perennial with deep red blooms; plants grow 5 to 6 inches tall Zones 5 to 8
J *Geranium renardii*	Perennial with small white flowers with violet veins; plants grow 1 foot tall Zones 4 to 10
K **Siberian carpet cypress** (*Microbiota decussata*)	Low juniperlike evergreen shrub grows 1 foot tall and spreads up to 15 feet wide Zones 2 to 8
L **'Vivelli' heath** (*Erica carnea* 'Vivelli')	Magenta flowers and dark green foliage on 9-inch-tall, 14-inch-wide plants Zones 4 to 7
M **'Alba Rigida' heather** (*Calluna vulgaris* 'Alba Rigida')	White flowers and bright green leaves on plants that are 6 inches tall and 10 inches wide Zones 4 to 10
N **'Allegro' heather** (*Calluna vulgaris* 'Allegro')	Ruby blooms and dark green foliage on 18-inch-tall and 24-inch-wide plants Zones 4 to 10
O **'Anthony Davis' heather** (*Calluna vulgaris* 'Anthony Davis')	White flowers and blue-gray-green leaves on 18-inch-tall and 20-inch-wide plants Zones 4 to 10
P **'Beoley Gold' heather** (*Calluna vulgaris* 'Beoley Gold')	White flowers and yellow foliage on 12- to 15-inch-tall plants that grow 20 inches wide Zones 4 to 10
Q **'Black Beauty' heather** (*Calluna vulgaris* 'Black Beauty')	Reddish buds and dark green leaves on 12-inch-tall plants that spread to 16 inches wide Zones 4 to 10

PLANT	🌿 DESCRIPTION ☀ HARDINESS ZONES
R 'Caerketton' heather (*Calluna vulgaris* 'Caerketton')	🌿 White blooms and medium green foliage on 10-inch-tall and 18-inch-wide plants ☀ Zones 4 to 10
S 'H. E. Beale' heather (*Calluna vulgaris* 'H. E. Beale')	🌿 Shell pink flowers and dark green leaves on plants that grow 2 feet tall and 2 feet wide ☀ Zones 4 to 10
T 'Hirsuta Typica' heather (*Calluna vulgaris* 'Hirsuta Typica')	🌿 Mauve blooms and silver-gray foliage on 16-inch-tall, 20-inch-wide plants ☀ Zones 4 to 10
U 'Minima Smith's Variety' heather (*Calluna vulgaris* 'Minima Smith's Variety')	🌿 Pink flowers and bright green foliage on 2- to 6-inch-tall plants that grow 15 inches wide ☀ Zones 4 to 10
V 'Mrs. R. H. Grey' heather (*Calluna vulgaris* 'Mrs. R. H. Grey')	🌿 Mauve blooms and dark green leaves on 2-inch-tall, 14-inch-wide plants ☀ Zones 4 to 10
W 'Palace Purple' heuchera (*Heuchera micrantha* var. *diversifolia* 'Palace Purple')	🌿 Purple-leaved perennial with clusters of greenish white flowers; plants grow 1 to 2 feet tall ☀ Zones 4 to 8
X Dwarf Japanese hollies (*Ilex crenata*, dwarf cultivars)	🌿 Evergreen shrub comes in a variety of heights, depending on the cultivar ☀ Zones 5 to 7
Y Paxistima (*Paxistima canbyi*)	🌿 Evergreen shrub with green or reddish flowers in spring; forms a groundcover 1 foot tall and 3 to 5 feet wide ☀ Zones 4 to 7
Z Pink tree peonies (*Paeonia suffruticosa*, pink cultivars)	🌿 Deciduous shrub with large crepe-paperlike blooms in pink (also comes in red, white, or yellow); plants grow 3 to 5 feet tall ☀ Zones 3 to 8
AA 'Scarlet Wonder' rhododendron (*Rhododendron* 'Scarlet Wonder')	🌿 Compact evergreen shrub with scarlet blooms; plants grow 2 feet tall ☀ Zones 5 to 8

Hot and Cold Cottage Garden

If your region swings from intense, dry heat in summer to blinding, dry cold in winter, you need plants that can take extremes. In his Santa Fe garden, writer Rand Lee, who is president of the American Dianthus Society and coeditor of *The American Cottage Gardener* magazine, grows a wide variety of annuals, perennials, biennials, and bulbs that thrive no matter what nature dishes out. Rand's garden features open-pollinated (naturally pollinated plants—not man-made hybrids), low-maintenance, drought-tolerant heirloom cultivars.

Ingredients and Supplies

The letter in front of each plant shows the plant's location in the plan on the facing page. The number of plants you'll need to order is in parentheses following each plant name. Plant quantities are approximate, but this should be enough for a 40-square-foot mixed cutting garden border.

Rand offers 4 different planting options for the space at each end of this border. Choose 2 of the bulleted options to fill the spots labeled A on the plan to extend the border's season of interest. Or choose only 1 of the bulleted items and repeat it at both ends of the border to give the garden a slightly more formal look.

- **A** Parrot tulips or other tall tulips for spring color or Asiatic lilies for early summer color (16 mixed bulbs)

- **A** Tall baby's-breath (*Gypsophila paniculata*) underplanted with small spring bulbs like crocuses (1 plant plus 10–15 small bulbs)

- **A** New England aster (*Aster novae-angliae*) for fall color (1 plant)

- **A** Reblooming lavender (*Lavandula angustifolia*), like 'Sharon Roberts,' for color in early and late summer (2 plants)

B 'Sonata' series cosmos (*Cosmos bipinnatus* 'Sonata' series) (6–8 plants)

C 'Rocket' series snapdragons (*Antirrhinum majus* 'Rocket' series) (4–6 plants)

D Calendulas (*Calendula officinalis*), like 'Radio' (4–6 plants)

E Stocks (*Matthiola incana*) like 'Excelsior Mammoth Column' (6–8 plants)

F Zinnias (*Zinnia elegans*), like 'State Fair' series (6 plants)

G Rocket larkspurs (*Consolida ambigua*) (6 plants)

Directions

1. Mix up your planting. When you plant lots of different kinds of plants together, it confuses pest insects, so grow as many of the ingredients listed above as possible.

2. Plant in soil that's well drained and slightly alkaline. "Relentless soil-building is the key to cottage gardening in New Mexico," says Rand. (For more information on soil preparation and planting, see "Getting Rid of Weeds and Sod" and "Improving the Soil" on page 267.)

3. Mulch plants well and use drip irrigation to keep plants supplied with water.

4. Be realistic. "Primroses, rhododendrons, and lily-of-the-valley will not thrive in a dry, alkaline Albuquerque garden," Rand notes. Wherever you live, grow plants that thrive in your climate for low-maintenance success.

Variation: If you have an extra 1-foot-wide band along the front of the bed (bringing the total area of the bed to 60 square feet), you can front the bed with one of the following plantings:

20 globe-type basil (*Ocimum basilicum* 'Spicy Globe' or other compact variety)
20 annual Dahlberg daisies (*Dyssodia tenuiloba*)
40 hyacinth bulbs
20 Johnny-jump-ups or other pansies
20 nasturtiums
10–16 perennial pinks (*Dianthus* spp.)

Hot and Cold Cottage Garden Plan

1'	Pinks, Dahlberg daisies, pansies, nasturtiums, basil, or hyacinths							
2'	A	B	C	D	E	F	G	A
	4'	2'	2'	2'	2'	2'	2'	4'

Create a long-lasting riot of color that can stand up to heat and cold with this cottage garden plan from Rand Lee. This mixture of plants means there's always something blooming in this garden, from spring well into fall.

Escape with a Xeriscape!

If you live in the West or Southwest where water is scarce, a xeriscape garden full of drought-tolerant plants is the way to go. But drought tolerance is just one benefit of this xeriscape garden. Landscape designer Mick Vann, who is president of the City of Austin's Xeriscape Advisory Board, also required that this planting provide color through at least three seasons, attract hummingbirds and butterflies, resist deer, be easy to maintain, consist of readily available plants, provide flowers for cutting, and be hardy to Zone 6! (See "Water-Saving Plants" beginning on page 282 for plant descriptions.)

Ingredients and Supplies

The letter in front of each plant shows the plant's location in the plan on the facing page. The number of plants you'll need to order is in parentheses following each plant name.

- **A** 'Goldsturm' black-eyed Susans or Shasta daisies (8 plants)
- **B** Butterfly weeds (2)
- **C** Rose campions (4)
- **D** Purple coneflowers (5)
- **E** Black-foot daisies (6)
- **F** Four-nerve daisies (12)
- **G** Society garlic bulbs (6)
- **H** Heron's bills (4)
- **I** Yellow African iris (2)
- **J** Mistflowers (4)
- **K** Obedient plants (2)
- **L** Penstemons (2)
- **M** 'Buff Beauty' hybrid musk roses (2)
- **N** 'Cramoisi Superieur' China rose (1)
- **O** Russian sages (2)
- **P** Canyon sages (3)
- **Q** Galeana sages (6)
- **R** Pitcher's sages (6)
- **S** Sea-pinks (8)
- **T** Pink skullcaps (6)
- **U** Desert willows (3)
- **V** Sprawling winecups (4)
- **W** 'Coronation Gold' yarrows (4)

Caliche (inexpensive limestone-based fill)

Compost or crushed or decomposed granite (for topdressing)

Mulching material, like hardwood chips, hay, or pine needles

Directions

1. Choose a spot in full to part sun—you'll need 160 square feet of space.

2. Drainage is essential for most drought-tolerant plants. To make sure that your garden drains well, add caliche to your existing soil or use it to help fill a raised bed. Use caliche as you would organic matter, mixing it with the soil up to a maximum of ¼ of the total volume of your planting area.

3. Prior to planting, topdress the area with ½ to 1 inch of crushed or decomposed granite. (Crushed granite contains potash, silicas, and trace minerals.) If crushed granite isn't available, you may substitute 2 to 3 inches of compost. As you dig holes and set plants in place, some of the material will work its way into the planting hole where it will enrich the soil.

4. Once the plants are in the ground, mulch with shredded hardwood bark, weed- and seed-free alfalfa hay, or pine needles. To encourage growth in the spring, rake aside the mulch so that the soil can warm up. Replace the mulch after growth begins.

5. The plants in this plan are drought-tolerant but need adequate water while they get established. During the first week after planting, water lightly every day. The second week, water every other day, for a little longer. Water 2 or 3 times during the third week, and once or twice during weeks 4 through 6. After week 6, water every 10 to 14 days. Skip a watering if it rains. If the weather is hot and dry, check plants often to see if they need water.

Xeriscape Garden Plan

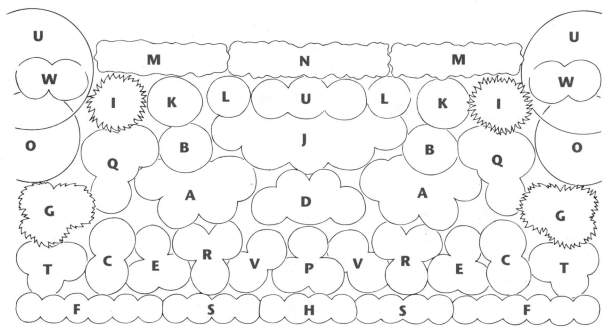

WATER-SAVING PLANTS

These drought-tolerant plants are commonly available at garden centers and nurseries in arid areas. For mail-order suppliers, see "Sources," beginning on page 308, or contact The Lady Bird Johnson Wildflower Center (formerly the National Wildflower Research Center), 4801 La Crosse Avenue, Austin, TX 78739.

Deadhead the perennial flowers if you want to stretch their bloom times to cover the entire bloom seasons listed in the descriptions.

PLANT	🌿 DESCRIPTION ☀ HARDINESS ZONES
A **'Goldsturm' black-eyed Susan** (*Rudbeckia fulgida* **var.** *sullivantii* **'Goldsturm'**)	🌿 Perennial with yellow daisylike blooms from May to September; flower centers are rusty-colored or brown; grows 2½ feet tall and 2 feet wide ☀ Zones 3 to 9
B **Butterfly weed** (*Asclepias tuberosa*)	🌿 Perennial with clusters of orange blooms from March to September; grows 1 to 3 feet tall and 2 feet wide ☀ Zones 3 to 9
C **Rose campion** (*Lychnis coronaria*)	🌿 Perennial with magenta Maltese-cross-shaped blooms from April to July; grows 2 feet tall and 2 feet wide ☀ Zones 4 to 10
D **Purple coneflower** (*Echinacea purpurea*)	🌿 Perennial with purple daisylike blooms from April to July; grows 2 to 4 feet tall and 1½ feet wide ☀ Zones 3 to 8
E **Black-foot daisy, melampodium** (*Melampodium leucanthum*)	🌿 Perennial with white, yellow-centered daisylike blooms from March to November; grows 1 foot tall and 2 feet wide ☀ Zones 6 to 10
F **Four-nerve daisy** (*Hymenoxys scaposa*)	🌿 Perennial with chrome yellow blooms from February to November; evergreen foliage has silvery accents; grows 8 inches tall and 12 inches wide ☀ Zones 5 to 10
A **Shasta daisy** (*Chrysanthemum* × *superbum*, **also sold as** *Leucanthemum* × *superbum*)	🌿 Perennial with white daisy blooms from April to October; grows 2 to 3 feet tall and 2 feet wide ☀ Zones 5 to 10
G **Society garlic** (*Tulbaghia violacea*)	🌿 Clusters of violet, urn-shaped blooms from March to November; foliage is evergreen to 20°F; mulch well in Zone 6; grows 1 foot tall and 2 feet wide ☀ Zones 6 to 10

PLANT	🌿 DESCRIPTION ☀ HARDINESS ZONES
H Heron's bill (*Erodium reichardii*)	🌿 Perennial with purple-veined white flowers from March to November; grows 6 inches tall and 12 inches wide ☀ Zones 6 to 10
I Yellow African iris (*Dietes bicolor*)	🌿 Perennial with creamy yellow flowers splotched with maroon; blooms from April to July; mulch well in Zones 6 and 7; grows 2½ feet tall and 2½ feet wide ☀ Zones 6 to 10
J Mistflower, hardy ageratum (*Eupatorium coelestinum*)	🌿 Perennial with clusters of blue to purple blooms from July to October; grows 2 to 3 feet tall and 3 feet wide ☀ Zones 6 to 10
K Obedient plant (*Physostegia virginiana*)	🌿 Perennial with spikes of purplish pink flowers that bloom from July to October; grows 3 to 4 feet tall and spreads ☀ Zones 3 to 10
L Penstemon (*Penstemon cobaea*)	🌿 Perennial with white foxglovelike flowers with violet stripes; blooms from March to May; grows 2 feet tall and 2 feet wide ☀ Zones 5 to 10
M 'Buff Beauty' hybrid musk rose (*Rosa* 'Buff Beauty')	🌿 Repeat-blooming rose blooms heavily in spring and fall with clusters of double, apricot-yellow flowers; mounded plants grow 6 feet tall and 6 feet wide ☀ Zones 5 to 10
N 'Cramoisi Superieur' China rose (*Rosa* 'Cramoisi Superieur')	🌿 Everblooming rose with fragrant, double, crimson blooms; grows 6 feet tall and 6 feet wide ☀ Zones 6 to 10
O Russian sage (*Perovskia atriplicifolia*)	🌿 Perennial with sprays of tiny blue blooms from July to October; grows 3 to 5 feet tall and 3 feet wide ☀ Zones 4 to 9
P Canyon sage (*Salvia lycioides*)	🌿 Perennial with cobalt-blue blooms in April and October to November; evergreen leaves are silvery-green; grows 1½ feet tall and 1½ feet wide ☀ Zones 6 to 10

(continued on page 284)

PLANT	🌿 DESCRIPTION ☀ HARDINESS ZONES
Q **Galeana sage** (*Salvia darcyi*)	🌿 Perennial with fire-engine-red blooms from April to November; mulch well in Zone 6; grows 2½ feet tall and 2½ feet wide ☀ Zones 6 to 10
R **Pitcher's sage, great azure sage** (*Salvia azurea* var. *grandiflora*)	🌿 Perennial with spikes of electric sky-blue blooms from May to October; grows 3 to 4 feet tall and 2 feet wide ☀ Zones 5 to 9
S **Sea-pink** (*Armeria maritima*)	🌿 Perennial with pink or red ball-like blooms from March to June (the species blooms rose pink, 'Dusseldorf Pride' is carmine red, and 'Laucheana' is deep rose red); blue-green grasslike evergreen foliage; grows 6 inches tall and 12 inches wide ☀ Zones 3 to 8
T **Pink skullcap** (*Scutellaria suffrutescens*)	🌿 Pink everblooming perennial with evergreen foliage; grows 1 foot tall and 2 feet wide ☀ Zones 6 to 10
U **Desert willow** (*Chilopsis linearis*)	🌿 Shrub or small tree with fragrant, trumpet-shaped pale purple blooms from May to October; leaves are long and willowlike; grows 15 feet tall and 8 to 10 feet wide ☀ Zones 6 to 10; may freeze to the ground in Zone 6 but will come back
V **Sprawling winecups** (*Callirhoe involucrata* var. *digitata*)	🌿 Groundcovering perennial with white to pale lavender blooms from February to July; evergreen foliage has silver splotches; plants grow 1 foot tall and 2 feet wide ☀ Zones 4 to 10
W **'Coronation Gold' yarrow** (*Achillea* 'Coronation Gold')	🌿 Perennial with mustard-yellow blooms from June to August; grows 3 feet tall and 2 feet wide ☀ Zones 3 to 9

All-American Wildflowers

Think of this as a one-size-fits-all wildflower mix. "You can grow it almost anywhere and under most conditions," explains Becky Schaff of Moon Mountain Wildflowers. Becky adds that you can adjust the mixture according to the types of seed that are available. Once your mix is planted, your climate and the amount of moisture in the soil will determine which wildflower species dominate your planting. (See "All-American Wildflowers You Can Grow" beginning on page 286 for descriptions of plants below.)

Ingredients and Supplies

1 seed packet baby-blue-eyes
1 seed packet black-eyed Susan
1 seed packet blanket flower
1 seed packet California blue-eyed grass
1 seed packet calliopsis
1 seed packet farewell-to-spring
1 seed packet 'Rubrum' scarlet flax
1 seed packet Mexican hat, red cultivar

1 seed packet lemon mint
1 seed packet Rocky mountain penstemon
1 seed packet mountain phlox
1 seed packet California poppy
1 seed packet tidy tips
1 seed packet white yarrow

Directions

1. Each seed packet contains about 100 seeds, which will cover an area of about 210 square feet altogether. For a smaller planting, reduce the amount of seed you use.

2. Prepare your planting site according to the information in "Getting Rid of Weeds and Sod" and "Improving the Soil" on page 267.

3. See "Growing Wildflowers from Seed" on page 287 for instructions on planting wildflower seeds.

4. Keep weeds under control while your wildflowers are getting established. Patrol your garden regularly and remove unwanted plants that may compete with your newly planted wildflowers.

ALL-AMERICAN WILDFLOWERS YOU CAN GROW

These adaptable wildflowers thrive in most areas of the United States. Although many seeds are widely available, you may find that the ones purchased from growers in your region—and preferably from local growers—perform better than seeds from distant sources. In addition to these stalwart and widespread standards, check to see what wildflowers are native in your area and add a few of those to your garden mix as well. See "Sources" beginning on page 308 for mail-order suppliers that carry wildflower seeds.

PLANT	✿ DESCRIPTION ☀ HARDINESS ZONES
Baby-blue-eyes (*Nemophila menziesii*)	✿ Clear blue bowl-shaped blooms on 4- to 12-inch-tall spreading plants ☀ Annual
Black-eyed Susan (*Rudbeckia hirta*)	✿ Biennial or short-lived perennial; yellow daisy flowers have brown centers. Grows 1 to 1½ feet tall ☀ Zones 2 to 9
Blanket flower (*Gaillardia aristata*)	✿ Perennial with daisylike yellow flowers often accented with burgundy; grows 2 to 3 feet tall ☀ Zones 2 to 10
California blue-eyed grass (*Sisyrinchium bellum*)	✿ Perennial with small blue star-shaped blooms on 2-foot-tall grasslike plants ☀ Zones 8 to 10
Calliopsis, plains coreopsis (*Coreopsis tinctoria*)	✿ Maroon, yellow, or bicolor petals around a red or purple center; grows 2 to 3 feet tall ☀ Annual
Farewell-to-spring (*Clarkia amoena*)	✿ Showy pink, red, salmon, white, or bicolored blooms on 1- to 3-foot-tall plants ☀ Annual
'Rubrum' scarlet flax (*Linum grandiflorum* 'Rubrum')	✿ Satiny red blooms on 1- to 2-foot tall stems ☀ Annual
Mexican hat (*Ratibida columnifera,* red cultivars)	✿ Perennial with an elongated cone surrounded by drooping red petals (Mexican hat also comes in yellow); grows 1 to 4 feet tall ☀ Zones 3 to 9
Lemon mint (*Monarda citriodora*)	✿ Annual or tender perennial with whorls of pink or white blooms spotted with purple; grows on 1- to 3-foot-tall stems ☀ Zones 5 to 9

PLANT	DESCRIPTION / HARDINESS ZONES
Rocky mountain penstemon (*Penstemon strictus*)	Perennial with spikes of blue blooms on 2½-foot-tall plants Zones 4 to 6
Mountain phlox (*Linanthus grandiflorus*)	Open clusters of white blooms which may be tinted lavender or pink on 1½-foot-tall stems Annual
California poppy (*Eschscholzia californica*)	Annual or tender perennial with deep orange cup-shaped blooms; grows 12 to 18 inches tall Annual
Tidy tips (*Layia platyglossa*)	Yellow and white daisy type blooms on 12-inch-tall plants Annual
White yarrow (*Achillea millefolium*, white cultivars)	Perennial with wide flattened white flower heads on 1½- to 3-foot-tall stems (yarrow also comes in yellow, pink and red) Zones 3 to 9

Growing Wildflowers from Seed

Sowing wildflower mixes is similar to sowing a lawn, but you don't have to improve the soil (unless it's really low on nutrients) or level the ground. Most wildflowers love sun, so choose a site that gets at least six hours of full sun a day. Well-drained soil is best, but you can find species that are adapted to wet sites, too.

If you live in the South or West (USDA Hardiness Zones 7 through 11), take advantage of the rainy season by sowing in autumn. In USDA Hardiness Zones 1 through 6, avoid the harsh winter by sowing in early spring.

Broadcast the seed by hand or use a spreader, making two passes, as shown in "Seeding a Lawn" on page 305. To make it easier to distribute the tiny seeds evenly, mix the seed with sand, perlite, finely screened compost, or potting soil, at a rate of 4 parts mixer to 1 part seed.

Press the seed into the soil surface—don't bury it—by walking over the area or dragging a board or light roller across it. Like all newly planted seeds, wildflower seeds germinate best if the soil is consistently moist. If you've planted an area that's small enough to irrigate, keep the soil damp for the first four to six weeks after planting by watering lightly but frequently. You can cut back on watering once the plants are about 2 inches tall.

Southern Heirloom Garden

You may be surprised to discover how modern looking an heirloom garden can be. "Old plants tend to be bold and undemanding," reveals Greg Grant, coauthor of *The Southern Heirloom Garden*. "I call this garden 'orange with an attitude.' It blooms in summer and will last forever in Zones 8a to 11." (See "Southern Heirloom Plants" on page 290 for plant descriptions.)

Ingredients and Supplies

The letter in front of each plant shows the plant's location in the plan below. The number of plants you'll need to order is in parentheses following each plant name.

A 'Orange Beauty' cannas (3 plants)
B 'Ellen Bosanquet' crinum lilies (3)

C Crocosmia bulbs (12)
D Campernelle jonquils (50)
E 'Kwanso' daylilies (12)
F 'Mutabilis' China rose (1)
G Turk's caps (5)

**Southern Heirloom
Garden Plan**

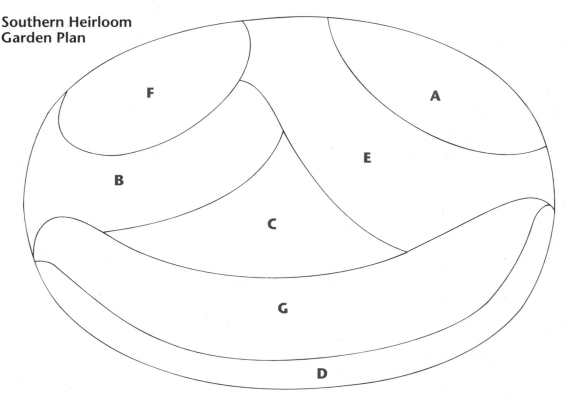

Directions

1. Choose a site in full sun with well-drained soil. Prepare the soil, as described in "Getting Rid of Weeds and Sod" and "Improving the Soil" on page 267. This bed covers an oval area about 8 feet wide and 15 feet long.

2. Plant in either spring or fall, following the layout shown in the plan on the facing page. Fall planting is preferable throughout most of the Deep South.

3. Mulch to prevent weeds and reduce the need for watering.

Without harsh winters to reduce their populations, insect pests can really thrive in southern gardens. A garden full of time-tested heirloom plants helps put a stop to pest problems. These tough-but-pretty customers have adapted over the years to resist or repel hungry bugs.

SOUTHERN HEIRLOOM PLANTS

Heirloom flowers are popular because they are often resistant to diseases and insects besides having beautifully colored blooms and/or fragrances.

See "Sources," beginning on page 308 for mail-order suppliers that carry a selection of heirloom flowers.

	PLANT	DESCRIPTION / HARDINESS ZONES
A	'Orange Beauty' canna (*Canna* × *generalis* 'Orange Beauty')	Tender perennial with large orange flowers from early summer to fall; grows 5 to 9 feet tall Zones 8 to 10 (grow as annuals elsewhere or store indoors over winter)
B	'Ellen Bosanquet' crinum lily (*Crinum* 'Ellen Bosanquet')	Tender perennial bulb with large fragrant lilylike flowers; grows 2 feet tall and 1 to 2 feet wide Zones 7 to 10
C	Crocosmia, montbretia (*Crocosmia* × *crocosmiiflora*)	Perennial bulb that produces sprays of bright yellow, orange, red, or bicolor flowers; grows 3 feet tall Zones 6 to 10
D	Campernelle jonquil (*Narcissus* × *odorus*)	Bulb with 2 to 3 fragrant golden yellow blooms per stem; grows 12 inches tall Zones 4 to 9
E	'Kwanso' tawny daylily (*Hemerocallis fulva* 'Kwanso')	Perennial with double orange flowers; grows 3 to 4 feet tall Zones 2 to 9
F	'Mutabilis' China rose (*Rosa chinensis* 'Mutabilis')	China rose with clusters of 3-inch-wide single flowers that open yellow, turn pink, and gradually deepen to red; grows 5 to 8 feet tall Zones 6 to 9
G	Turk's cap (*Malvaviscus arboreus* var. *drummondii*)	Shrubby perennial with bright red tubular flowers; grows into a mound 3 feet tall and 5 feet wide Hardy to Zone 7 but can be grown as an annual elsewhere

How Sweet the Night

If your job keeps you away from your garden all day (what an outrage!), create a garden that you can enjoy in the evening. "This planting features annuals that are fragrant at night," explains Ed Rasmussen of The Fragrant Path, a seed company that specializes in seeds of fragrant, old-fashioned, and rare plants. "And because the plants are white, they seem almost luminous in the dark." (See "Night-Blooming Flowers" on page 292 for plant descriptions.)

Ingredients and Supplies

The letter in front of each plant shows the plant's location in the plan on page 293. The number of plants you'll need to fill in the plan is in parentheses following each plant name.

- **A** Large, old-fashioned type of sweet alyssum (10) or smaller modern cultivars (12–15)
- **B** White angel's trumpet (2 plants)
- **C** Sweet four-o'clock (1–3)
- **D** White Marvel-of-Peru (1–3)
- **E** White heliotrope (3–5)
- **F** White or purple horn-of-plenty (1)
- **G** Compact white petunia (12–16)
- **H** 'Loveliness Hybrids' pinks (to fill in gaps between other plants)
- **I** Evening stock (3–5)
- **J** Cream-white jasmine tobacco (5–7)
- **K** 'Lime Green' winged tobacco (5)
- **L** Pure white woodland tobacco (3)

Directions

1. Buy 1 packet of seed for each type of plant listed in Ingredients and Supplies. Some of these plants are old-fashioned, so you may need to order seeds if your garden center offers mostly modern, run-of-the-mill fare.

2. Choose an area in full sun and prepare the soil as described in "Getting Rid of Weeds and Sod" and "Improving the Soil" on page 267. This planting covers about 150 square feet.

3. Two weeks after the last frost date, sow the seeds directly in the soil, at the depth shown on the seed packet (or about 3 times deeper than the diameter of the seed). Sow 2 or 3 times as many seeds as the number of plants called for in Ingredients and Supplies to guarantee enough plants to fill the plan.

4. Keep the soil moist while the seeds germinate and make their first few inches of growth. When plants are growing well and are several inches tall, thin to the correct spacing. Or grow plants from seed indoors and set out transplants after the average date of the last frost in your area.

NIGHT-BLOOMING FLOWERS

Turn your yard into an after-hours paradise with white or light-colored versions of these plants. After a long day at work, a visit to this fragrant garden offers a soothing diversion from the cares of the day. Don't be surprised if you find you're not alone in your garden as dusk falls—fragrant white flowers are moth magnets, and these furry-bodied insects can be every bit as spectacular and showy as their butterfly cousins.

	PLANT		DESCRIPTION / HARDINESS ZONES
A	Sweet alyssum (*Lobularia maritima*)		Tiny white blooms on mounded plants (flowers also come in rose and purple); grows to 12 inches tall / Annual
B	Angel's trumpet (*Datura inoxia*)		Tender perennial grown as an annual; long, white tubular blooms grow on 3-foot-tall plants (flowers also come in pink and lavender) / Zone 9
C	Sweet four-o'clock (*Mirabilis longiflora*)		Tender perennial grown as an annual; long white, pink, or violet trumpet-shaped blooms are fragrant and open after sunset; grows 1½ to 3 feet tall / Zones 8 to 10
D	Marvel-of-Peru, four-o'clock (*Mirabilis jalapa*)		Tender perennial grown as an annual; red, pink, yellow, or white blooms open in the afternoon; grows 1½ to 3 feet tall / Zones 8 to 10
E	White heliotrope (*Heliotropium arborescens* 'Alba')		Tender perennial grown as an annual; fragrant white blooms grow on 12-inch-tall plants / Zones 9 to 10
F	Horn-of-plenty (*Datura metel*)		Long, tubular white, violet, or yellow blooms; grows 5 feet tall; seeds are poisonous / Annual
G	Petunia (*Petunia* × *hybrida*)		White trumpet-shaped blooms (flowers also come in blue, pink, purple, red, and yellow); grows 8 to 18 inches tall / Annual
H	'Loveliness Hybrids' pinks (*Dianthus* 'Loveliness Hybrids')		Perennial grown as a biennial (plants are short-lived); fringed white blooms open on mounded 15-inch-tall plants (flowers also come in pink, purple, and red) / Zones 4 to 8

| PLANT | 🌿 DESCRIPTION |
	☀ HARDINESS ZONES
I **Evening stock** (*Matthiola longipetala*)	🌿 Fragrant purple or white blooms on 1½-foot-tall plants ☀ Annual
J **Jasmine tobacco, flowering tobacco** (*Nicotiana alata*)	🌿 Fragrant white trumpet-shaped blooms (flowers also come in green, pink, purple, and red); plants can reach 5 feet tall ☀ Annual
K **'Lime Green' winged tobacco or flowering tobacco** (*Nicotiana alata* 'Lime Green')	🌿 Green blooms on 2½-foot-tall plants ☀ Annual
L **Woodland tobacco** (*Nicotiana sylvestris*)	🌿 Tender plant grown as a biennial; large white trumpet-shaped blooms are pollinated by hawk-moths; grows 3 to 4 feet tall ☀ Annual

Night Garden Plan

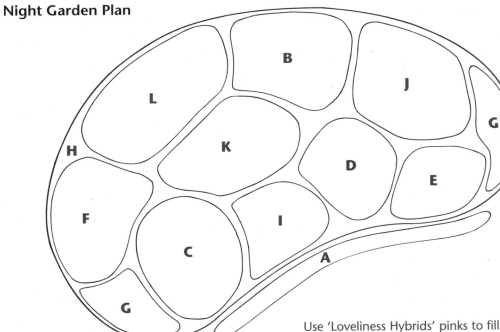

Use 'Loveliness Hybrids' pinks to fill the spaces between other plants in this glowing evening garden.

Cafeteria-Style Meadow Mixes for Average and Dry Soils

The supply of specific wildflower seeds varies from year to year. That's why Neil Diboll of Prairie Nursery in Westfield, Wisconsin, uses flexible formulas for the mixes he sells—he can exclude some plants when seed isn't available. On the following pages, you'll find plant choices for two of his most popular shortgrass prairie mixes: one for soil with average moisture and one for dry soil. Both are best suited to the north-eastern quarter of the United States and to southern Ontario. For each, he recommends including about a dozen of the long-lived flowering perennials listed in "Wildflowers for a Meadow Mix" beginning on page 296 and at least two of the grasses.

Ingredients and Supplies

Wildflowers for Average Moisture Soil

3 grams heart-leaved Alexander seeds
1 gram sky blue aster seeds
1 gram smooth aster seeds
2 grams black-eyed Susan seeds
5 grams prairie blazing-star seeds
3 grams purple prairie clover seeds
5 grams pale purple coneflower seeds
5 grams purple coneflower seeds
2 grams lance-leaved coreopsis seeds
2 grams stiff goldenrod seeds
4 grams nodding wild onion seeds
2 grams smooth penstemon seeds
2 grams wild quinine seeds
3 grams rattlesnake master seeds
5 grams great Solomon's seal seeds

Nodding onion   Pale purple coneflower   Prairie blazing-star

For the first 2 years after you plant your wildflower meadow, keep an eye out for invading weeds so that wildflowers and grasses can get established and thrive.

Wildflowers for Dry Soil

1 gram sky blue aster seeds

2 grams rough blazing-star seeds

3 grams large-flowered beardtongue seeds

2 grams spotted bee balm seeds

2 grams black-eyed Susan seeds

2 grams butterfly weed seeds

5 grams pale purple coneflower seeds

2 grams lance-leaved coreopsis seeds

1 gram showy goldenrod seeds

2 grams stiff goldenrod seeds

12 grams wild lupine seeds

2 grams Canada milk vetch seeds

3 grams purple prairie clover seeds

2 grams Ohio spiderwort seeds

3 grams flowering spurge seeds

1 gram western sunflower seeds

Meadow Grasses

25 grams little bluestem seeds

20 grams prairie dropseed seeds

25 grams side oats grama seeds

Directions

1. Choose a sunny site for your wildflower meadow and prepare the soil using the directions in "Getting Rid of Weeds and Sod" and "Improving the Soil" on page 267.

2. Select 12 to 15 of the wildflowers for average moisture soil or dry soil, depending on your site's conditions. Choose at least 2 of the grasses. (See "Wildflowers for a Meadow Mix" starting on page 296 and "Grasses for Your Meadow Mix" on page 299 for descriptions.)

3. Combine recommended amounts of wildflower and grass seeds, then mix the seed with sand, vermiculite, compost, or other material to make it easier to spread.

4. Plant your mix of wildflower and grass seed using the "Growing Wildflowers from Seed" instructions on page 287.

5. Tend your wildflower meadow planting until the young plants are well-established. Although most of the plants in these mixes need little care, your meadow will thrive if you give it moisture and a hand in the battle against weeds while it's getting started.

Note: Neil gives the quantities of seeds in grams (0.035 ounces), but you can convert them to whatever weight measurement you like, as long as the relative amounts are about the same. As given, the mix covers about 1,000 square feet. Neil notes, "The quantities are for very clean seed. If the seed contains chaff, you'll need to use more—maybe many times as much." He recommends asking the supplier what percentage of the product is clean seed.

WILDFLOWERS FOR A MEADOW MIX—MOIST OR DRY

Whether your yard's moist or dry, you can use the plants described here to create a showy and durable wildflower meadow. Select about a dozen wildflowers from either the plants for average moisture soil or those for dry soil—some are suitable for either condition. Choose a couple of grasses from those described on page 299 and get ready to sow.

If your yard gets an average amount of moisture (it's not wet or dry) and is average in fertility (not rich or poor), you can grow your own shortgrass prairie using plants listed for average moisture soil. This mix of beautiful wildflowers does best in well-drained loam or clay soils. Check your yard after a hard rain—if standing water drains away within a short time, your soil qualifies as well drained.

In sandy or gravelly soils, the plants listed for dry soil will bloom and thrive. Try these tough customers in very well-drained sites where water never stands.

PLANT	DESCRIPTION / HARDINESS ZONES
Nodding wild onion (*Allium cernuum*)	Perennial with globe-shaped pink flowers; grows 1½ to 2 feet tall. Zones 4 to 9
Sky blue aster (*Aster oolentangiensis*, formerly known as *A. azureus*)	Perennial with brilliant blue daisylike blooms; grows 2 to 3 feet tall. Zones 3 to 9
Smooth aster (*Aster laevis*)	Perennial with lavender-pink daisylike blooms; grows 2 to 4 feet tall. Zones 2 to 7
Lance-leaved coreopsis (*Coreopsis lanceolata*)	Perennial with yellow daisylike blooms; grows 1 to 2 feet tall. Zones 3 to 8
Pale purple coneflower (*Echinacea pallida*)	Perennial with large pale purple daisylike blooms, grows 3 to 5 feet tall. Zones 4 to 8
Purple coneflower (*Echinacea purpurea*)	Perennial with pink-purple daisylike blooms; grows 3 to 4 feet tall. Zones 3 to 8
Rattlesnake master (*Eryngium yuccifolium*)	Perennial with long flowerstalks topped with clusters of pale green ball-shaped blooms; yuccalike foliage; grows 3 to 4 feet tall. Zones 4 to 9
Prairie blazing-star (*Liatris pycnostachya*)	Perennial with tall spikes of flowers; grows 3 to 4 feet tall. Zones 3 to 9
Wild quinine (*Parthenium integrifolium*)	Perennial with flat-topped clusters of small white and yellow blooms; grows 2 to 4 feet tall. Zones 4 to 8

AVERAGE MOISTURE SOIL

PLANT	🌿 DESCRIPTION ☀ HARDINESS ZONES
AVERAGE MOISTURE SOIL	
Smooth penstemon, foxglove penstemon (*Penstemon digitalis*)	🌿 Perennial with clusters of white blooms on tall flowerstalks; grows 2 to 3 feet tall ☀ Zones 4 to 8
Purple prairie clover (*Dalea purpurea,* may also be sold as *Petalostemon purpureum*)	🌿 Perennial with small elongated clusters of bright purple blooms; grows 2 feet tall ☀ Zones 3 to 9
Great Solomon's seal (*Polygonatum biflorum* var. *commutatum,* may also be sold as *Polygonatum commutatum*)	🌿 Perennial with clusters of small greenish white flowers; grows 3 to 7 feet tall ☀ Zones 3 to 7
Black-eyed Susan (*Rudbeckia hirta*)	🌿 Biennial or short-lived perennial grown as an annual; yellow daisylike blooms; grows 1 to 3 feet tall ☀ Zones 2 to 9
Stiff goldenrod (*Solidago rigida*)	🌿 Perennial with flat-topped clusters of yellow flowers; grows 3 to 5 feet tall ☀ Zones 3 to 9
Heart-leaved Alexander (*Zizia aptera*)	🌿 Perennial with flattened clusters of bright yellow blooms; grows 1 to 2 feet tall ☀ Zones 3 to 9
DRY SOIL	
Sky blue aster (*Aster oolentangiensis,* formerly known as *A. azureus*)	🌿 Perennial with brilliant blue daisylike blooms; grows 2 to 3 feet tall ☀ Zones 3 to 9
Rough blazing-star (*Liatris aspera*)	🌿 Perennial with clusters of pale purple or pink buttonlike flowers; grows 4 to 6 feet tall ☀ Zones 3 to 9
Large-flowered beardtongue (*Penstemon grandiflorus*)	🌿 Perennial with large lavender-blue flowers; grows 2 to 4 feet tall ☀ Zones 3 to 8
Spotted bee balm, dotted mint (*Monarda punctata*)	🌿 Perennial with tiered clusters of small, spotted yellow-green blooms above whorls of pink bracts; grows to 3 feet tall ☀ Zones 3 to 9
Black-eyed Susan (*Rudbeckia hirta*)	🌿 Biennial or short-lived perennial grown as an annual; yellow daisy blooms; grows 1 to 3 feet tall ☀ Zones 2 to 9

(continued on page 298)

PLANT	☙ DESCRIPTION ☀ HARDINESS ZONES
Butterfly weed (*Asclepias tuberosa*)	☙ Perennial with flat clusters of bright orange blooms; grows 1 to 3 feet tall ☀ Zones 3 to 9
Pale purple coneflower (*Echinacea pallida*)	☙ Perennial with large pale purple daisylike blooms, grows 3 to 5 feet tall ☀ Zones 4 to 8
Lance-leaved coreopsis (*Coreopsis lanceolata*)	☙ Perennial with yellow daisylike blooms; grows 1 to 2 feet tall ☀ Zones 3 to 9
Showy goldenrod (*Solidago speciosa*)	☙ Perennial with long clusters of bright yellow blooms; grows 1 to 3 feet tall ☀ Zones 3 to 8
Stiff goldenrod (*Solidago rigida*)	☙ Perennial with flat-topped clusters of yellow flowers; grows 3 to 5 feet tall ☀ Zones 3 to 9
Wild lupine (*Lupinus perennis*)	☙ Perennial with spikes of blue pealike blooms; grows 1 to 2 feet tall ☀ Zones 3 to 9
Canada milk vetch (*Astragalus canadensis*)	☙ Perennial with creamy yellow lupinelike blooms; grows 2 to 4 feet tall ☀ Zones 1 to 6
Purple prairie clover (*Dalea purpurea,* may also be sold as *Petalostemon purpureum*)	☙ Perennial with small elongated clusters of bright purple blooms; grows 2 feet tall ☀ Zones 3 to 9
Ohio spiderwort (*Tradescantia ohiensis*)	☙ Perennial with deep blue, rose, or white 3-petaled flowers; grows 1 to 3 feet tall ☀ Zones 3 to 9
Flowering spurge (*Euphorbia corollata*)	☙ Perennial with clusters of little white blooms; grows 1 to 3 feet tall ☀ Zones 3 to 9
Western sunflower (*Helianthus occidentalis*)	☙ Perennial with bright yellow daisy flowers; grows 2 to 3 feet tall ☀ Zones 4 to 8

DRY SOIL

GRASSES FOR YOUR MEADOW MIX

Choose 2 or more of the following grasses to mix with your wildflower choices from the lists for average moisture soil or dry soil in "Wildflowers for a Meadow Mix—Moist or Dry."

PLANT	🌿 DESCRIPTION ☀ HARDINESS ZONES
Side oats grama (*Bouteloua curtipetala*)	🌿 Tiny purple petals dangle from long stems; grows 2 to 3 feet tall ☀ Zones 4 to 9
Little bluestem (*Schizachyrium scoparium*)	🌿 Ripening seedheads look like fluffy plumes; leaves are blue to green and turn reddish orange in fall; plants grow 2 to 3 feet tall ☀ Zones 3 to 10
Prairie dropseed (*Sporobolus heterolepis*)	🌿 Long airy panicles of flowers rise above arching emerald green leaves which turn gold or orange in fall; grows 2 to 3 feet tall ☀ Zones 3 to 9

DEALING WITH WEEDS

Wildflower meadows don't require much care, but they do need a little to keep them looking their best. White sweet clover (*Melilotus alba*) is often troublesome, as are weedy grasses, such as Johnson grass (*Sorghum halapense*), crabgrass (*Digitaria* spp.), and whatever lawn grasses you may have killed off when preparing the site.

Once the wildflower planting is about a year old, you can start cutting it back annually to get rid of woody weeds and to help spread the seeds that the plants produce. In autumn, when most of the plants are looking brown, cut them to a height of about 6 inches, preferably using a scythe or string trimmer. You can mow it, but most mowers cut too low, which weakens the perennial wildflowers. 🌿

Clip off the weeds rather than pulling them so that you don't disturb wildflower seedlings.

Sweet clover   **Johnson grass**   **Crabgrass**

A Native Mix for the Southeast

The native wildflowers that Wildseed Farms of Fredericksburg, Texas, includes in its Texas/Oklahoma wildflower mix are species that do well throughout most of the Southeast, says staff botanist Tom Kramer. If you're lucky enough to live in Texas or Oklahoma, you might just want to mix up a batch of these durable natives and sow them in your garden in the quantities shown below. Elsewhere in the Southeast, replace the Texas bluebonnets and Texas paintbrush with larger amounts of other natives on the list or with some of the colorful non-natives listed in "Add a Splash of Color" on the facing page.

Tom explains that Wildseed Farms creates its seed mixes on a percentage-by-weight basis. Weighing wildflower seeds can be tricky—many of these plants have tiny seeds, while others feature seeds the size of small pebbles. Note the relative amounts of each type of seed in this mix and substitute accordingly. But don't fret too much over precise weights—nature leaves ample room for fudging, and a mixed wildflower garden allows for plenty of adjustment. If you have too much of one plant, dig out some and share the extras with a friend. If things look sparse, add a few more seeds to the mix. (See "Wildflowers for the Southeast" on page 302 for plant descriptions.)

Ingredients and Supplies

- 55 grams Texas bluebonnet seeds
- 36 grams Indian blanket seeds
- 29 grams lance-leaved coreopsis seeds
- 26 grams purple coneflower seeds
- 24 grams Drummond phlox seeds
- 17 grams lemon mint seeds
- 10 grams calliopsis seeds
- 9 grams clasping coneflower seeds
- 8 grams black-eyed Susan seeds
- 7 grams Mexican hat seeds
- 4 grams showy primrose seeds
- 1 gram Texas paintbrush seeds

Directions

1. Prepare the soil according to the directions in "Getting Rid of Weeds and Sod" and "Improving the Soil" on page 267.

2. The ideal time to plant wildflower seeds in the Southeast is fall, between September and December, with October usually being the best month. For general planting and care directions for wildflowers, see "Growing Wildflowers from Seed" on page 287 and "Dealing with Weeds" on page 299.

Note: The quantities of seeds in this mix are expressed in grams (0.035 ounces), but you can convert them to any unit of weight you prefer, as long as the relative amounts of seed remain similar. A table of conversion factors appears on pages 320–321. If you mix the seeds in the amounts shown here, you'll end up with approximately 227 grams of seed (about ½ pound)—enough to sow 1,000 square feet of garden space.

Southeastern heat and sun won't wilt wildflowers like
lance-leaved coreopsis (*A*), lemon mint (*B*), purple coneflower (*C*),
black-eyed Susan (*D*), and Mexican hat (*E*).

ADD A SPLASH OF COLOR

To add more color to your wildflower garden and to fill in around slower-starting perennials, toss the seeds of some annuals into your mix. These annuals are among the seeds that Wildseed Farms includes in its wildflower mix for the Southeast. Some of these plants will self-sow and return to brighten your garden year after year; others will require annual sowing to make repeat appearances. To guarantee that your favorites keep coming back, it's worth it to add a few seeds to your garden each fall.

African daisy (*Dimorphotheca aurantiaca*)
Sweet alyssum (*Lobularia maritima*)
Cornflower (*Centaurea cyanus*)
Corn poppy (*Papaver rhoeas*)
Cosmos (*Cosmos bipinnatus*)
Evening primrose (*Oenothera lamarckiana*)
Five spot (*Nemophila maculata*)
Scarlet flax (*Linum rubrum*)
Rocket larkspur (*Consolida ambigua*)
Toadflax (*Linaria maroccana*)

WILDFLOWERS FOR THE SOUTHEAST

Plant beautiful native wildflowers instead of a lawn! You'll gain a yardful of beautiful flowers, and best of all, you'll need to cut back these plants only once a year.

PLANT	❧ DESCRIPTION ☀ HARDINESS ZONES
Black-eyed Susan (*Rudbeckia hirta*)	❧ Biennial or short-lived perennial grown as an annual; yellow daisylike blooms; 1 to 3 feet tall ☀ Zones 2 to 9
Texas bluebonnet (*Lupinus texensis*)	❧ Deep blue blooms, will reseed in favorable conditions; 16 inches tall ☀ Annual
Calliopsis, plains coreopsis (*Coreopsis tinctoria*)	❧ Maroon, yellow, or bicolor petals around a red or purple center; 2 to 3 feet tall ☀ Annual
Clasping coneflower (*Dracopis amplexicaulis*, **may be sold as** *Rudbeckia amplexicaulis*)	❧ Yellow coneflowerlike blooms, leaf clasps around the stem; 1 to 2 feet tall ☀ Annual
Purple coneflower (*Echinacea purpurea*)	❧ Perennial with red-violet daisylike blooms that have orange centers; 2 to 4 feet tall ☀ Zones 3 to 8
Lance-leaved coreopsis (*Coreopsis lanceolata*)	❧ Perennial with yellow daisylike blooms; 1 to 2 feet tall ☀ Zones 3 to 8
Indian blanket (*Gaillardia pulchella*)	❧ Annual or short-lived perennial with yellow daisylike blooms that have purple-brown centers; 1 to 1½ feet tall ☀ Zones 2 to 10
Texas paintbrush (*Castilleja indivisa*)	❧ Annual, biennial, or tender perennial, with tiny pale yellow blooms surrounded by showy red-orange bracts; 8 to 24 inches tall ☀ Zones 6 to 9
Mexican hat (*Ratibida columnifera*)	❧ Perennial with an elongated cone surrounded by drooping yellow petals; 1 to 4 feet tall ☀ Zones 3 to 9
Lemon mint (*Monarda citriodora*)	❧ Annual or tender perennial with white or pinkish blooms; lemon-scented plant 1 to 3 feet tall ☀ Zones 5 to 9
Drummond phlox, annual phlox (*Phlox drummondii*)	❧ Clusters of pink, red, or white blooms; 6 to 18 inches tall ☀ Annual
Showy evening primrose (*Oenothera speciosa*)	❧ Perennial with cup-shaped pink blooms; 1 to 2 feet tall; plants may be invasive—particularly in rich soil ☀ Zones 5 to 8

Easy-Being-Green Mesclun Mix

You don't have to wait until the salad greens are in the bowl to toss them. By tossing the seeds of different greens together before planting them, you can grow a ready-made salad, called mesclun. Iowa-based freelance garden writer Veronica Fowler offers her formula for a mesclun mix that pleases the eyes as well as the tastebuds.

There's no need to hide this instant salad in your vegetable garden—it's pretty enough to plant in a patio pot or at the edge of your flower border! Some of the "greens" in Veronica's mix are actually red, for a splash of color, and the mix includes a selection of leaf shapes and textures, too. But don't let its appearance keep it out of your salad bowl—Veronica's mesclun mix tastes as good as it looks. "The flavor is mostly mild," Veronica says, "with just a little bite from the arugula."

Ingredients and Supplies

1 seed packet 'Tres Fine' curly endive
2 seed packets 'Salad Bowl' lettuce
1 seed packet 'Red Oak Leaf' or 'Red Salad Bowl' lettuce
1 seed packet 'Lollo Rossa' lettuce
1 seed packet 'Rouge d'Hiver' lettuce
1 seed packet arugula
Sand or potting soil
Fertilizer (optional)

Directions

1. Pour the seeds into a clean, dry container.
2. To make the mix easier to sow, combine the seeds with sand or potting soil.
3. Scatter the seeds evenly over prepared soil (see "Improving the Soil" on page 267 for instructions on preparing soil).
4. Firm the soil with your hand and keep it evenly moist.

5. To speed up growth, water weekly with a diluted fertilizer, such as fish emulsion or liquid kelp.
6. Begin harvesting while leaves are still young and tender—usually in 3 to 4 weeks.
7. Sow more of this mix every 2 weeks or so to enjoy a steady supply of salad through the growing season.

Note: Veronica stretches the outdoor growing season by starting her mesclun in a cold frame in early March and again in August. "I can harvest well past Thanksgiving," she says. To maximize space, time, and supplies, Veronica uses the cut-and-come-again harvest method—instead of pulling up the whole plant, she just cuts off the leaves she needs, or cuts the whole plant a little above the soil surface and lets it grow back for another harvest.

Ecologize Your Lawn

Tired of your demanding lawn? Switch to an ecology lawn. "An ecological approach to the traditional American lawn is long overdue," insists Rose Marie Nichols McGee, president of Nichols Garden Nursery in Albany, Oregon. According to Rose Marie, an ecological lawn will still provide you with a soft and inviting turf, but it's more self-sustaining than a traditional lawn. Envision a mixed tapestry of grasses and plants like clovers, yarrow, and English daisies, she says. An occasional mowing is all it takes to keep the nongrass plants in check.

Ingredients and Supplies

Amounts are per 1,000 square feet

   2 ounces Dutch white clover seed

   ½ ounce seed yarrow (*Achillea millefolium*)

   ¼ ounce seed wild or species English
         daisy (*Bellis perennis*)

Directions

1. Overseed in the fall in areas with mild winters. In the East and Midwest, sow as early as possible in the spring.

2. Keep the soil moist (not soggy) for at least 4 to 6 weeks after sowing. Once your ecology lawn is established, you can water or not, depending on the look you like. If you want your lawn to stay green, water during the hot, dry days of summer. If watering is restricted or if you don't mind the look of dormant plants, don't water—your lawn will grow again when the rains come. There's no need to fertilize because the clover adds enough nitrogen to keep the grass healthy.

Note: This mix is for overseeding an existing healthy lawn and is adapted throughout the United States, except for the Southeast as far west as central Texas. If your present lawn is little more than dandelions and annual grasses, Rose Marie recommends starting fresh with a commercial ecology lawn developed for your region. (See "Sources," beginning on page 308, for mail-order suppliers that carry lawn seed mixes.)

Seeding a Lawn

Early autumn is the best time to seed a lawn, since it's often rainy and weeds are less frisky than in the spring and summer. Spring is the second best time, since the weather is cool and rain is frequent. You can seed in the summer, but it's a lot more work because you have to water much more often.

Level it out. Once you've cleared the planting area of plants, make it as level as possible. If it hasn't been graded, grade it—or hire someone with a bulldozer to grade it—so that it slopes away from the house. (Check with friends and neighbors to find a bulldozer operator with good references.) After the area has been graded, use a rake or spade to move soil from small raised areas into small depressions. Then rake the whole area to loosen the soil.

Spread seed evenly. Use a rotary or drop spreader to sow your lawn seed. Mix the seed half-and-half with sand or potting soil to help spread it more evenly across the planting area.

Cover the seed lightly with soil by dragging a push broom or a metal rake across the ground. Then tamp down the ground with your feet or a roller that weighs about 50 pounds. Cover the area with ½ inch of straw mulch to help keep moisture in the soil.

Water as needed to keep the soil moist until the grass is a few inches tall. Typically, you'll need to water every 2 to 3 days, but if rain is scarce, you may need to lightly sprinkle more often—once or twice a day. 🌾

To seed your lawn evenly, plant in 2 directions. Using half of your lawn seed, make parallel lines to cover the area to be planted. Then spread the rest of the seed by moving in a direction that is perpendicular to your first pass.

Sustainable Warm-Region Lawn

If you live in the Southwest—Texas, Oklahoma, Louisiana, or New Mexico—you can enjoy a nearly nonstop green lawn by growing well-adapted cool and warm season grasses. "With this combination, you get year-round growth," says Richard Fadal, president of Texascapes, an all-organic landscape design and maintenance firm in Austin, Texas. "Having a diversity of species helps combat diseases and insects. And because there's so much competition from the grasses, weeds are rarely noticeable."

The only time the lawn goes off color, Richard explains, is during a brief period in spring when the cool-season grasses begin to die out and the warm-season ones are still getting going. He suggests adding white clover for green color in winter and spring and to add nitrogen. This formula is adaptable: Use it to start a new lawn or to improve an existing one.

Ingredients and Supplies

Seed rates are per 1,000 square feet. Use the lower rate on healthy soil.

- 2 pounds Bermuda grass (*Cynodon dactylon*)
- 2–4 pounds buffalo grass (*Buchloe dactyloides*)
- 2–4 pounds locally available perennial ryegrass (*Lolium perenne*)
- 2–4 pounds locally available fine fescue (*Festuca rubra*) and/or 'Kentucky 31' fescue (*Festuca arundinacea* 'Kentucky 31', may be offered as *F. elatior* 'Kentucky 31')
- ½ pound white clover seed (optional)

Directions

1. Add good quality topsoil if your existing soil is shallow. For a new lawn on bare soil, Richard recommends starting with 6 inches

LAID-BACK LAWN CARE

To care for your lawn once it's established, mow high and fertilize seldom. Here's how.

Set your mower on high. Mow to a height of 3 to 4 inches, removing only ⅓ of the height of the grass in a single mowing. Letting your lawn grow a little taller reduces the stress on the grass and helps shade out weeds.

With fertilizer, once is enough. Fertilize once a year for a low-care lawn (one that's seldom watered and mowed only when 3 to 4 inches tall) and 2 to 3 times a year for a regular care program. Use an organic fertilizer with an analysis of about 6–1–1 at a rate of 20 pounds per 1,000 square feet.

of good, crumbly soil, either native or purchased. Have the soil tested and add nutrients if any are deficient.

2. Cover the soil with a ½-inch-thick layer of finely textured organic matter, like compost, composted manure, rice hulls, or leaf mold.

3. Till to a depth of 2 to 4 inches and rake the surface smooth.

4. Plant the Bermuda grass and buffalo grass between May 1 and September 15. You'll need to sow these grasses only once. For help, see "Seeding a Lawn" on page 305. For an established lawn, use a spreader to evenly distribute the seed over the existing grass.

5. Seed annually with the perennial ryegrass, fescue, and clover between September 16 and April 30.

Note: Richard recommends 'Sahara' Bermuda grass because, compared to common Bermuda grass, it's very drought tolerant, is slightly shorter, and stays green longer. Common Bermuda grass is an acceptable substitute, but do not use hybrid Bermuda grass. If it's available, Richard recommends 'Top Gun' buffalo grass because it germinates quickly, but any cultivar will work.

KEEP YOUR LAWN IN CLOVER

Use the lower rates of grass seed in this mixture if you're using clover. And make sure that you coat the clover seed with inoculant before planting. This seed treatment (available where clover seed is sold) contains beneficial soil bacteria. When the roots of legume plants (like clover) and the soil bacteria are in contact with each other, they can capture nitrogen from the air and convert it to a form that plants can use.

Inoculate clover seeds before you plant them. Spread out the seeds in a bucket, moisten them with a spray of water or kelp solution, then pour in the inoculant.

Shake the bucket lightly to thoroughly cover the clover seeds with inoculant.

Sources

The following companies and organizations carry products or offer services related to formulas in this book. Simply look under a topic of interest, and you'll find sources for what you need.

Associations

American Dianthus Society
Rand B. Lee
P.O. Box 22232
Santa Fe, NM 87502-2232
phone: (505) 438-7038
e-mail: randbear@nets.com

American Rose Society
P.O. Box 30000
Shreveport, LA 71130-0030
phone: (318) 938-5402
fax: (318) 938-5405
e-mail: ars@ars-hq.org
Web site: http://www.ars.org

Garlic Seed Foundation
Rose Valley Farm
Rose, NY 14542-0419
phone: (315) 587-9787

**The Lady Bird Johnson
  Wildflower Center**
4801 La Crosse Avenue
Austin, TX 78739
phone: (512) 292-4100
e-mail: nwrc@onr.com
Web site:
    http://www.wildflower.org

**North American Butterfly
  Association (NABA)**
4 Delaware Road
Morristown, NJ 07960
phone: (973) 285-0907
fax: (973) 285-0936
e-mail: naba@naba.org
Web site: http://www.naba.org

**Rodale Institute
  Experimental Farm**
611 Siegfriedale Road
Kutztown, PA 19530
phone: (610) 683-1400
fax: (610) 683-8548

Beneficial Insects

Bountiful Gardens
18001 Shafer Ranch Road
Willits, CA 95490-9626
phone/fax: (707) 459-6410

Gardens Alive!
5100 Schenley Place
Lawrenceburg, IN 47025
phone: (812) 537-8650
fax: (812) 537-5108

The Green Spot
Department of Bio-Ingenuity
93 Priest Road
Nottingham, NH 03290-6204
phone: (603) 942-8925
fax: (603) 942-8932

Gurney's Seed & Nursery Co.
110 Capital Street
Yankton, SD 57079
phone: (605) 665-1930
fax: (605) 665-9718

Harmony Farm Supply
P.O. Box 460
Grafton, CA 95444
phone: (707) 823-9125
fax: (707) 823-1734

The Natural Gardening Company
217 San Anselmo Avenue
San Anselmo, CA 94960
phone: (707) 766-9303
fax: (707) 766-9747

Peaceful Valley Farm Supply
P.O. Box 2209
Grass Valley, CA 95945
phone: (916) 272-4769
fax: (916) 272-4794

Territorial Seed Company
P.O. Box 157
Cottage Grove, OR 97424
phone: (541) 942-9547
fax: (888) 657-3131
Web site:
    http://www.territorialseed.com

Bird Seed and Supplies

Duncraft
102 Fisherville Road
Penacook, NH 03303-9020
phone: (800) 593-5656
fax: (603) 226-3735

Bulbs

American Daylily & Perennials
P.O. Box 210
Grain Valley, MO 64029
phone: (816) 224-2852
fax: (816) 443-2849

The Daffodil Mart
30 Irene Street
Torrington, CT 06790
phone: (800) ALL-BULB
fax: (800) 420-2852

Dutch Gardens
P.O. Box 200
Adelphia, NJ 07710-0200
phone: (800) 818-3861
fax: (908) 780-7720

Gurney's Seed & Nursery Co.
110 Capital Street
Yankton, SD 57079
phone: (605) 665-1930
fax: (605) 665-9718

McClure & Zimmerman
P.O. Box 368
108 W. Winnebago
Friesland, WI 53935-0368
phone: (920) 326-4220
fax: (800) 692-5864

Van Bourgondien Bros.
P.O. Box 1000
245 Route 109
Babylon, NY 11702-9004
phone: (800) 622-9997
fax: (516) 669-1228
e-mail: blooms@dutchbulbs.com
Web site:
    http://www.dutchbulbs.com

Compost Equipment

ComposTumbler
160 Koser Road
Lititz, PA 17543
phone: (800) 880-2345

Gardener's Supply Company
128 Intervale Road
Burlington, VT 05401
phone: (800) 863-1700
fax: (800) 551-6712
e-mail: info@gardeners.com
Web site:
    http://www.gardeners.com

Gardens Alive!
5100 Schenley Place
Lawrenceburg, IN 47025
phone: (812) 537-8650
fax: (812) 537-5108

Harmony Farm Supply
P.O. Box 460
Grafton, CA 95444
phone: (707) 823-9125
fax: (707) 823-1734

Johnny's Selected Seeds
Foss Hill Road
Albion, ME 04910-9731
phone: (207) 437-4301
fax: (800) 437-4290
e-mail:
    homegarden@johnnyseeds.com
Web site:
    http://www.johnnyseeds.com

The Natural Gardening Company
217 San Anselmo Avenue
San Anselmo, CA 94960
phone: (707) 766-9303
fax: (707) 766-9747

Peaceful Valley Farm Supply
P.O. Box 2209
Grass Valley, CA 95945
phone: (916) 272-4769
fax: (916) 272-4794

Seeds of Change
P.O. Box 15700
Sante Fe, NM 87506-5700
phone: (888) 762-7333
fax: (888) 329-4762
Web site:
    http://www.seedsofchange.com

Worm's Way
7850 N. Highway 37
Bloomington, IN 47404
phone: (800) 274-9676
fax: (800) 316-1264

Cover Crops

Bountiful Gardens
18001 Shafer Ranch Road
Willits, CA 95490-9626
phone/fax: (707) 459-6410

Gardens Alive!
5100 Schenley Place
Lawrenceburg, IN 47025
phone: (812) 537-8650
fax: (812) 537-5108

Harmony Farm Supply
P.O. Box 460
Grafton, CA 95444
phone: (707) 823-9125
fax: (707) 823-1734

Nichols Garden Nursery
1190 N. Pacific Highway
Albany, OR 97321-4580
phone: (541) 928-9280
fax: (541) 967-8406
e-mail:
    nichols@gardennursery.com
Web site: http://www.
    pacificharbor.com/nichols

Peaceful Valley Farm Supply
P.O. Box 2209
Grass Valley, CA 95945
phone: (916) 272-4769
fax: (916) 272-4794

Pinetree Garden Seeds
Box 300
New Gloucester, ME 04260
phone: (888) 527-3337
fax: (207) 926-3886
e-mail:
    superseeds@worldnet.att.net

Seeds of Change
P.O. Box 15700
Sante Fe, NM 87506-5700
phone: (888) 762-7333
fax: (888) 329-4762
Web site:
    http://www.seedsofchange.com

Territorial Seed Company
P.O. Box 157
Cottage Grove, OR 97424
phone: (541) 942-9547
fax: (888) 657-3131
Web site:
    http://www.territorialseed.com

Fertilizers and Soil Care

Harmony Farm Supply
P.O. Box 460
Grafton, CA 95444
phone: (707) 823-9125
fax: (707) 823-1734

Ohio Earth Food, Inc.
5488 Swamp Street, NE
Hartville, OH 44632
phone: (330) 877-9356
fax: (330) 877-4237

Peaceful Valley Farm Supply
P.O. Box 2209
Grass Valley, CA 95945
phone: (916) 272-4769
fax: (916) 272-4794

Worm's Way
7850 N. Highway 37
Bloomington, IN 47404
phone: (800) 274-9676
fax: (800) 316-1264

Annual Flowers

Abundant Life Seed Foundation
P.O. Box 772
Port Townsend, WA 98368
phone: (360) 385-5660
fax: (360) 385-7455
Web site:
http://csf.Colorado.edu/perma/
abundant

Bountiful Gardens
18001 Shafer Ranch Road
Willits, CA 95490-9626
phone/fax: (707) 459-6410

W. Atlee Burpee & Co.
300 Park Avenue
Warminster, PA 18991-0001
phone: (800) 888-1447
fax: (800) 487-5530
Web site:
http://garden.burpee.com

The Cook's Garden
P.O. Box 535
Londonderry, VT 05148
phone: (800) 457-9703
fax: (800) 457-9705
Web site:
http://www.cooksgarden.com

Ferry-Morse Seeds
P.O. Box 488
Fulton, KY 42041-0488
phone: (800) 283-3400
fax: (800) 283-2700

The Fragrant Path
P.O. Box 328
Fort Calhoun, NE 68023
*A seed company that specializes in seeds
of fragrant, old-fashioned, and rare plants*

Gurney's Seed & Nursery Co.
110 Capital Street
Yankton, SD 57079
phone: (605) 665-1930
fax: (605) 665-9718

Johnny's Selected Seeds
Foss Hill Road
Albion, ME 04910-9731
phone: (207) 437-4301
fax: (800) 437-4290
e-mail: homegarden@johnny-
seeds.com
Web site:
http://www.johnnyseeds.com

J. W. Jung Seed Co.
335 S. High Street
Randolph, WI 53957
phone: (800) 247-5864
fax: (800) 692-5864

Logee's Greenhouses, Ltd.
141 North Street
Danielson, CT 06239-1939
phone: (860) 774-8038
fax: (888) 774-9932

Geo. W. Park Seed Co., Inc.
1 Parkton Avenue
Greenwood, SC 29647-0001
phone: (800) 845-3369
fax: (800) 275-9941
e-mail: catalog@parkseed.com

Pinetree Garden Seeds
Box 300
New Gloucester, ME 04260
phone: (888) 527-3337
fax: (207) 926-3886
e-mail: superseeds@worldnet.att.net

Seeds Blüm
HC 33 Idaho City Stage
Boise, ID 83706
phone: (800) 528-3658
fax: (208) 338-5658
e-mail:
103774.167@compuserv.com

Seeds of Change
P.O. Box 15700
Sante Fe, NM 87506-5700
phone: (888) 762-7333
fax: (888) 329-4762
Web site:
http://www.seedsofchange.com

Shepherd's Garden Seeds
30 Irene Street
Torrington, CT 06790
phone: (860) 482-3638
Web site:
http://www.shepherds.com

Stokes Seeds, Inc.
P.O. Box 548
Buffalo, NY 14240-0548
phone: (716) 695-6980
fax: (888) 834-3334

Territorial Seed Company
P.O. Box 157
Cottage Grove, OR 97424
phone: (541) 942-9547
fax: (888) 657-3131
Web site:
http://www.territorialseed.com

Thompson & Morgan, Inc.
P.O. Box 1308
Jackson, NJ 08527-0308
phone: (800) 274-7333
fax: (888) 466-4769

Heirloom Flowers

The Fragrant Path
P.O. Box 328
Fort Calhoun, NE 68023
*A seed company that specializes in seeds
of fragrant, old-fashioned, and rare plants*

Louisiana Nursery
5833 Highway 182
Opelousas, LA 70570
phone: (318) 948-3696
fax: (318) 942-6404

Seeds Blüm
HC 33 Idaho City Stage
Boise, ID 83706
phone: (800) 528-3658
fax: (208) 338-5658
e-mail:
103774.167@compuserv.com

Seeds of Change
P.O. Box 15700
Sante Fe, NM 87506-5700
phone: (888) 762-7333
fax: (888) 329-4762
Web site:
http://www.seedsofchange.com

Select Seeds Antique Flowers
180 Stickney Road
Union, CT 06076-4617
phone: (860) 684-9310
fax: (860) 684-9224
e-mail: select@neca.com
Web site: http://trine.com/
GardenNet/SelectSeeds

Perennial Flowers

Kurt Bluemel, Inc.
2740 Greene Lane
Baldwin, MD 21013-9523
phone: (410) 557-7229
fax: (410) 557-9785
e-mail: kbi@bluemel.com
Web site:
http://www/bluemel.com/kbi

Bountiful Gardens
18001 Shafer Ranch Road
Willits, CA 95490-9626
phone/fax: (707) 459-6410

W. Atlee Burpee & Co.
300 Park Avenue
Warminster, PA 18991-0001
phone: (800) 888-1447
fax: (800) 487-5530
Web site:
http://garden.burpee.com

Carroll Gardens
444 E. Main Street
Westminster, MD 21157
phone: (800) 638-6334
fax: (410) 857-4112

Forestfarm
Ray and Peg Prag
990 Tetherow Road
Williams, OR 97544-9599
phone: (541) 846-7269
fax: (541) 846-6963

The Fragrant Path
P.O. Box 328
Fort Calhoun, NE 68023
*A seed company that specializes in seeds
of fragrant, old-fashioned, and rare plants*

Goodness Grows, Inc.
Highway 77 N
P.O. Box 311
Lexington, GA 30648
phone: (706) 743-5055
fax: (706) 743-5112

Greer Gardens
1280 Goodpasture Island Road
Eugene, OR 97401-1794
phone: (541) 686-8266
fax: (541) 686-0910

Ellen Hornig
Seneca Hill Perennials
3712 Co. Route 57
Oswego, NY 13126
phone: (315) 342-5915
e-mail: hornig@oswego.edu
*Specializes in hardy aroids, species
cyclamen, and unusual perennials;
plant list is $1.00.*

Johnny's Selected Seeds
Foss Hill Road
Albion, ME 04910-9731
phone: (207) 437-4301
fax: (800) 437-4290
e-mail:
homegarden@johnnyseeds.com
Web site: http://www.johnny-
seeds.com

J. W. Jung Seed Co.
335 S. High Street
Randolph, WI 53957
phone: (800) 247-5864
fax: (800) 692-5864

Logee's Greenhouses, Ltd.
141 North Street
Danielson, CT 06239-1939
phone: (860) 774-8038
fax: (888) 774-9932

Louisiana Nursery
5833 Highway 182
Opelousas, LA 70570
phone: (318) 948-3696
fax: (318) 942-6404

Milaeger's Gardens
4838 Douglas Avenue
Racine, WI 53402-2498
phone: (800) 669-9956
fax: (414) 639-1855

Miniature Plant Kingdom
4125 Harrison Grade Road
Sebastopol, CA 95472
phone: (707) 874-2233
fax: (707) 874-3242

The Natural Garden
38W443 Highway 64
St. Charles, IL 60175
phone: (630) 584-0150
fax: (630) 584-0185

Nichols Garden Nursery
1190 N. Pacific Highway
Albany, OR 97321-4580
phone: (541) 928-9280
fax: (541) 967-8406
e-mail:
    nichols@gardennursery.com
Web site: http://www.
    pacificharbor.com/nichols

Pinetree Garden Seeds
P.O. Box 300
New Gloucester, ME 04260
phone: (888) 527-3337
fax: (207) 926-3886
e-mail: superseeds@worldnet.att.net

Prairie Nursery
P.O. Box 306
Westfield, WI 53964
phone: (608) 296-3679
fax: (608) 296-2741

Roslyn Nursery
211 Burrs Lane
Dix Hills, NY 11746
phone: (516) 643-9347
fax: (516) 427-0894
e-mail: roslyn@concentric.net
Web site:
    http://www.cris.com/~Roslyn

Seeds Blüm
HC 33 Idaho City Stage
Boise, ID 83706
phone: (800) 528-3658
fax: (208) 338-5658
e-mail:
    103774.167@compuserv.com

Seeds of Change
P.O. Box 15700
Sante Fe, NM 87506-5700
phone: (888) 762-7333
fax: (888) 329-4762
Web site:
    http://www.seedsofchange.com

Shepherd's Garden Seeds
30 Irene Street
Torrington, CT 06790
phone: (860) 482-3638
Web site:
    http://www.shepherds.com

Southern Perennials and Herbs
98 Bridges Road
Tylertown, MS 39667-9338
phone: (800) 774-0079
fax: (601) 684-3729
e-mail: sph@neosoft.com
Web site: http://www.s-p-h.com

Stokes Seeds, Inc.
P.O. Box 548
Buffalo, NY 14240-0548
phone: (716) 695-6980
fax: (888) 834-3334

Thompson & Morgan, Inc.
P.O. Box 1308
Jackson, NJ 08527-0308
phone: (800) 274-7333
fax: (888) 466-4769

Van Ness Water Gardens
2460 North Euclid Avenue
Upland, CA 91784-1199
phone: (909) 982-2425
fax: (909) 949-7217

We-Du Nurseries
Route 5, Box 724
Marion, NC 28752
phone: (704) 738-8300
fax: (704) 738-8131

Wildseed Farms
P.O. Box 3000
425 Wildflower Hills
Fredericksburg, TX 78624
phone: (800) 848-0078
fax: (830) 990-8090
Web site:
    http://www.wildseedfarms.com

Woodlanders, Inc.
1128 Colleton Avenue
Aiken, SC 29801
phone/fax: (803) 648-7522

Ornamental Grasses

Kurt Bluemel, Inc.
2740 Greene Lane
Baldwin, MD 21013-9523
phone: (410) 557-7229
fax: (410) 557-9785
e-mail: kbi@bluemel.com
Web site:
    http://www/bluemel.com/kbi

Greer Gardens
1280 Goodpasture Island Road
Eugene, OR 97401-1794
phone: (541) 686-8266
fax: (541) 686-0910

**Limerock Ornamental
    Grasses, Inc.**
70 Sawmill Road
Port Matilda, PA 16870
phone: (814) 692-2272
fax: (814) 692-9848

Prairie Nursery
P.O. Box 306
Westfield, WI 53964
phone: (608) 296-3679
fax: (608) 296-2741

Roslyn Nursery
211 Burrs Lane
Dix Hills, NY 11746
phone: (516) 643-9347
fax: (516) 427-0894
e-mail: roslyn@concentric.net
Web site:
    http://www.cris.com/~Roslyn

Wayside Gardens
1 Garden Lane
Hodges, SC 29695-0001
phone: (800) 845-1124
fax: (800) 457-9712
e-mail:
    catalog@waysidegardens.com
Web site:
    http://www.waysidegardens.com

White Flower Farm
P.O. Box 50
Litchfield, CT 06759-0050
phone: (800) 503-9624
fax: (860) 496-1418
Web site:
    http://www.whiteflowerfarm.com

Heaths and Heathers

Heaths & Heathers
E 502 Haskell Hill Road
Shelton, WA 98584-8429
phone/fax: (360) 427-5318
e-mail:
    handh@heathsandheathers.com

Rock Spray Nursery
P.O. Box 693
Truro, MA 02666
phone: (508) 349-6769
fax: (508) 349-2732
e-mail:
    kherrick@rockspray.com
Web site:
    http://www.rockspray.com

Herbs, Herbal Products and Supplies, and Herbal Education

Aubrey Organics
4419 N. Manhattan Avenue
Tampa, FL 33614
phone: (813) 877-4186
100% natural hand crafted cosmetics preserved with citrus seed extract

Avena Botanicals
Deb Soule
219 Mill Street
Rockport, ME 04856
phone: (207) 594-0694
fax: (207) 594-2975
Organic herbal extracts, custom formulations, herb teas, oils, and salves

Blazing Star Herbal School
Gail Ulrich
P.O. Box 6
Shelburne Falls, MA 01370
phone: (413) 625-6875

Blue Mountain Herbal Apothecary
R. Lynn Shumake, PD
P.O. Box 216
Glenelg, MD 21737
phone/fax: (410) 992-8554
Pharmacy-prepared custom compounded natural remedies; herbal tinctures, tonics, therapeutic massage creams/oils

Patricia Carrigan
Herbalist and Founder of Mystic
    Hollow Center for Holistic
    Healing
P.O. Box 696
Shepherdstown, WV 25443
phone: (304) 876-8137
Handmade herbal salves

Dandelion Designs
JoAnn Stak
12 Ferguson Avenue
Burlington, VT 05401-5313
phone: (802) 863-9521
Homemade candles, soaps, essential oil blends, potpourri

Barb Dawson
921 Hidden Branches Trail
Canton, GA 30115
phone: (770) 479-4993
fax: (770) 479-7432
e-mail: noahsapothecary@
    mindspring.com
Animal herbalist offering consultations, herbal supplements, and books

Dry Creek Herb Farm and Learning Center
Shatoiya and Rick de la Tour
13935 Dry Creek Road
Auburn, CA 95602
phone: (916) 878-2441
fax: (916) 878-6772
Teas, bulk herbs, skin care products, oils, soaps, and herb crafting supplies

Heart's Ease Herb Shop & Gardens
Sharon Lovejoy, founder and
    consultant
Susan Pendergast, proprietor
4101 Burton Drive
Cambria, CA 93428
phone: (800) 266-HERB (4372)
    (805) 927-5224 *local calls*
fax: (805) 927-1420
Wide range of herbal products

Hill Woman Productions
Sue-Ryn Burns
44027 Cross Island Road
Wellesley Island, NY 13640
phone: (315) 482-2985
Specializes in blended herbs, oils, and incense

Horizon Herbs
Richo Cech
P.O. Box 69
Williams, OR 97544
phone: (541) 846-6704
Seed, rootstock, and live plants of medicinal herbs

Lily of the Valley Herbs
Paul Carmichael
3969 Fox Avenue
Minerva, OH 44657
phone: (330) 862-3920
Herbal products and homemade herbal remedies; herbs available locally

Logee's Greenhouses, Ltd.
141 North Street
Danielson, CT 06239-1939
phone: (860) 774-8038
fax: (888) 774-9932

Lunar Farms Herbal Specialist
Rita C. Karydas
#3 Highland-Greenhills
Gilmer, TX 75644
phone: (903) 734-5893
Herbal salves, oils, and personal care products

Alison Melotti-Cormack
62 N. 4th Street
Chambersburg, PA 17201
phone: (717) 261-0698
Natural grain warmers

Mountain Rose Herbs
Julie Bailey
20818 High Street
North San Juan, CA 95960
phone: (800) 879-3337
fax: (916) 292-9138
Organically grown herbs, handcrafted herbal body care products, and supplies

Naomi's Herbs
Laurieann Quiry
11 Housatonic Street
Lenox, MA 01420
phone: (413) 637-0616
Organic medicinal and culinary herbs, tea blends, therapeutic essential oils, Chinese medicinals, and homeopathics

Nichols Garden Nursery
1190 N. Pacific Highway
Albany, OR 97321-4580
phone: (541) 928-9280
fax: (541) 967-8406
e-mail: nichols@gardennursery.com
Web site: http://www.
    pacificharbor.com/nichols

Richters Herb Catalogue
Goodwood, Ontario L0C 1A0
Canada
phone: (905) 640-6677
fax: (905) 640-6641
e-mail: orderdesk@richters.com
Web site:
    http://www.richters.com

Sage Mountain Herbs
Rosemary Gladstar
P.O. Box 420
E. Barre, VT 05649
phone: (802) 479-9825
fax: (802) 476-3722
Ongoing classes, apprenticeship program, and correspondence course

The Sandy Mush Herb Nursery
316 Surrett Cove Road
Leicester, NC 28748
phone: (704) 683-2014

Sedler's Mother Earth Herbs
Kathy McQuade-Sedler, Herbalist
12036 Nevada City Highway #191
Grass Valley, CA 95945
phone: (916) 788-0138
fax: (916) 788-0849
Dried herbs, custom tea blends, books, candles, herbcrafting supplies, homemade body care products; catalog available

Seeds Blüm
HC 33 Idaho City Stage
Boise, ID 83706
phone: (800) 528-3658
fax: (208) 338-5658
e-mail:
    103774.167@compuserv.com

Select Seeds Antique Flowers
180 Stickney Road
Union, CT 06076-4617
phone: (860) 684-9310
fax: (860) 684-9224
e-mail: select@neca.com
Web site: http://trine.com/
    GardenNet/SelectSeeds

**September's Sun Herbal
    Soap Company**
Stephanie Tourles,
    Licensed Aesthetician
P.O. Box 772
West Hyannisport, MA 02672
phone: (508) 862-9955
Handmade herbal soaps and herbal craft books. For brochure, send self-addressed, stamped envelope

Shepherd's Garden Seeds
30 Irene Street
Torrington, CT 06790
phone: (860) 482-3638
Web site:
    http://www.shepherds.com

Carolyn Lee Tubman
P.O. Box 470
Milford, VA 22514
phone: (804) 633-1370

Walk in Beauty
Kathy Lee
P.O. Box 1331
Colfax, CA 95713
phone: (916) 346-7143
Custom blended herbs, spices, and teas

Well-Sweep Herb Farm
205 Mt. Bethel Road
Port Murray, NJ 07865
phone: (908) 852-5390

**WiseWays Herbals—Singing
    Brook Farm**
Mariam Massaro
99 Harvey Road
Worthington, MA 01098
phone: (413) 238-4268
fax: (413) 238-5978
Aromatherapy and body care products, medicinal formulas, extracts, teas, and salves

Woodsong Herbals
Julie Manchester
P.O. Box 301
Randolph, VT 05060
phone: (802) 728-4941
Medicinal and culinary herbal products

Lawn Mixes

Prairie Nursery
P.O. Box 306
Westfield, WI 53964
phone: (608) 296-3679
fax: (608) 296-2741

Pest, Disease, and Weed Control

Gardener's Supply Company
128 Intervale Road
Burlington, VT 05401
phone: (800) 863-1700
fax: (800) 551-6712
e-mail: info@gardeners.com
Web site:
    http://www.gardeners.com

Gardens Alive!
5100 Schenley Place
Lawrenceburg, IN 47025
phone: (812) 537-8650
fax: (812) 537-5108

Harmony Farm Supply
P.O. Box 460
Grafton, CA 95444
phone: (707) 823-9125
fax: (707) 823-1734

The Natural Gardening Company
217 San Anselmo Avenue
San Anselmo, CA 94960
phone: (707) 766-9303
fax: (707) 766-9747

Ohio Earth Food, Inc.
5488 Swamp Street, NE
Hartville, OH 44632
phone: (330) 877-9356
fax: (330) 877-4237

Peaceful Valley Farm Supply
P.O. Box 2209
Grass Valley, CA 95945
phone: (916) 272-4769
fax: (916) 272-4794

Safety Equipment

A. M. Leonard, Inc.
241 Fox Drive
P.O. Box 816
Piqua, OH 45356
phone: (800) 543-8955
fax: (800) 433-0633

Soil Testing

Cook's Consulting
R.D. 2, Box 13
Lowville, NY 13367
phone: (315) 376-3002
Provides organic recommendations, offers free soil testing kit

Peaceful Valley Farm Supply
P.O. Box 2209
Grass Valley, CA 95945
phone: (916) 272-4769
fax: (916) 272-4794
Offers basic soil test as well as one for micronutrients; organic recommendations provided

Timberleaf Soil Testing Services
39648 Old Spring Road
Murrieta, CA 92563
phone: (909) 677-7510
Offers several soil tests, including for basic and trace minerals; organic recommendations included

Wallace Laboratories
365 Coral Circle
El Segundo, CA 90245
phone: (310) 615-0116
fax: (310) 640-6863
Provides analyses for soil fertility (essential nutrients) along with nonessential potentially toxic heavy metals; recommendations provided; provides analyses of water, plant tissues, composts, fertilizers, and building materials

Woods End Research Laboratory
P.O. Box 297
Mt. Vernon, ME 04352
phone: (207) 293-2457
fax: (207) 293-2488
This is a compost & soil research lab; performs soil testing for homeowners and soil life testing; offers compost testing kit

Tools and Supplies

Gardener's Supply Company
128 Intervale Road
Burlington, VT 05401
phone: (800) 863-1700
fax: (800) 551-6712
e-mail: info@gardeners.com
Web site: http://www.gardeners.com

Kinsman Company, Inc.
River Road
Point Pleasant, PA 18950
phone: (800) 733-4146
fax: (215) 297-0450

A. M. Leonard, Inc.
241 Fox Drive
P.O. Box 816
Piqua, OH 45356
phone: (800) 543-8955
fax: (800) 433-0633

The Natural Gardening Company
217 San Anselmo Avenue
San Anselmo, CA 94960
phone: (707) 766-9303
fax: (707) 766-9747

Smith & Hawken
2 Arbor Lane
Box 6900
Florence, KY 41022-6900
phone: (800) 981-9888
    catalog requests only
fax: (606) 727-1166

Trees, Shrubs, and Vines

Carroll Gardens
444 E. Main Street
Westminster, MD 21157
phone: (800) 638-6334
fax: (410) 857-4112

Forestfarm
Ray and Peg Prag
990 Tetherow Road
Williams, OR 97544-9599
phone: (541) 846-7269
fax: (541) 846-6963

Greer Gardens
1280 Goodpasture Island Road
Eugene, OR 97401-1794
phone: (541) 686-8266
fax: (541) 686-0910

Gurney's Seed & Nursery Co.
110 Capital Street
Yankton, SD 57079
phone: (605) 665-1930
fax: (605) 665-9718

Miniature Plant Kingdom
4125 Harrison Grade Road
Sebastopol, CA 95472
phone: (707) 874-2233
fax: (707) 874-3242

Pickering Nurseries, Inc.
670 Kingston Road
Pickering, Ontario L1V 1A6
Canada
phone: (905) 839-2111
fax: (905) 839-4807
Roses

Roslyn Nursery
211 Burrs Lane
Dix Hills, NY 11746
phone: (516) 643-9347
fax: (516) 427-0894
e-mail: roslyn@concentric.net
Web site:
    http://www.cris.com/~Roslyn

Wayside Gardens
1 Garden Lane
Hodges, SC 29695-0001
phone: (800) 845-1124
fax: (800) 457-9712
e-mail:
    catalog@waysidegardens.com
Web site:
    http://www.waysidegardens.com

White Flower Farm
P.O. Box 50
Litchfield, CT 06759-0050
phone: (800) 503-9624
fax: (860) 496-1418
Web site:
    http://www.whiteflowerfarm.com

Woodlanders, Inc.
1128 Colleton Avenue
Aiken, SC 29801
phone/fax: (803) 648-7522

Vegetables

Abundant Life Seed Foundation
P.O. Box 772
Port Townsend, WA 98368
phone: (360) 385-5660
fax: (360) 385-7455
Web site: http://csf.Colorado.edu/
    perma/abundant

W. Atlee Burpee & Co.
300 Park Avenue
Warminster, PA 18991-0001
phone: (800) 888-1447
fax: (800) 487-5530
Web site:
    http://garden.burpee.com

The Cook's Garden
P.O. Box 535
Londonderry, VT 05148
phone: (800) 457-9703
fax: (800) 457-9705
Web site:
    http://www.cooksgarden.com

Ferry-Morse Seeds
P.O. Box 488
Fulton, KY 42041-0488
phone: (800) 283-3400
fax: (800) 283-2700

Gurney's Seed & Nursery Co.
110 Capital Street
Yankton, SD 57079
phone: (605) 665-1930
fax: (605) 665-9718

Johnny's Selected Seeds
Foss Hill Road
Albion, ME 04910-9731
phone: (207) 437-4301
fax: (800) 437-4290
e-mail:
    homegarden@johnnyseeds.com
Web site:
    http://www.johnnyseeds.com

Native Seeds/Search
2509 N. Campbell Avenue, #325
Tucson, AZ 85719
phone: (520) 327-9123 *no orders*
fax: (520) 327-5821 *orders welcome*
Web site:
    http://desert.net/seeds/home.htm

Geo. W. Park Seed Co., Inc.
1 Parkton Avenue
Greenwood, SC 29647-0001
phone: (800) 845-3369
fax: (800) 275-9941
e-mail:
    catalog@parkseed.com

Pinetree Garden Seeds
Box 300
New Gloucester, ME 04260
phone: (888) 527-3337
fax: (207) 926-3886
e-mail:
    superseeds@worldnet.att.net

Seeds Blüm
HC 33 Idaho City Stage
Boise, ID 83706
phone: (800) 528-3658
fax: (208) 338-5658
e-mail:
    103774.167@compuserv.com

Seeds of Change
P.O. Box 15700
Sante Fe, NM 87506-5700
phone: (888) 762-7333
fax: (888) 329-4762
Web site:
    http://www.seedsofchange.com

Shepherd's Garden Seeds
30 Irene Street
Torrington, CT 06790
phone: (860) 482-3638
Web site:
    http://www.shepherds.com

Wildflowers

Abundant Life Seed Foundation
P.O. Box 772
Port Townsend, WA 98368
phone: (360) 385-5660
fax: (360) 385-7455
Web site: http://csf.Colorado.edu/
    perma/abundant

The Fragrant Path
P.O. Box 328
Fort Calhoun, NE 68023
*A seed company that specializes in seeds
of fragrant, old-fashioned, and rare plants*

Moon Mountain Wildflowers
P.O. Box 725
Carpinteria, CA 93014-0725
phone: (805) 684-2565

Native Seeds/Search
2509 N. Campbell Avenue, #325
Tucson, AZ 85719
phone: (520) 327-9123 *no orders*
fax: (520) 327-5821 *orders welcome*
Web site:
    http://desert.net/seeds/home.htm

The Natural Garden
38W443 Highway 64
St. Charles, IL 60175
phone: (630) 584-0150
fax: (630) 584-0185

Plants of the Southwest
Agua Fria, Route 6, Box 11A
Santa Fe, NM 87501
phone: (800) 788-7333
fax: (505) 438-8800
e-mail: contact@plantsofthesouth-
    west.com
Web site: http://www.plantsofthe-
    southwest.com

Prairie Nursery
P.O. Box 306
Westfield, WI 53964
phone: (608) 296-3679
fax: (608) 296-2741

Clyde Robin Seed Company
P.O. Box 2366
Castro Valley, CA 94546
phone: (510) 785-0425
fax: (510) 785-6463

Seeds Blüm
HC 33 Idaho City Stage
Boise, ID 83706
phone: (800) 528-3658
fax: (208) 338-5658
e-mail:
    103774.167@compuserv.com

Thompson & Morgan, Inc.
P.O. Box 1308
Jackson, NJ 08527-0308
phone: (800) 274-7333
fax: (888) 466-4769

Wildseed Farms
P.O. Box 3000
425 Wildflower Hills
Fredericksburg, TX 78624
phone: (800) 848-0078
fax: (830) 990-8090
Web site:
    http//:www.wildseedfarms.com

The Vermont Wildflower Farm
Reservation Center
Wildflower Lane
P.O. Box 1400
Louisiana, MO 63353-8400
phone: (800) 424-1165
fax: (573) 754-5290

We-Du Nurseries
Route 5, Box 724
Marion, NC 28752
phone: (704) 738-8300
fax: (704) 738-8131

Worms

The following carry worms
and worm composting supplies.
Redworms (*Eisenia foetida* and
Lumbricus rubellus) are best for compost.

Bountiful Gardens
18001 Shafer Ranch Road
Willits, CA 95490-9626
phone/fax: (707) 459-6410

Gardener's Supply Company
128 Intervale Road
Burlington, VT 05401
phone: (800) 863-1700
fax: (800) 551-6712
e-mail: info@gardeners.com
Web site:
    http://www.gardeners.com

Gardens Alive!
5100 Schenley Place
Lawrenceburg, IN 47025
phone: (812) 537-8650
fax: (812) 537-5108

The Natural Gardening Company
217 San Anselmo Avenue
San Anselmo, CA 94960
phone: (707) 766-9303
fax: (707) 766-9747

Peaceful Valley Farm Supply
P.O. Box 2209
Grass Valley, CA 95945
phone: (916) 272-4769
fax: (916) 272-4794

Worm's Way
7850 N. Highway 37
Bloomington, IN 47404
phone: (800) 274-9676
fax: (800) 316-1264

Recommended Reading

Bird and Butterfly Gardens

Adams, George. *Birdscaping Your Garden.* Emmaus, PA: Rodale Press, 1994.

Ellis, Barbara. *Attracting Birds and Butterflies.* New York: Houghton Mifflin, 1997.

Lewis, Alcinda, ed. *Butterfly Gardens.* Brooklyn, NY: Brooklyn Botanic Garden, 1996.

Proctor, Noble. *Garden Birds: How to Attract Birds to Your Garden.* Emmaus, PA: Rodale Press, 1986.

Roth, Sally. *Natural Landscaping.* Emmaus, PA: Rodale Press, 1997.

Tufts, Craig, and Peter Lower. *The National Wildlife Federation's Guide to Gardening for Wildlife.* Emmaus, PA: Rodale Press, 1995.

Warton, Susan. *An Illustrated Guide to Attracting Birds.* Menlo Park, CA: Sunset Publishing, 1995.

Composting and Soil

Appelhof, Mary. *Worms Eat My Garbarge.* Kalamazoo, MI: Flower Press, 1982.

Beck, Malcolm. *The Secret Life of Compost.* Metairie, LA: Acres U.S.A., 1997.

Campbell, Stu. *Let It Rot: The Gardener's Guide to Composting.* Charlotte, VT: Storey Communications, 1975.

Greshuny, Grace. *Start with the Soil.* Emmaus, PA: Rodale Press, 1993.

Hynes, Erin, *Rodale's Successful Organic Gardening: Improving the Soil.* Emmaus, PA: Rodale Press, 1994.

Martin, Deborah, and Grace Gershuny, eds. *The Rodale Book of Composting.* Emmaus, PA: Rodale Press, 1992.

General Gardening

Abraham, Doc, and Katy Abraham. *Green Thumb Wisdom.* Pownal, VT: Storey Communications, 1996.

Bender, Steve, and Felder Rushing. *Passalong Plants.* Chapel Hill, NC: University of North Carolina Press, 1993.

Benjamin, Joan, ed. *Great Garden Shortcuts.* Emmaus, PA: Rodale Press, 1996.

Bradley, Fern Marshall, and Barbara Ellis, eds. *Rodale's All-New Encyclopedia of Organic Gardening.* Emmaus, PA: Rodale Press, 1992.

Coleman, Elliot. *The New Organic Grower.* White River Junction, VT: Chelsea Green Publishing Co, 1995.

Mackey, Betty B., et al. *The Gardener's Home Companion.* New York: Macmillan Publishing Co., Inc., 1991.

Michalak, Patricia S., and Cass Peterson. *Rodale's Successful Organic Gardening: Vegetables.* Emmaus, PA: Rodale Press, 1993.

Nick, Jean, and Fern Marshall Bradley. *Growing Fruits & Vegetables Organically.* Emmaus, PA: Rodale Press, 1994.

Perlmutter, Mary. *How Does Your Garden Grow…Organically?.* Ottawa, Canada: The Salvation Army Triumph Press, 1990 (out of print).

Yang, Linda. *The City and Town Gardener.* New York: Random House, 1995.

Yeomans, Kathleen. *The Able Gardener.* Pownal, VT: Storey Communications, 1993.

Herbs and Crafts

Blose, Nora. *Herb Drying Handbook.* New York: Sterling Publishing Co., 1993.

Bremness, Lesley. *The Eyewitness Book of Herbs.* New York: Dorling Kindersley Publishing, 1994.

Clark, Marge. *The Best of Thymes.* West Lebanon, IN: Thyme Cookbooks, 1997.

Clark, Marge. *It's About Thyme!* West Lebanon, IN: Thyme Cookbooks, 1988.

Cusick, Dawn. *Potpourri Crafts.* New York: Sterling Publishing Co., Inc., 1992.

Duke, James A. *The Green Pharmacy.* Emmaus, PA: Rodale Press, 1997.

Gladstar, Rosemary. *Herbal Healing for Women.* New York: Simon & Schuster, 1993.

Gruenberg, Louise. *Potpourri: The Art of Fragrance Crafting.* Norway, IA: Frontier Herbs, 1984.

Hampton, Aubrey. *What's in Your Cosmetics? A Complete Consumer's Guide to Natural & Synthetic Ingredients.* Tuscon, AZ: Odonian Press, 1993.

Kowalchik, Claire, and William H. Hylton. *Rodale's Illustrated Encyclopedia of Herbs.* Emmaus, PA: Rodale Press, 1987.

Lovejoy, Sharon. *Sunflower Houses.* Loveland, CO: Interweave Press, 1995.

Marcin, Marietta Marshall. *The Herbal Tea Garden.* Pownal, VT: Storey Communications, 1993.

McClure, Susan. *The Herb Gardener: A Guide for All Seasons.* Pownal, VT: Storey Communications, 1995.

Oster, Maggie. *Herbal Vinegar.* Pownal, VT: Storey Communications, 1994.

Oster, Maggie, and Sal Gilbertie. *The Herbal Palate Cookbook.* Pownal, VT: Storey Communications, 1996.

Smith, Miranda. *Your Backyard Herb Garden.* Emmaus, PA: Rodale Press, 1997.

Soule, Deb. *The Roots of Healing: A Woman's Book of Herbs.* Secaucas, NJ: Carol Publishing Group, 1994.

Toomay, Mindy. *A Cozy Book of Herbal Teas.* Rocklin, CA: Prima Publishing, 1994.

Tourles, Stephanie. *The Herbal Body Book.* Pownal, VT: Storey Communications, 1994.

Ulrich, Gail. *Herbs to Boost Immunity.* New Canaan, CT: Keats Publishing, 1997.

Williams, Betsy. *Potpourri and Fragrant Projects.* New York: The Reader's Digest Association, Inc., 1996.

Wood, Matthew. *The Book of Herbal Wisdom.* Berkeley, CA: North Atlantic Books, 1997.

Wood, Rob, and Lucy Wood. *The Art of Dried Flowers.* Philadelphia: Running Press, 1991.

Landscape and Flower Gardening

Benjamin, Joan, and Barbara Ellis, eds. *Rodale's No-Fail Flower Garden.* Emmaus, PA: Rodale Press, 1994.

Binetti, Marianne. *Shortcuts for Accenting Your Garden: Over Five Hundred Easy & Inexpensive Tips.* Pownal, VT: Storey Communications, 1993.

Bradley, Fern Marshall, ed. *Gardening with Perennials.* Emmaus, PA: Rodale Press, 1996.

Garrett, Howard. *Howard Garrett's Plants for Texas.* Austin, TX: University of Texas Press, 1993.

McKeon, Judy. *The Encyclopedia of Roses.* Emmaus, PA: Rodale Press, 1995.

Phillips, Ellen, and C. Colston Burrell. *Rodale's Illustrated Encyclopedia of Perennials.* Emmaus, PA: Rodale Press, 1993.

Sombke, Laurence. *Beautiful Easy Flower Gardens.* Emmaus, PA: Rodale Press, 1995.

Taylor, Norman. *Taylor's Guide to Annuals.* Rev. ed. Boston: Houghton Mufflin Co., 1986.

Taylor, Norman. *Taylor's Guide to Perennials.* Rev. ed. Boston: Houghton Mifflin Co., 1986.

Welch, William C., and Greg Grant. *The Southern Heirloom Garden.* Dallas, TX: Taylor Publishing Company, 1995.

Pest Management

Carr, Anna, et al. *Rodale's Chemical-Free Yard and Garden.* Emmaus, PA: Rodale Press, 1991.

Ellis, Barbara W., and Fern Marshall Bradley. *The Organic Gardener's Handbook of Natural Insect and Disease Control.* Emmaus, PA: Rodale Press, 1992.

Gilkeson, Linda, et. al. *Rodale's Pest & Disease Problem Solver.* Emmaus, PA: Rodale Press, 1996.

Michalak, Patricia S., and Linda Gilkeson. *Rodale's Successful Organic Gardening: Controlling Pests and Diseases.* Emmaus, PA: Rodale Press, 1994.

Weed Management

Agricultural Research Service, USDA. *Common Weeds of The United States Department of Agriculture.* New York: Dover Publications, 1971.

Hynes, Erin. *Rodale's Successful Organic Gardening: Controlling Weeds.* Emmaus, PA: Rodale Press, 1995.

Magazines and Newsletters

American Cottage Gardener, 1306 Lujan Street, Santa Fe, NM 87505-3220

Common Sense Pest Control Quarterly, Bio-Integral Resource Center (BIRC), P.O. Box 7414, Berkeley, CA 94707-0414

Fine Gardening, The Taunton Press, Inc., Newtown, CT 06470-5506

The Garden Sampler, P.O. Box 7, Peru, VT 05152

Horticulture, P.O. Box 51455, Boulder, CO 80323-1455

HortIdeas, 750 Black Lick Road, Gravel Switch, KY 40328

Organic Gardening, Rodale Press Inc., 33 E. Minor Street, Emmaus, PA 18098

Metric Conversion Tables

LIQUID AND HOUSEHOLD MEASUREMENTS

	To	From	Use
TO CONVERT	milliliters	teaspoons	____ teaspoons × 5 = ____ milliliters
	teaspoons	milliliters	____ milliliters × 0.201 = ____ teaspoons
	liters	cups	____ cups × 0.24 = ____ liters
	cups	liters	____ liters × 4.17 = ____ cups

	U.S.	Metric
COMMON EQUIVALENTS	¼ teaspoon	1.25 milliliters
	½ teaspoon	2.5 milliliters
	1 teaspoon	5 milliliters
	1 tablespoon (3 teaspoons)	15 milliliters
	2 tablespoons (1 fluid ounce)	30 milliliters
	¼ cup (2 fluid ounces)	60 milliliters
	⅓ cup (2.67 fluid ounces)	80 milliliters
	½ cup (4 fluid ounces)	120 milliliters
	⅔ cup (5.33 fluid ounces)	160 milliliters
	¾ cup (6 fluid ounces)	180 milliliters
	1 cup (8 fluid ounces)	240 milliliters
	1 pint (2 cups)	480 milliliters
	1 quart (2 pints or 4 cups)	960 milliliters (0.96 liters)
	1 gallon (4 quarts, 8 pints, or 16 cups)	3,840 milliliters (3.84 liters)

WEIGHTS

	To	From	Use
TO CONVERT	grams	ounces	____ ounces × 28.35 = ____ grams
	ounces	grams	____ grams × 0.035 = ____ ounces
	kilograms	pounds	____ pounds × 0.454 = ____ kilograms
	pounds	kilograms	____ kilograms × 2.2 = ____ pounds

WEIGHTS — CONTINUED

<table>
<tr><td rowspan="13" style="writing-mode: vertical-rl">COMMON EQUIVALENTS</td><td>U.S.</td><td>METRIC</td></tr>
<tr><td>1 ounce</td><td>28 grams</td></tr>
<tr><td>2 ounces</td><td>57 grams</td></tr>
<tr><td>4 ounces (¼ pound)</td><td>113 grams</td></tr>
<tr><td>5 ounces (⅓ pound)</td><td>142 grams</td></tr>
<tr><td>6 ounces</td><td>170 grams</td></tr>
<tr><td>7 ounces</td><td>198 grams</td></tr>
<tr><td>8 ounces (½ pound)</td><td>227 grams</td></tr>
<tr><td>10 ounces</td><td>284 grams</td></tr>
<tr><td>12 ounces (¾ pound)</td><td>340 grams</td></tr>
<tr><td>14 ounces</td><td>397 grams</td></tr>
<tr><td>16 ounces (1 pound)</td><td>454 grams</td></tr>
<tr><td>32 ounces (2 pounds)</td><td>908 grams (.908 kilogram)</td></tr>
</table>

LENGTH

	TO	**FROM**	**USE**
TO CONVERT	inches	centimeters	____ centimeters × 0.394 = ____ inches
	centimeters	inches	____ inches × 0.254 = ____ centimeters
	feet	centimeters	____ centimeters × 0.033 = ____ feet
	centimeters	feet	____ feet × 30.48 = ____ centimeters

	U.S.	**METRIC**
COMMON EQUIVALENTS	1 inch	2.54 centimeters
	6 inches	15.24 centimeters
	12 inches (1 foot)	30.48 centimeters
	18 inches (1½ feet)	45.72 centimeters
	24 inches (2 feet)	60.96 centimeters
	36 inches (3 feet or 1 yard)	91.44 centimeters
	60 inches (5 feet)	152.4 centimeters (1.524 meters)
	72 inches (6 feet or 2 yards)	182.88 centimeters (1.829 meters)

Index

NOTE: Page references in **boldface** indicate illustrations.

D

E

Marigolds, 100, 165, 186, 271, 273
Marvel-of-Peru, about, 292
Massage oils, 245
Matthiola longipetala, about, 292
Meadow foam, about, 181
Mealybug Death Drench, 93
Mealybugs, controlling, 93, **93**, 97
Medicine Cabinet Micronutrients, 50
Melampodium, about, 282
Mentha species, 114, 187, 259
Metric conversion tables, 320–21
Mexican bean beetles, 86, 104
Mexican hat, about, 286, **301**, 302
Mexican oregano, about, 114
Mice, deterring, 107
Microbes (microorganisms)
    conditions encouraging, 1, 8, 34, 38, 49, 68
    usefulness in soil, 61, 65
Microbiota decussata, about, 276
Mighty-Milk Tomato Blight Cure, 130
Mighty Oak Leaf Tea, 47, **47**
Milkweeds, about, 188
Milky disease spore, 111
Mint, 114, **155**, 187
Mirabilis species, 292
Mistflower, about, 283
Mites (spider mites), 46, 97
Mix-and-Match Bouquet Garden, 272–73, **272**
Mix-and-Match Organic Fertilizer, 29
Moisture, in composting, 1–3, **2**, **3**, 16
Molasses, 106, 140
Mole-Med, 110
Moles, deterring, 110–11, **110**, **111**
Molybdenum, 26
Monarda species, 286, 297, **301**, 302
Montbretia, about, 290
Mosaic, symptoms of, 120

Mosquitoes, deterring, 35
Moth-Chasing Marvels, 224
Mowing, 37, 299
Mulch
    and disease prevention, 130
    materials for, 11, 37, 47, 51, 145, 160, **160**, 162
    for soil-building, 58, 59
    sour mulch syndrome, 14
    for weed control, 160–62, **160**, **161**, **162**, 164, **164**
20 Mule Team Borax, 157
Mullein, **153**, 196, 220, **220**
Mullein-Stalk Candlesticks, 220, **220**
Murphy's Oil Soap, 134, 146
Mustard greens, in salads, 168, **169**

N

Narcissus × odorus, about, 290
Native Mix for the Southeast, A, 300–302, **301**
Necrotic ring spot, prevention of, 127
Nectar plants, 186–87
Neem, for controlling fungus gnats, 99
Nematodes, controlling, 86, 106
Nemophila menziesii, about, 286
Nepeta × faassenii, about, 181
Newspaper, 17, 160, 161, **161**

T

Verbena species, 187

Vermiculite, defined, 71

Vervain, Brazilian, 187, 268, 269

Vetch, 63, 106, 268, 269, 298

Vinca major, as herbal remedy, 260

Vinegar. *See also* Herbal vinegars
    as household cleanser, 221
    using in gardens, 48, 99, 117, 152, **152**

Vinegar Cure for Acid-Loving Plants, The, 48

Vinegar Foils Fungus Gnats, 99

Vinegar Spray Keeps Cats Away, 117

Vinegar Tonic Tea for Houseplants, 55, **55**

Vines, 79, 115, 315–16

Violets, 168, **169**, 189, 211, **211**

W

Warm and Spicy Tea, 194

Wash Away Fungi with Garrett's Spray, 141

Water
    acidifying alkaline, 47, **47**
    hot as weed killer, 154
    for insect control, 46, 94, 97

Watermelons, compost tea and, 121

Weed control
    of broad-leaved plants, 152, **152**, 153, **153**
    cover crops for, 63, 164–65, **164**
    cultivating for, 155, **155**, 163, **163**, 267
    formulas for, 150, 152, **152**, 154, 156–60, **158**, **159**, **160**, 162–66, **162**, **163**, **164**
    mulches for, 160–62, **160**, **161**, **162**, 164, **164**
    in pavement cracks, **152**, 154, 157
    sources for materials for, 315
    in wildflower meadows, 299

Weed-Free Lawn Formula, 166

Weeds, 17
    cooking with, 168–69, 204, 211, **211**

Weeds in Hot Water, 154

Wet-Weather Compost, 3, **3**

Whiteflies, 48, 97, 98, **98**, 99

Wildflowers
    formulas for mixes, 285–87, 294–99, **294**, 300–302, **301**
    sources for, 317

Wild petunias, about, 188

Willows, 34, 189

Wilted Weed Salad, 168

Wilts, symptoms of, 120

Winecups, about sprawling, 284

Win the Weed War with Gin, 156

Wipe Out Black Spot with Tomato Leaf Tonic, 131

Wisterias, about, 115

Wood ashes, 43, 78

Wood chips, 14, **14**, 17, 68, 161, **161**

World's EASIEST Compost, The, 4, **4**

Worms
    castings of, 42, **42**, 69, **69**
    composting with, 18–21, **19, 21**
    raising, 42, 64, **64**
Worms' Turn, The, 42, **42**
Worm tea, defined, 20
Wormwood, about, 114

X

Xeriscaping, 280–84, **281**

Y

Yarrow, 181, 252, 260, **260**, 284, 287

Z

Zephyr Farm's High Fertility Seed-Starting
   Mix, 74
Zephyr Farm's Original Fertility Mix, 75
Zinc, 26
Zingiber officinale, 261
Zinnia, about, 187, 271, 273
Zizia aptera, about, 297

USDA Plant Hardiness Zone Map

This map was revised in 1990 to reflect changes in climate since the original USDA map, done in 1965. It is now recognized as the best estimator of minimum temperatures available. Look at the map to find your area, then match its pattern to the key on the right. When you've found your pattern, the key will tell you what hardiness zone you live in. Remember that the map is a general guide; your particular conditions may vary.

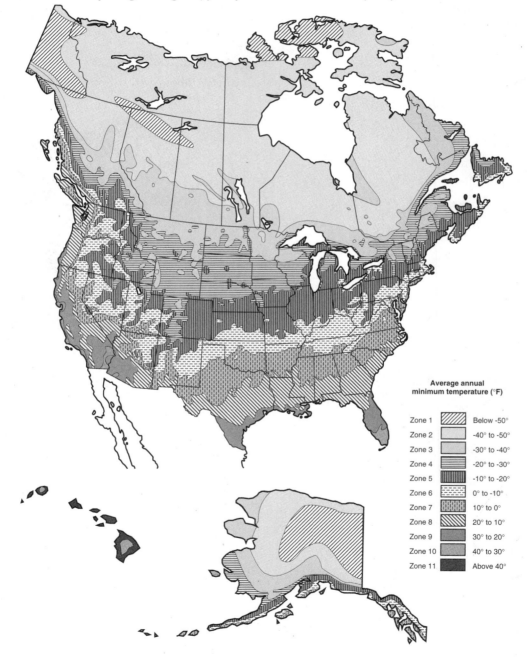

Average annual minimum temperature (°F)

Zone 1		Below -50°
Zone 2		-40° to -50°
Zone 3		-30° to -40°
Zone 4		-20° to -30°
Zone 5		-10° to -20°
Zone 6		0° to -10°
Zone 7		10° to 0°
Zone 8		20° to 10°
Zone 9		30° to 20°
Zone 10		40° to 30°
Zone 11		Above 40°